Vol. 2

Beyblade Extreme Rotation Shoot

Beyblade
Vol. 2
Beyblade Extreme Rotation Shoot

Story and Art by Takao Aoki

English Adaptation/Fred Burke
Translation/Akira Watanabe
Touch-up Art & Lettering/Dave Lanphear
Cover & Interior Design/Andrea Rice
Editor/Ian Robertson

Managing Editor/Annette Roman
Director of Production/Noboru Watanabe
Editorial Director/Alvin Lu
Sr. Director of Licensing & Acquisitions/Rika Inouye
Vice President of Sales & Marketing/Liza Coppola
Executive Vice President/Hyoe Narita
Publisher/Seiji Horibuchi

Published by VIZ, LLC
P.O. Box 77010
San Francisco, CA 94107

10 9 8 7 6 5 4 3 2 1
First printing, November 2004

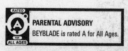

PARENTAL ADVISORY
BEYBLADE is rated A for All Ages.

store.viz.com   www.viz.com

story thus far

Tyson is an Elementay School student who loves Beyblades. He enjoys a good fight, but he cares for his friends and has their trust. One day Tyson helped out his friends by battling the Blade Sharks, a Beyblade group specializing in rough tactics. Tyson was able to win the Battle with the use of the Dragoon, a Beyblade given to him by the masked stranger, Jin. But now Tyson is a target for the leader of the Blade Sharks, Kai Hiwatari. Kai plans to take the Dragoon—one of the four legendary Beyblades said to exist in the world—away from Tyson.

Now that an American-born Beyblader, Max, has joined Tyson's group, the battle between Tyson and Kai is finally ready to begin!

Tyson: an energetic youth with a passionate Beyblader spirit!

Gramps: Tyson's Grandfather, a master swordsman.

Max: Tyson's American-born Beyblading pal!

The Chief: Tyson's best friend, Kenny, loves science more than battling.

Ray: a mysterious, skilled Beyblader from China.

Jin: a very mysterious character whose true identity is unknown

Kai Hiwatari: Kai will do anything to get Tyson's Dragoon!

Contents

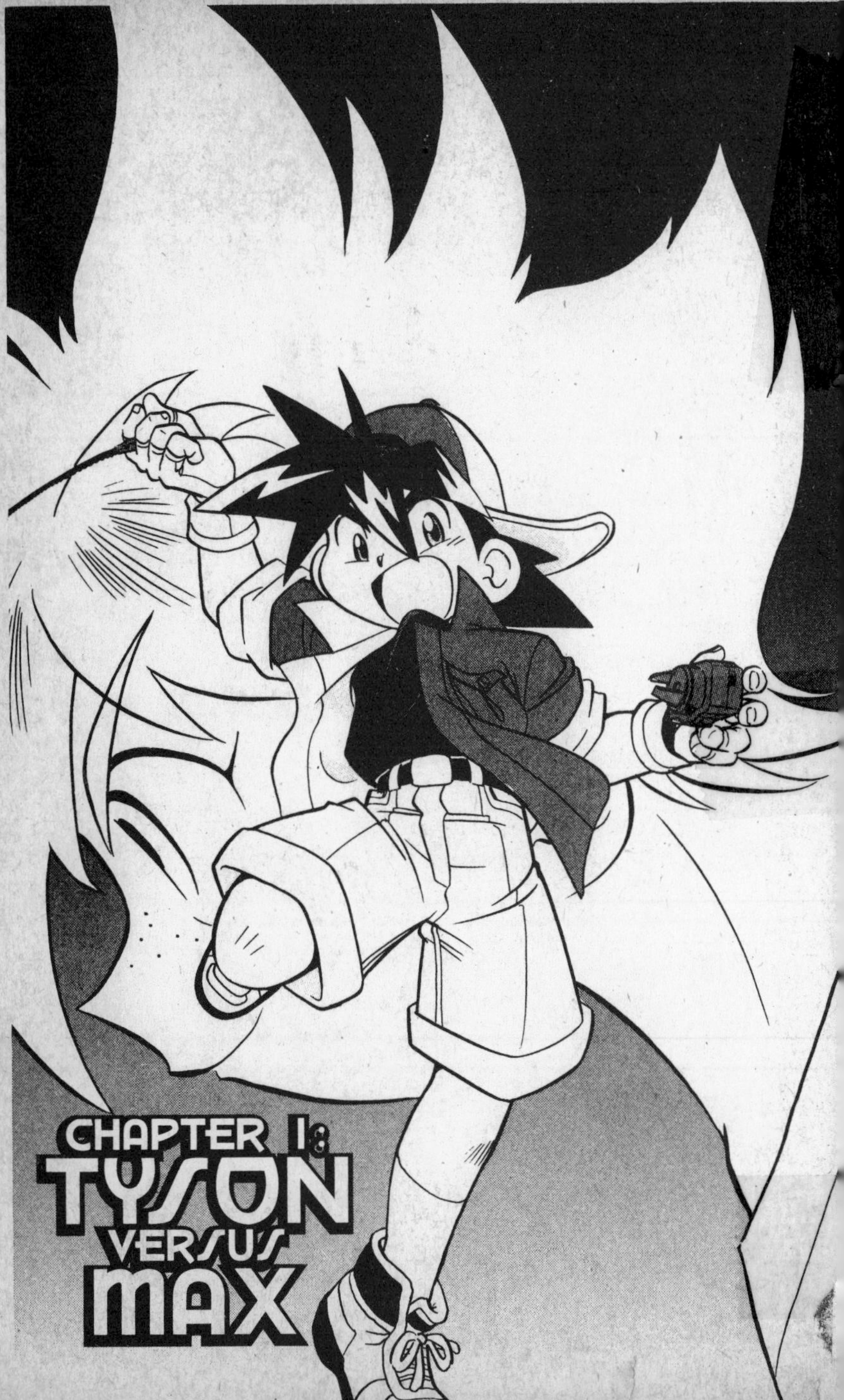
CHAPTER 1:
TYSON
VERSUS
MAX

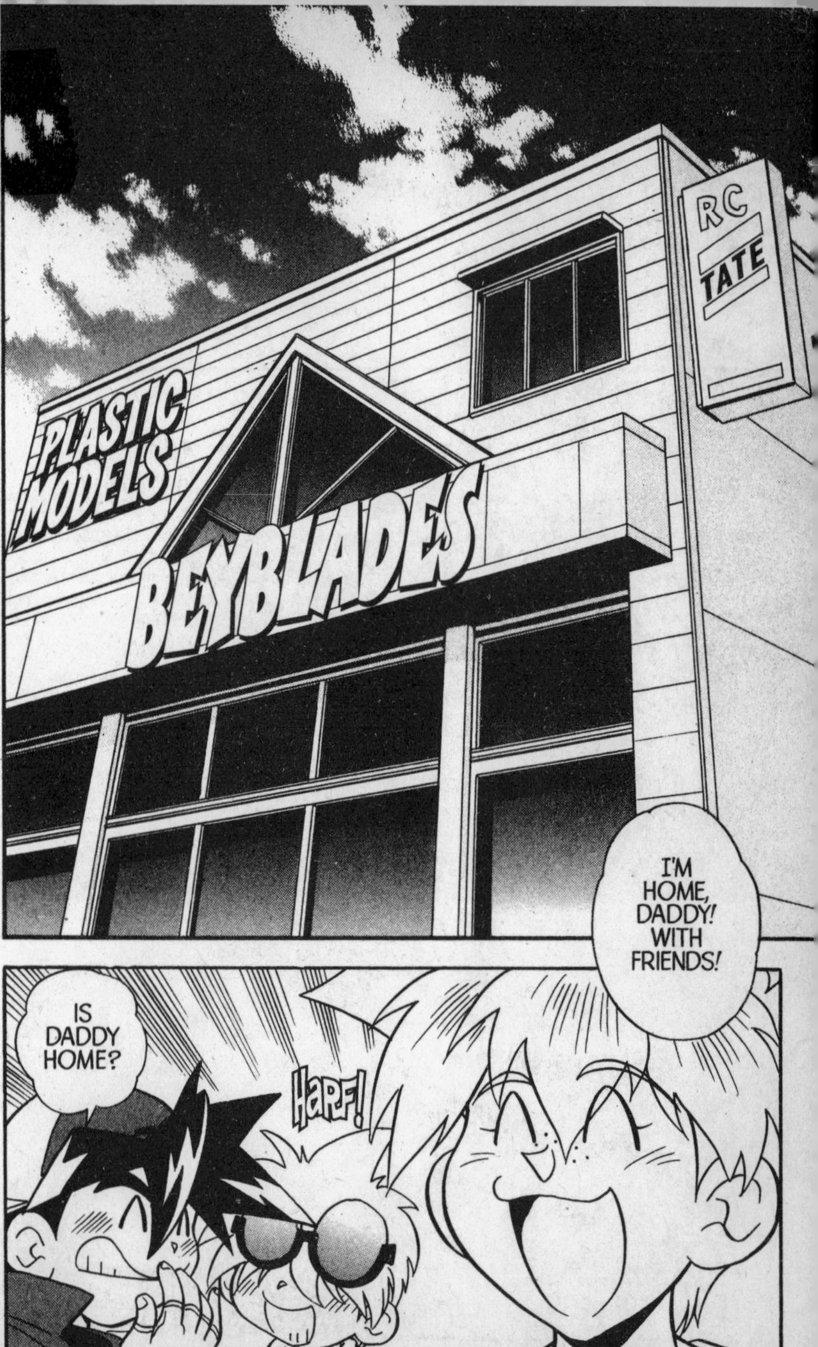
RC TATE
PLASTIC MODELS
BEYBLADES
I'M HOME, DADDY! WITH FRIENDS!
HARF!
IS DADDY HOME?

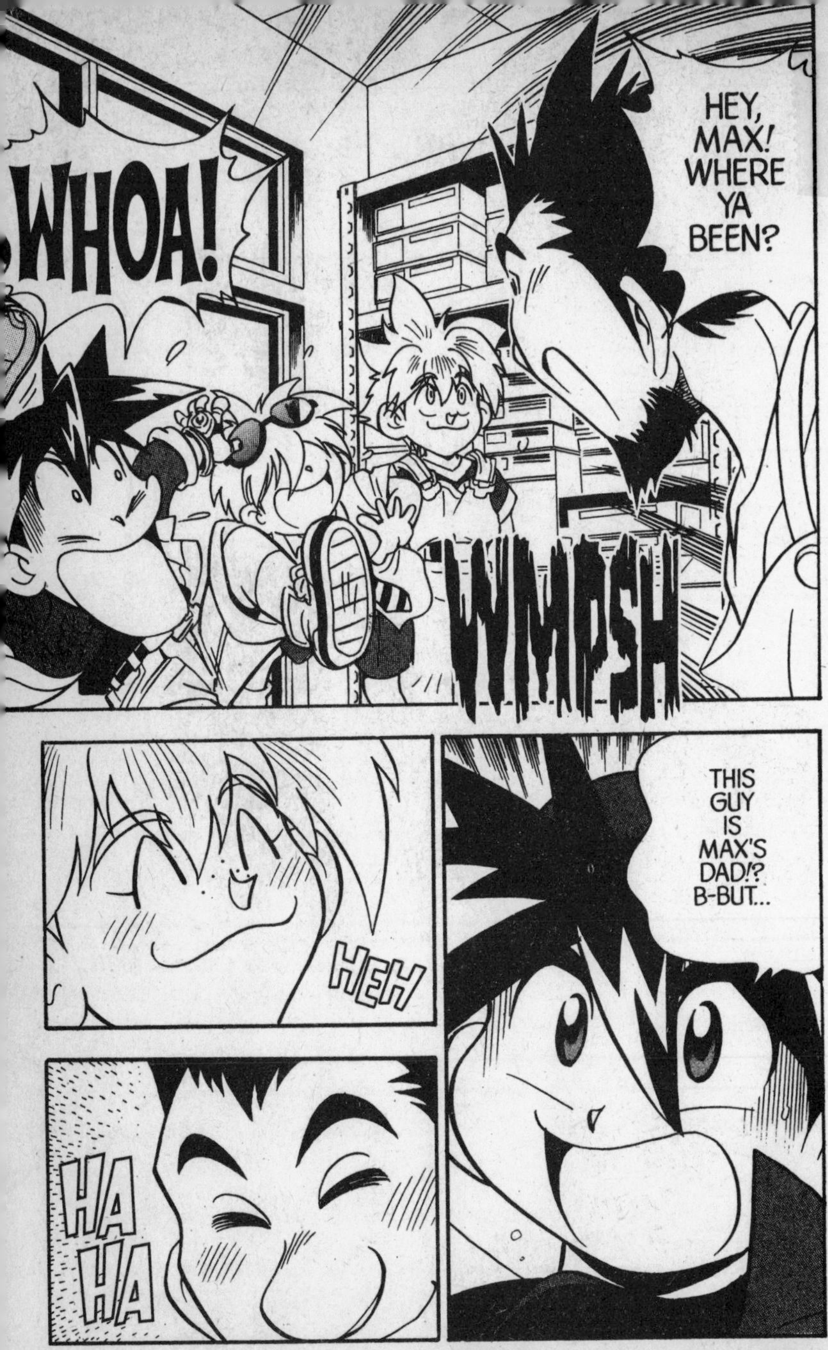
HEY, MAX! WHERE YA BEEN?
WHOA!
WMPSH
THIS GUY IS MAX'S DAD!? B-BUT...
HEH
HA HA

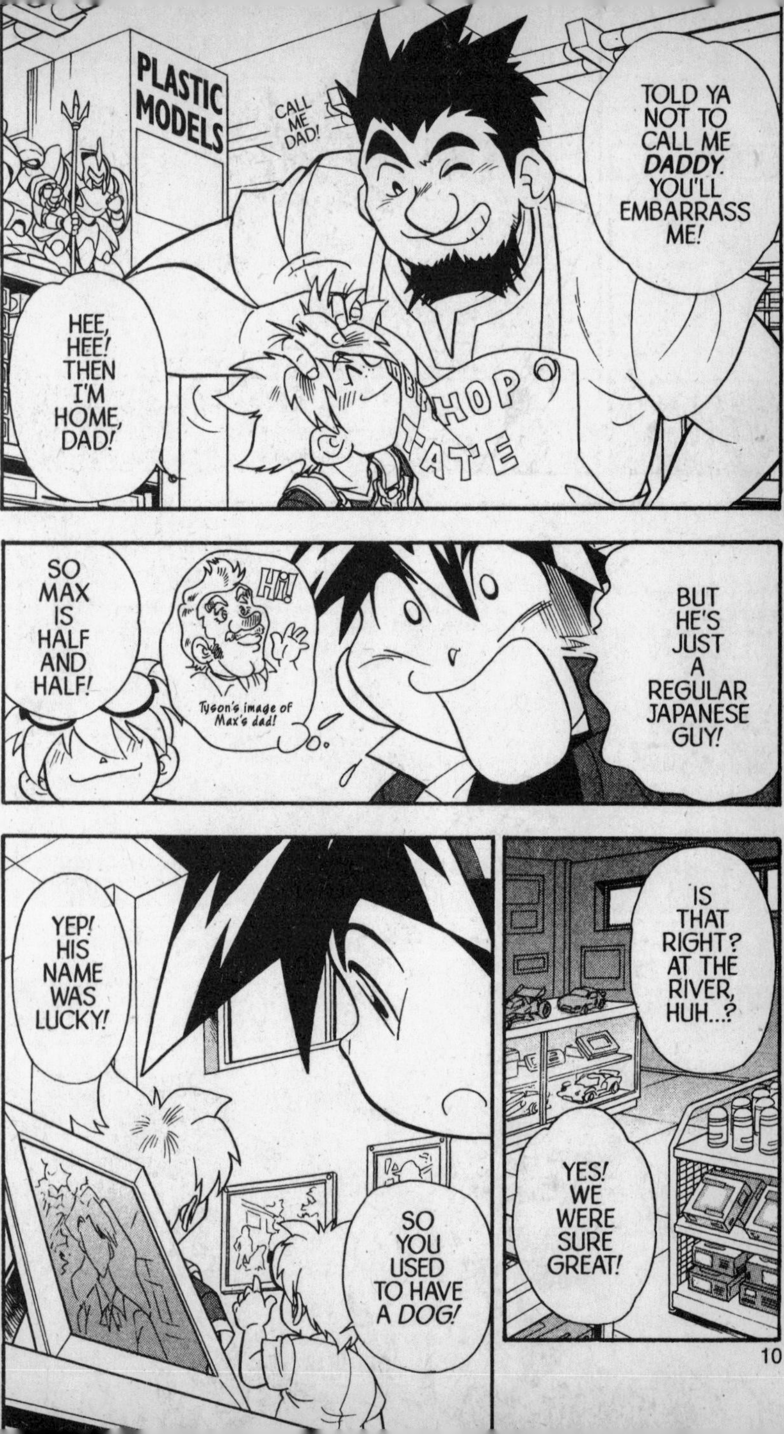
TOLD YA NOT TO CALL ME *DADDY*. YOU'LL EMBARRASS ME!
CALL ME DAD!
PLASTIC MODELS
HEE, HEE! THEN I'M HOME, DAD!
BUT HE'S JUST A REGULAR JAPANESE GUY!
Hi!
Tyson's image of Max's dad!
SO MAX IS HALF AND HALF!
IS THAT RIGHT? AT THE RIVER, HUH...?
YES! WE WERE SURE GREAT!
SO YOU USED TO HAVE A *DOG!*
YEP! HIS NAME WAS LUCKY!

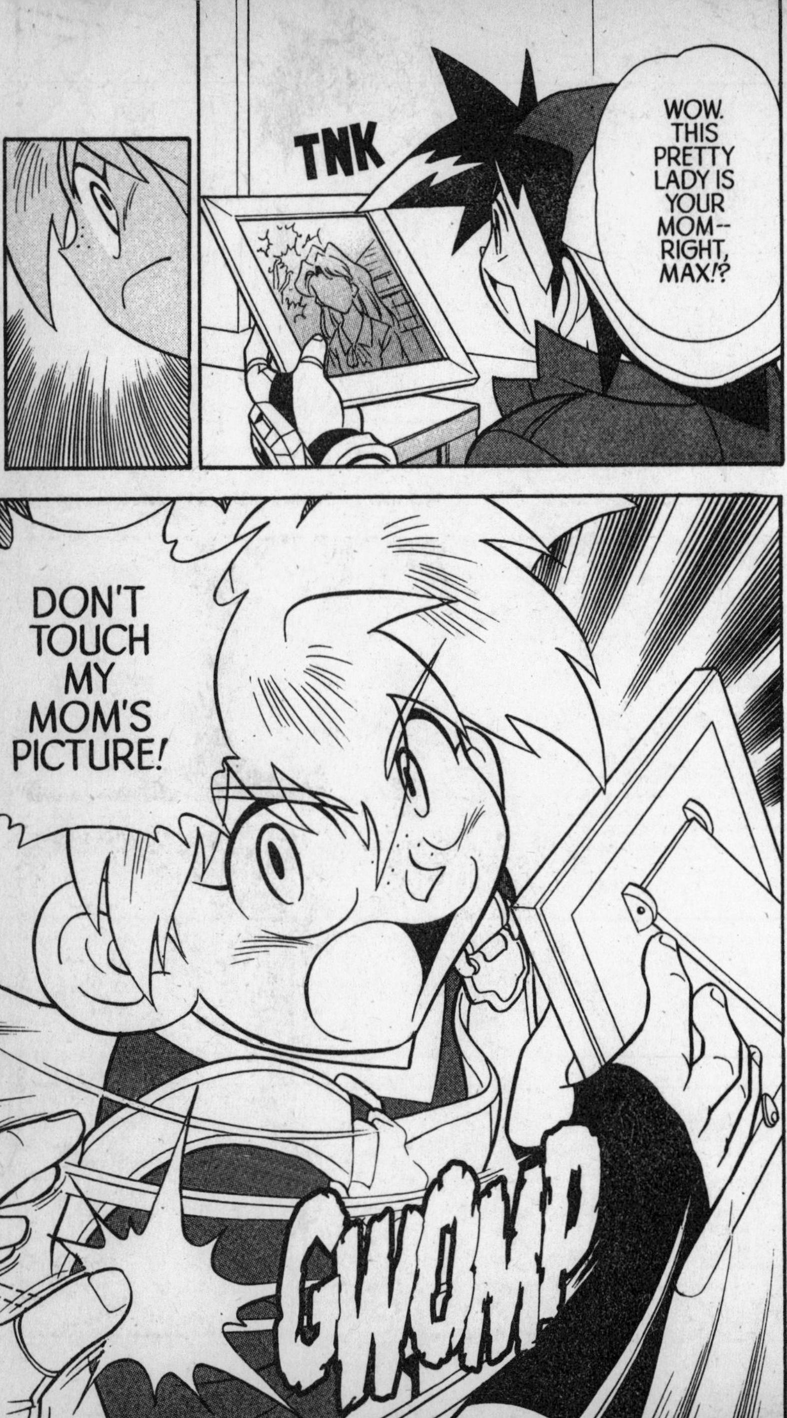
TNK
WOW. THIS PRETTY LADY IS YOUR MOM-- RIGHT, MAX!?
DON'T TOUCH MY MOM'S PICTURE!
GWOMP

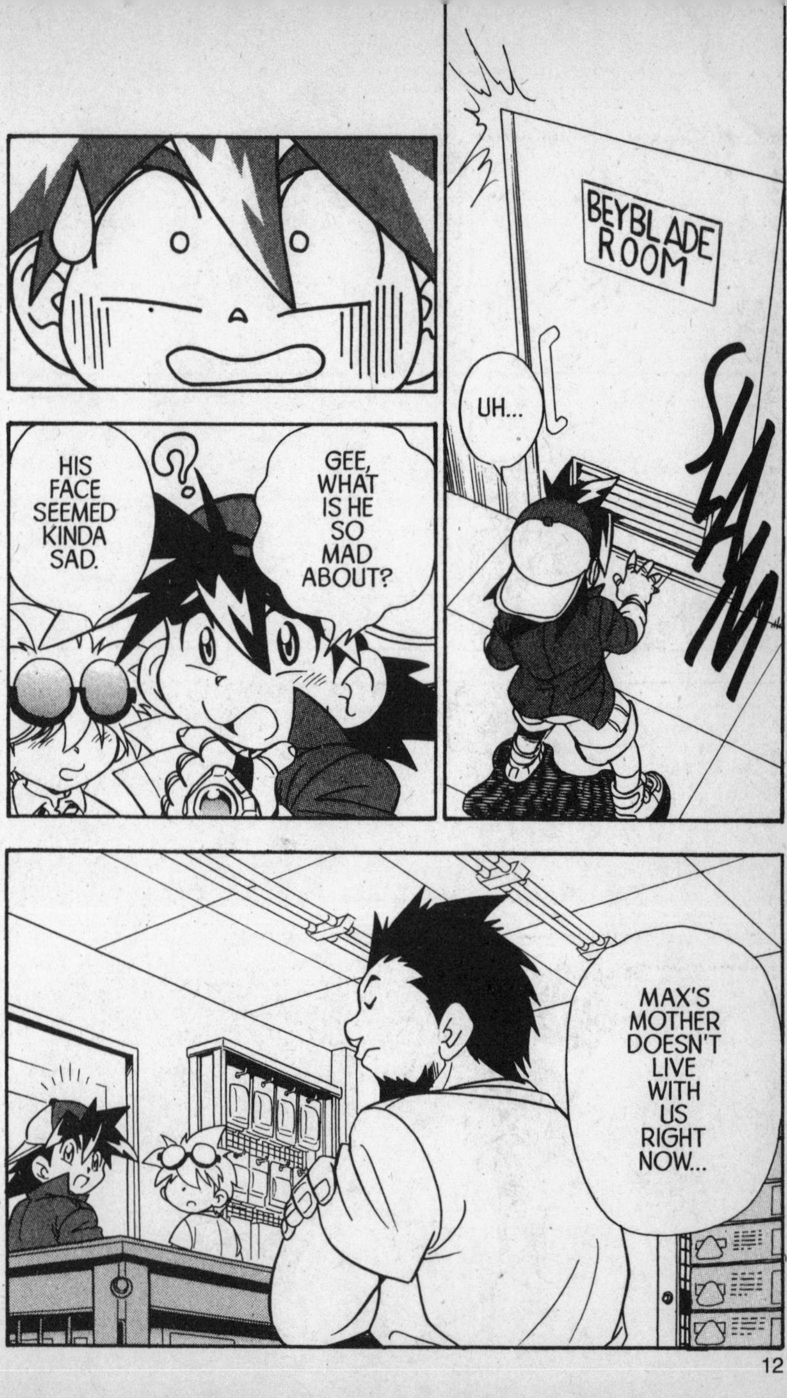

BEYBLADE ROOM
UH...
SLAM
GEE, WHAT IS HE SO MAD ABOUT?
HIS FACE SEEMED KINDA SAD.
MAX'S MOTHER DOESN'T LIVE WITH US RIGHT NOW...

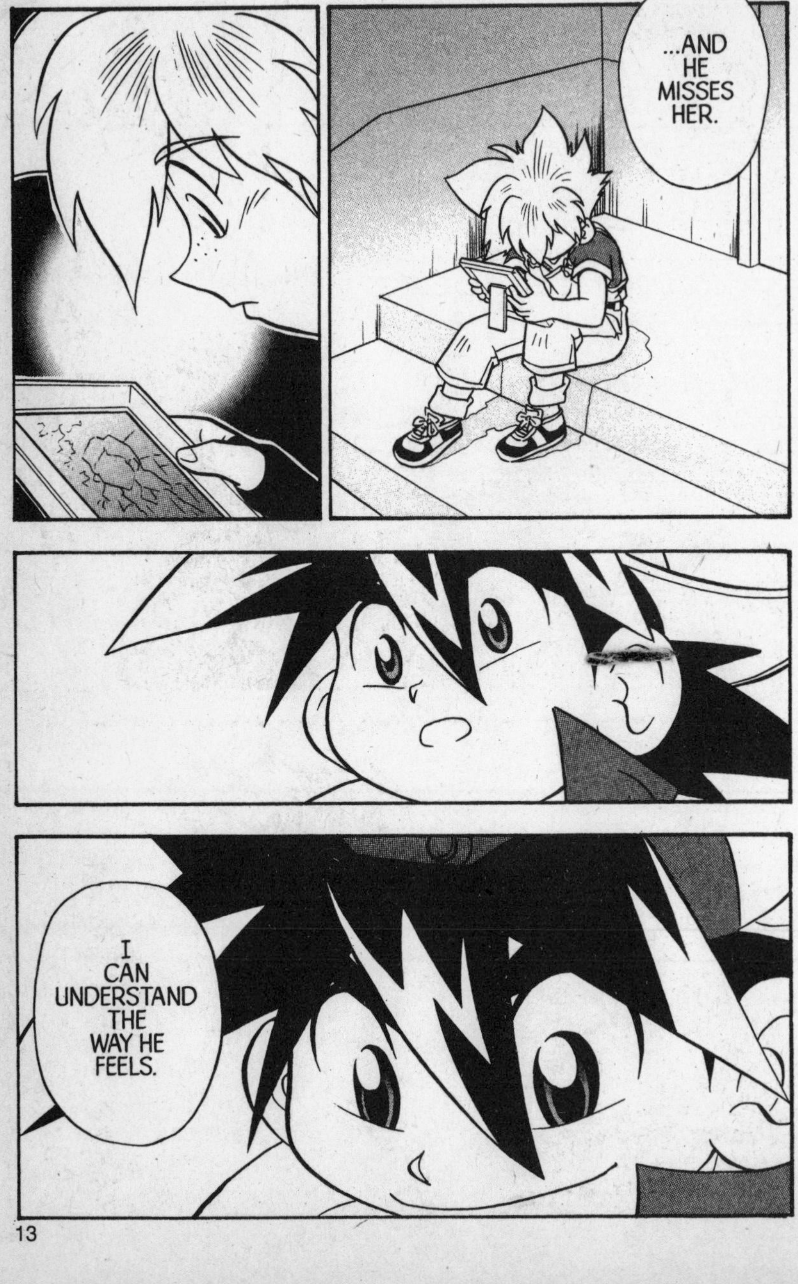
...AND HE MISSES HER.
I CAN UNDERSTAND THE WAY HE FEELS.

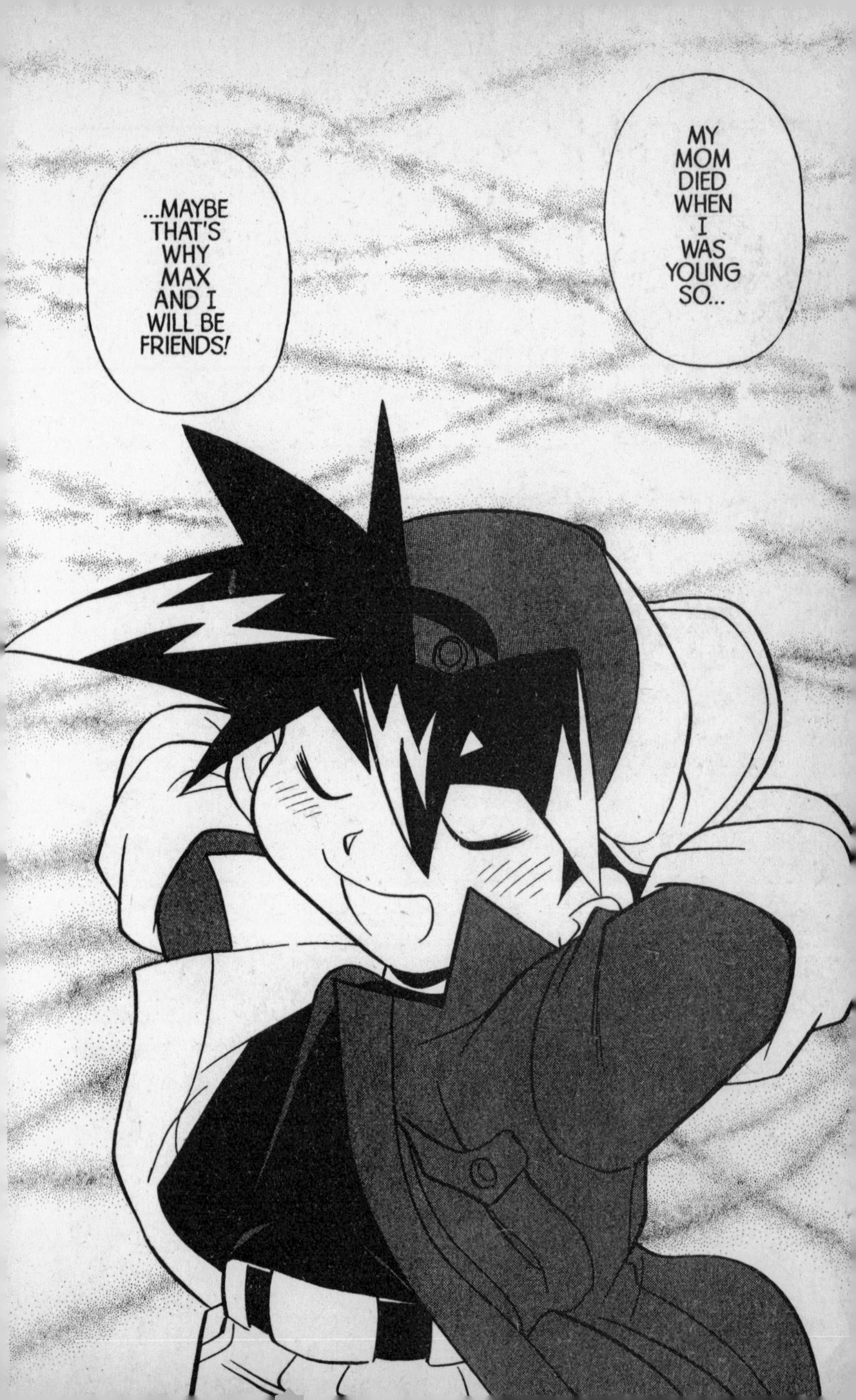
MY MOM DIED WHEN I WAS YOUNG SO...
...MAYBE THAT'S WHY MAX AND I WILL BE FRIENDS!

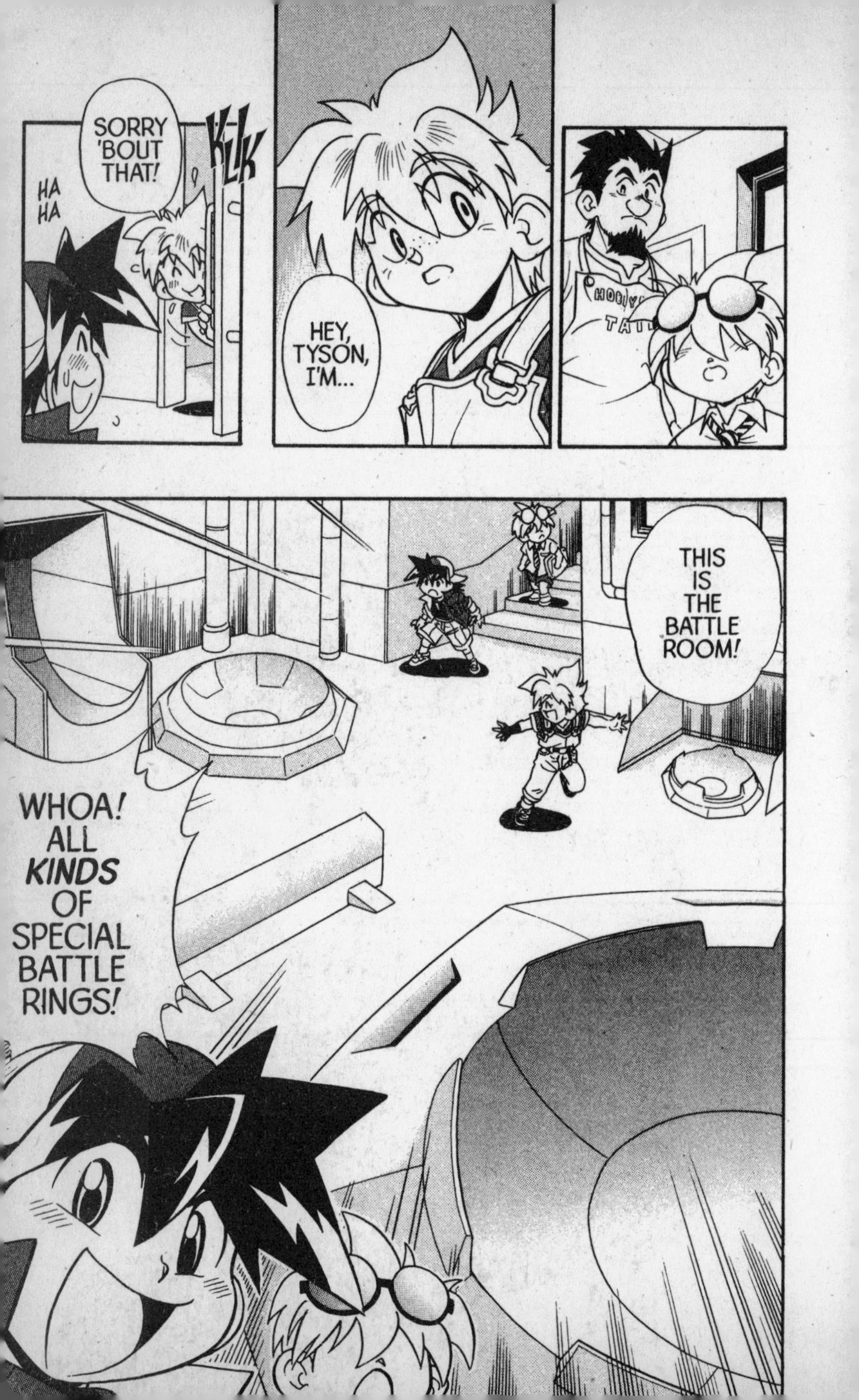
HEY, TYSON, I'M...
KLIK
SORRY 'BOUT THAT!
HA HA
THIS IS THE BATTLE ROOM!
WHOA! ALL **KINDS** OF SPECIAL BATTLE RINGS!

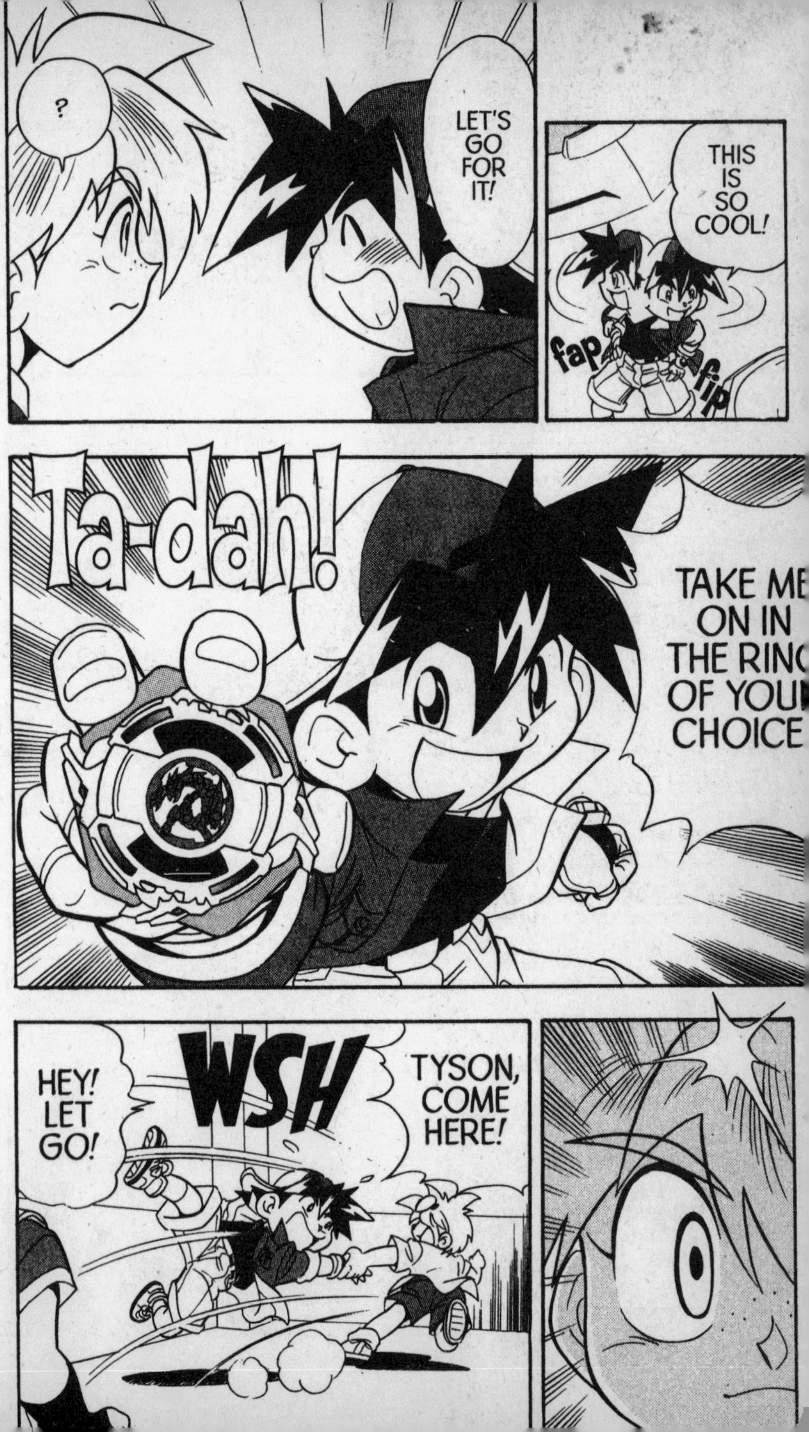
THIS IS SO COOL!
fap
fip
LET'S GO FOR IT!
?
TAKE ME ON IN THE RING OF YOUR CHOICE
Ta-dah!
TYSON, COME HERE!
WSH
HEY! LET GO!

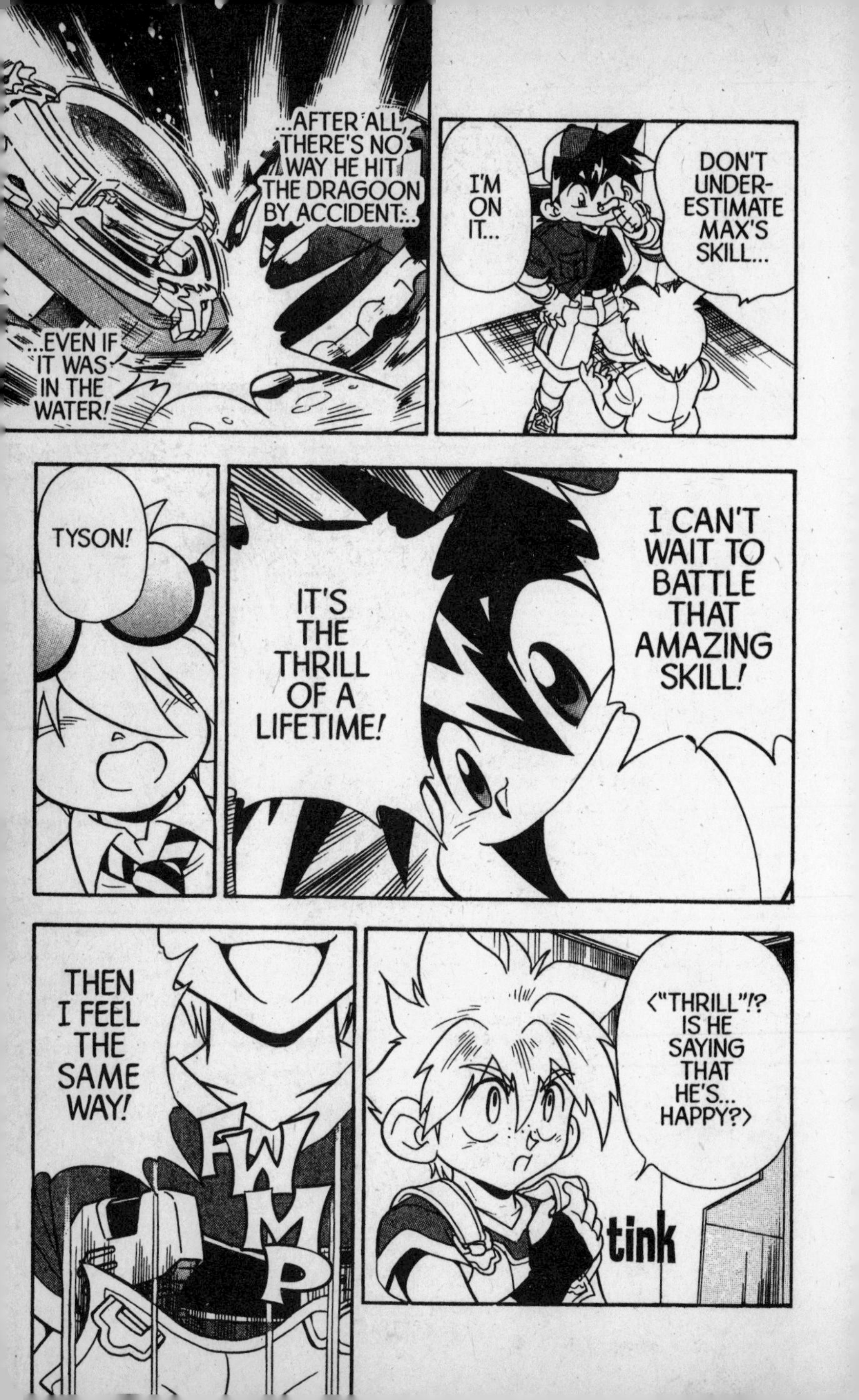
DON'T UNDER-ESTIMATE MAX'S SKILL...
I'M ON IT...
...AFTER ALL, THERE'S NO WAY HE HIT THE DRAGOON BY ACCIDENT...
...EVEN IF IT WAS IN THE WATER!
I CAN'T WAIT TO BATTLE THAT AMAZING SKILL!
IT'S THE THRILL OF A LIFETIME!
TYSON!
<"THRILL"!? IS HE SAYING THAT HE'S... HAPPY?>
tink
THEN I FEEL THE SAME WAY!
FWMP

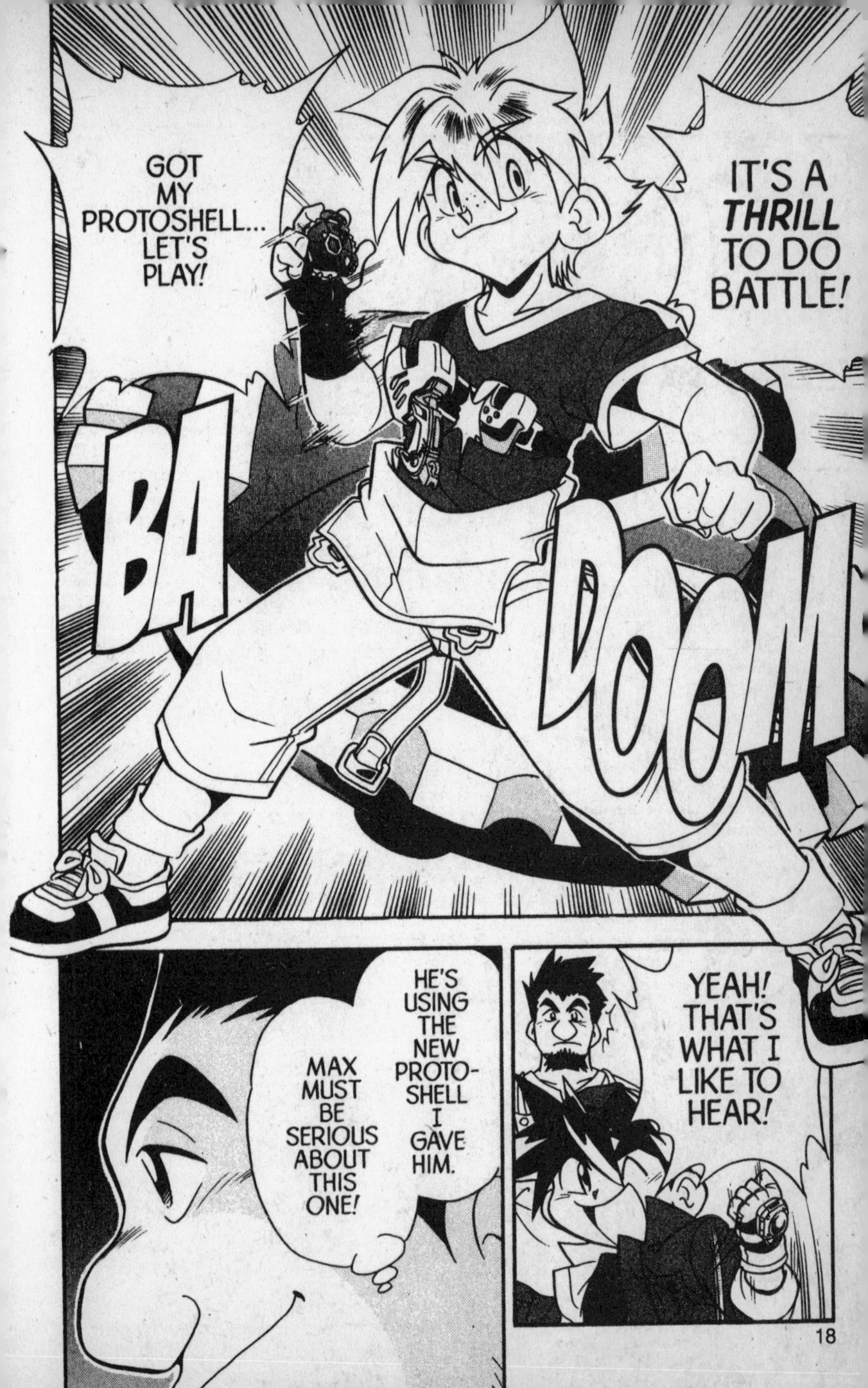
IT'S A *THRILL* TO DO BATTLE!
GOT MY PROTOSHELL... LET'S PLAY!
BA DOOM
YEAH! THAT'S WHAT I LIKE TO HEAR!
HE'S USING THE NEW PROTO-SHELL I GAVE HIM.
MAX MUST BE SERIOUS ABOUT THIS ONE!

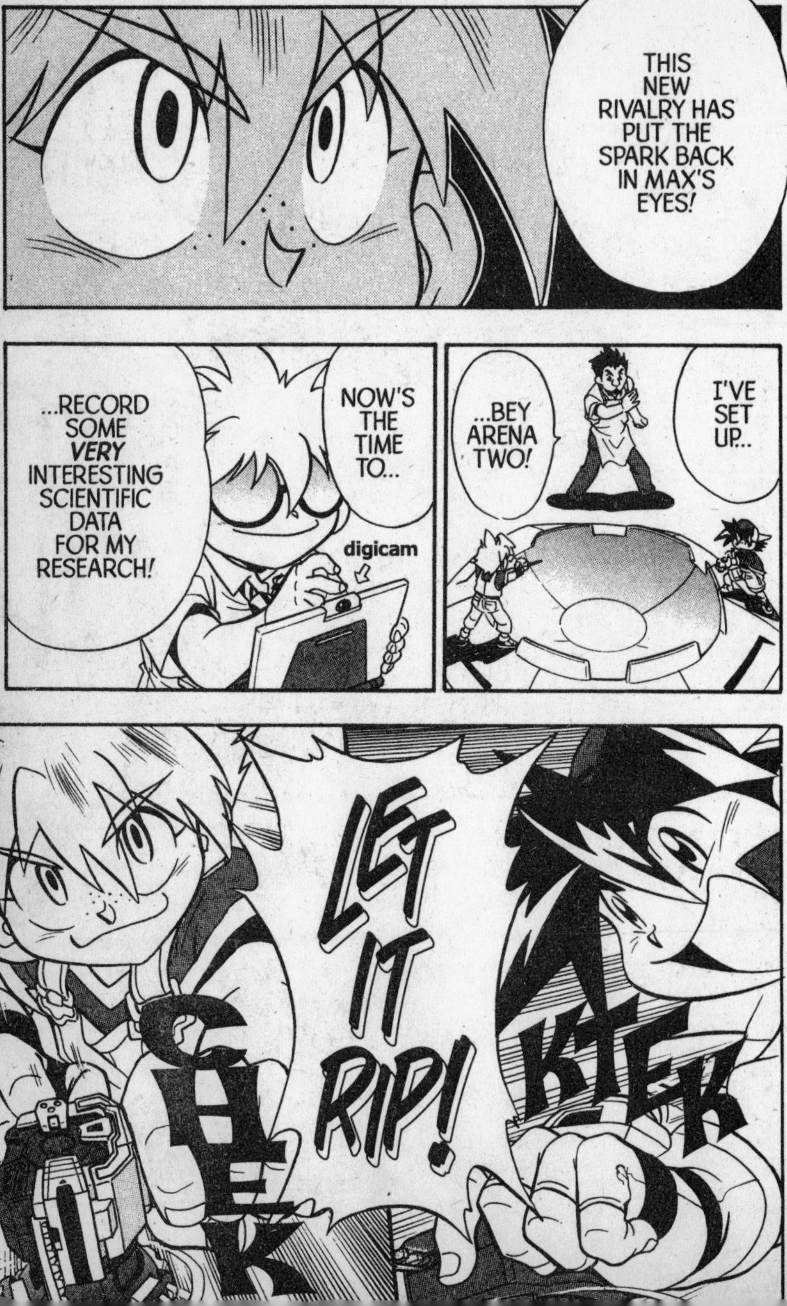
THIS NEW RIVALRY HAS PUT THE SPARK BACK IN MAX'S EYES!
I'VE SET UP...
...BEY ARENA TWO!
NOW'S THE TIME TO...
...RECORD SOME *VERY* INTERESTING SCIENTIFIC DATA FOR MY RESEARCH!
digicam
LET IT RIP!

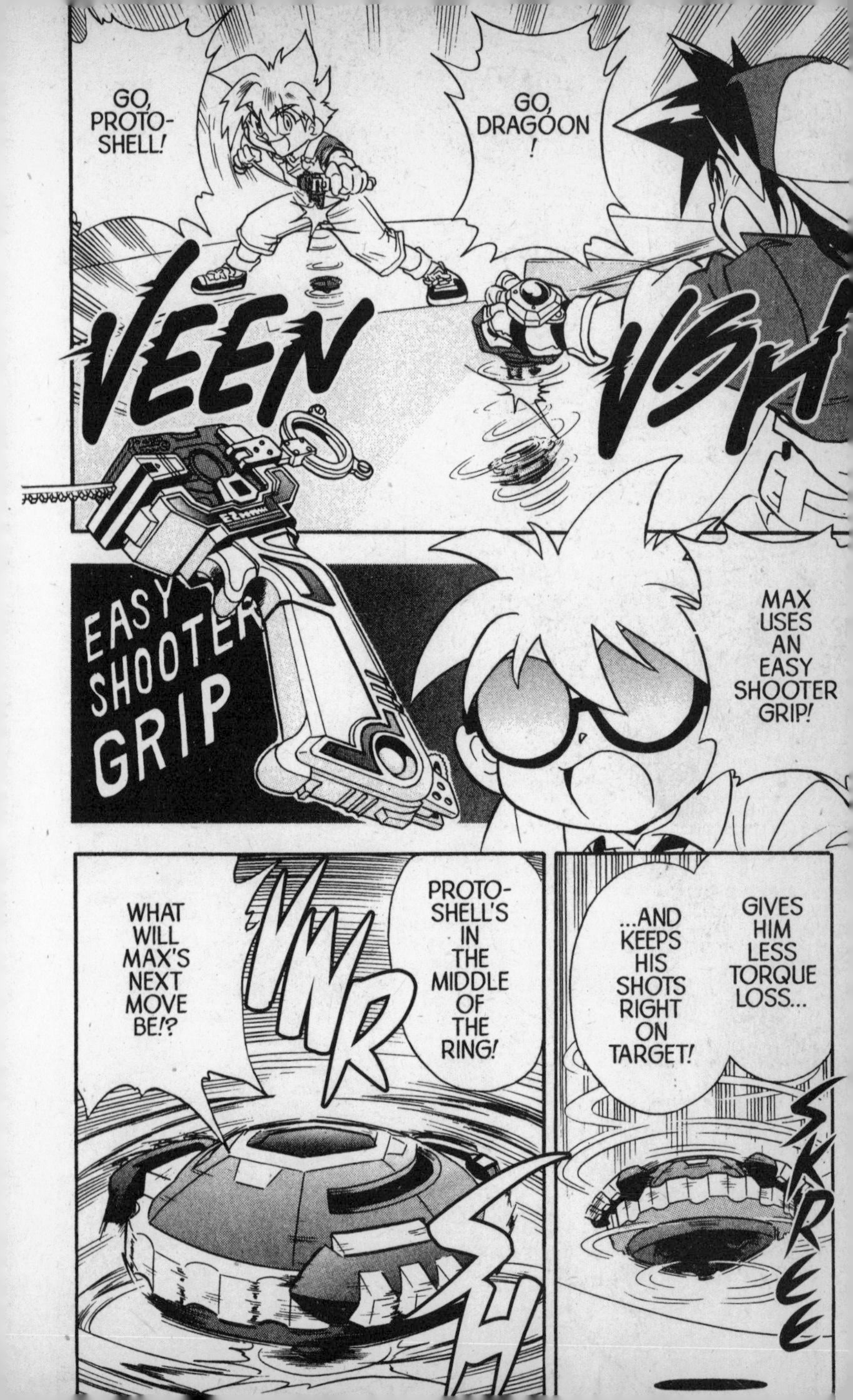
GO, DRAGOON!
GO, PROTO-SHELL!
VSH
VEEN
MAX USES AN EASY SHOOTER GRIP!
EASY SHOOTER GRIP
GIVES HIM LESS TORQUE LOSS...
...AND KEEPS HIS SHOTS RIGHT ON TARGET!
SKREE
PROTO-SHELL'S IN THE MIDDLE OF THE RING!
VWR
WHAT WILL MAX'S NEXT MOVE BE!?
SH

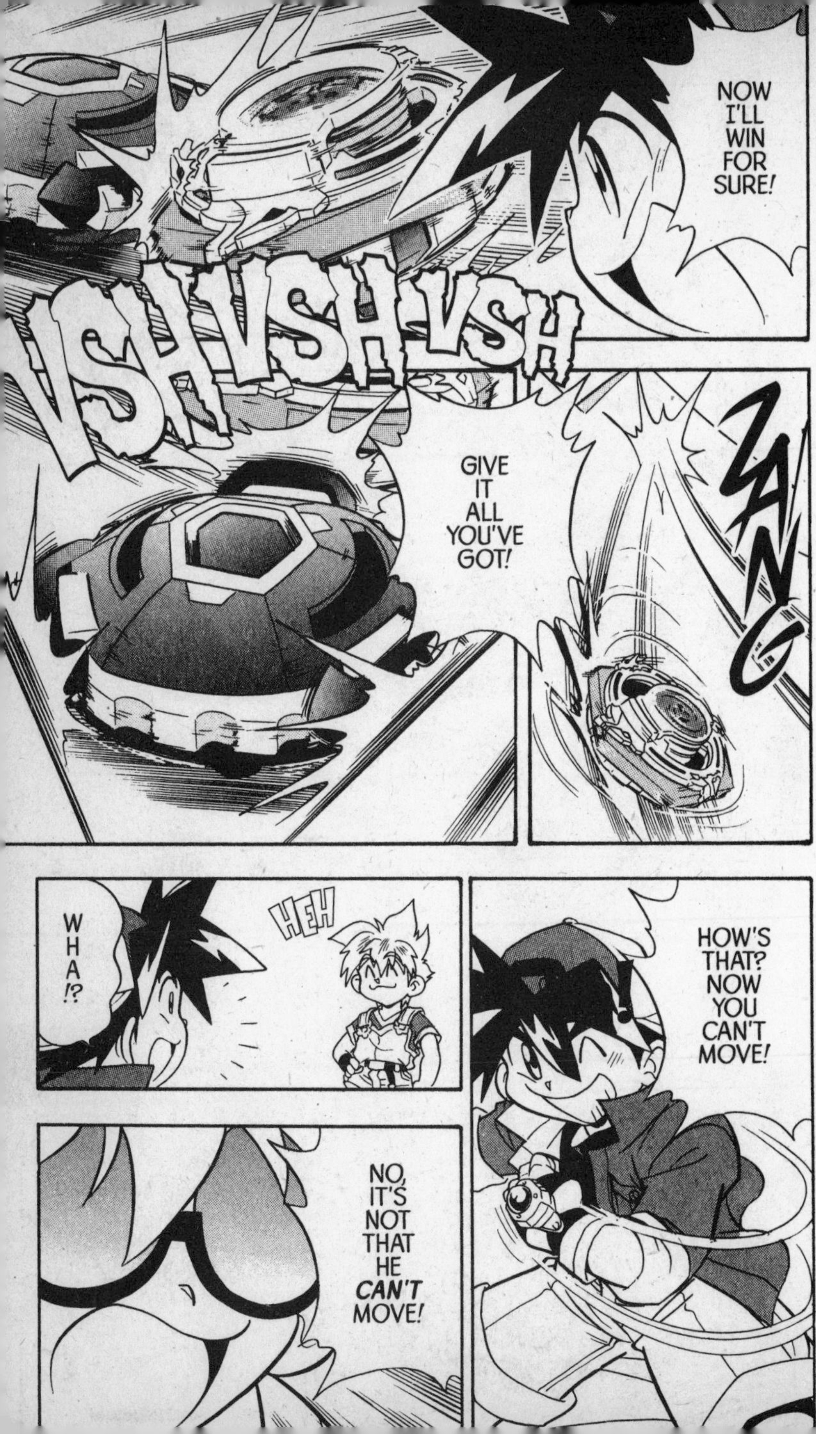
NOW I'LL WIN FOR SURE!
VSH VSH VSH
ZANG
GIVE IT ALL YOU'VE GOT!
HOW'S THAT? NOW YOU CAN'T MOVE!
WHA!?
HEH
NO, IT'S NOT THAT HE ***CAN'T*** MOVE!

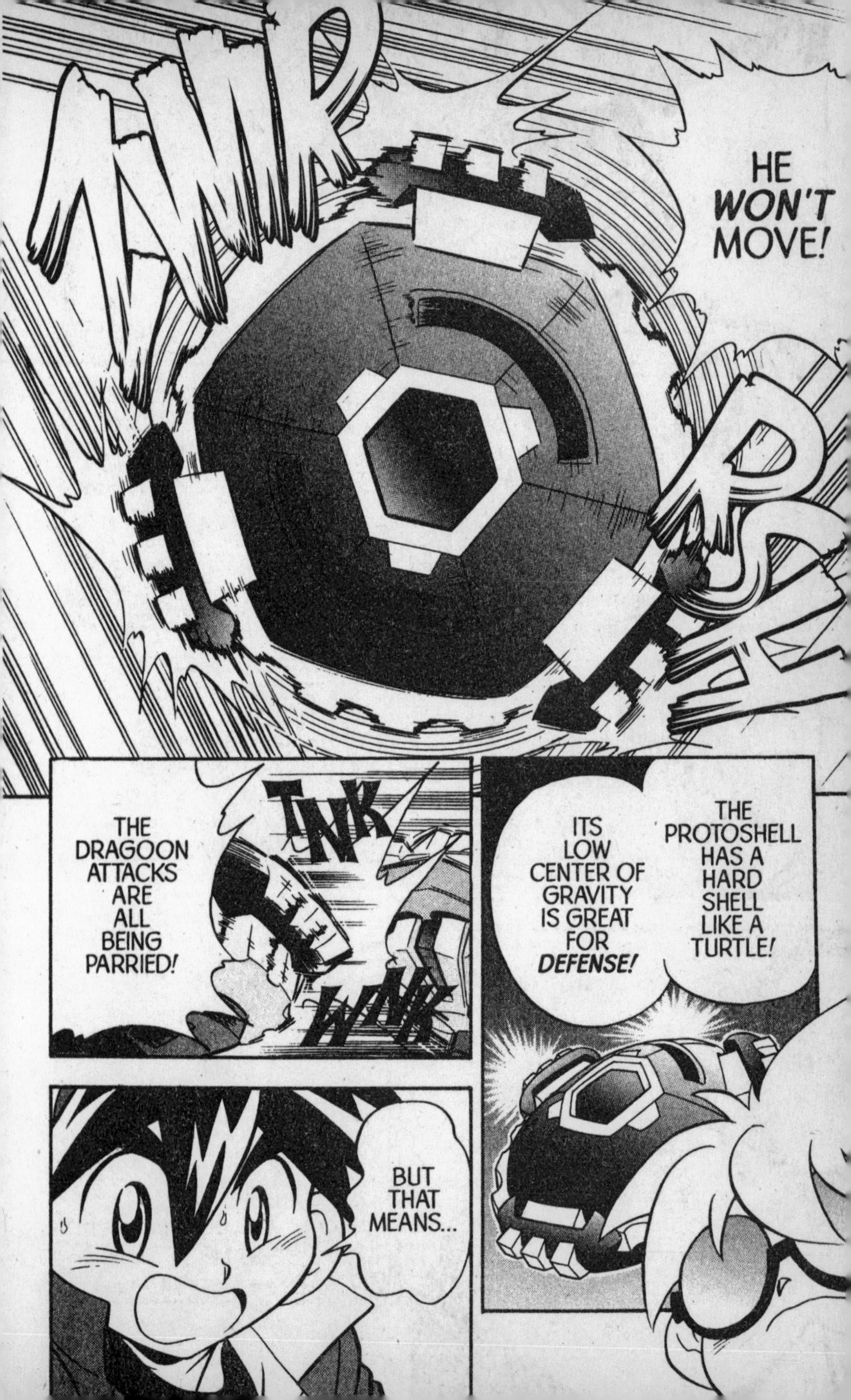
HE WON'T MOVE!
THE PROTOSHELL HAS A HARD SHELL LIKE A TURTLE!
ITS LOW CENTER OF GRAVITY IS GREAT FOR DEFENSE!
THE DRAGOON ATTACKS ARE ALL BEING PARRIED!
TINK
WINK
BUT THAT MEANS...

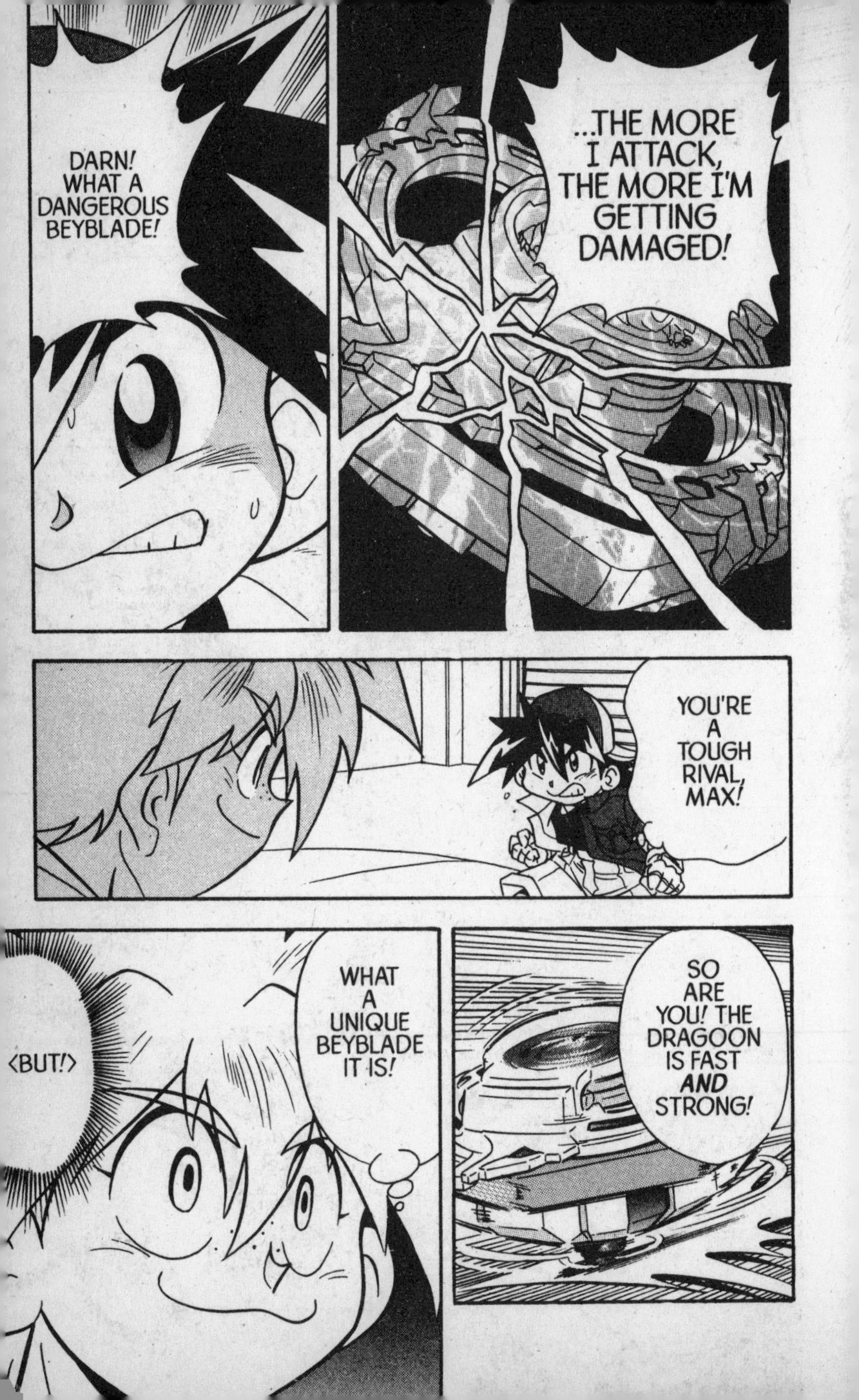
...THE MORE I ATTACK, THE MORE I'M GETTING DAMAGED!
DARN! WHAT A DANGEROUS BEYBLADE!
YOU'RE A TOUGH RIVAL, MAX!
SO ARE YOU! THE DRAGOON IS FAST ***AND*** STRONG!
WHAT A UNIQUE BEYBLADE IT IS!
<BUT!>

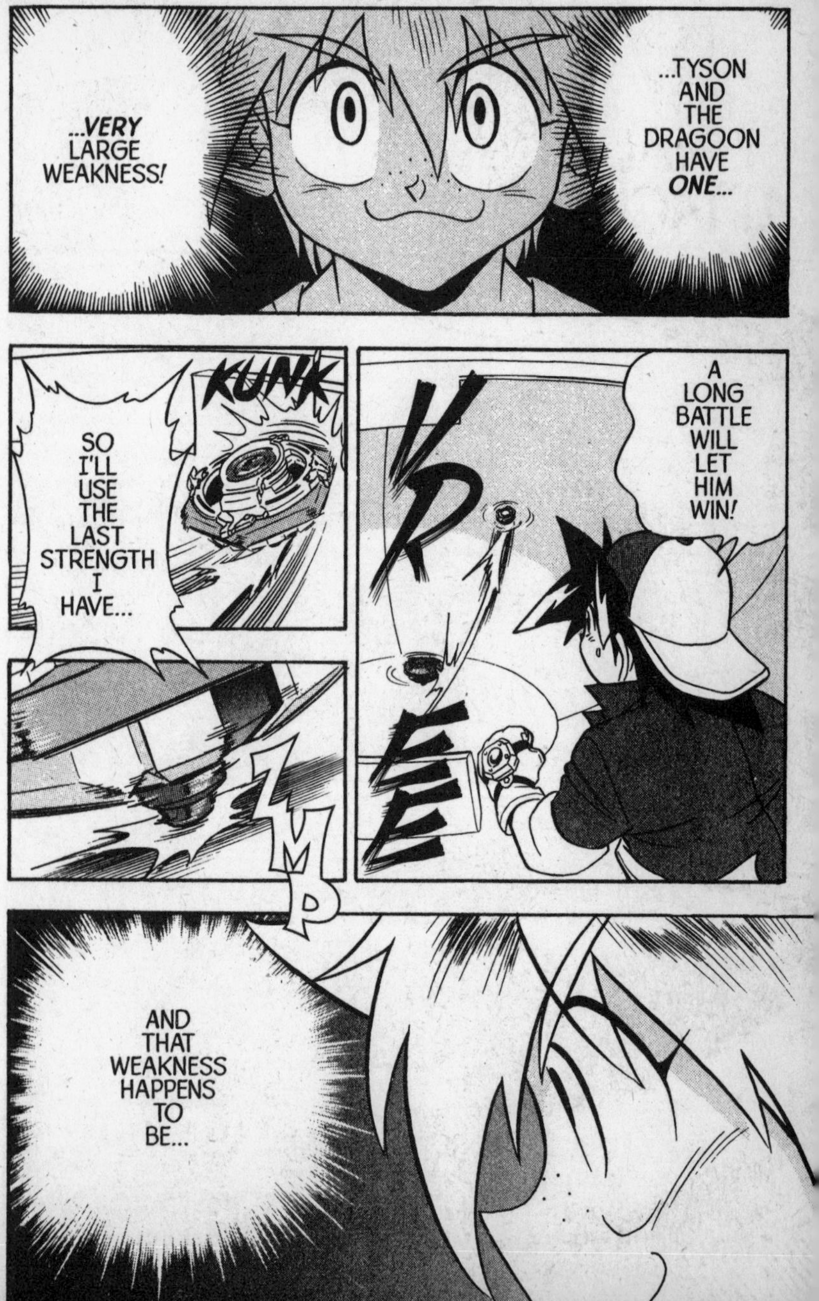
...TYSON AND THE DRAGOON HAVE *ONE*...
...*VERY* LARGE WEAKNESS!
A LONG BATTLE WILL LET HIM WIN!
VREEE
KUNK
SO I'LL USE THE LAST STRENGTH I HAVE...
AND THAT WEAKNESS HAPPENS TO BE...

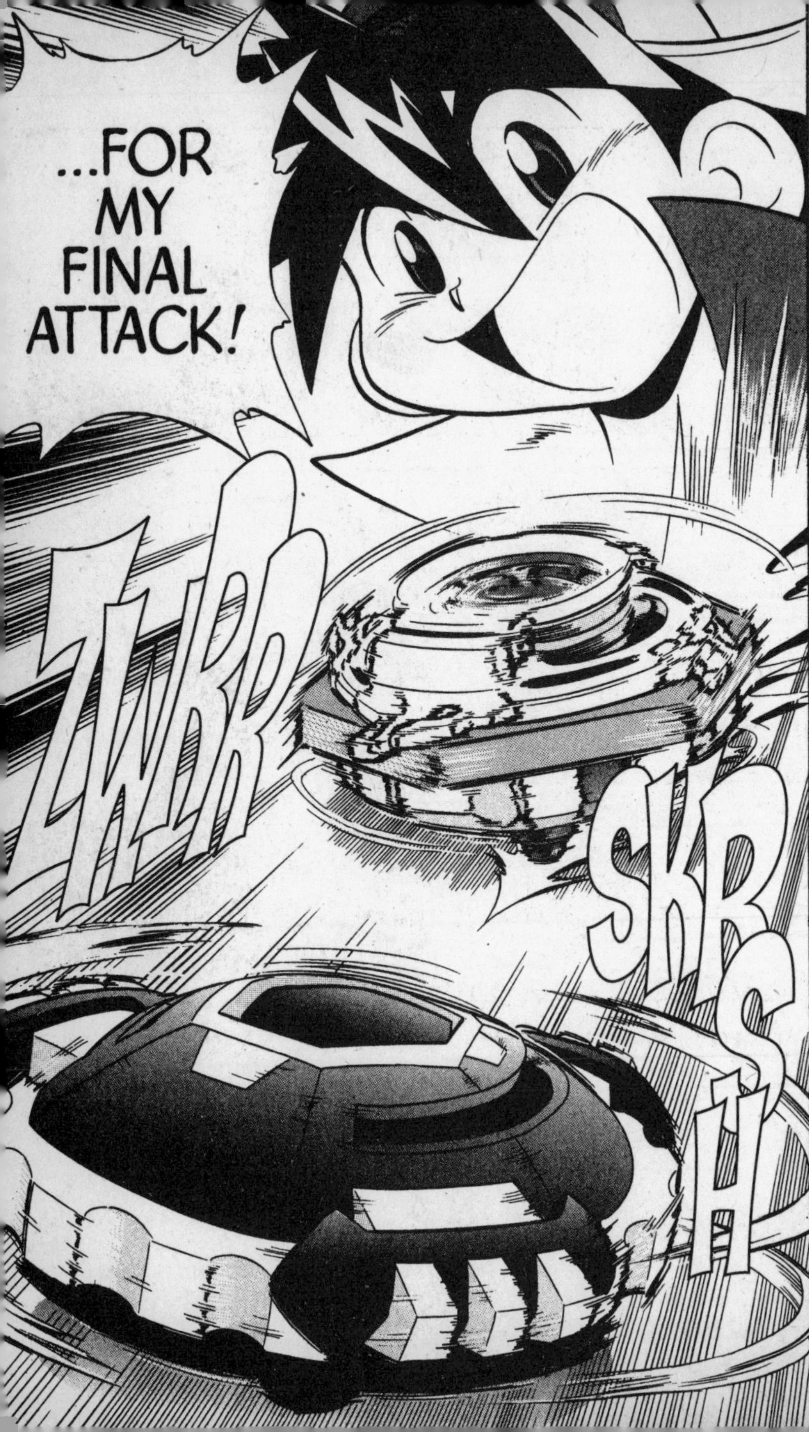
...FOR MY FINAL ATTACK!
ZWRRR
SKRSSH

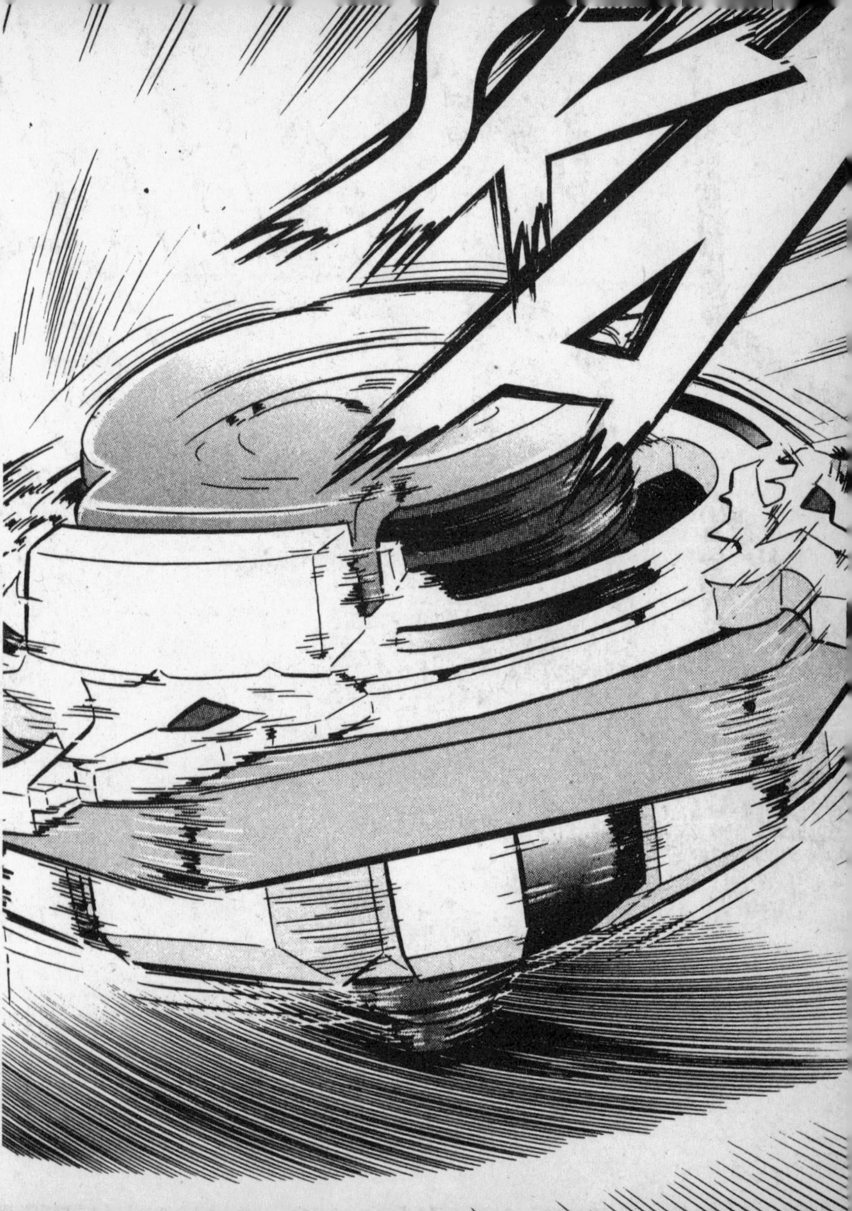

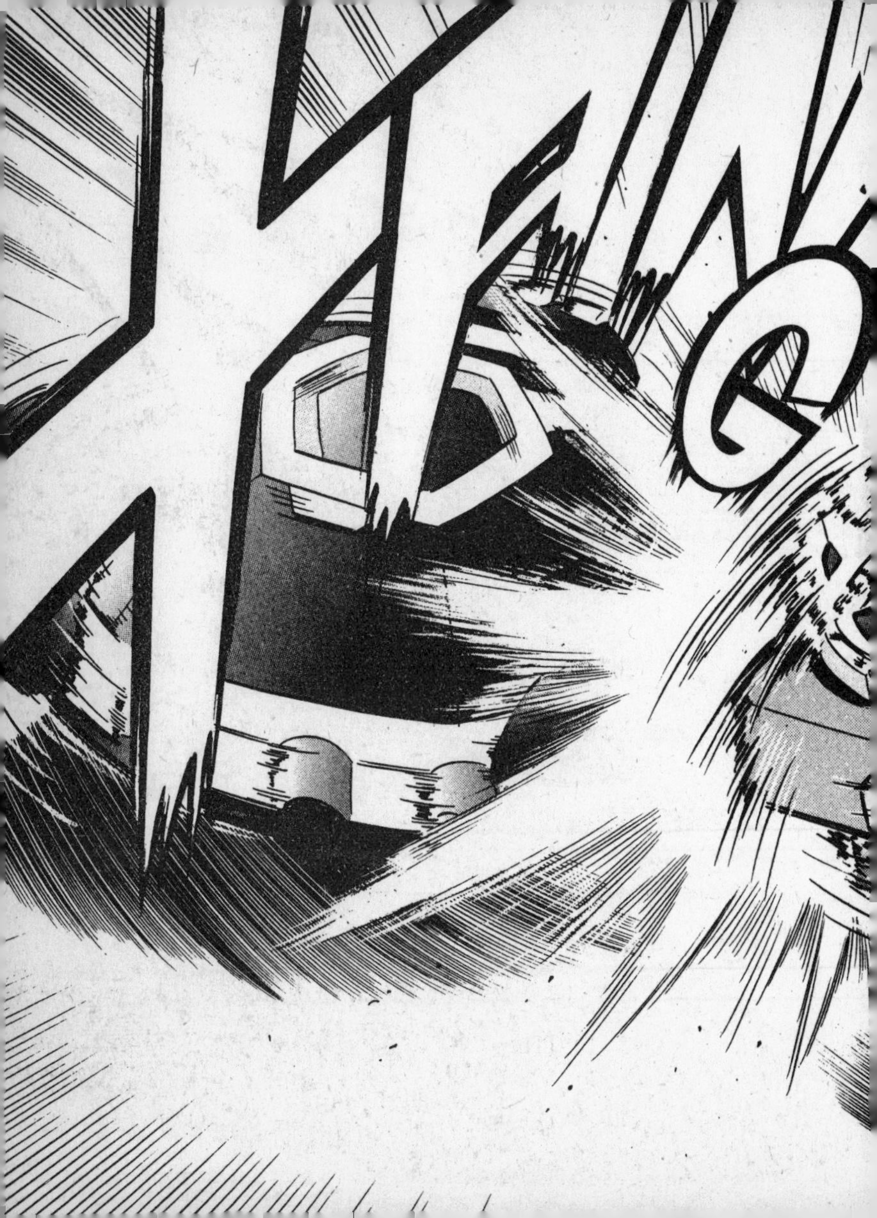

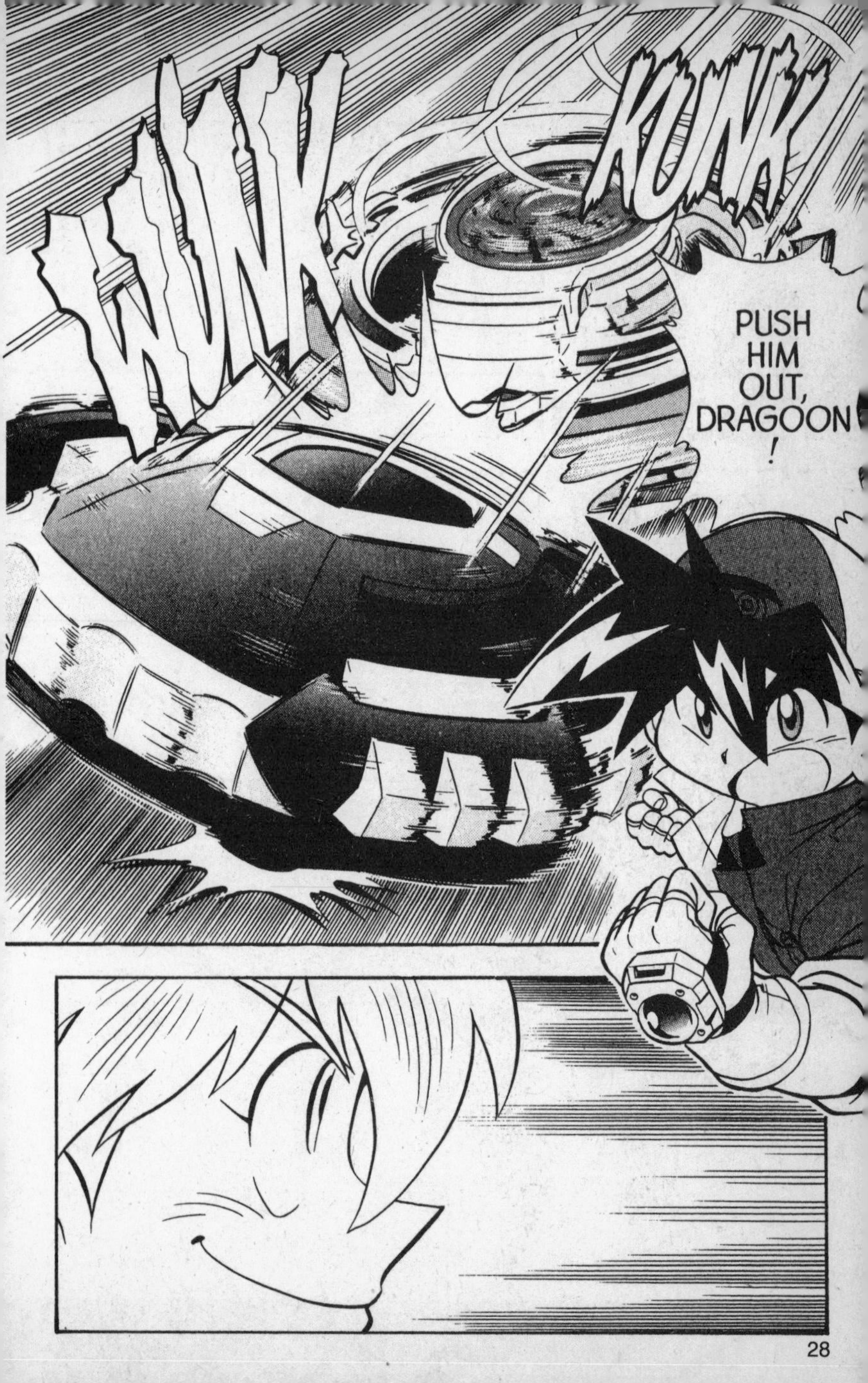
KONK
WUNK
PUSH HIM OUT, DRAGOON!

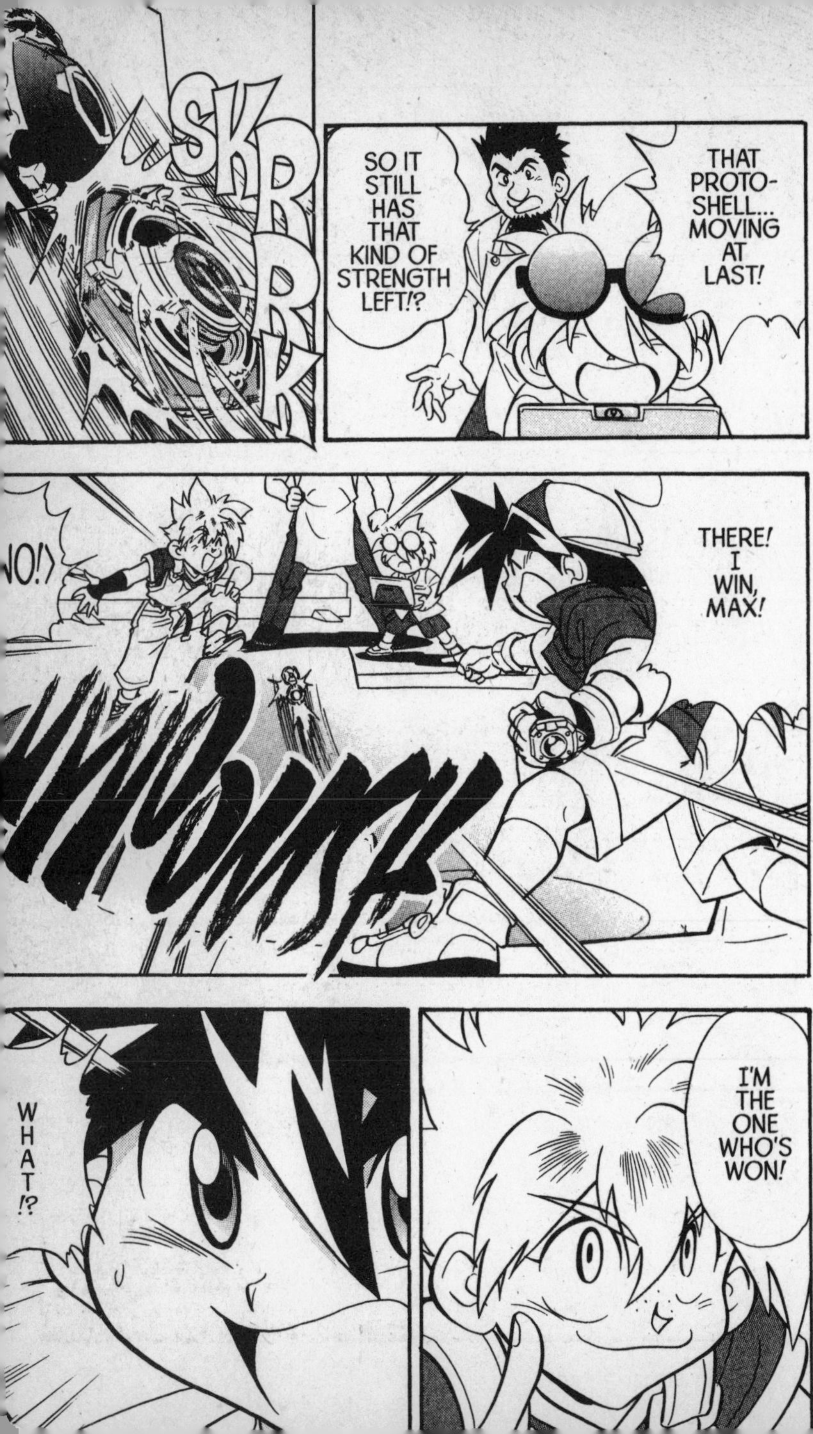

THAT PROTO-SHELL... MOVING AT LAST!
SO IT STILL HAS THAT KIND OF STRENGTH LEFT!?
SKRRRK
THERE! I WIN, MAX!
I'M THE ONE WHO'S WON!
WHAT!?

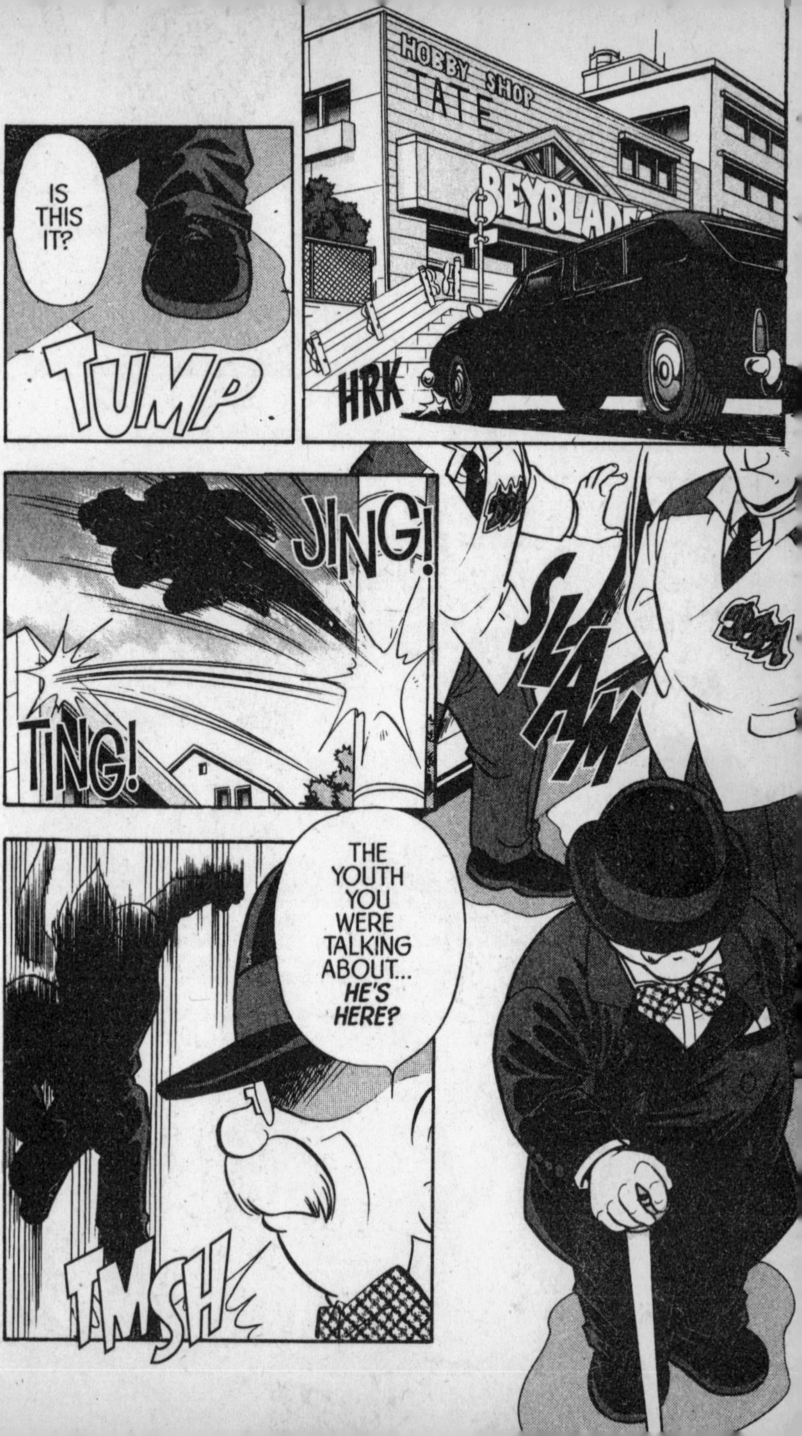
HOBBY SHOP
TATE
HRK
IS THIS IT?
TUMP
SLAM
JING!
TING!
THE YOUTH YOU WERE TALKING ABOUT... *HE'S HERE?*
TMSH

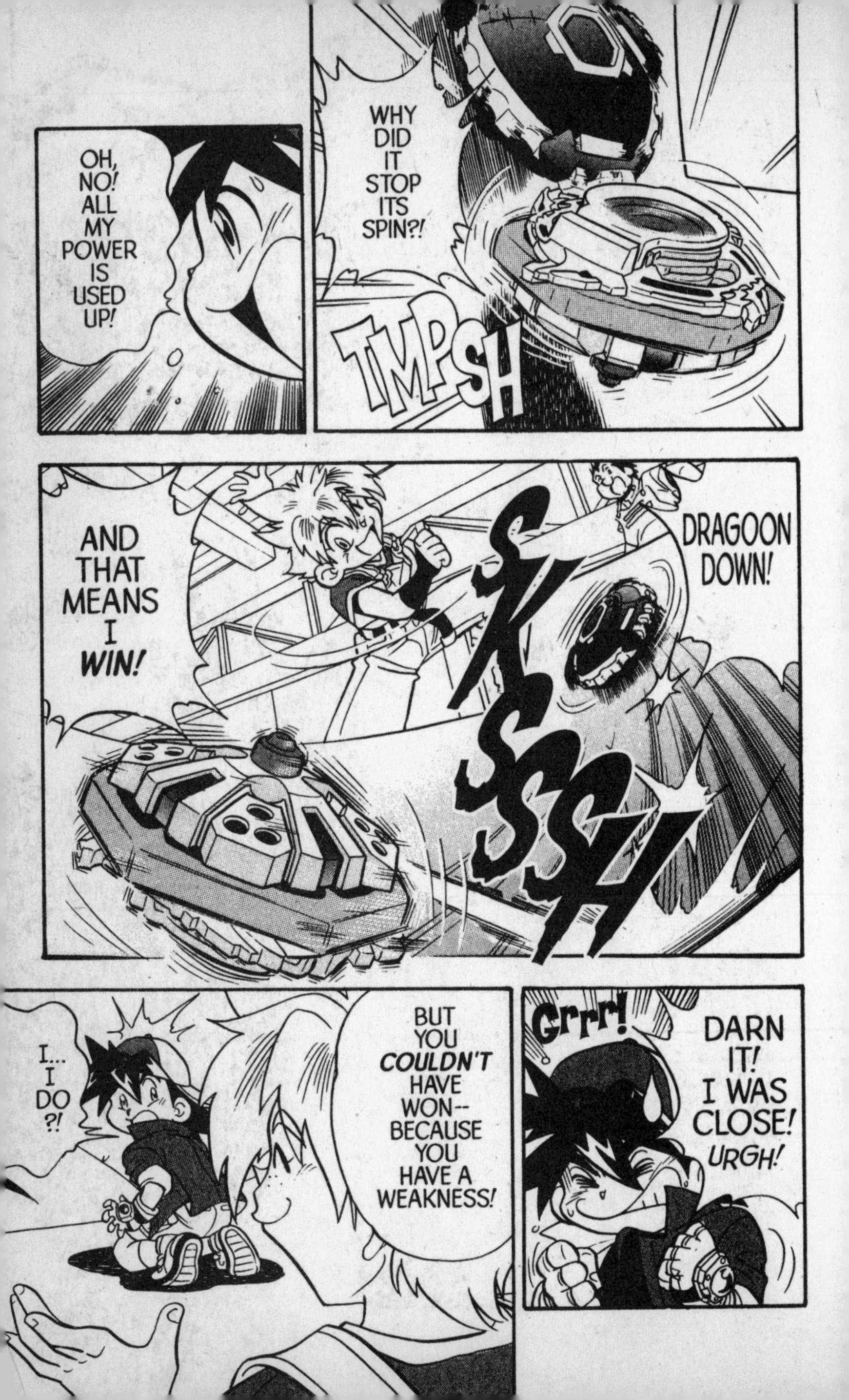
WHY DID IT STOP ITS SPIN?!
TMPSH
OH, NO! ALL MY POWER IS USED UP!
DRAGOON DOWN!
AND THAT MEANS I *WIN!*
Grrr!
DARN IT! I WAS CLOSE!
URGH!
BUT YOU *COULDN'T* HAVE WON-- BECAUSE YOU HAVE A WEAKNESS!
I... I DO?!

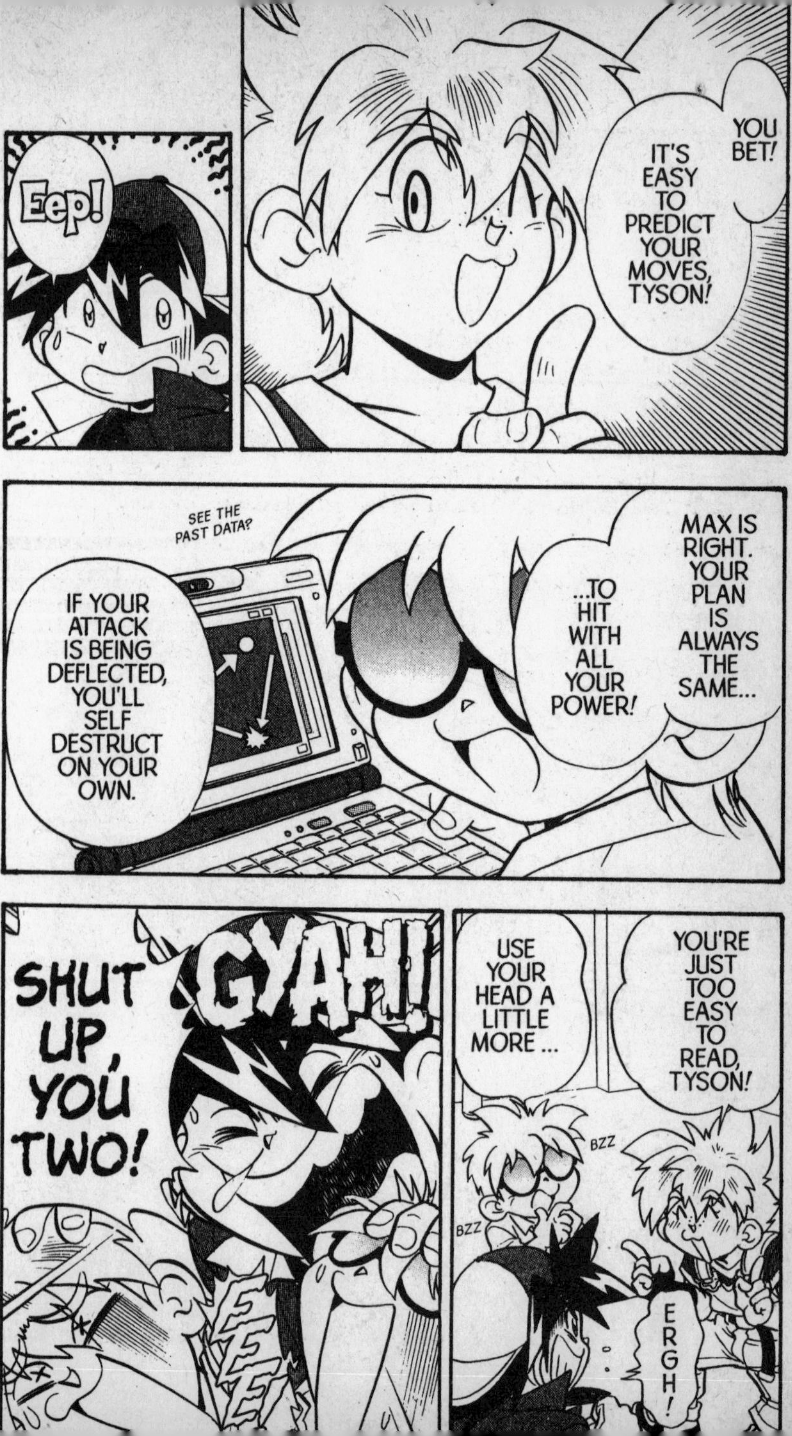
YOU BET!
IT'S EASY TO PREDICT YOUR MOVES, TYSON!
Eep!
MAX IS RIGHT. YOUR PLAN IS ALWAYS THE SAME...
...TO HIT WITH ALL YOUR POWER!
SEE THE PAST DATA?
IF YOUR ATTACK IS BEING DEFLECTED, YOU'LL SELF DESTRUCT ON YOUR OWN.
YOU'RE JUST TOO EASY TO READ, TYSON!
USE YOUR HEAD A LITTLE MORE ...
BZZ
BZZ
ERGH!
GYAH!
SHUT UP, YOU TWO!

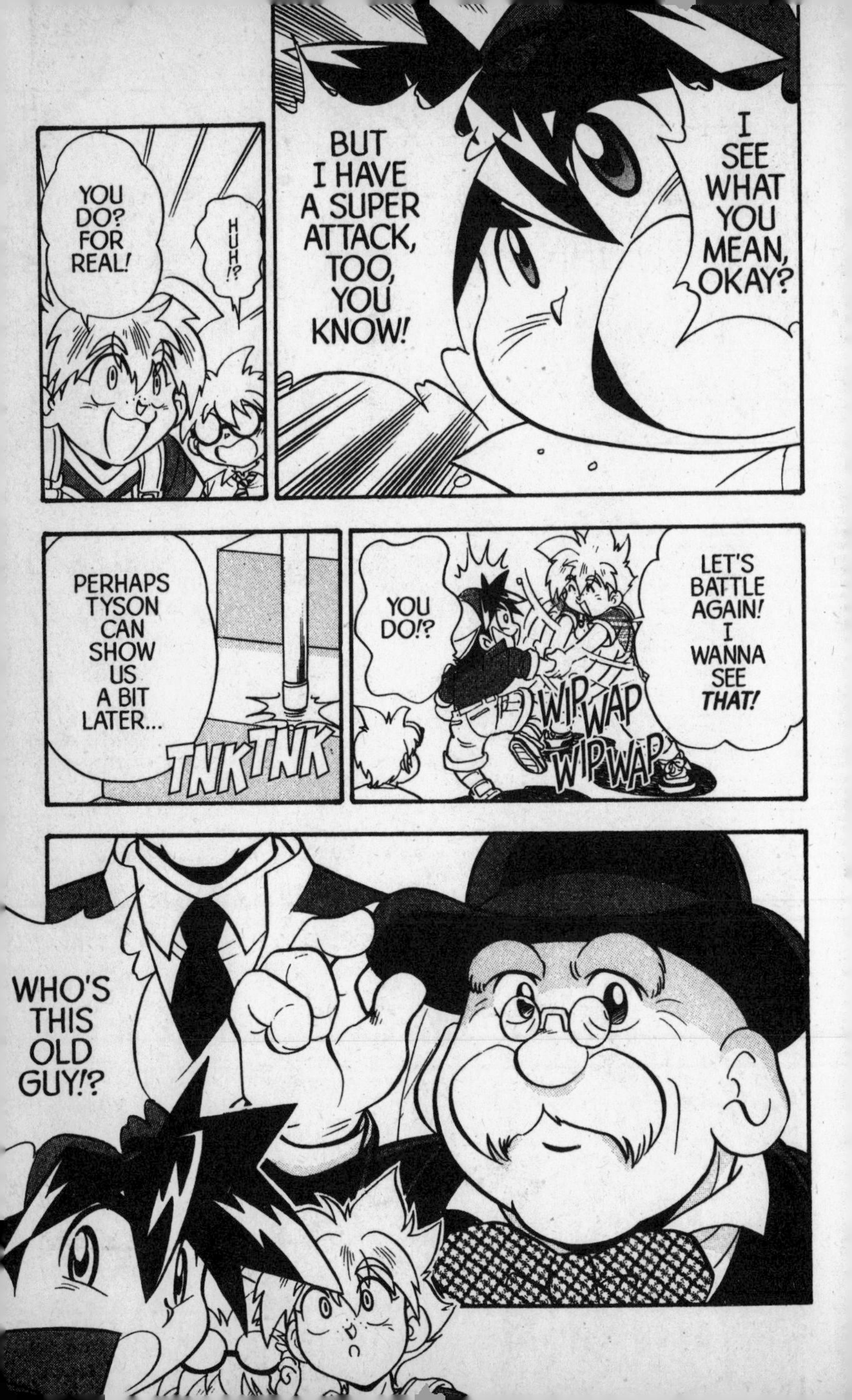
I SEE WHAT YOU MEAN, OKAY?
BUT I HAVE A SUPER ATTACK, TOO, YOU KNOW!
HUH!?
YOU DO? FOR REAL!
LET'S BATTLE AGAIN! I WANNA SEE *THAT!*
WIP WAP
WIP WAP
YOU DO!?
PERHAPS TYSON CAN SHOW US A BIT LATER...
TNK TNK
WHO'S THIS OLD GUY!?

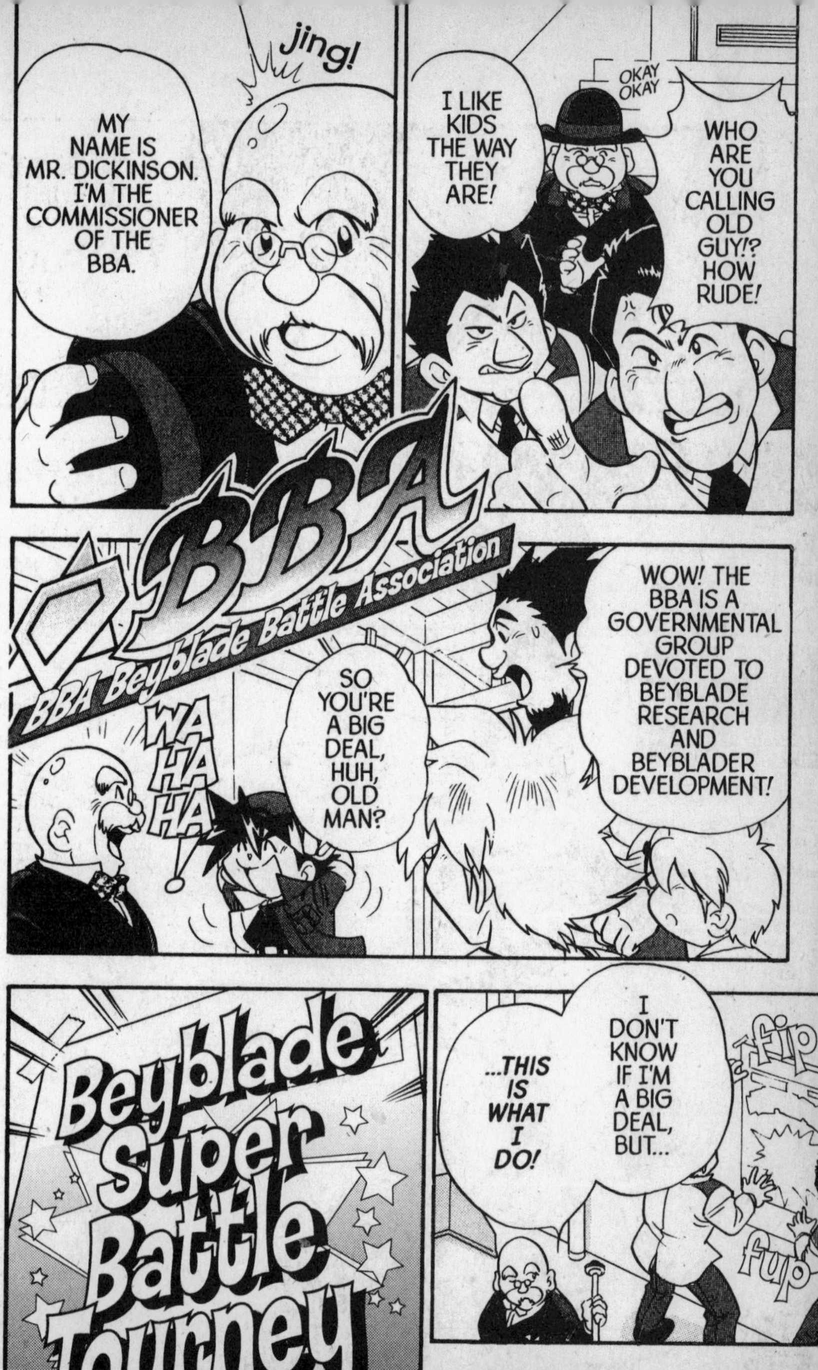
WHO ARE YOU CALLING OLD GUY!? HOW RUDE!
OKAY OKAY
I LIKE KIDS THE WAY THEY ARE!
jing!
MY NAME IS MR. DICKINSON. I'M THE COMMISSIONER OF THE BBA.
WOW! THE BBA IS A GOVERNMENTAL GROUP DEVOTED TO BEYBLADE RESEARCH AND BEYBLADER DEVELOPMENT!
BBA
BBA Beyblade Battle Association
SO YOU'RE A BIG DEAL, HUH, OLD MAN?
WA HA HA!
fip
I DON'T KNOW IF I'M A BIG DEAL, BUT...
...THIS IS WHAT I DO!
fup
Beyblade Super Battle Tourney

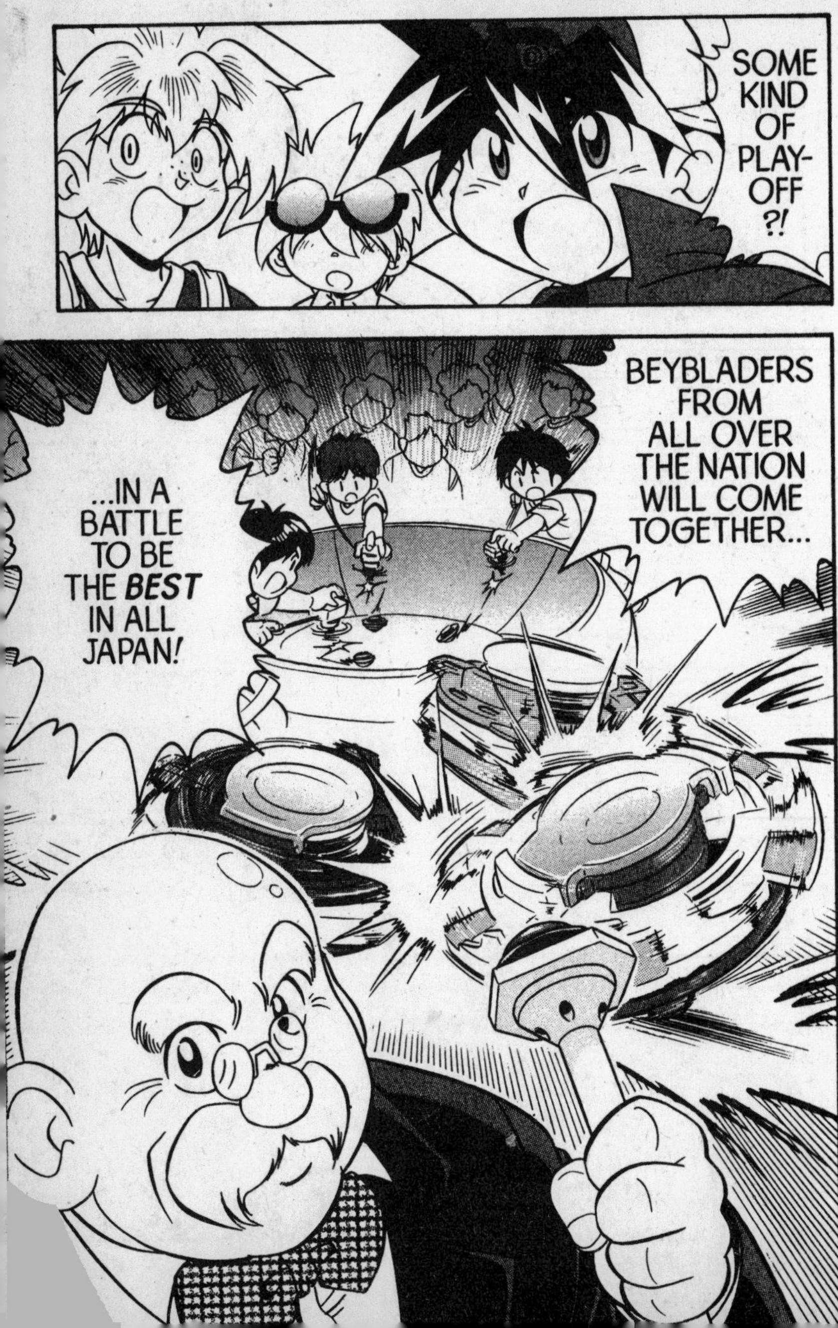
SOME KIND OF PLAY-OFF ?!
BEYBLADERS FROM ALL OVER THE NATION WILL COME TOGETHER...
...IN A BATTLE TO BE THE *BEST* IN ALL JAPAN!

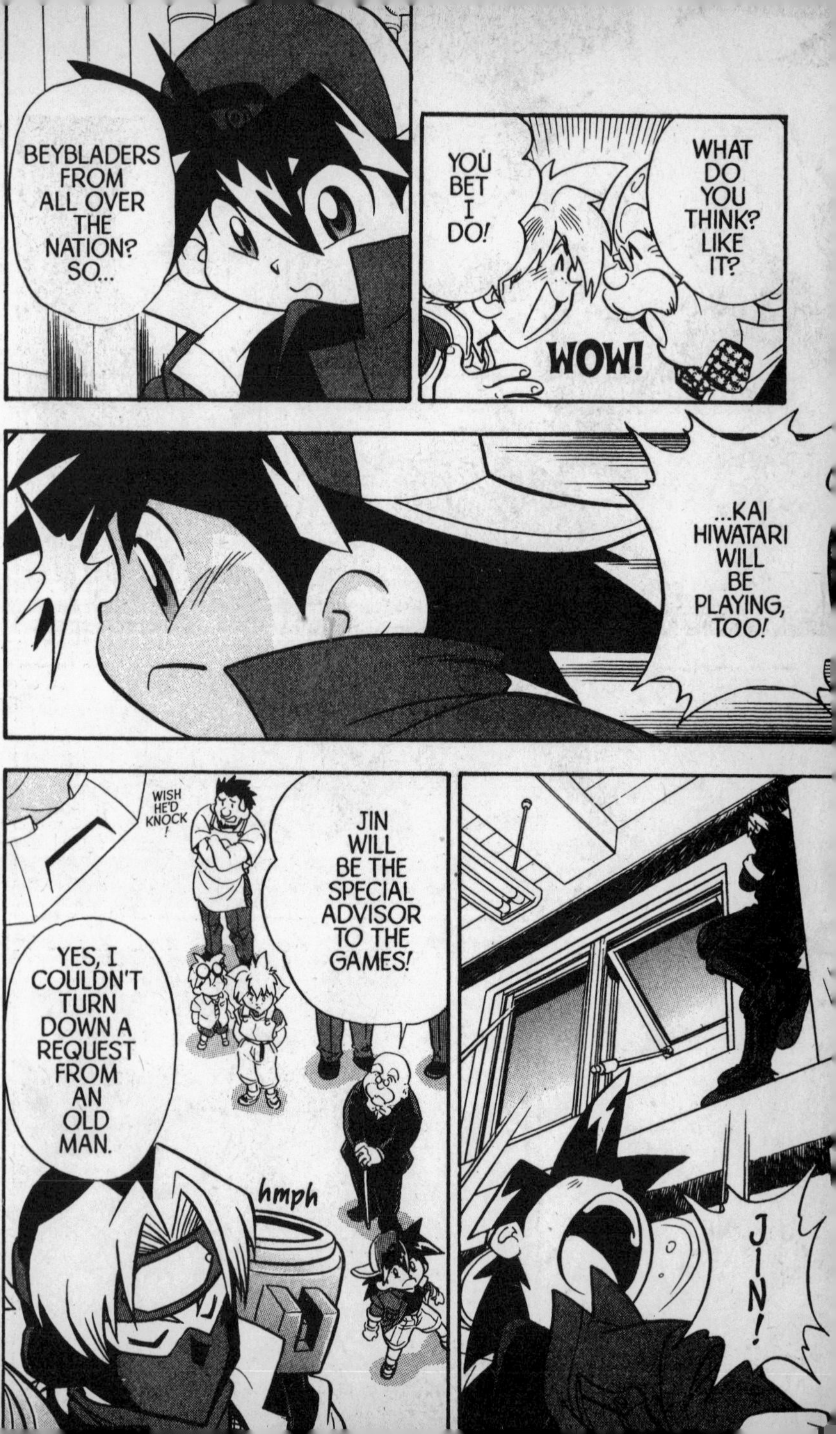
WHAT DO YOU THINK? LIKE IT?
YOU BET I DO!
WOW!
BEYBLADERS FROM ALL OVER THE NATION? SO...
...KAI HIWATARI WILL BE PLAYING, TOO!
JIN!
JIN WILL BE THE SPECIAL ADVISOR TO THE GAMES!
WISH HE'D KNOCK!
YES, I COULDN'T TURN DOWN A REQUEST FROM AN OLD MAN.
hmph

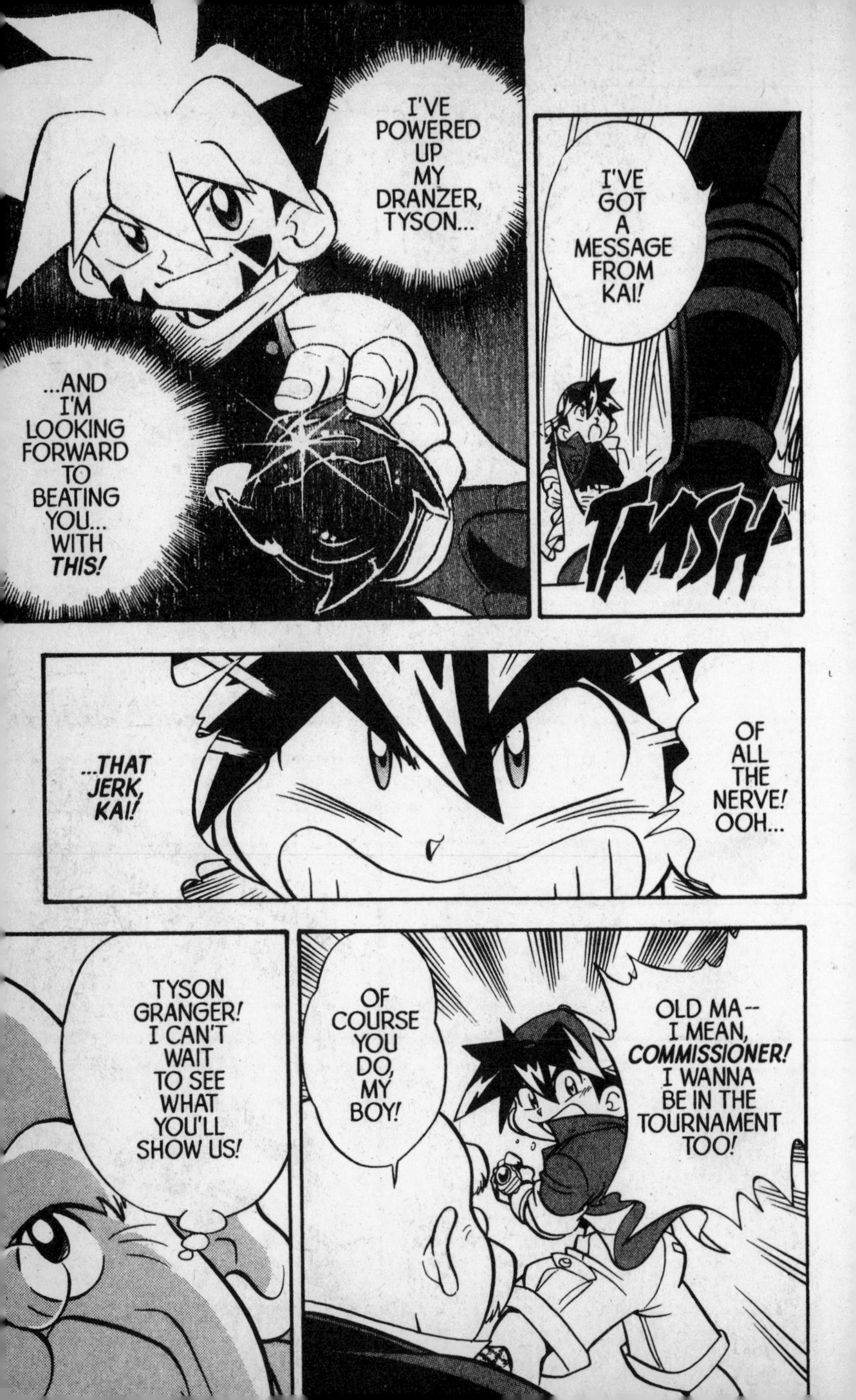
I'VE GOT A MESSAGE FROM KAI!
TMSH
I'VE POWERED UP MY DRANZER, TYSON...
...AND I'M LOOKING FORWARD TO BEATING YOU... WITH *THIS!*
OF ALL THE NERVE! OOH...
...THAT JERK, KAI!
OLD MA-- I MEAN, *COMMISSIONER!* I WANNA BE IN THE TOURNAMENT TOO!
OF COURSE YOU DO, MY BOY!
TYSON GRANGER! I CAN'T WAIT TO SEE WHAT YOU'LL SHOW US!

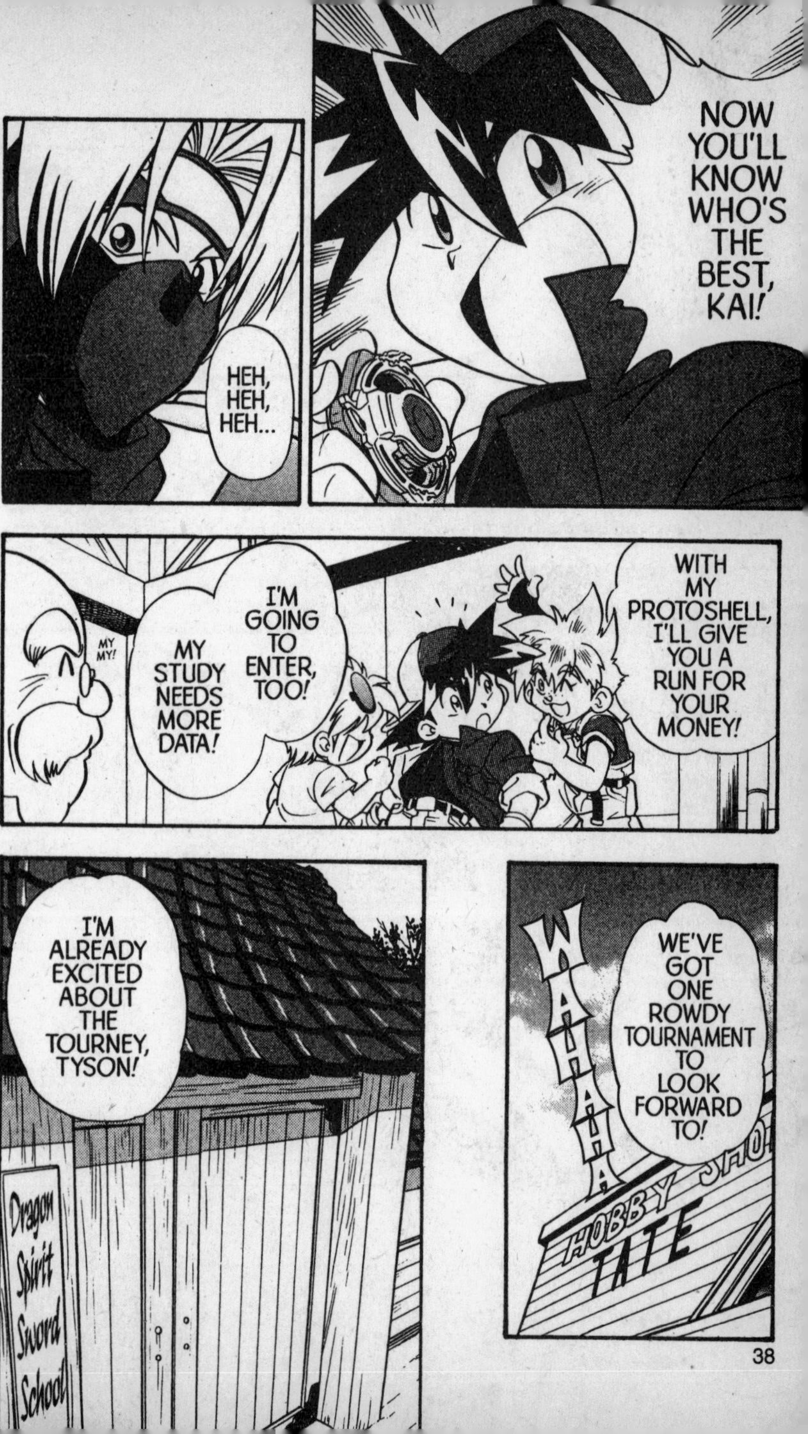
NOW YOU'LL KNOW WHO'S THE BEST, KAI!
HEH, HEH, HEH...
WITH MY PROTOSHELL, I'LL GIVE YOU A RUN FOR YOUR MONEY!
I'M GOING TO ENTER, TOO!
MY STUDY NEEDS MORE DATA!
MY MY!
WAHAHAHA
WE'VE GOT ONE ROWDY TOURNAMENT TO LOOK FORWARD TO!
HOBBY SHO
TATE
I'M ALREADY EXCITED ABOUT THE TOURNEY, TYSON!
Dragon Spirit Sword School

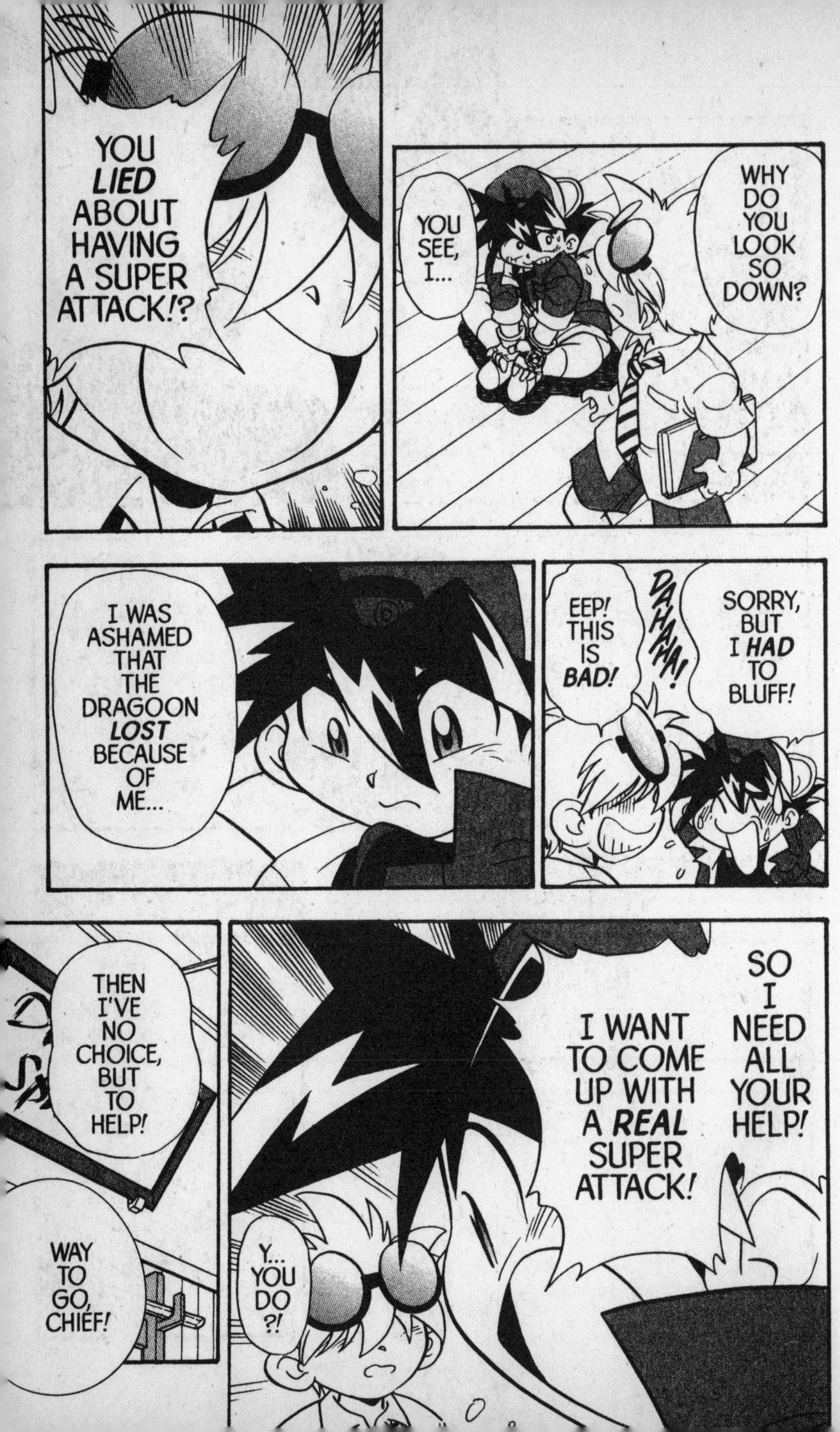
WHY DO YOU LOOK SO DOWN?
YOU SEE, I...
YOU LIED ABOUT HAVING A SUPER ATTACK!?
SORRY, BUT I HAD TO BLUFF!
DAHAHA!
EEP! THIS IS BAD!
I WAS ASHAMED THAT THE DRAGOON LOST BECAUSE OF ME...
I WANT TO COME UP WITH A REAL SUPER ATTACK!
SO I NEED ALL YOUR HELP!
Y... YOU DO?!
THEN I'VE NO CHOICE, BUT TO HELP!
WAY TO GO, CHIEF!

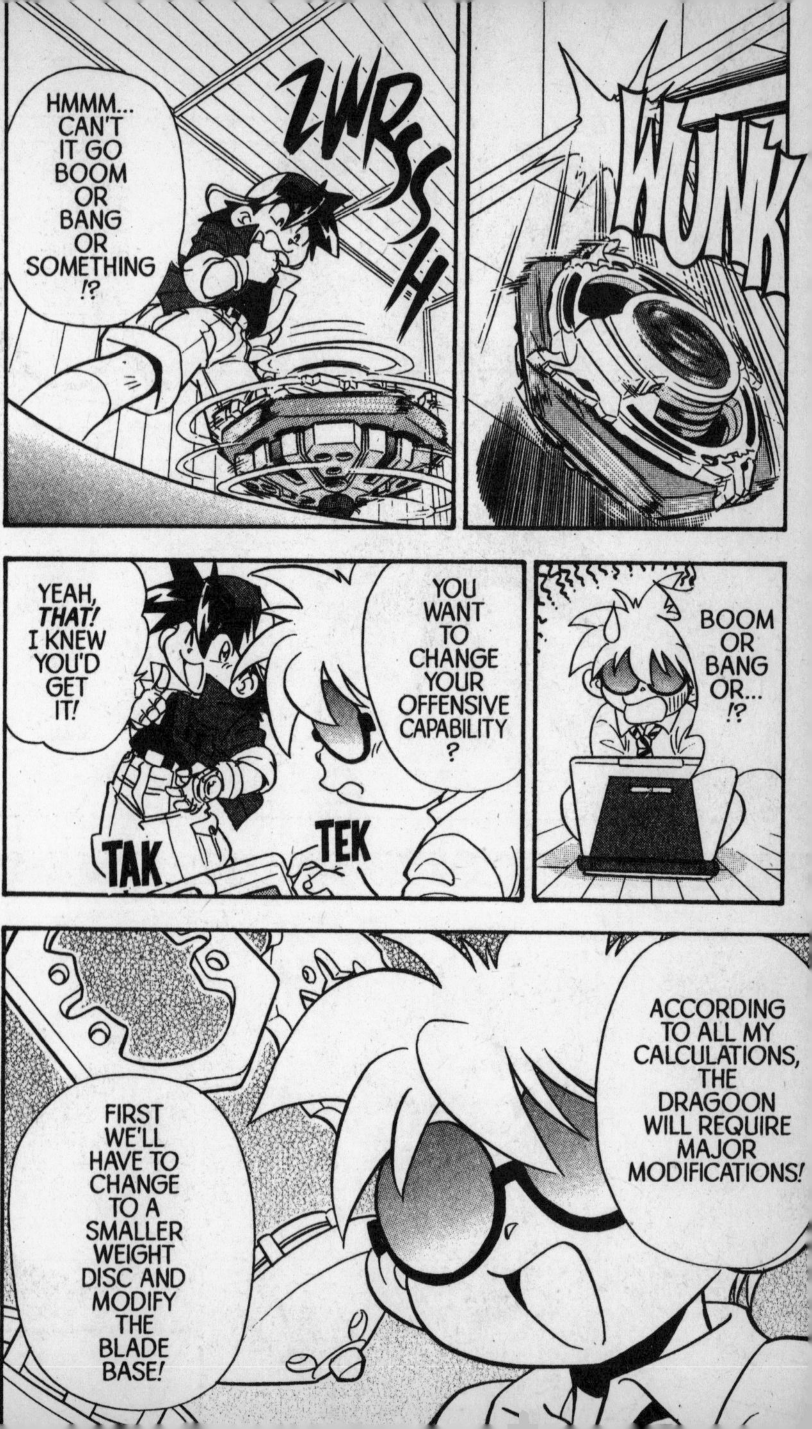
WUNK
ZWRSSH
HMMM... CAN'T IT GO BOOM OR BANG OR SOMETHING !?
BOOM OR BANG OR... !?
YOU WANT TO CHANGE YOUR OFFENSIVE CAPABILITY ?
YEAH, *THAT!* I KNEW YOU'D GET IT!
TEK
TAK
ACCORDING TO ALL MY CALCULATIONS, THE DRAGOON WILL REQUIRE MAJOR MODIFICATIONS!
FIRST WE'LL HAVE TO CHANGE TO A SMALLER WEIGHT DISC AND MODIFY THE BLADE BASE!

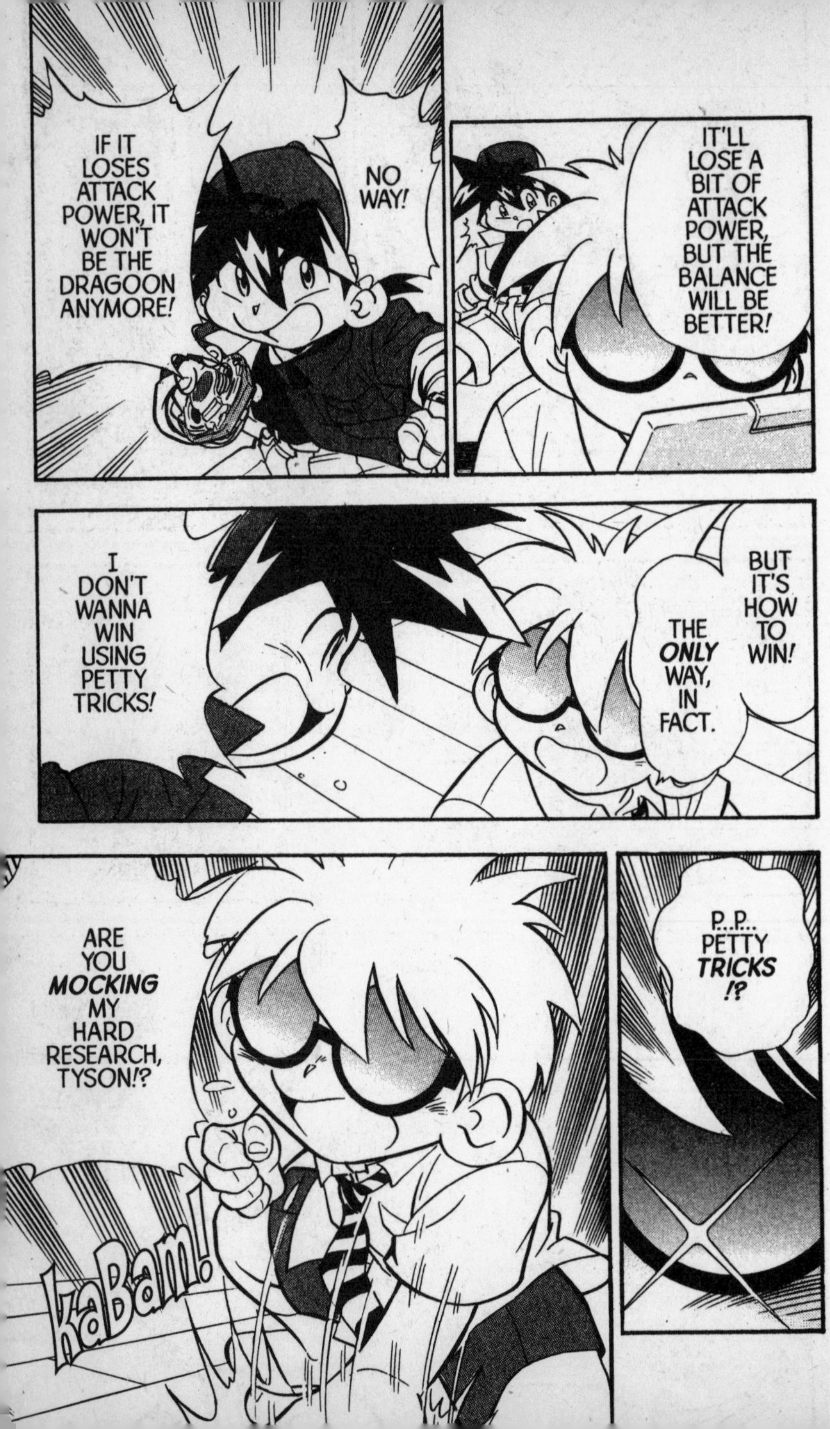

IT'LL LOSE A BIT OF ATTACK POWER, BUT THE BALANCE WILL BE BETTER!
NO WAY!
IF IT LOSES ATTACK POWER, IT WON'T BE THE DRAGOON ANYMORE!
BUT IT'S HOW TO WIN!
THE *ONLY* WAY, IN FACT.
I DON'T WANNA WIN USING PETTY TRICKS!
P..P... PETTY *TRICKS* !?
ARE YOU *MOCKING* MY HARD RESEARCH, TYSON!?
KaBam!

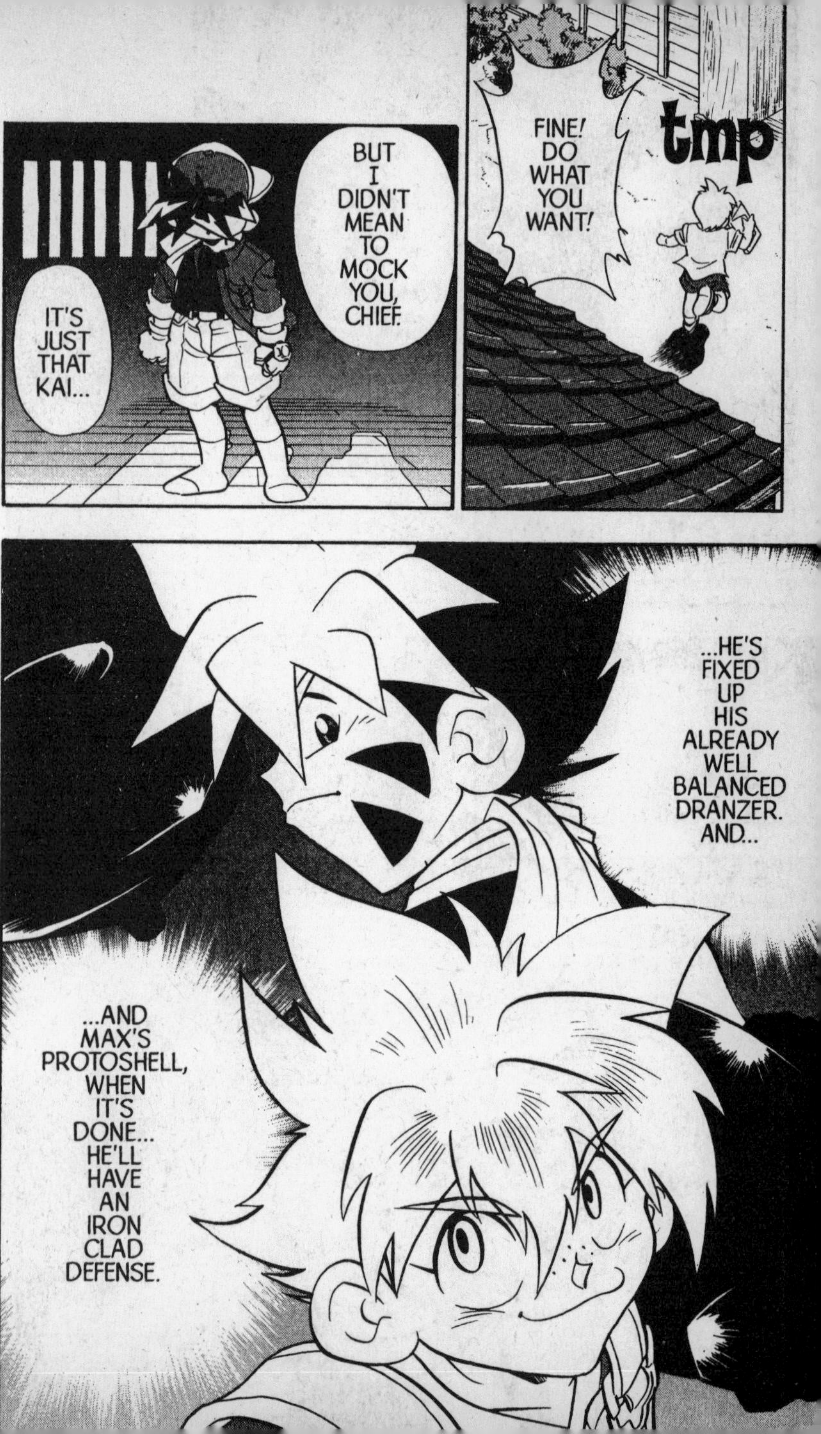
FINE! DO WHAT YOU WANT!
tmp
BUT I DIDN'T MEAN TO MOCK YOU, CHIEF.
IT'S JUST THAT KAI...
...HE'S FIXED UP HIS ALREADY WELL BALANCED DRANZER. AND...
...AND MAX'S PROTOSHELL, WHEN IT'S DONE... HE'LL HAVE AN IRON CLAD DEFENSE.

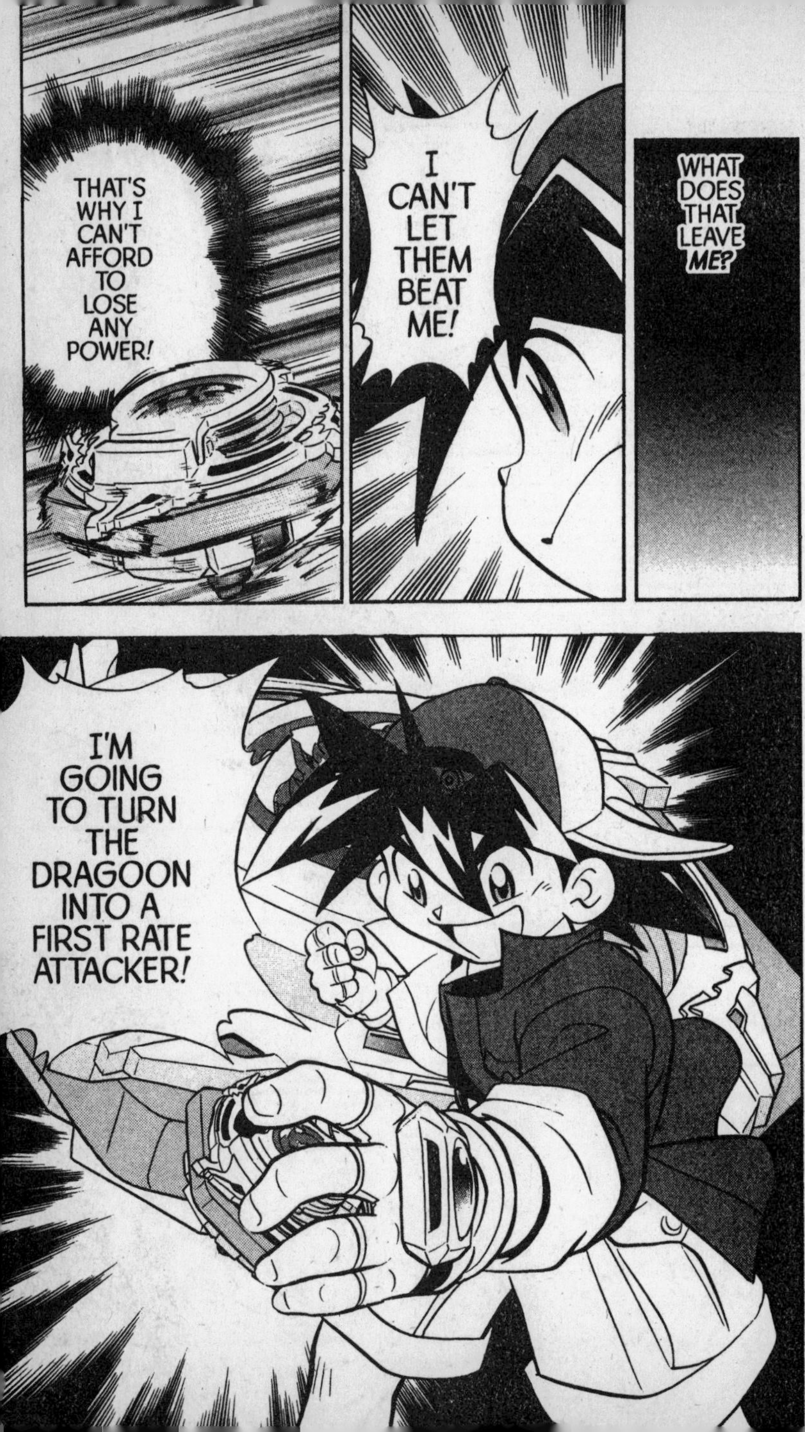
WHAT DOES THAT LEAVE ME?
I CAN'T LET THEM BEAT ME!
THAT'S WHY I CAN'T AFFORD TO LOSE ANY POWER!
I'M GOING TO TURN THE DRAGOON INTO A FIRST RATE ATTACKER!

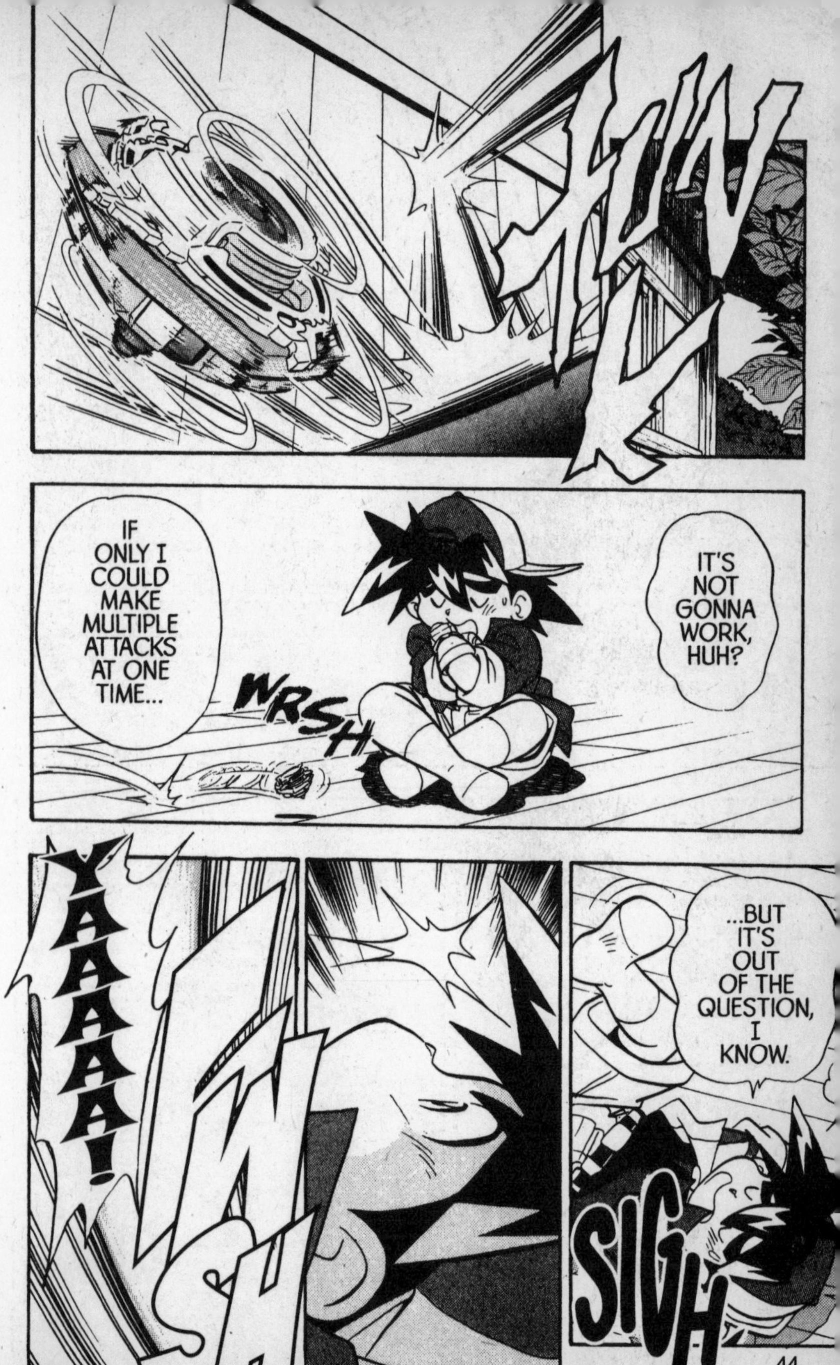

IT'S NOT GONNA WORK, HUH?
WRSH
IF ONLY I COULD MAKE MULTIPLE ATTACKS AT ONE TIME...
...BUT IT'S OUT OF THE QUESTION, I KNOW.
SIGH
YAAAAAI!

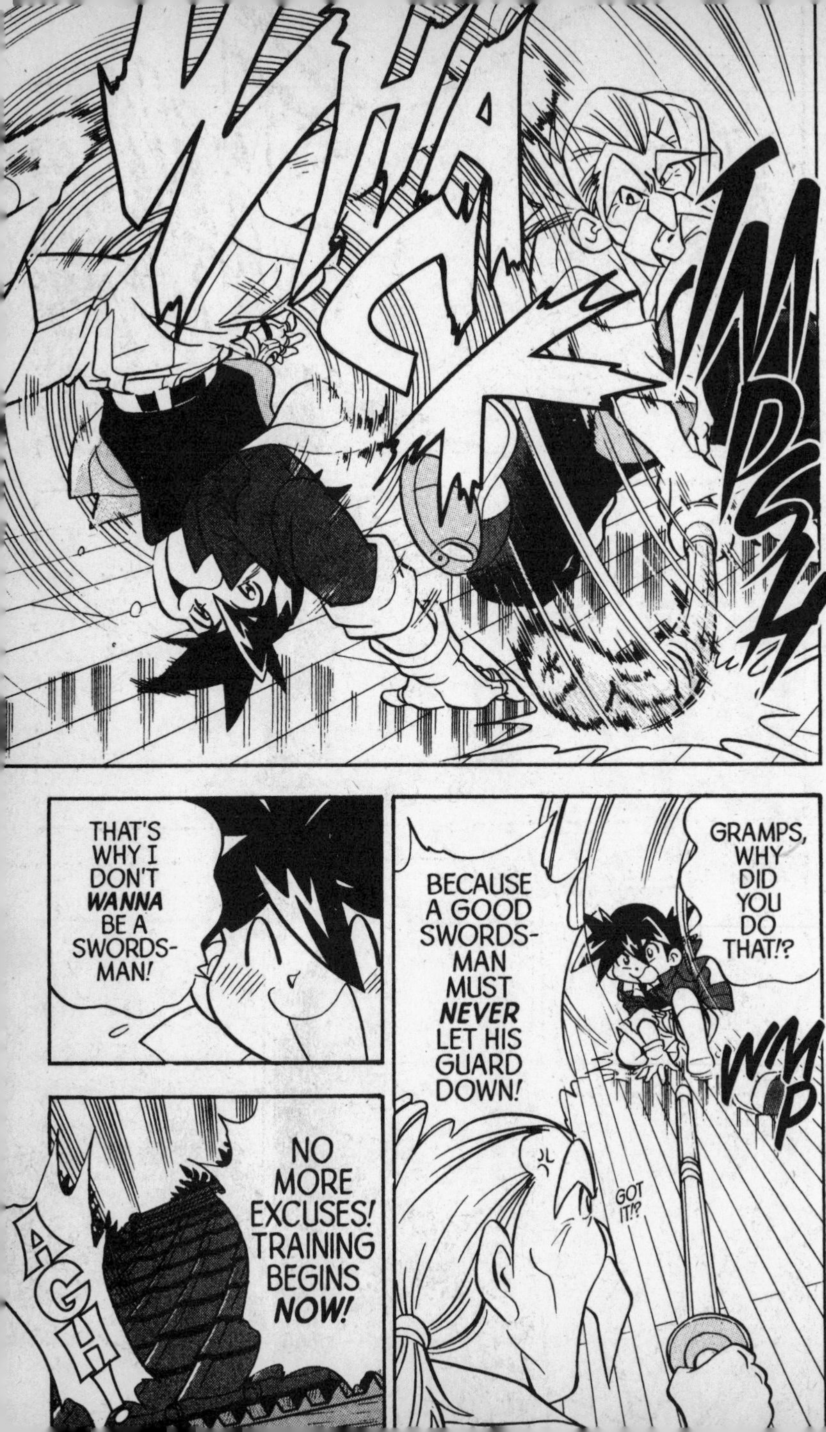
WHACK
TWDSH
GRAMPS, WHY DID YOU DO THAT!?
BECAUSE A GOOD SWORDSMAN MUST NEVER LET HIS GUARD DOWN!
WMP
GOT IT!?
THAT'S WHY I DON'T WANNA BE A SWORDSMAN!
NO MORE EXCUSES! TRAINING BEGINS NOW!
AGH!!

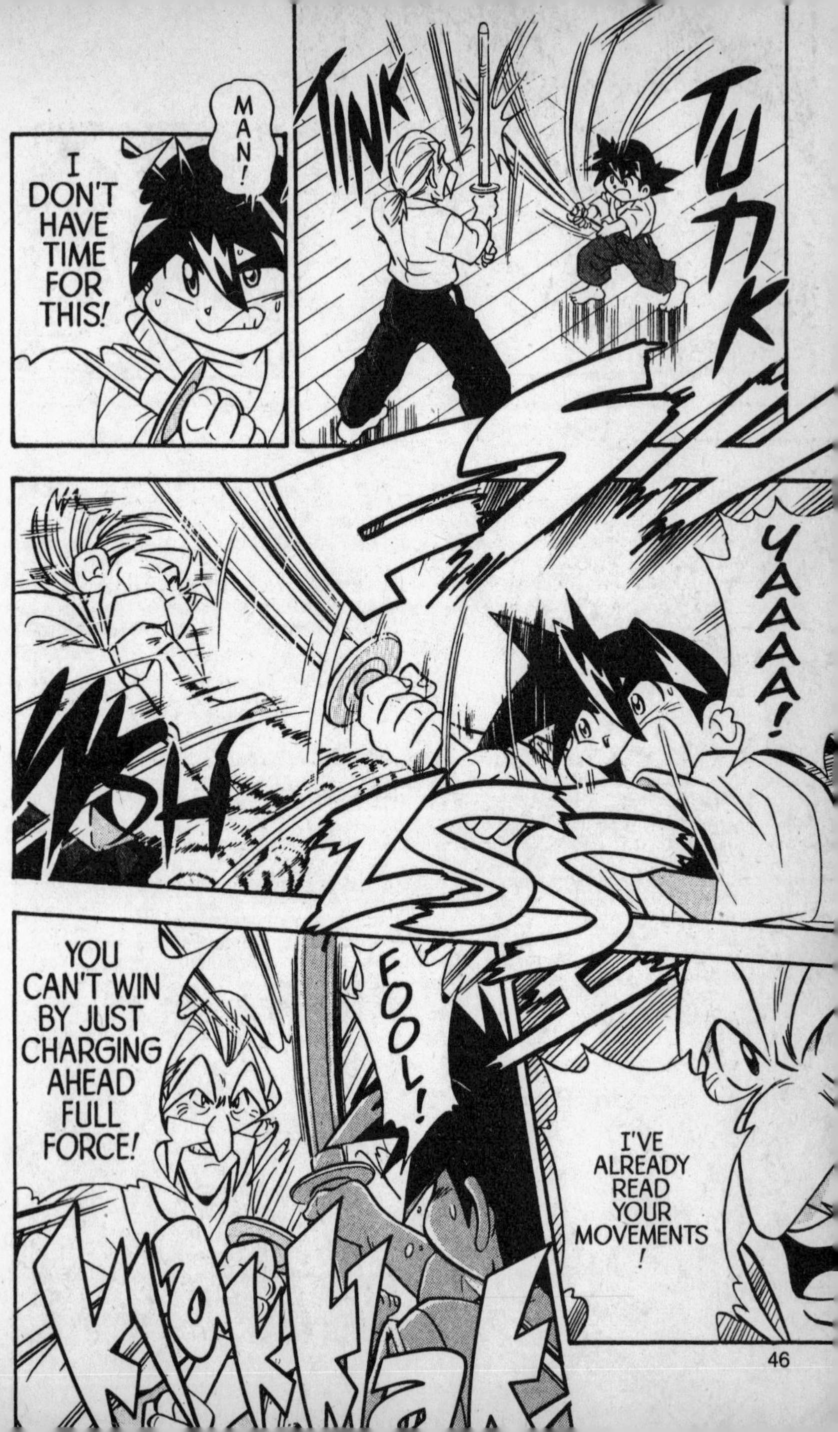
TUNK
TINK
MAN!
I DON'T HAVE TIME FOR THIS!
YAAAAA!
WSH
I'VE ALREADY READ YOUR MOVEMENTS!
FOOL!
YOU CAN'T WIN BY JUST CHARGING AHEAD FULL FORCE!

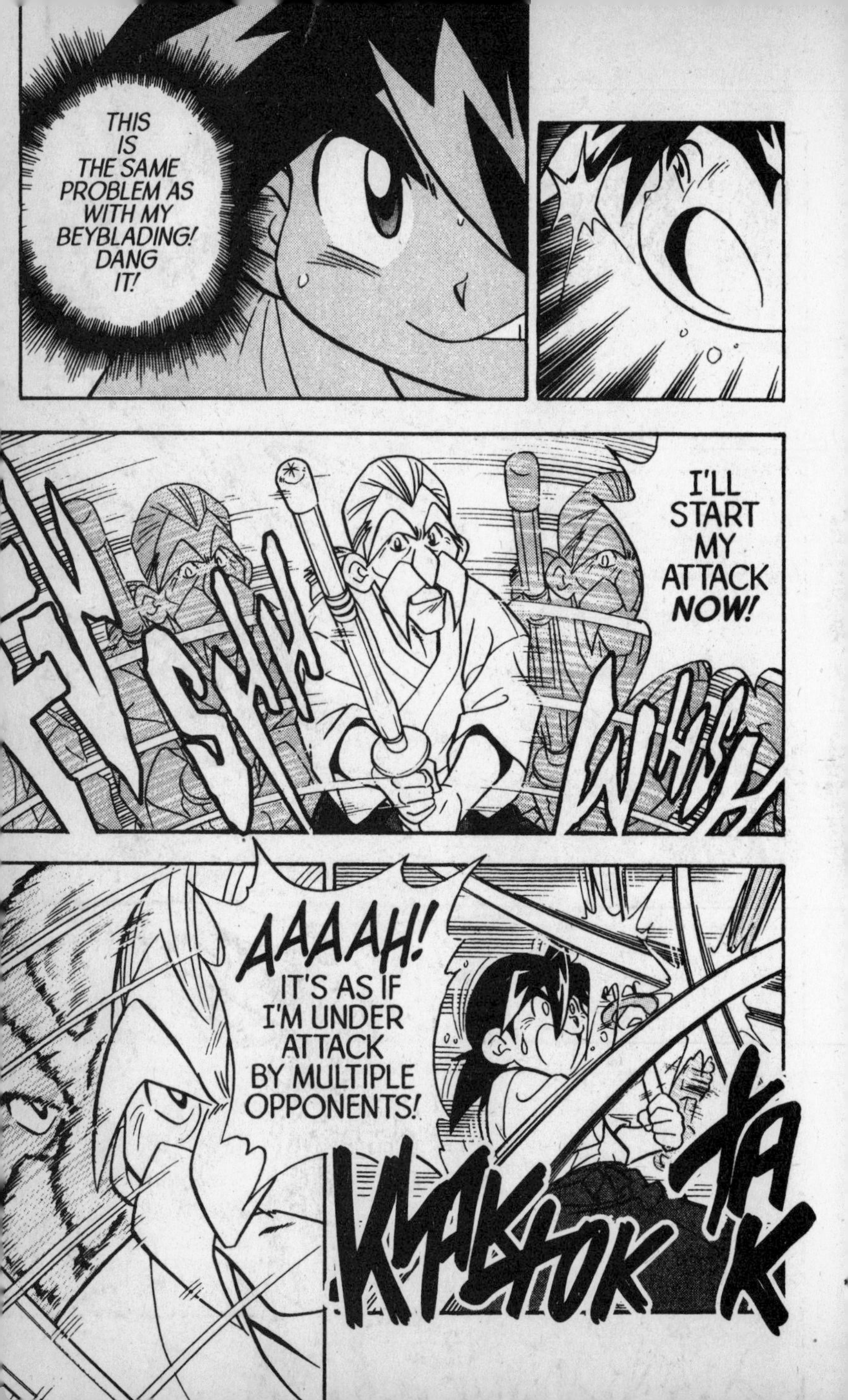
THIS IS THE SAME PROBLEM AS WITH MY BEYBLADING! DANG IT!
I'LL START MY ATTACK NOW!
AAAAH!
IT'S AS IF I'M UNDER ATTACK BY MULTIPLE OPPONENTS!

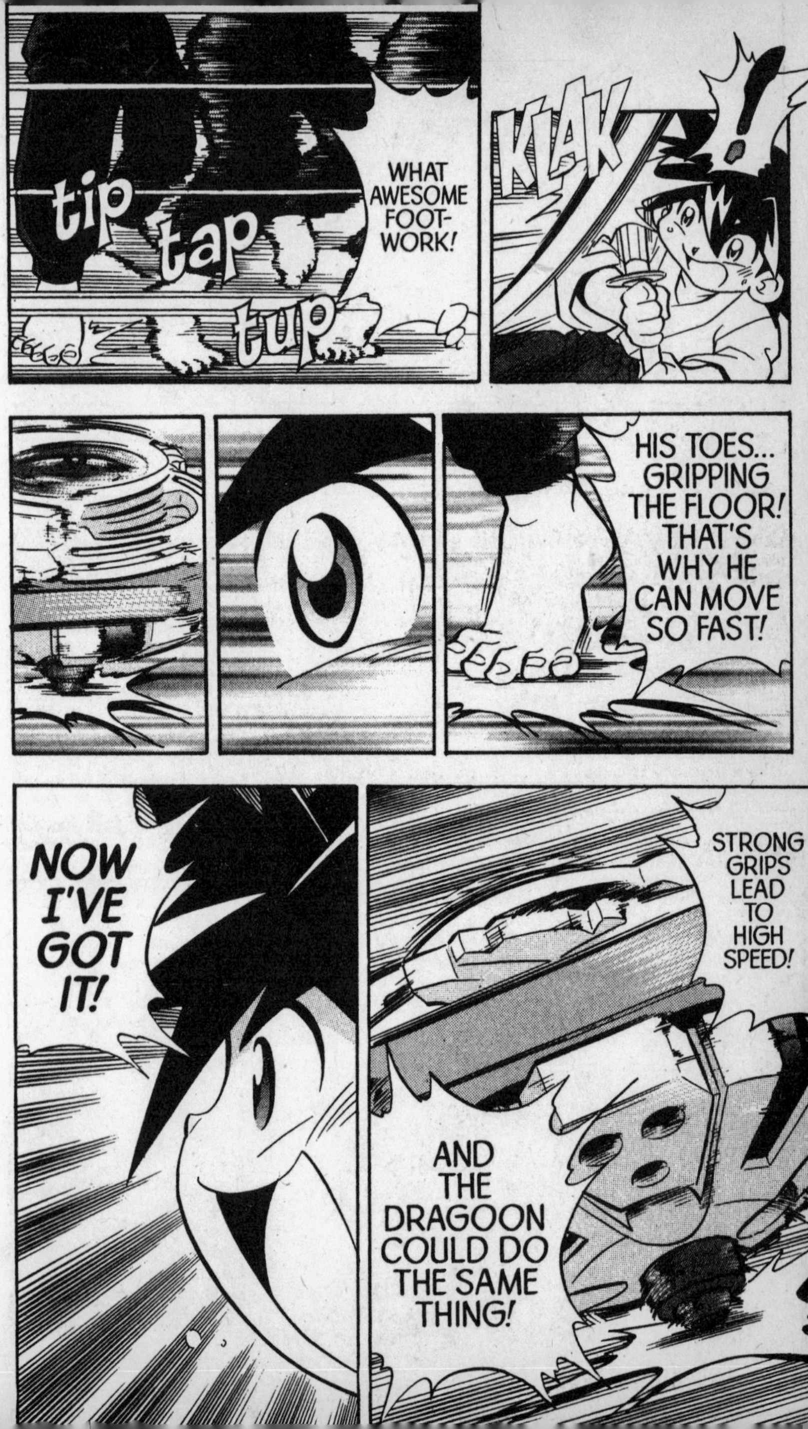
KLAK
!
WHAT AWESOME FOOT-WORK!
tip
tap
tup
HIS TOES... GRIPPING THE FLOOR! THAT'S WHY HE CAN MOVE SO FAST!
STRONG GRIPS LEAD TO HIGH SPEED!
AND THE DRAGOON COULD DO THE SAME THING!
NOW I'VE GOT IT!

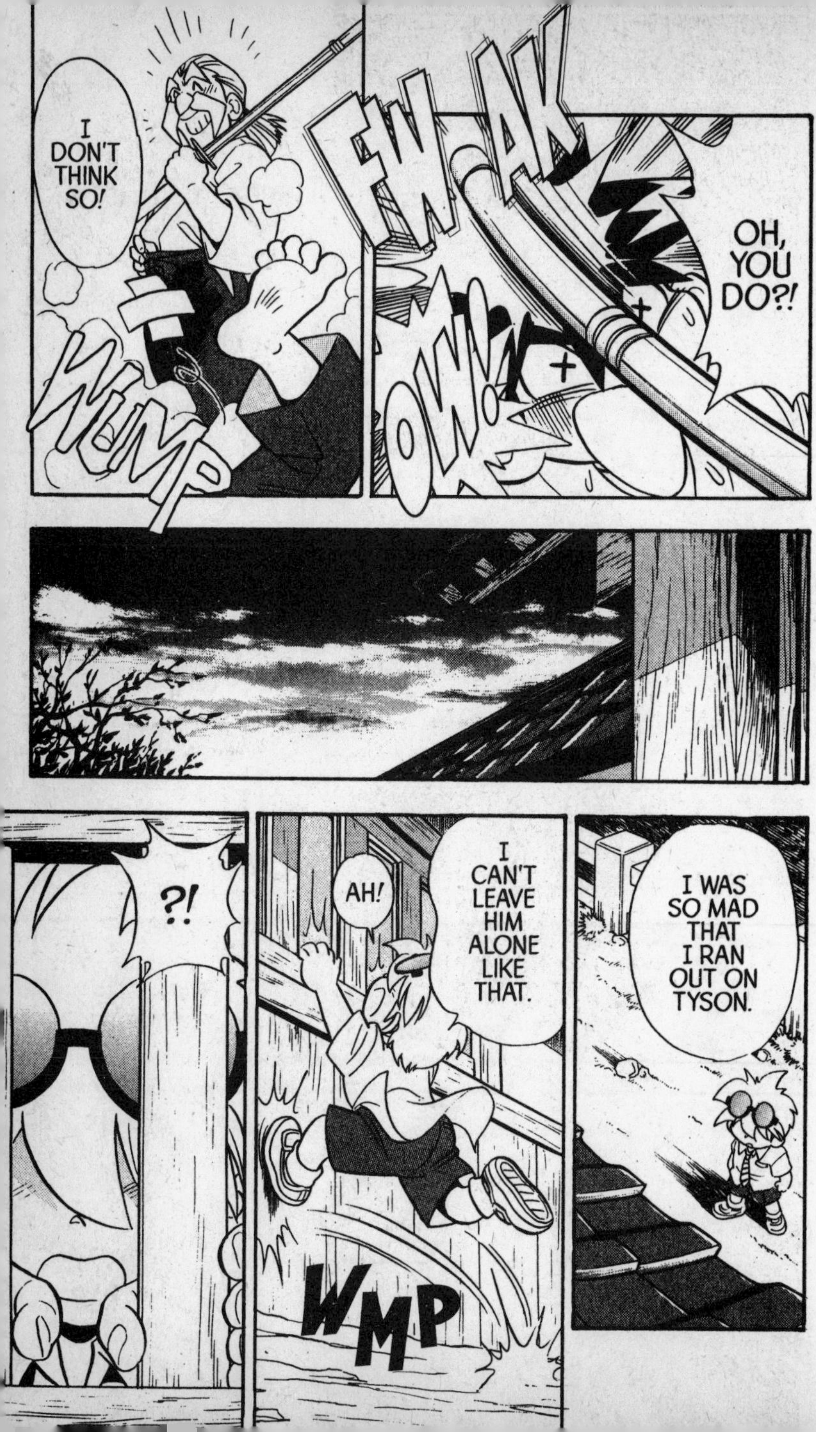
FWAK
OH, YOU DO?!
OWW!
I DON'T THINK SO!
WUMP
I WAS SO MAD THAT I RAN OUT ON TYSON.
I CAN'T LEAVE HIM ALONE LIKE THAT.
AH!
WMP
?!

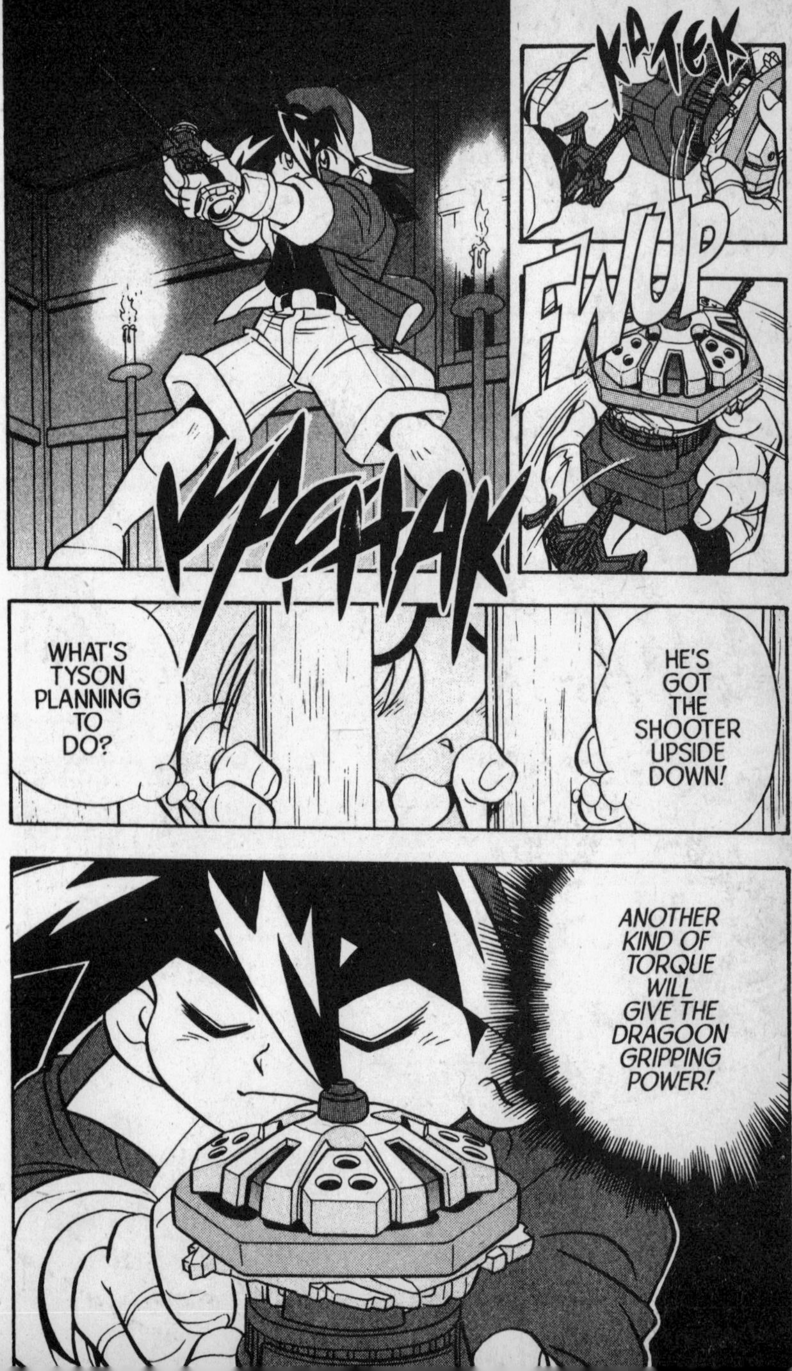
KATEK
FWUP
WACHAK
HE'S GOT THE SHOOTER UPSIDE DOWN!
WHAT'S TYSON PLANNING TO DO?
ANOTHER KIND OF TORQUE WILL GIVE THE DRAGOON GRIPPING POWER!

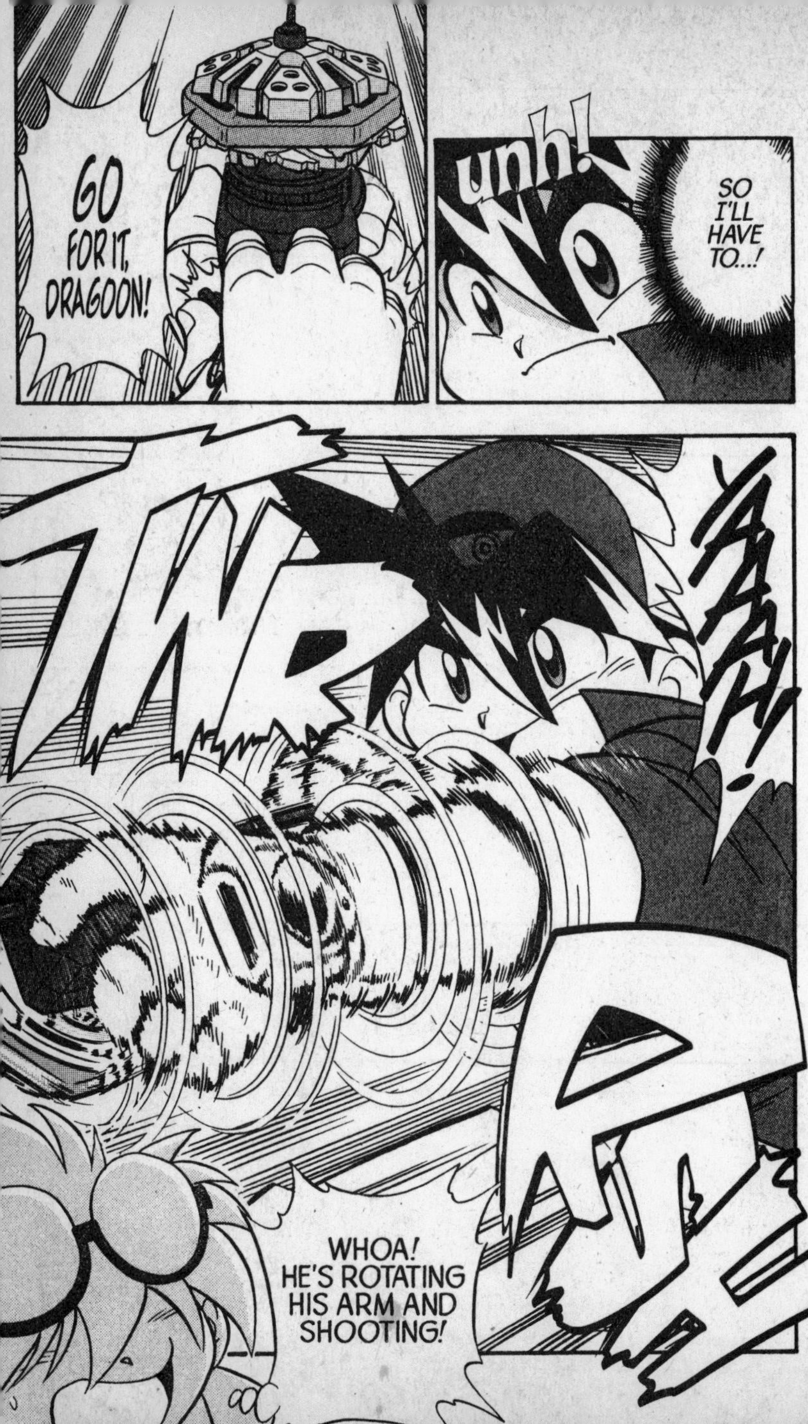
unh!
SO I'LL HAVE TO...!
GO FOR IT, DRAGOON!
WHOA! HE'S ROTATING HIS ARM AND SHOOTING!

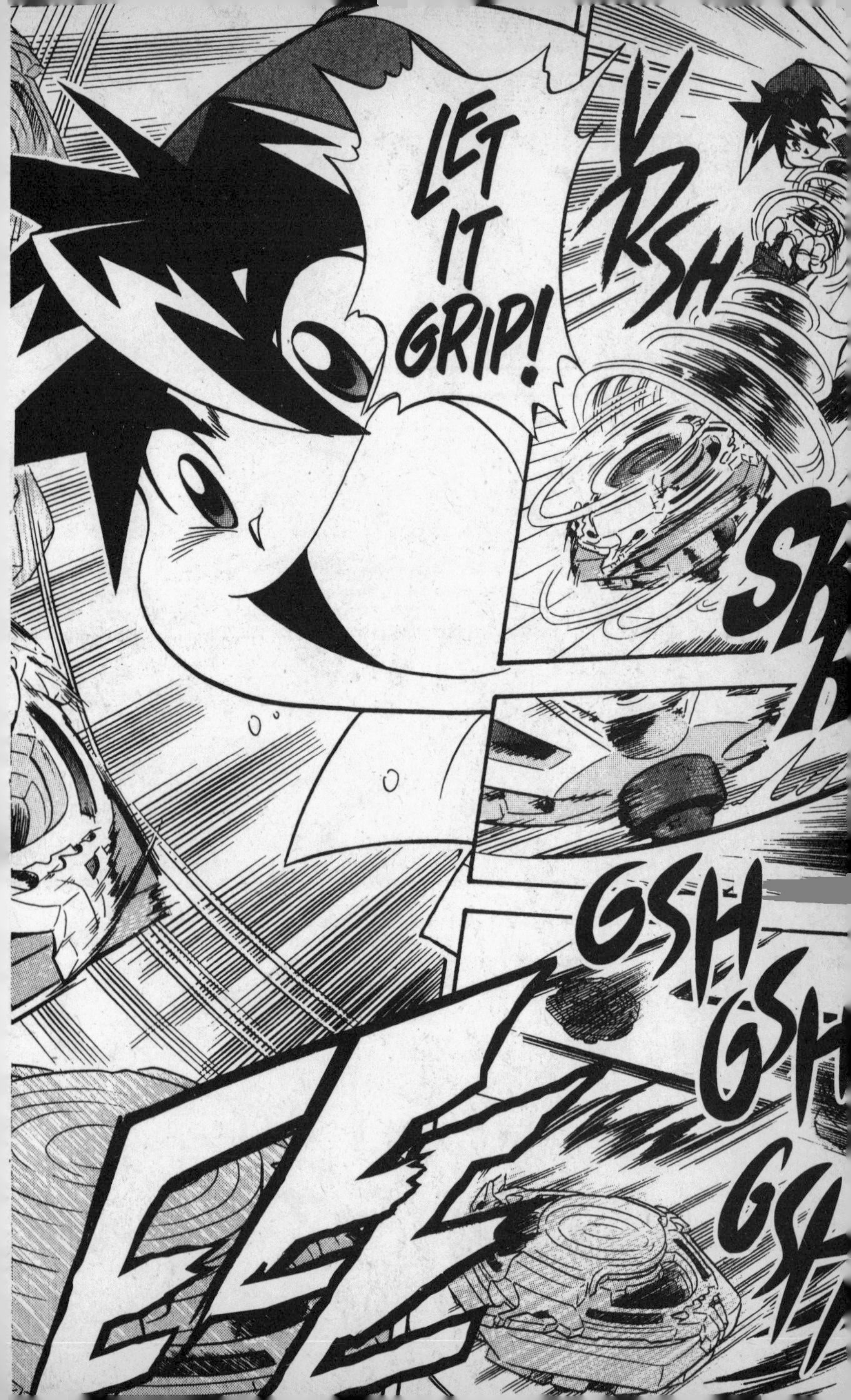
VRSH
LET IT GRIP!
GSH!

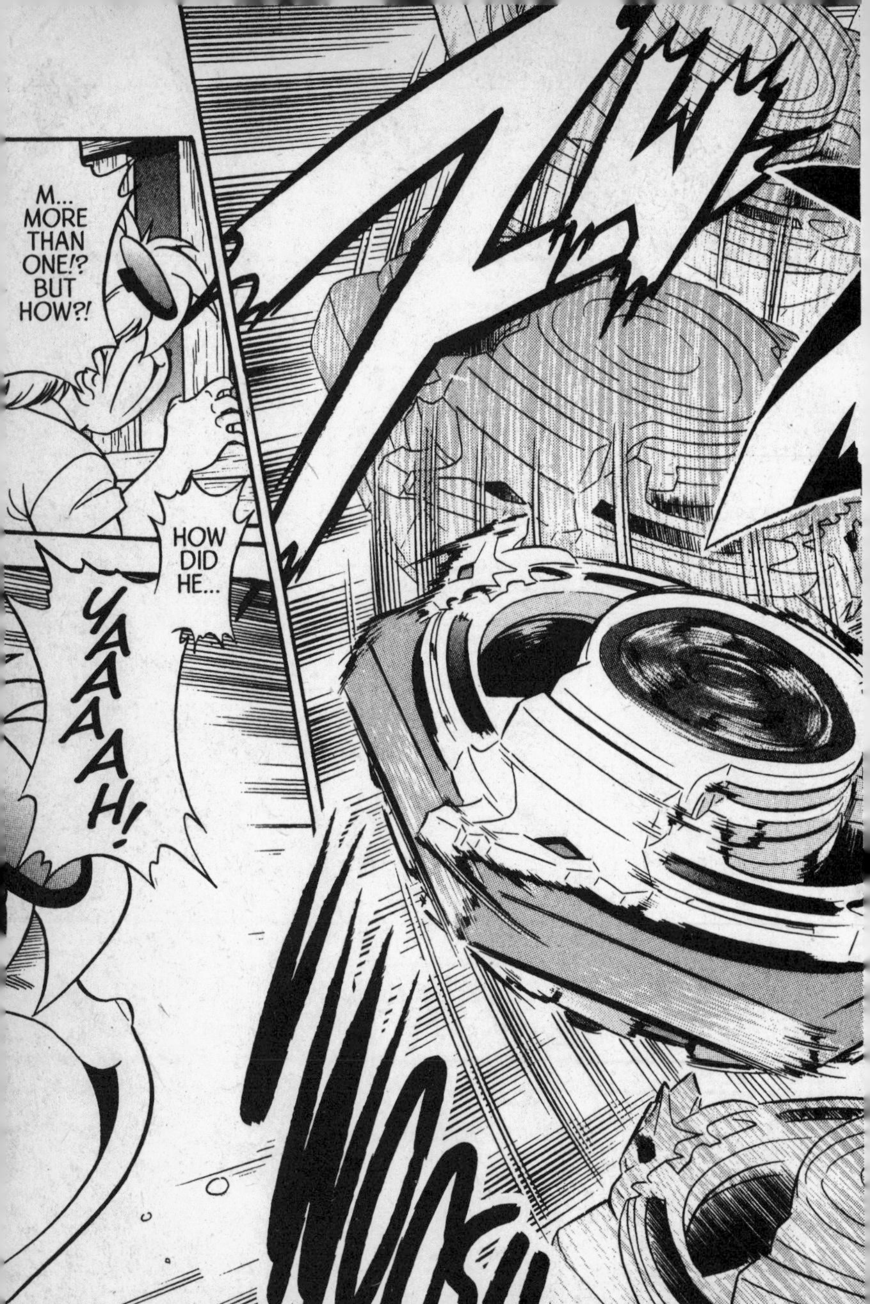
WHOOSH
M... MORE THAN ONE!? BUT HOW?!
HOW DID HE...
YAAAAH!

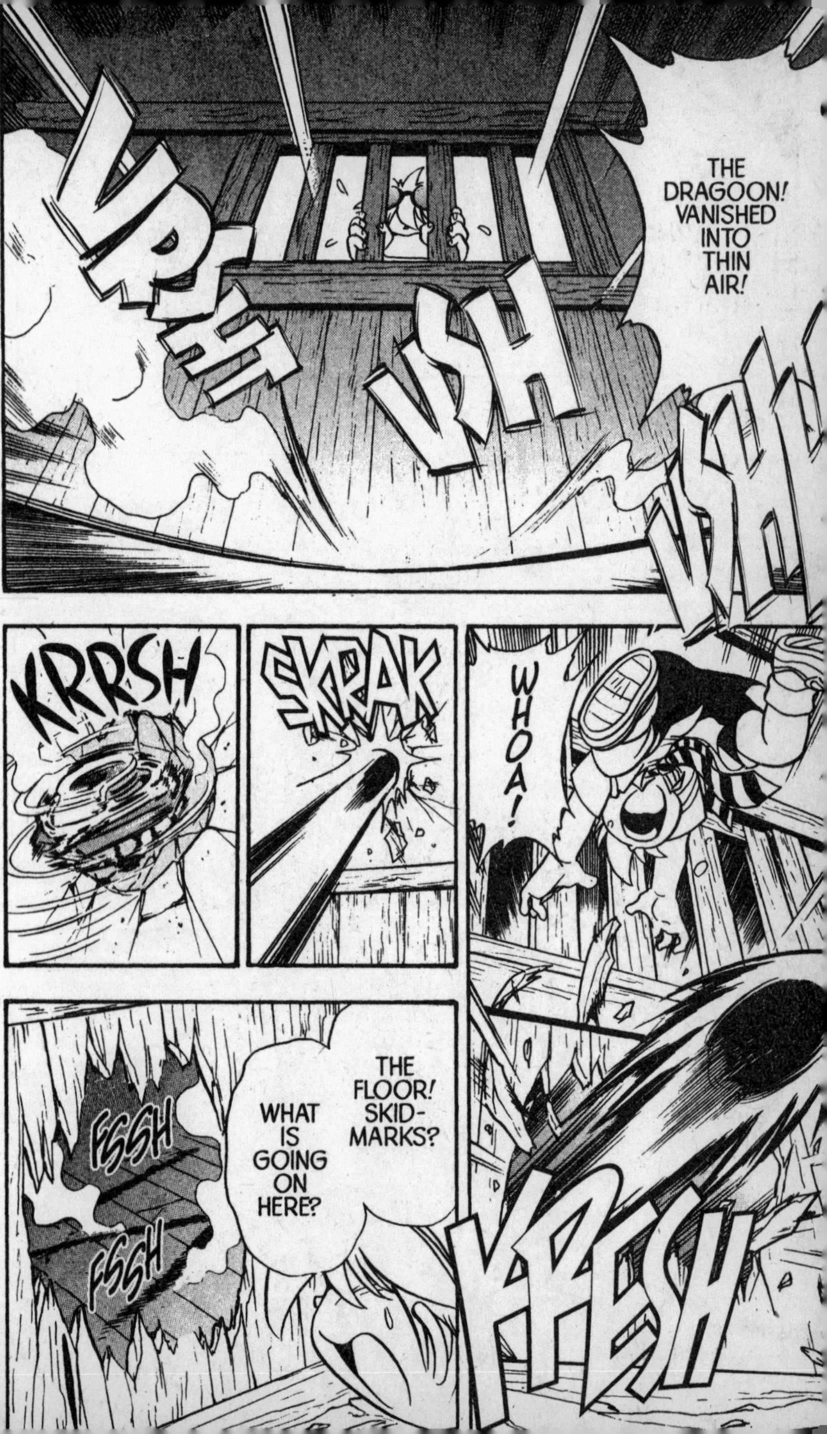
THE DRAGOON! VANISHED INTO THIN AIR!
VSH
WHOA!
SKRAK
KRRSH
KRESH
THE FLOOR! SKID-MARKS?
WHAT IS GOING ON HERE?
FSSH
FSSH

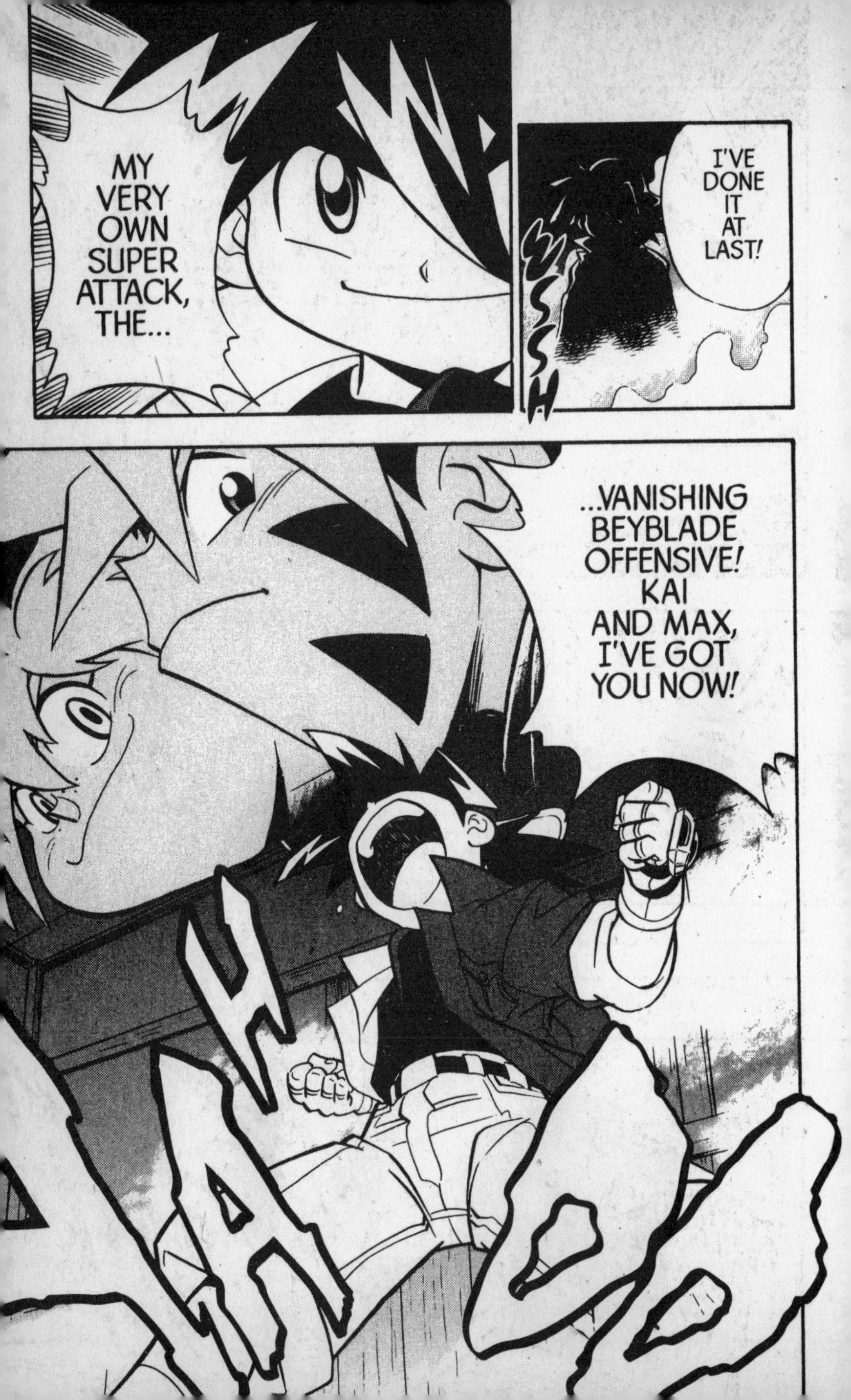
I'VE DONE IT AT LAST!
MY VERY OWN SUPER ATTACK, THE...
...VANISHING BEYBLADE OFFENSIVE! KAI AND MAX, I'VE GOT YOU NOW!

CHAPTER 2: A MEETING OF THE POWERS

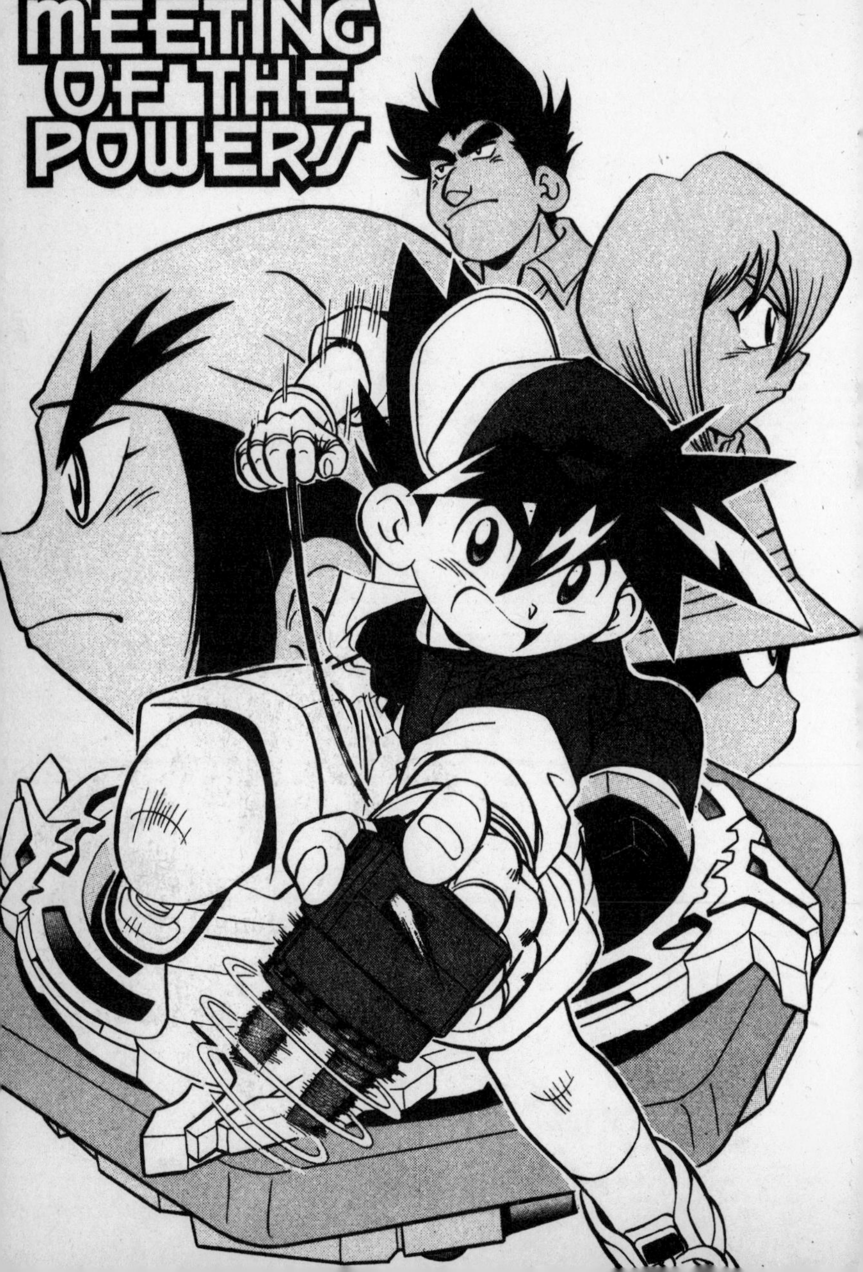

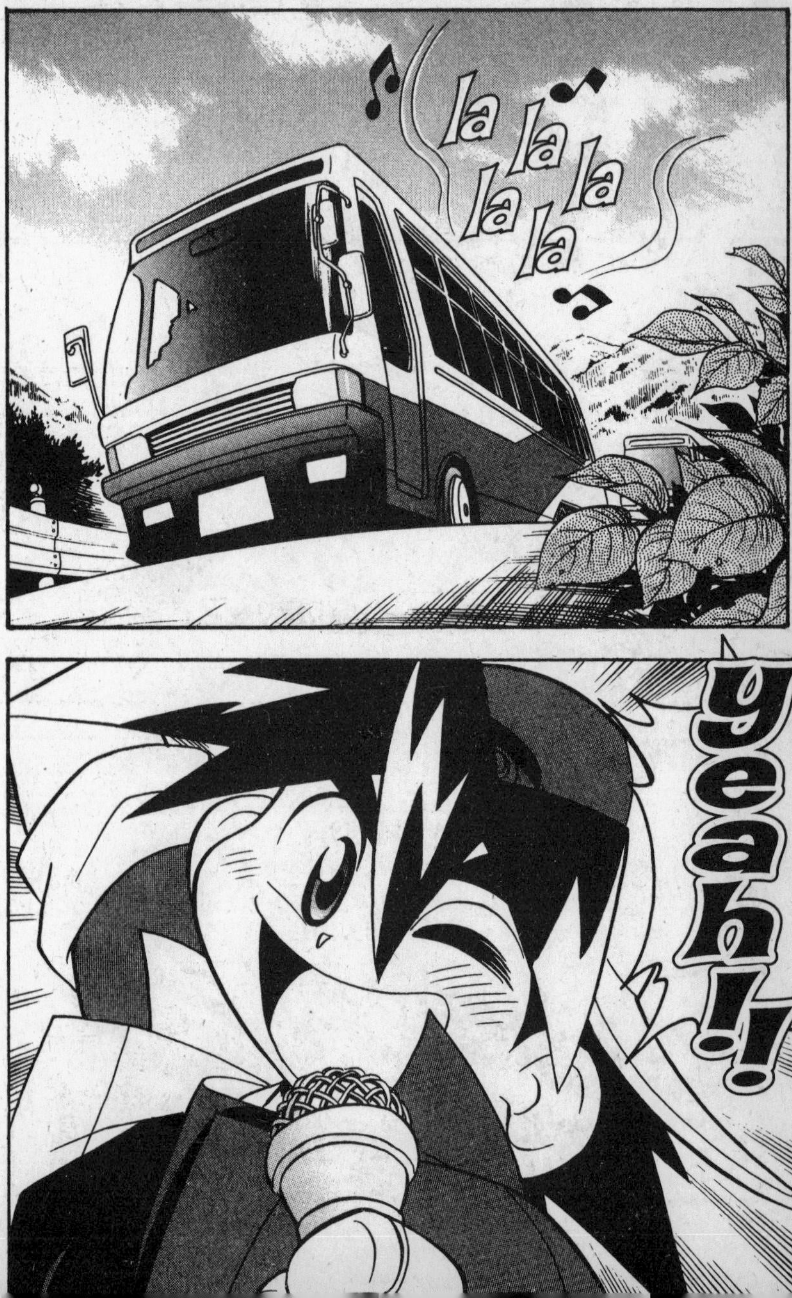

la la la la la la
yeah!!

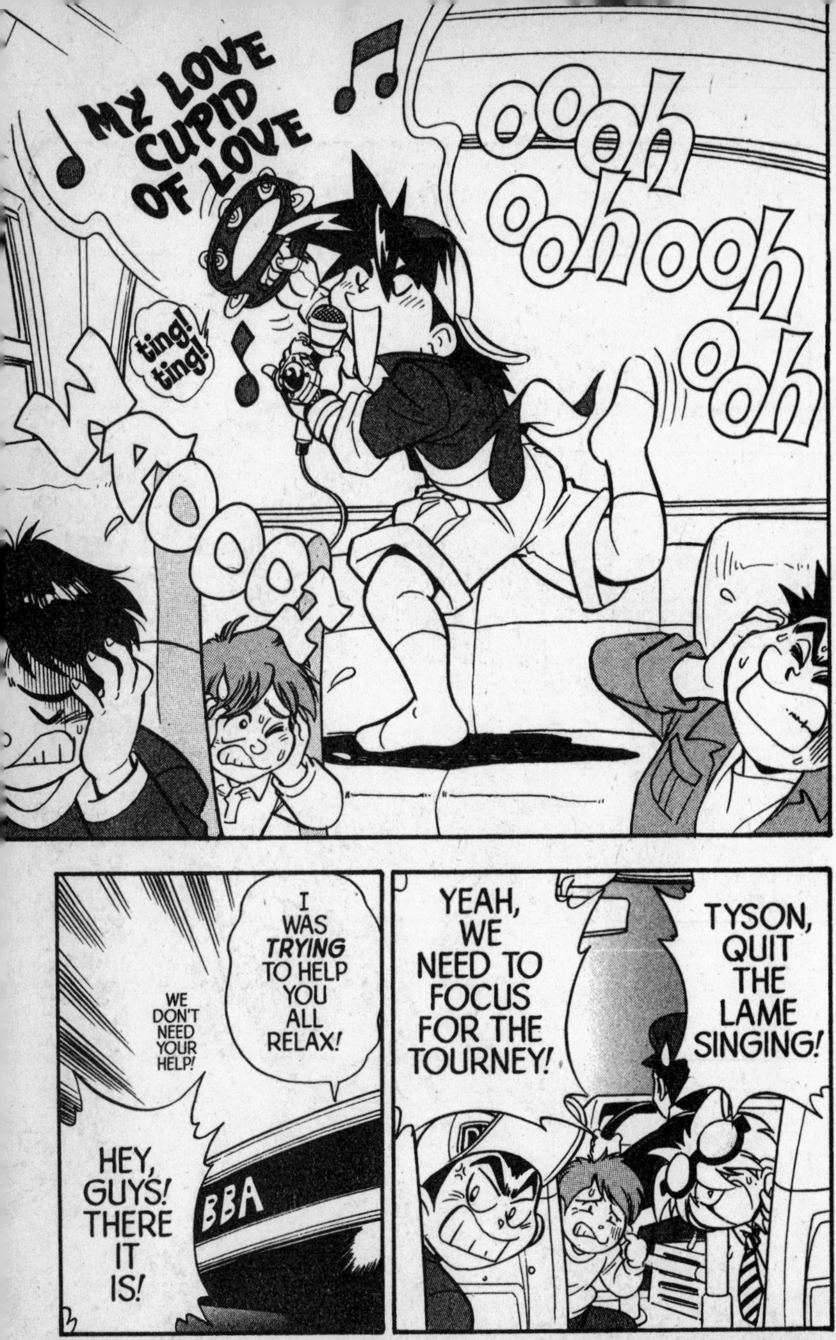
oooh oohooh ooh
MY LOVE CUPID OF LOVE
ting! ting!
WAOOOH
TYSON, QUIT THE LAME SINGING!
YEAH, WE NEED TO FOCUS FOR THE TOURNEY!
I WAS *TRYING* TO HELP YOU ALL RELAX!
WE DON'T NEED YOUR HELP!
HEY, GUYS! THERE IT IS!
BBA

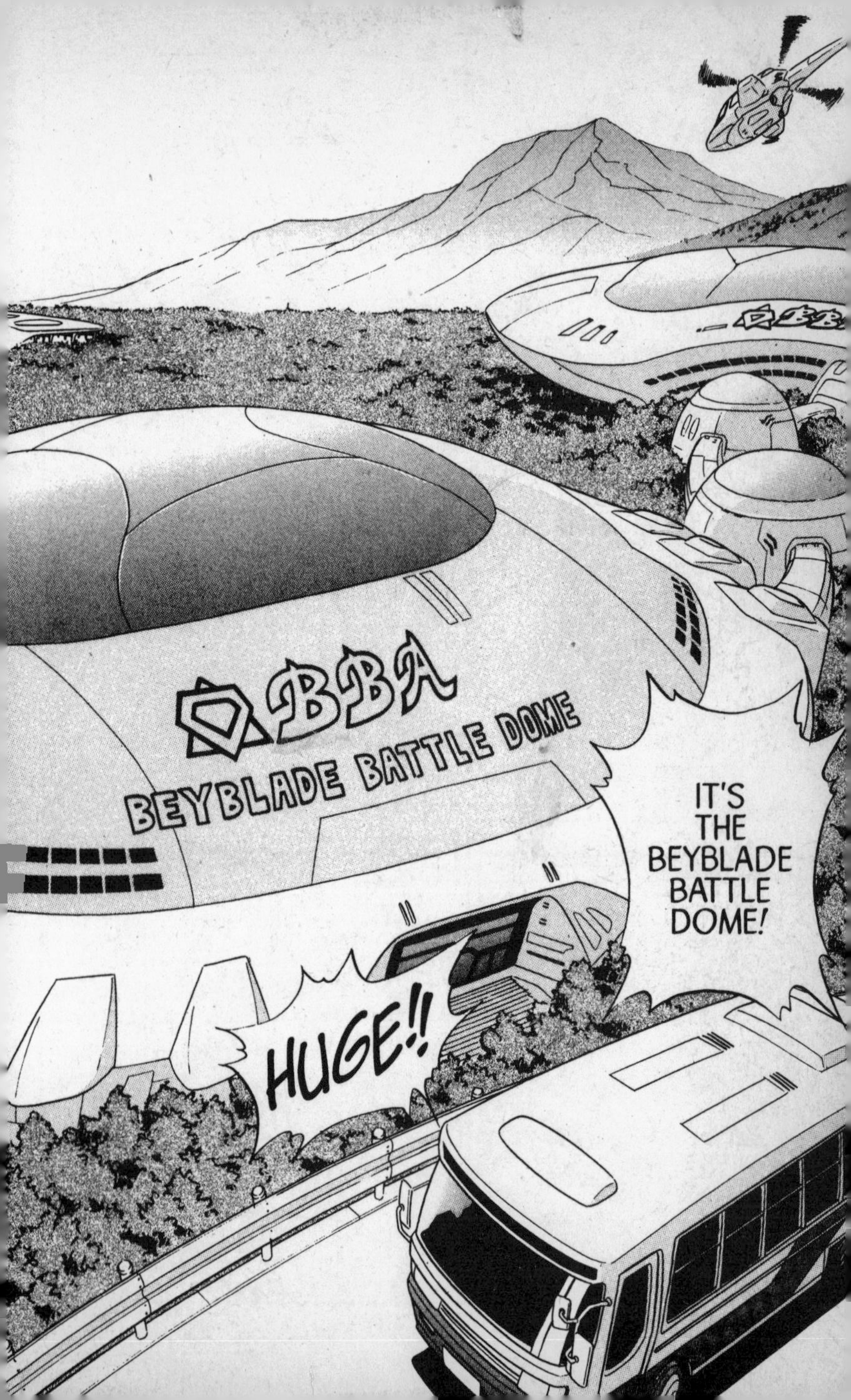
BBA
BEYBLADE BATTLE DOME
IT'S THE BEYBLADE BATTLE DOME!
HUGE!!

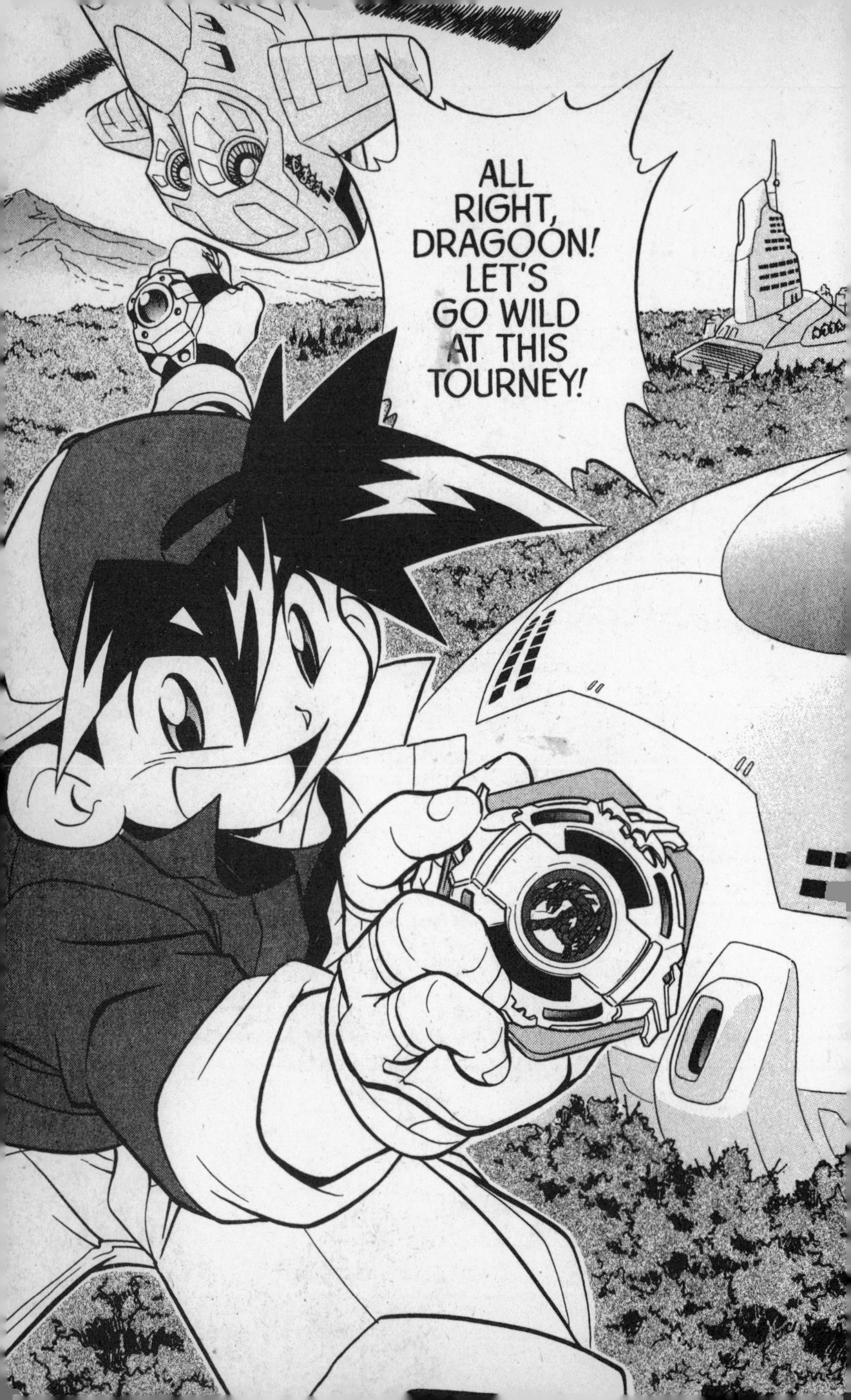
ALL RIGHT, DRAGOON! LET'S GO WILD AT THIS TOURNEY!

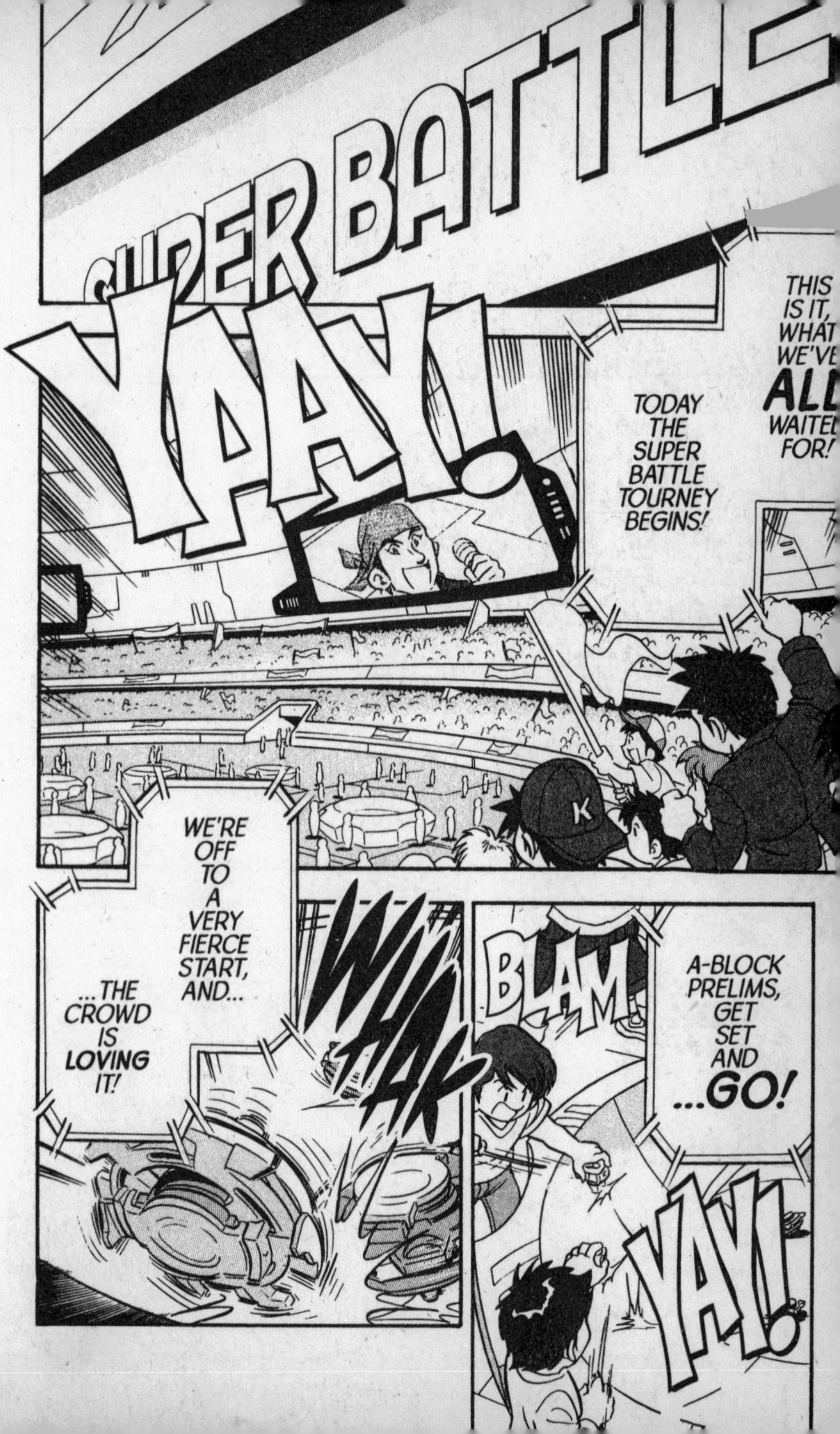
SUPER BATTL
YAY!
THIS IS IT, WHAT WE'VE ALL WAITED FOR!
TODAY THE SUPER BATTLE TOURNEY BEGINS!
A-BLOCK PRELIMS, GET SET AND ...GO!
BLAM
YAY!
WE'RE OFF TO A VERY FIERCE START, AND...
...THE CROWD IS LOVING IT!

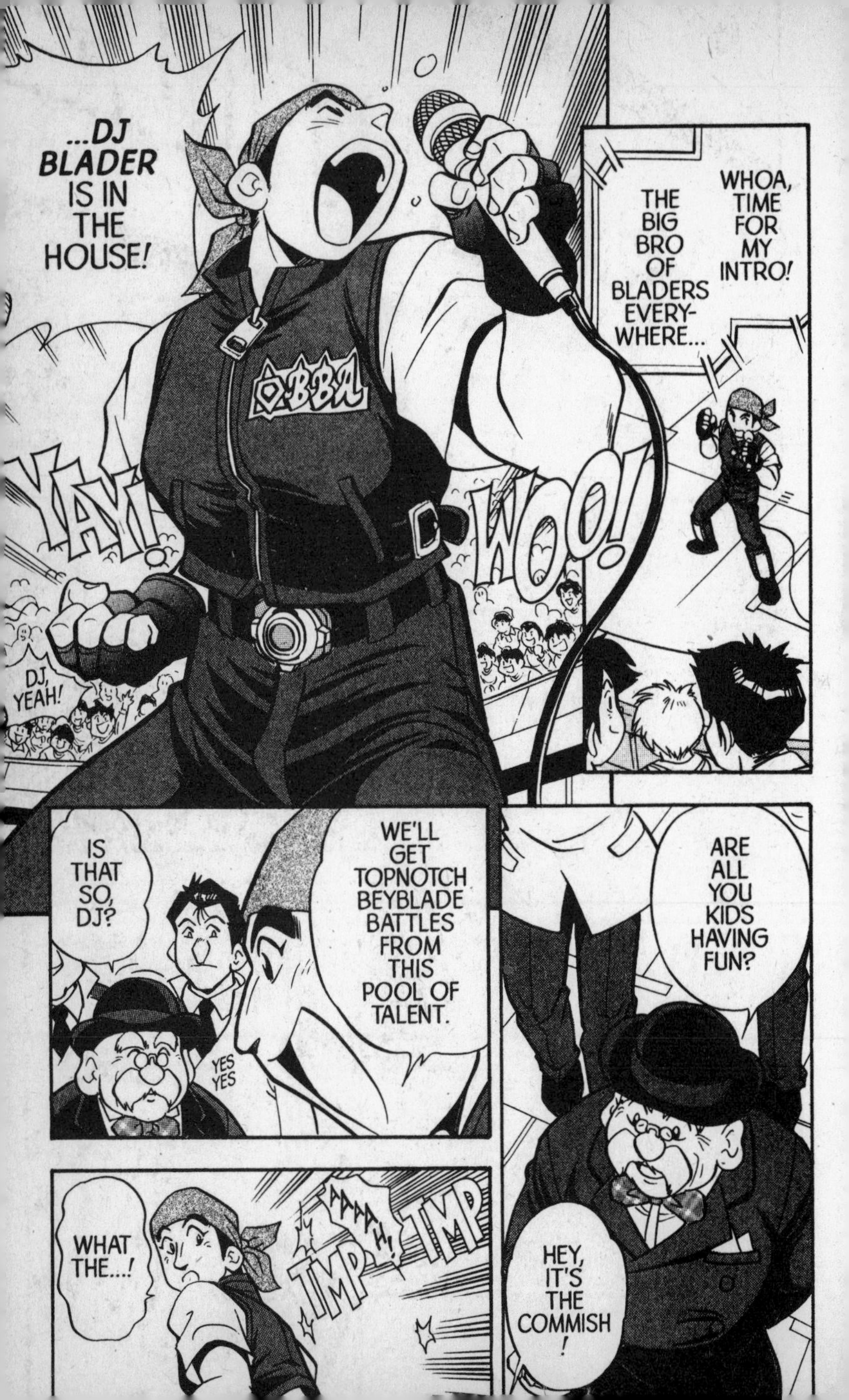
WHOA, TIME FOR MY INTRO!
THE BIG BRO OF BLADERS EVERY-WHERE...
...DJ BLADER IS IN THE HOUSE!
WOO!
YAY!
DJ, YEAH!
ARE ALL YOU KIDS HAVING FUN?
HEY, IT'S THE COMMISH!
WE'LL GET TOPNOTCH BEYBLADE BATTLES FROM THIS POOL OF TALENT.
IS THAT SO, DJ?
YES YES
TMP
PAAAH!
TMP
WHAT THE...!

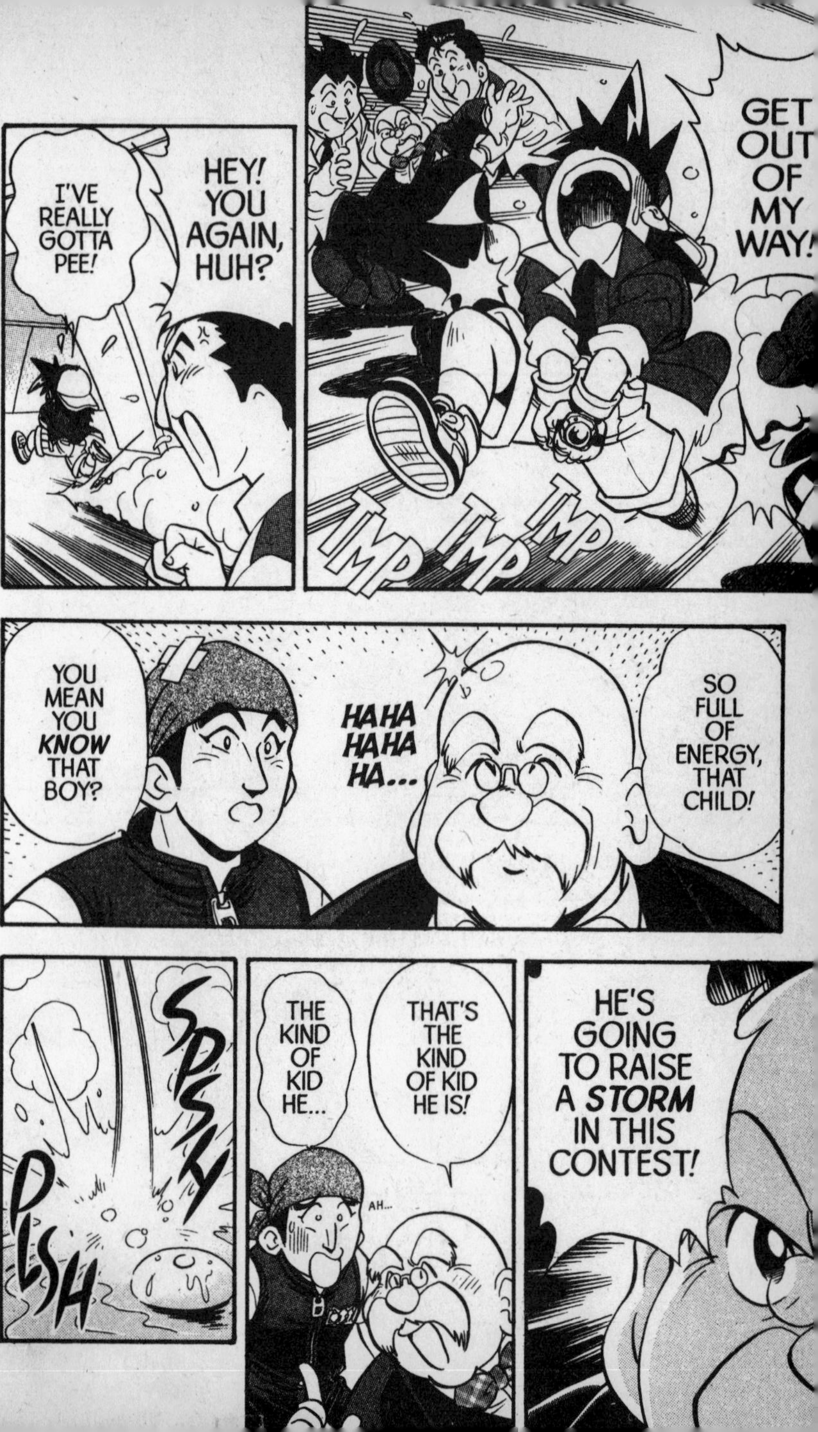
GET OUT OF MY WAY!
TMP TMP TMP
HEY! YOU AGAIN, HUH?
I'VE REALLY GOTTA PEE!
SO FULL OF ENERGY, THAT CHILD!
HAHA HAHA HA...
YOU MEAN YOU KNOW THAT BOY?
HE'S GOING TO RAISE A STORM IN THIS CONTEST!
THAT'S THE KIND OF KID HE IS!
THE KIND OF KID HE...
AH...
SPSH
PLSH

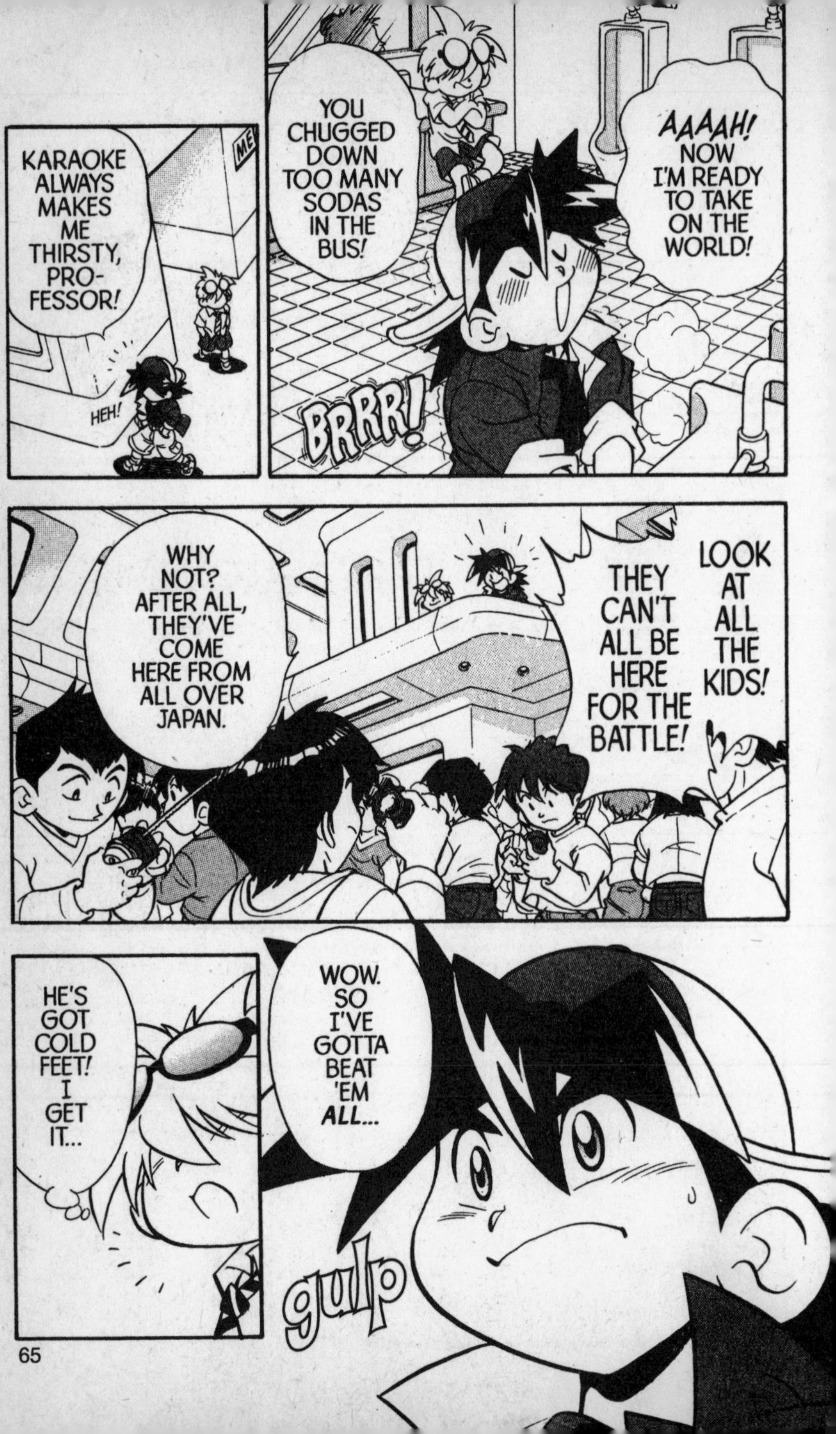
AAAAH! NOW I'M READY TO TAKE ON THE WORLD!
YOU CHUGGED DOWN TOO MANY SODAS IN THE BUS!
BRRR!
KARAOKE ALWAYS MAKES ME THIRSTY, PRO-FESSOR!
HEH!
LOOK AT ALL THE KIDS!
THEY CAN'T ALL BE HERE FOR THE BATTLE!
WHY NOT? AFTER ALL, THEY'VE COME HERE FROM ALL OVER JAPAN.
WOW. SO I'VE GOTTA BEAT 'EM *ALL*...
gulp
HE'S GOT COLD FEET! I GET IT...

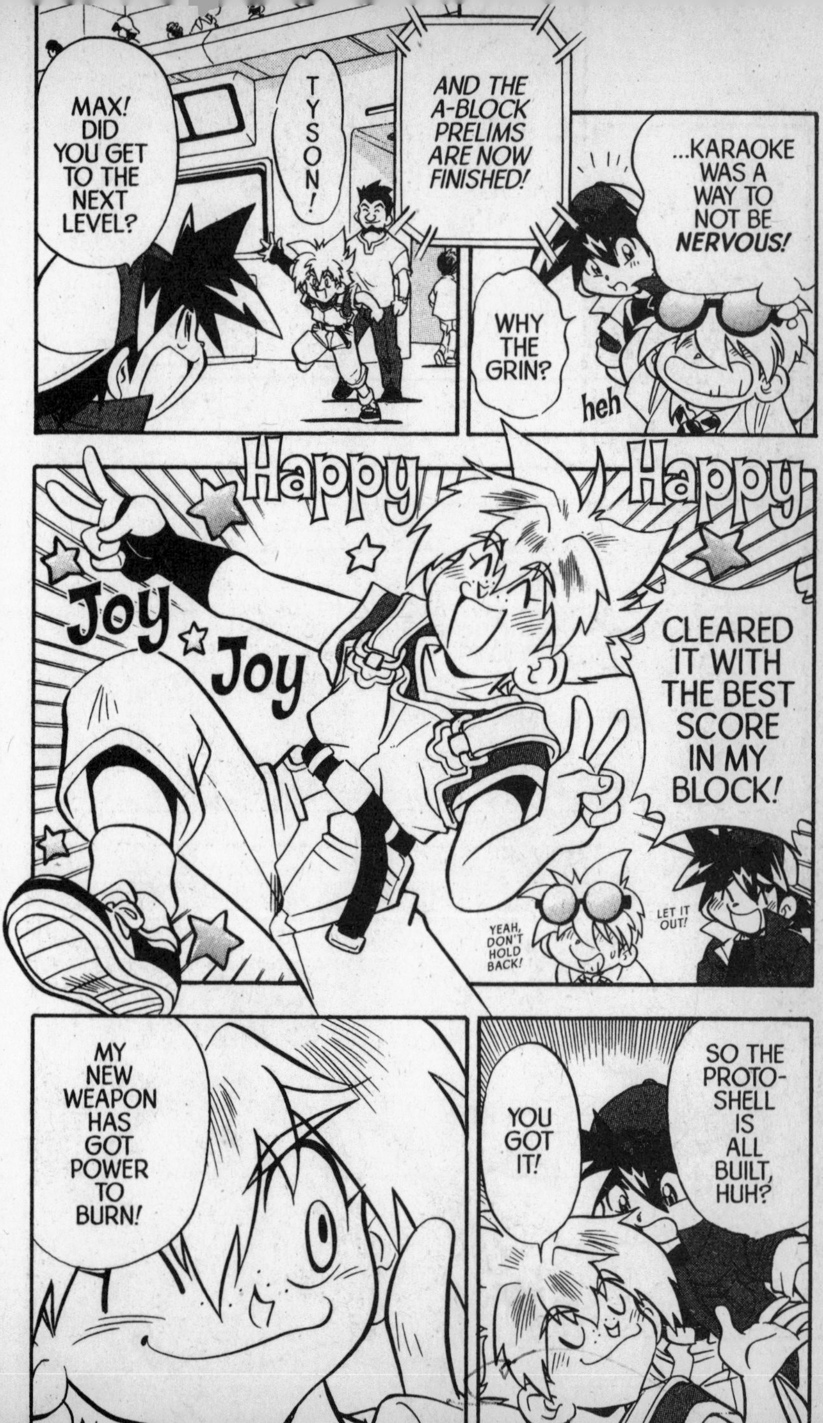
AND THE A-BLOCK PRELIMS ARE NOW FINISHED!
...KARAOKE WAS A WAY TO NOT BE NERVOUS!
WHY THE GRIN?
heh
TYSON!
MAX! DID YOU GET TO THE NEXT LEVEL?
Happy Happy
Joy Joy
CLEARED IT WITH THE BEST SCORE IN MY BLOCK!
LET IT OUT!
YEAH, DON'T HOLD BACK!
SO THE PROTO-SHELL IS ALL BUILT, HUH?
YOU GOT IT!
MY NEW WEAPON HAS GOT POWER TO BURN!

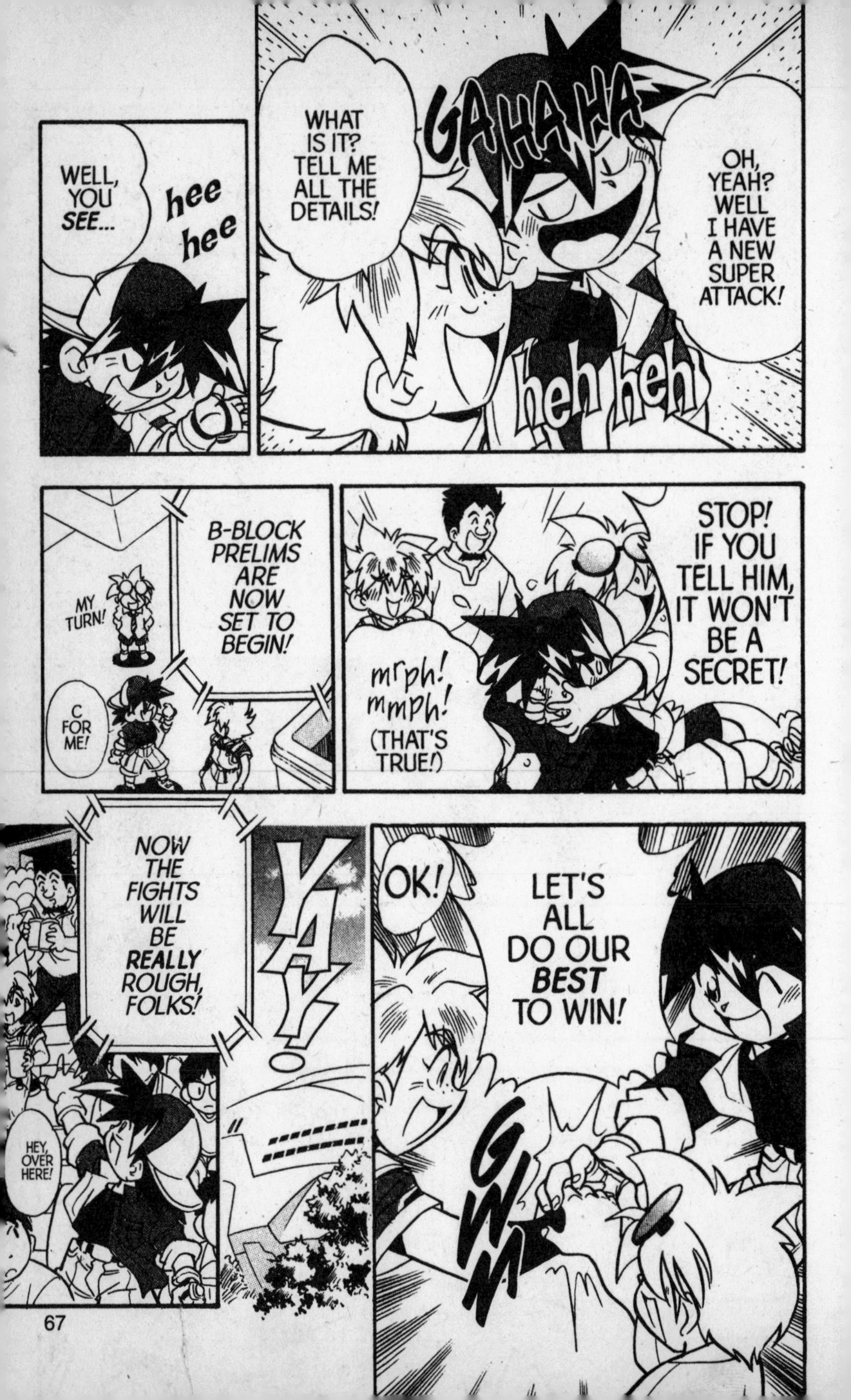
WHAT IS IT? TELL ME ALL THE DETAILS!
GAHAHA
OH, YEAH? WELL I HAVE A NEW SUPER ATTACK!
heh heh
WELL, YOU *SEE*...
hee hee
STOP! IF YOU TELL HIM, IT WON'T BE A SECRET!
mrph! mmph! (THAT'S TRUE!)
B-BLOCK PRELIMS ARE NOW SET TO BEGIN!
MY TURN!
C FOR ME!
OK!
LET'S ALL DO OUR *BEST* TO WIN!
YAY!
NOW THE FIGHTS WILL BE ***REALLY*** ROUGH, FOLKS!
HEY, OVER HERE!

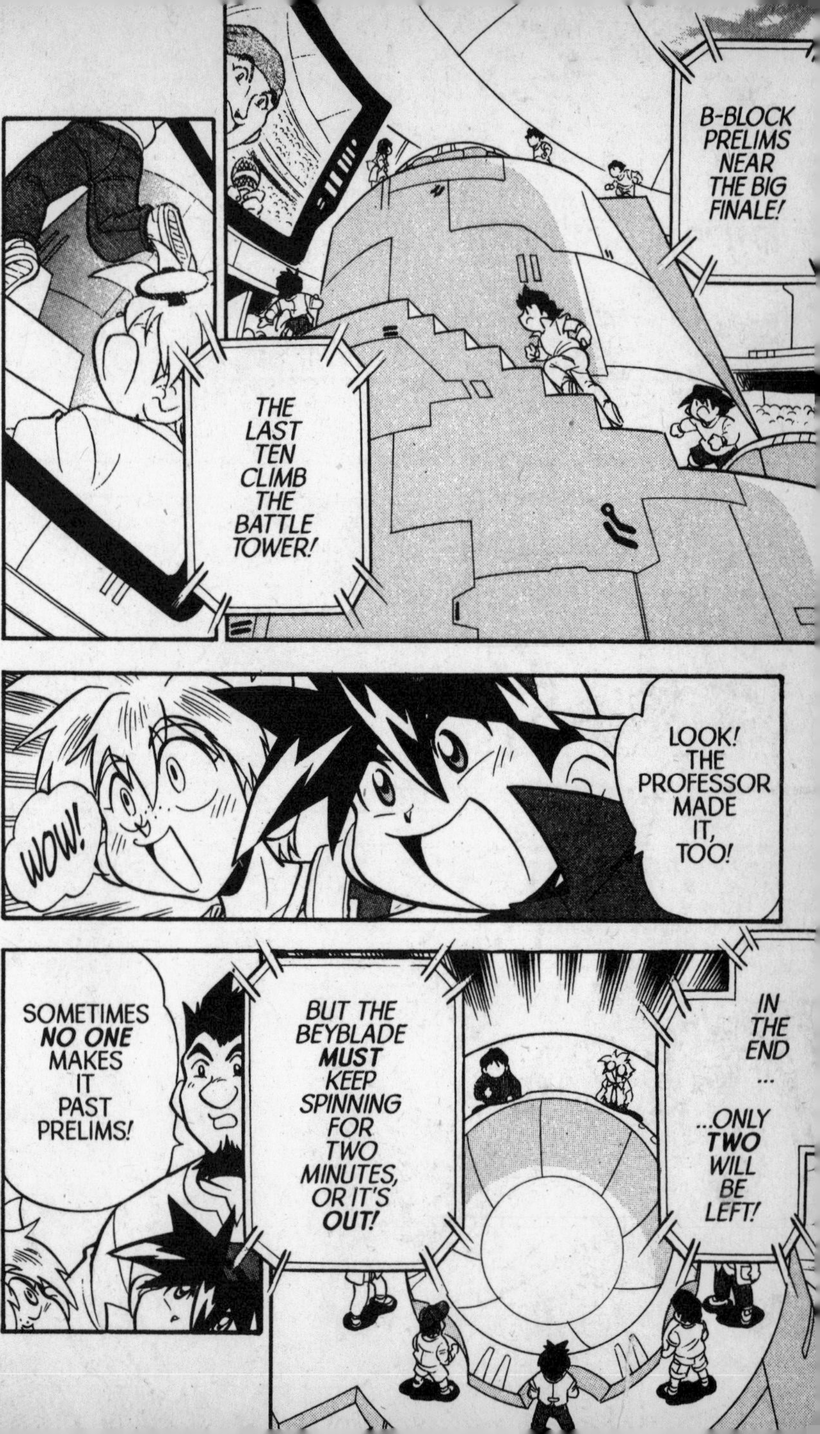
B-BLOCK PRELIMS NEAR THE BIG FINALE!
THE LAST TEN CLIMB THE BATTLE TOWER!
LOOK! THE PROFESSOR MADE IT, TOO!
WOW!
IN THE END...
...ONLY TWO WILL BE LEFT!
BUT THE BEYBLADE MUST KEEP SPINNING FOR TWO MINUTES, OR IT'S OUT!
SOMETIMES NO ONE MAKES IT PAST PRELIMS!

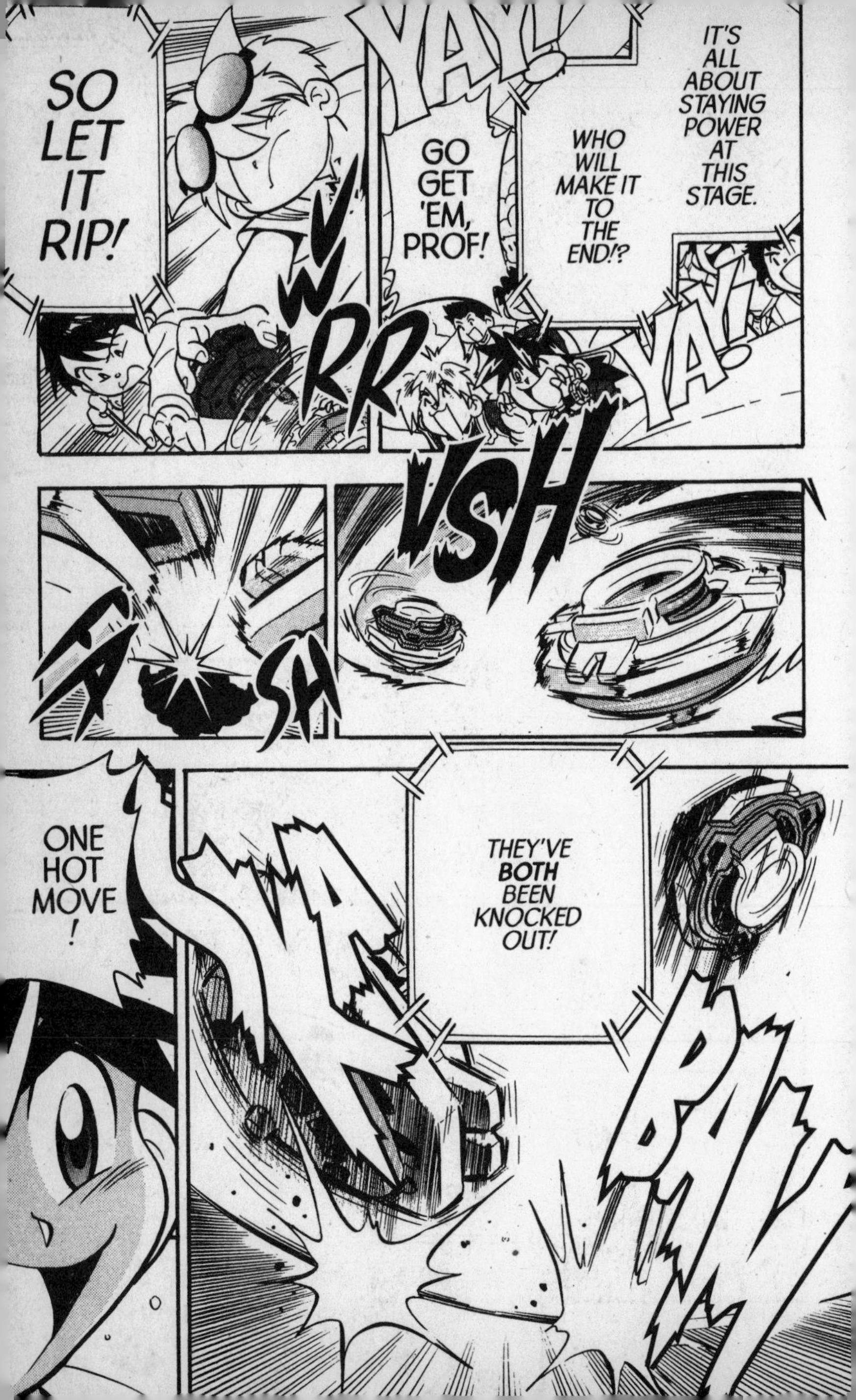
IT'S ALL ABOUT STAYING POWER AT THIS STAGE.
WHO WILL MAKE IT TO THE END!?
YA!
GO GET 'EM, PROF!
YAY!
SO LET IT RIP!
WRRR
VSH
SH
THEY'VE **BOTH** BEEN KNOCKED OUT!
ONE HOT MOVE!

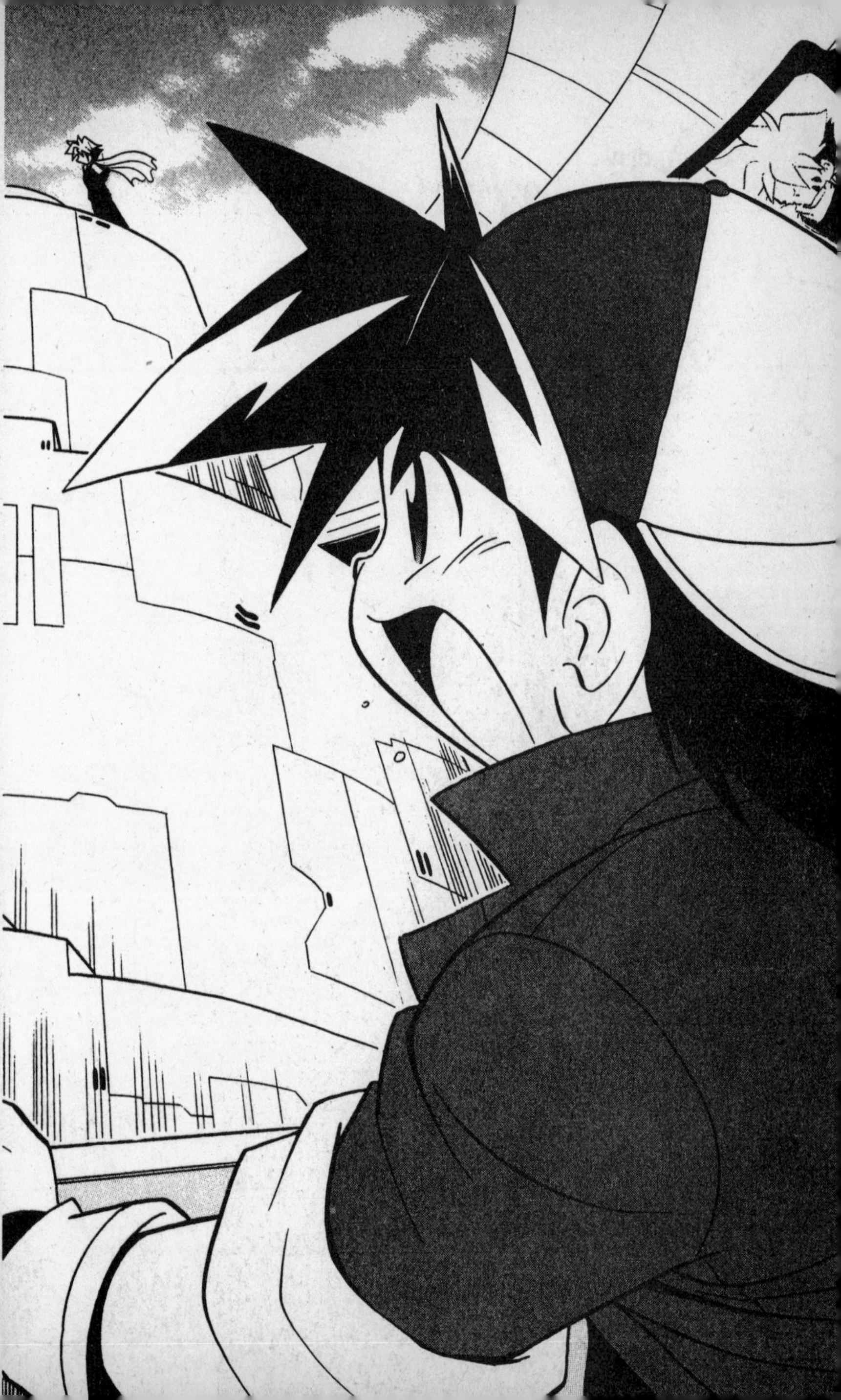

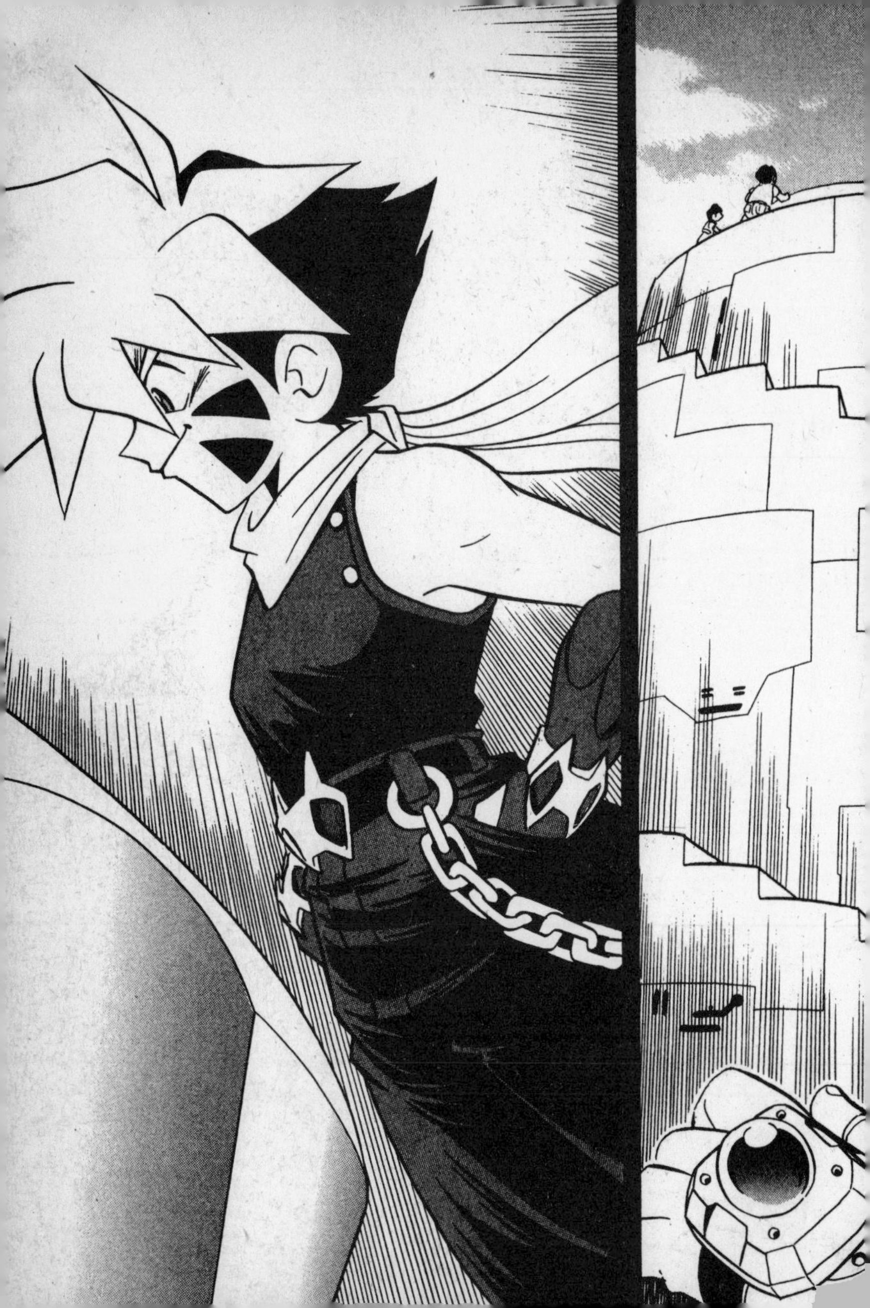

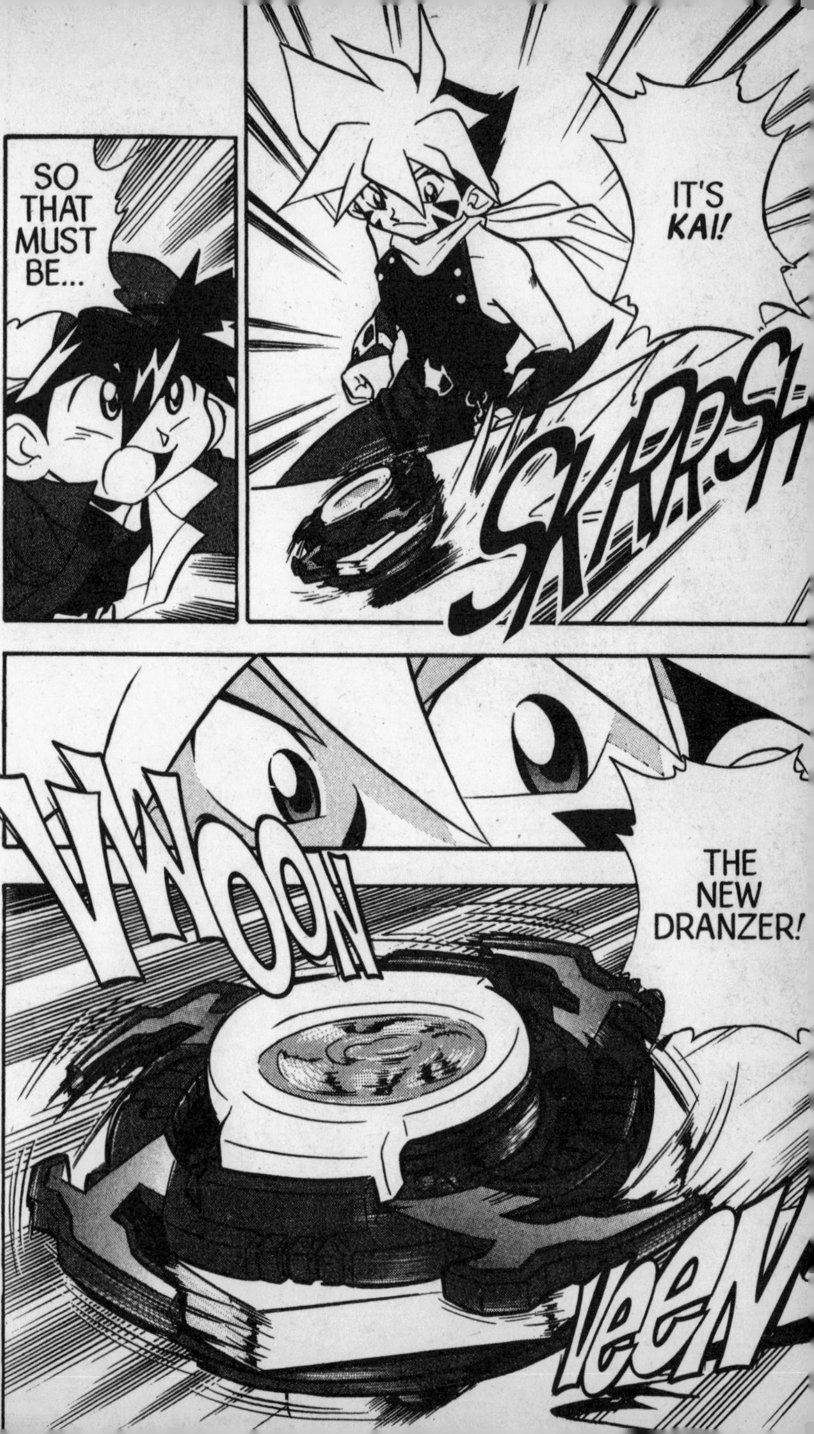
SO THAT MUST BE...
IT'S KAI!
SKARRSH
THE NEW DRANZER!
VWOOON
VEEN

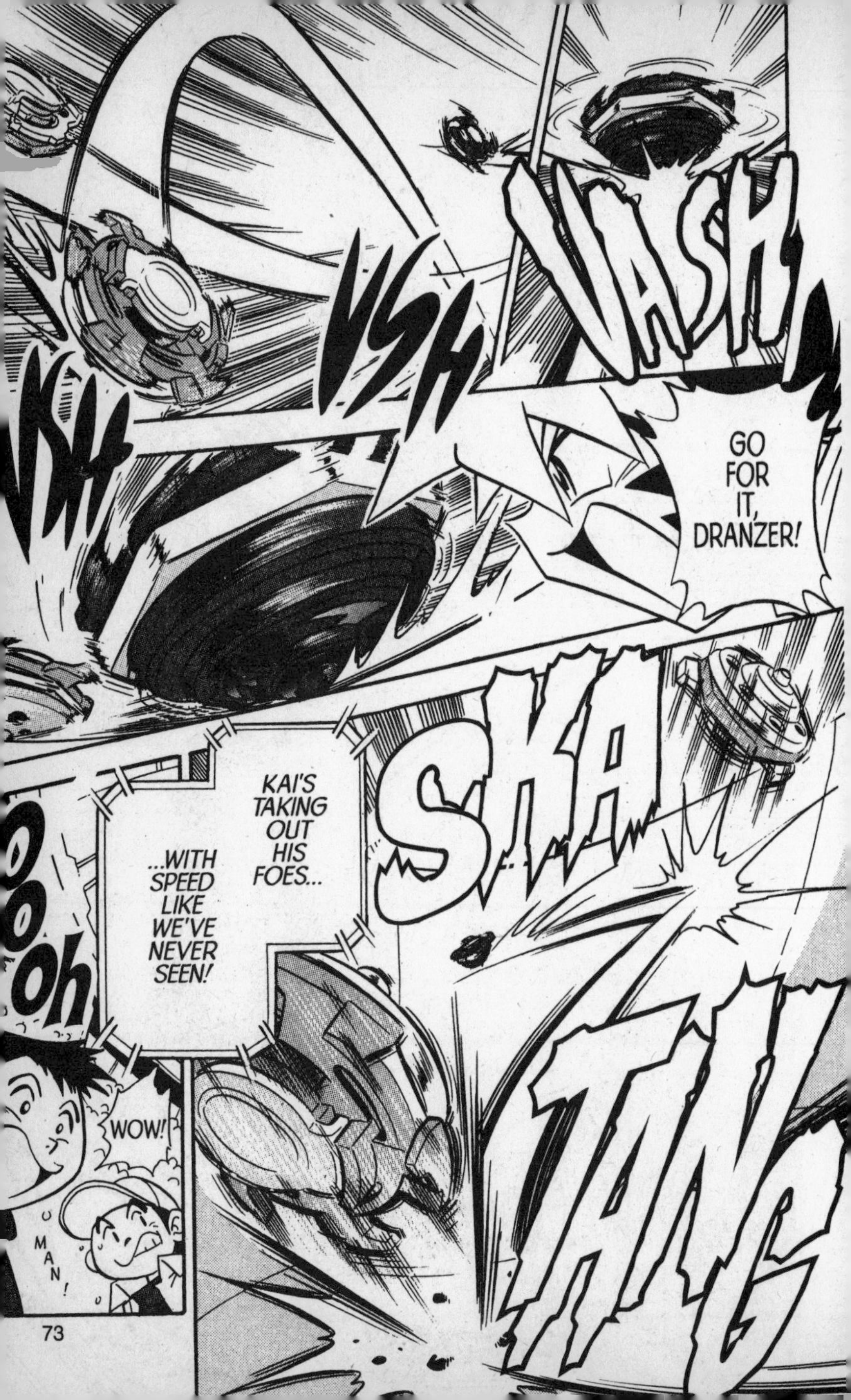
VASH
VSH
VSH
GO FOR IT, DRANZER!
SHA
TANG
KAI'S TAKING OUT HIS FOES...
...WITH SPEED LIKE WE'VE NEVER SEEN!
Ooooh
WOW!
MAN!

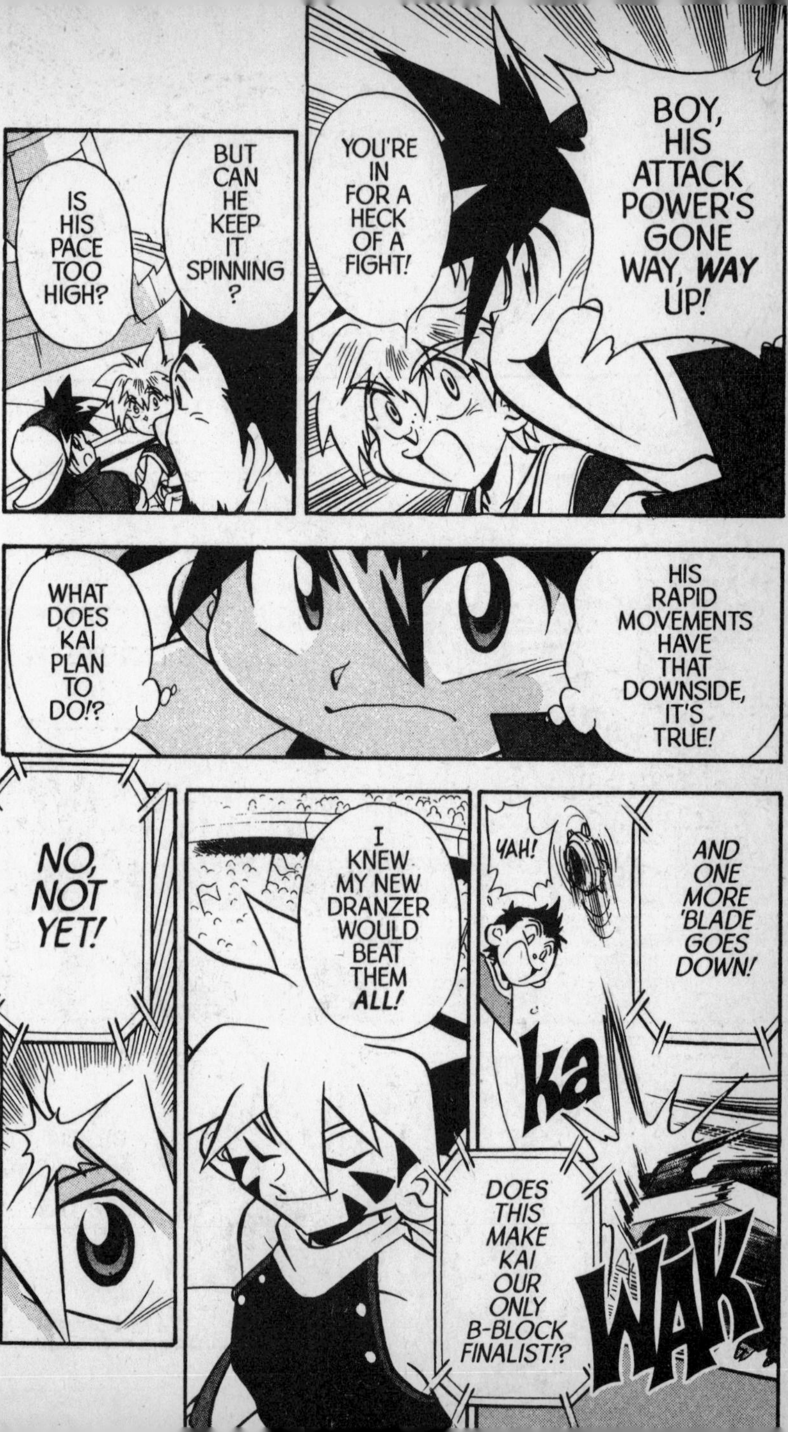
BOY, HIS ATTACK POWER'S GONE WAY, **WAY** UP!
YOU'RE IN FOR A HECK OF A FIGHT!
BUT CAN HE KEEP IT SPINNING?
IS HIS PACE TOO HIGH?
HIS RAPID MOVEMENTS HAVE THAT DOWNSIDE, IT'S TRUE!
WHAT DOES KAI PLAN TO DO!?
AND ONE MORE 'BLADE GOES DOWN!
YAH!
ka
WAK
DOES THIS MAKE KAI OUR ONLY B-BLOCK FINALIST!?
I KNEW MY NEW DRANZER WOULD BEAT THEM **ALL!**
NO, NOT YET!

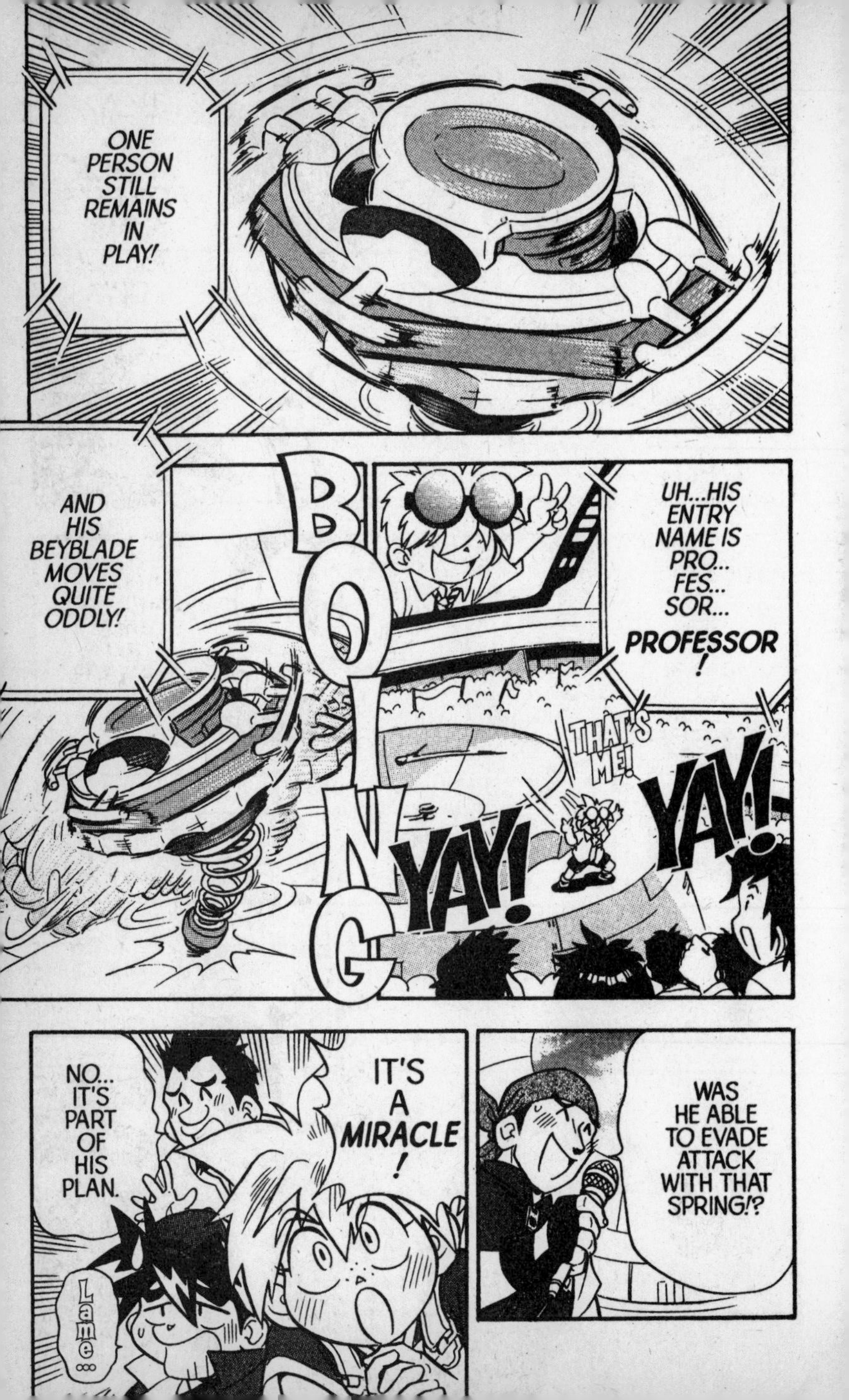
ONE PERSON STILL REMAINS IN PLAY!
UH...HIS ENTRY NAME IS PRO... FES... SOR... PROFESSOR!
AND HIS BEYBLADE MOVES QUITE ODDLY!
BOING
THAT'S ME!
YAY!
YAY!
WAS HE ABLE TO EVADE ATTACK WITH THAT SPRING!?
IT'S A MIRACLE!
NO... IT'S PART OF HIS PLAN.
Lame...

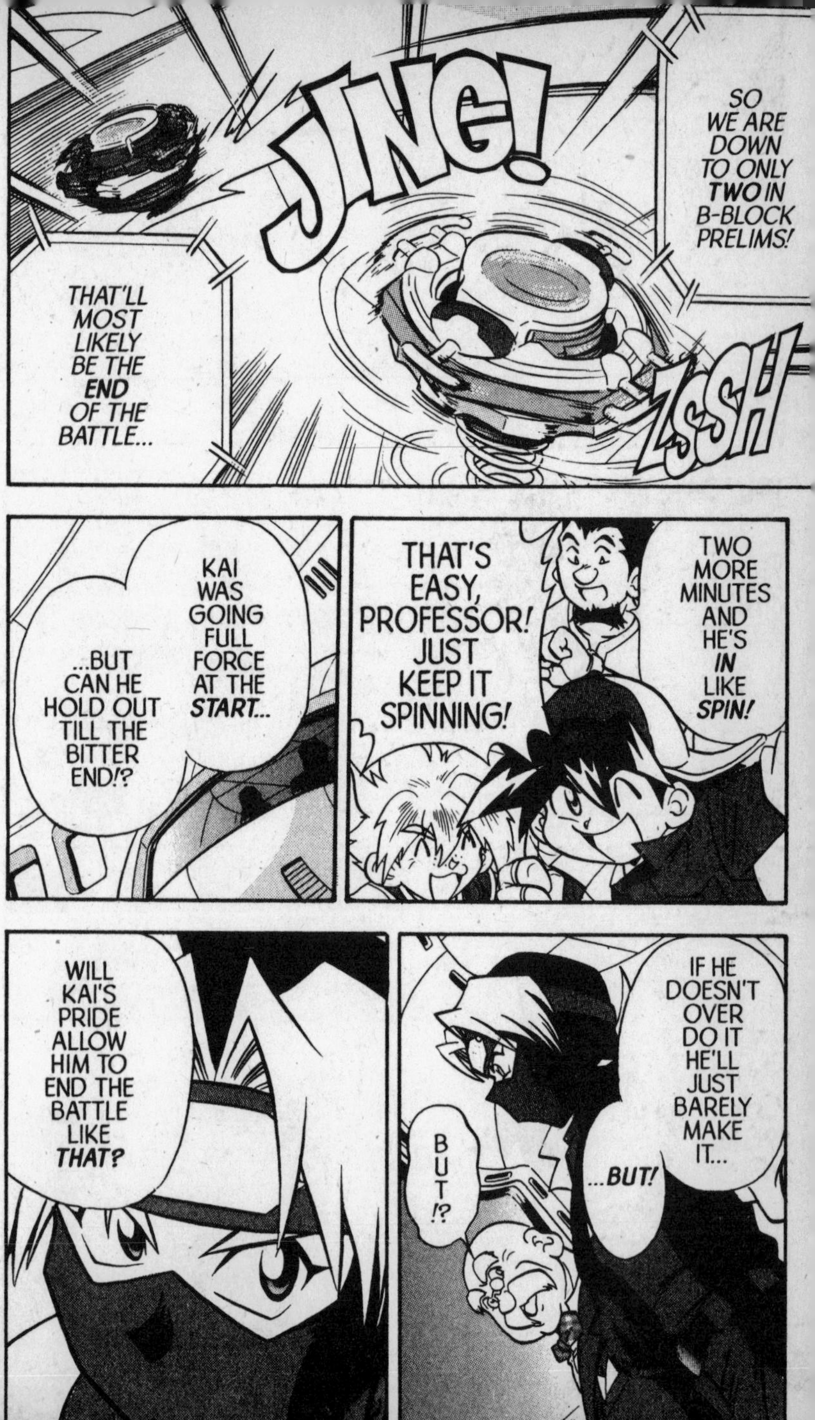
SO WE ARE DOWN TO ONLY TWO IN B-BLOCK PRELIMS!
JING!
ZSSH
THAT'LL MOST LIKELY BE THE END OF THE BATTLE...
TWO MORE MINUTES AND HE'S IN LIKE SPIN!
THAT'S EASY, PROFESSOR! JUST KEEP IT SPINNING!
KAI WAS GOING FULL FORCE AT THE START...
...BUT CAN HE HOLD OUT TILL THE BITTER END!?
IF HE DOESN'T OVER DO IT HE'LL JUST BARELY MAKE IT...
...BUT!
BUT!?
WILL KAI'S PRIDE ALLOW HIM TO END THE BATTLE LIKE THAT?

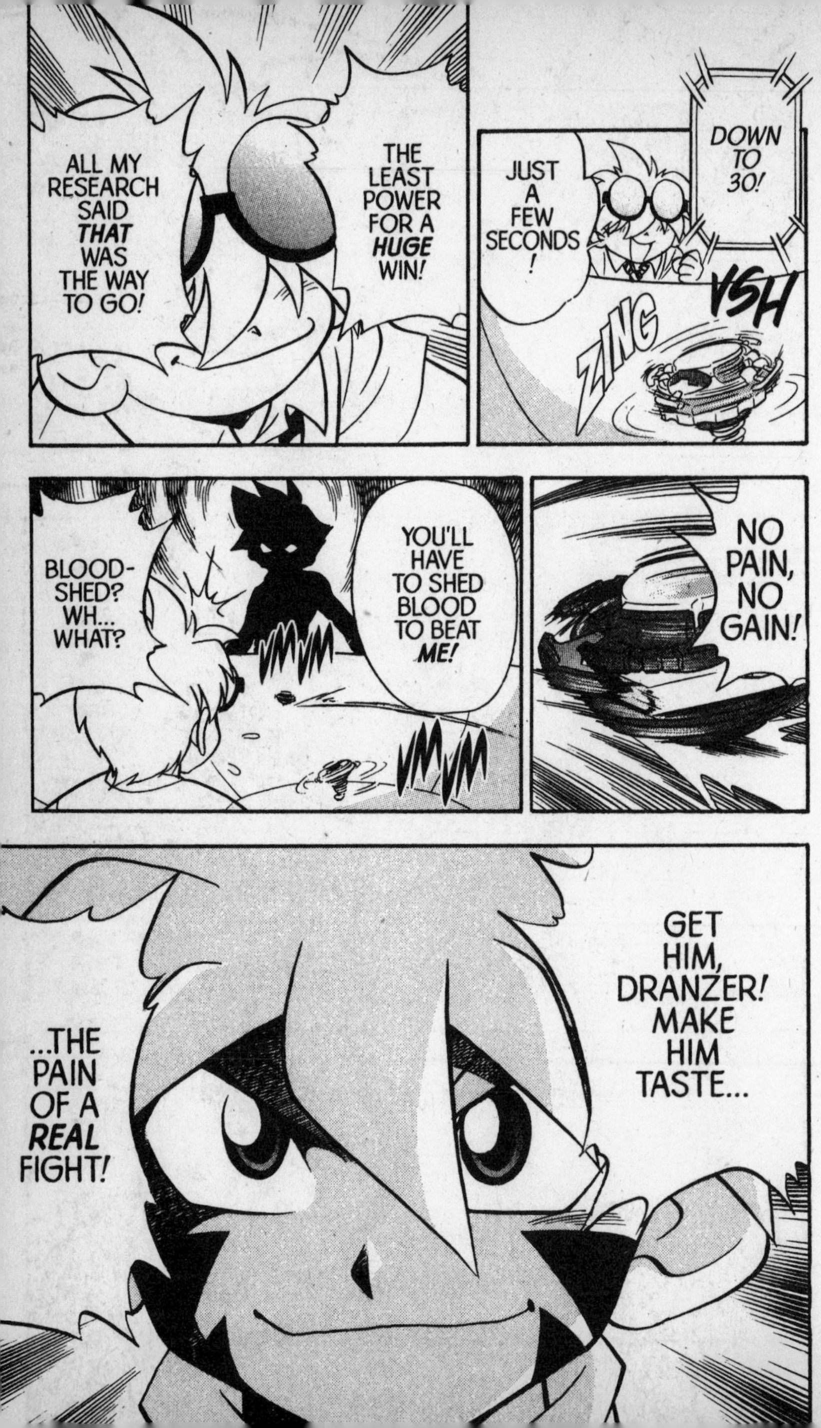
DOWN TO 30!
JUST A FEW SECONDS!
VSH
ZING
THE LEAST POWER FOR A HUGE WIN!
ALL MY RESEARCH SAID THAT WAS THE WAY TO GO!
NO PAIN, NO GAIN!
YOU'LL HAVE TO SHED BLOOD TO BEAT ME!
VMVM
BLOOD-SHED? WH... WHAT?
VMVM
GET HIM, DRANZER! MAKE HIM TASTE...
...THE PAIN OF A REAL FIGHT!

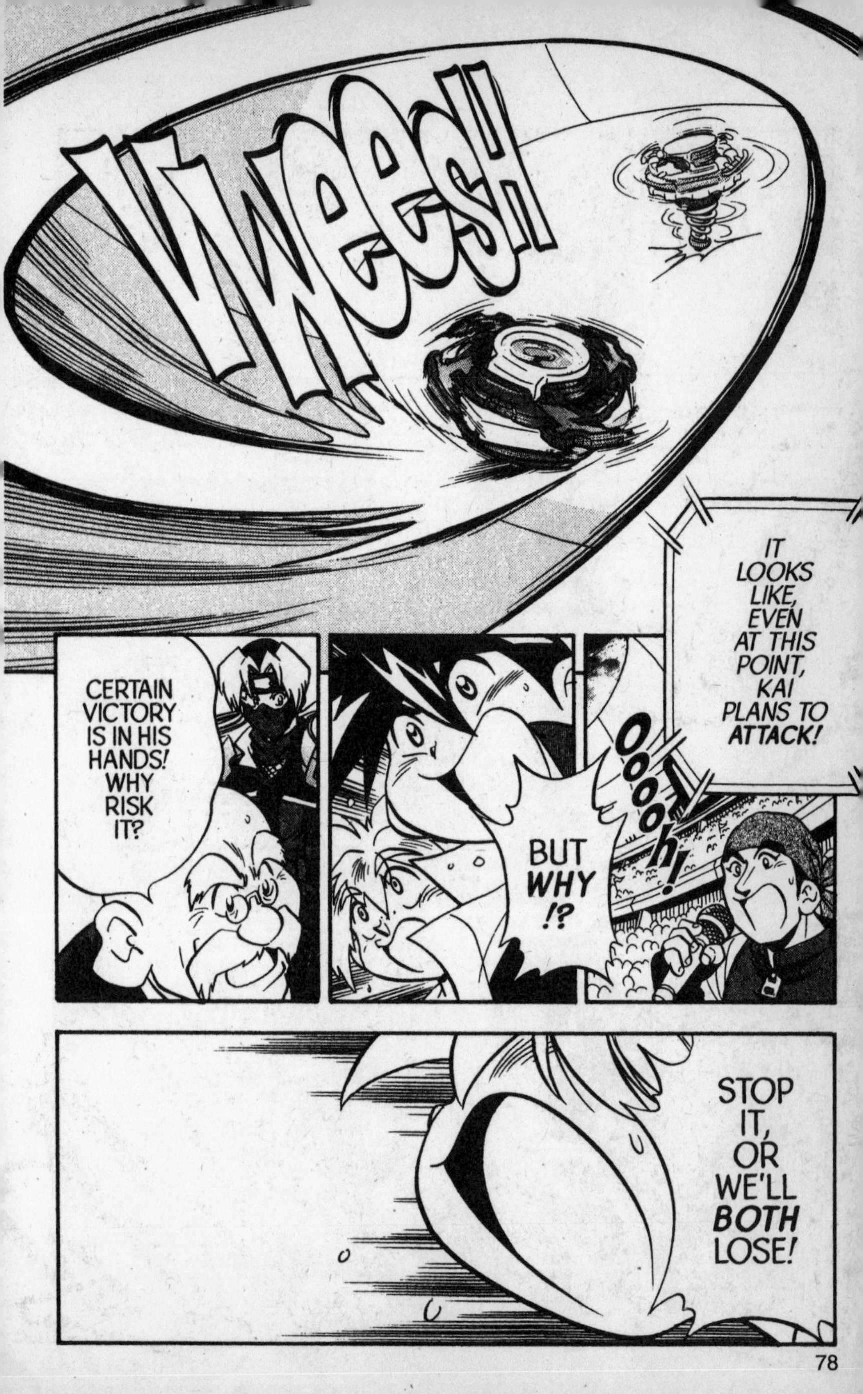
WHEESH!
IT LOOKS LIKE, EVEN AT THIS POINT, KAI PLANS TO ATTACK!
OOOOH!
BUT WHY!?
CERTAIN VICTORY IS IN HIS HANDS! WHY RISK IT?
STOP IT, OR WE'LL BOTH LOSE!

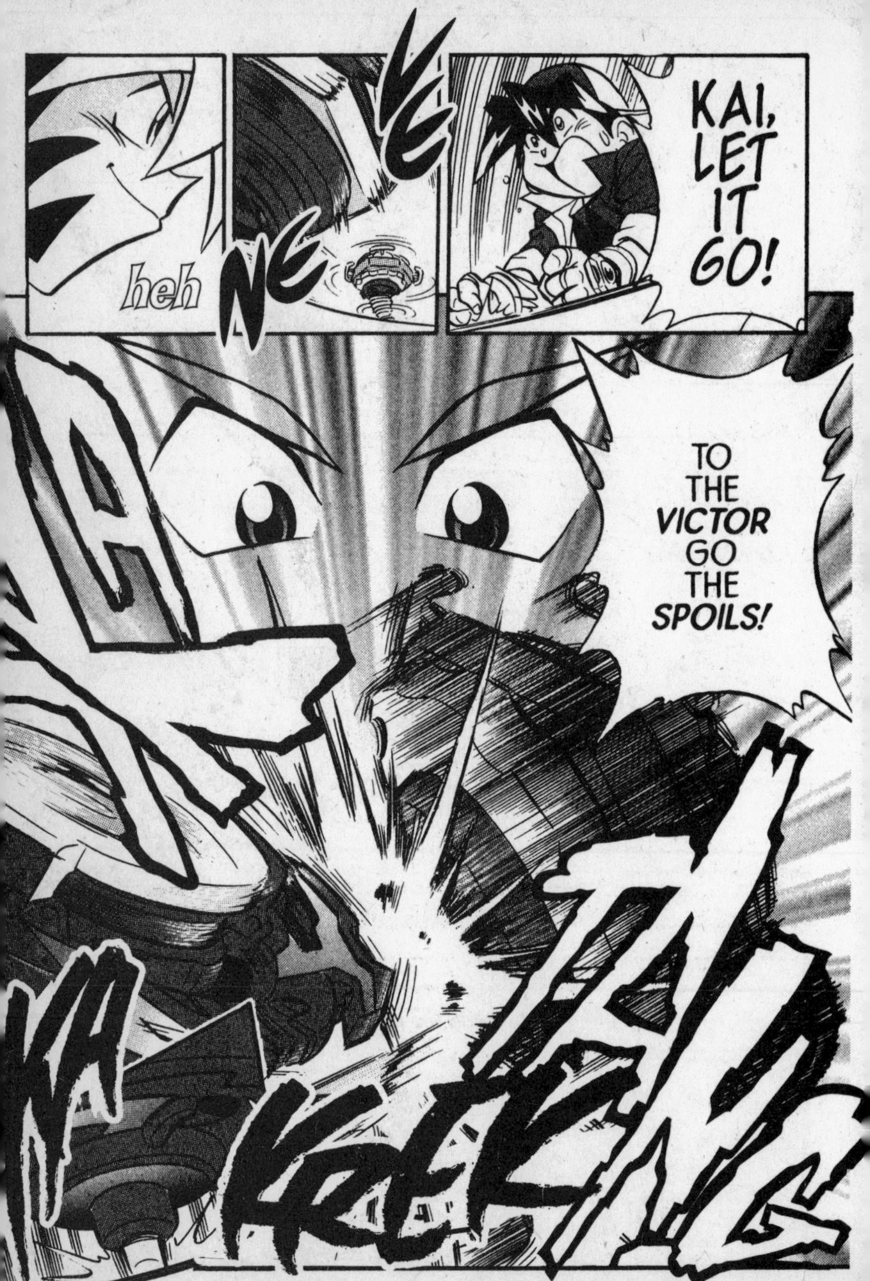
KAI, LET IT GO!
heh
TO THE VICTOR GO THE SPOILS!

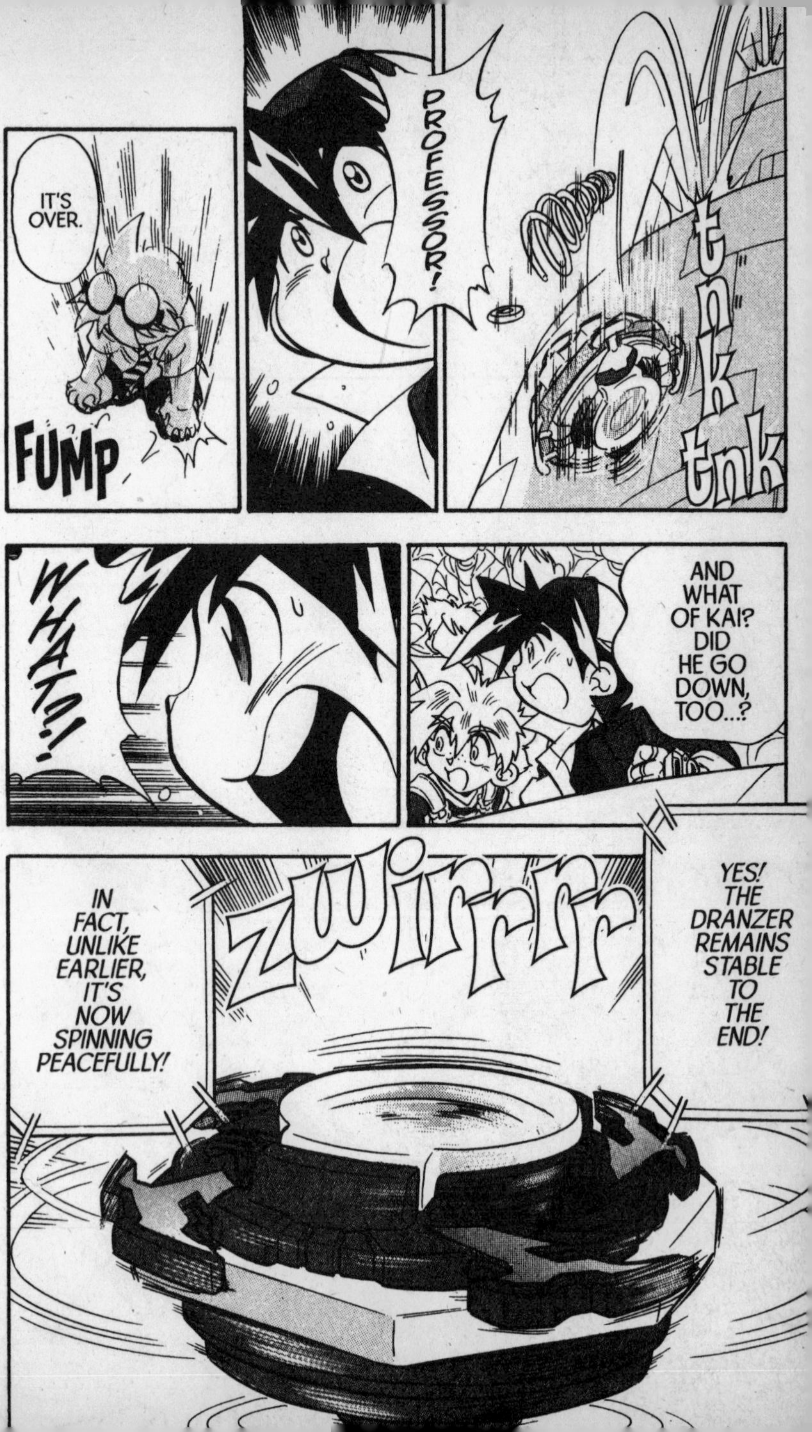
tnk tnk
PROFESSOR!
IT'S OVER.
FUMP
AND WHAT OF KAI? DID HE GO DOWN, TOO...?
WHAA?!!
YES! THE DRANZER REMAINS STABLE TO THE END!
zwirrr
IN FACT, UNLIKE EARLIER, IT'S NOW SPINNING PEACEFULLY!

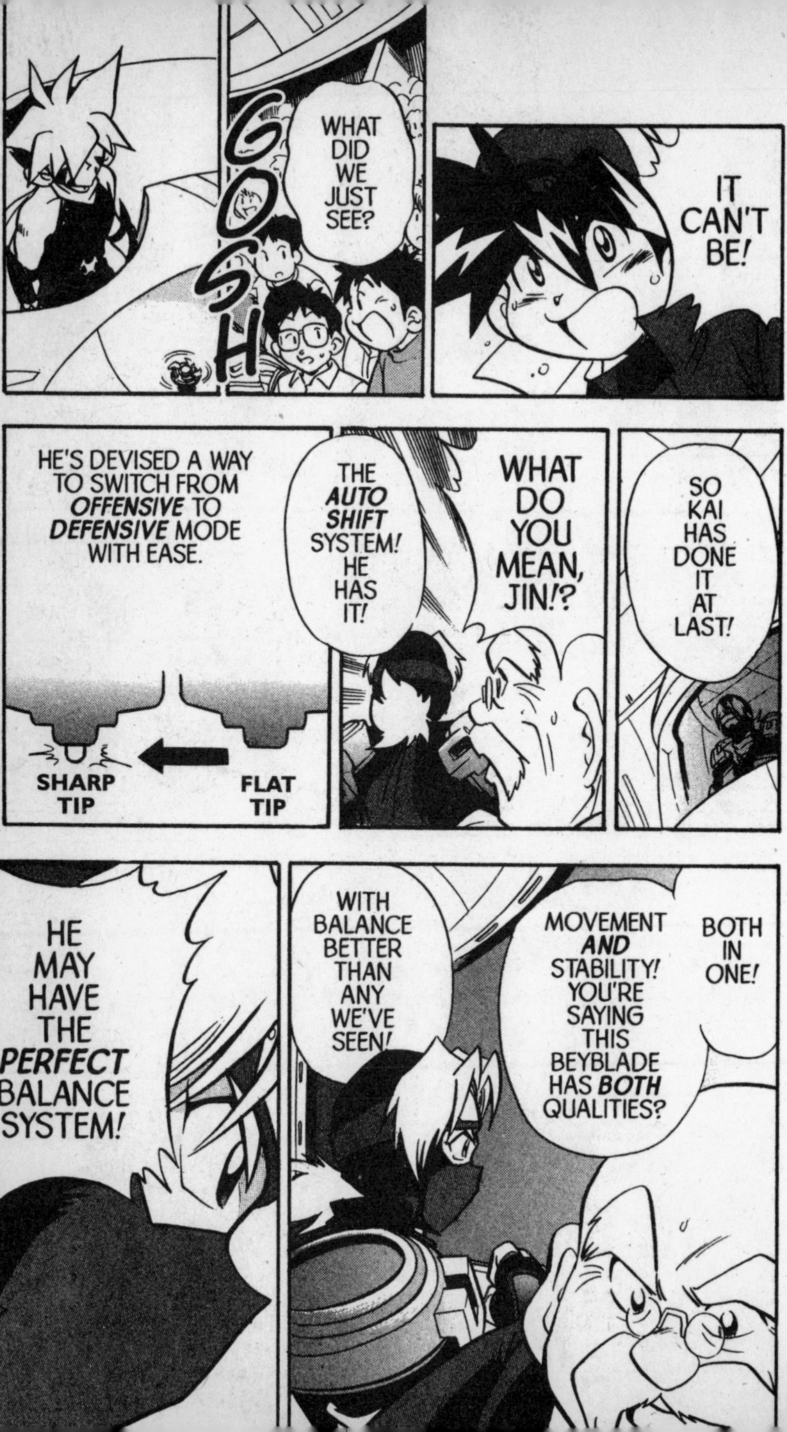
IT CAN'T BE!
WHAT DID WE JUST SEE?
GOSH
SO KAI HAS DONE IT AT LAST!
WHAT DO YOU MEAN, JIN!?
THE *AUTO SHIFT* SYSTEM! HE HAS IT!
HE'S DEVISED A WAY TO SWITCH FROM *OFFENSIVE* TO *DEFENSIVE* MODE WITH EASE.
FLAT TIP
SHARP TIP
BOTH IN ONE!
MOVEMENT *AND* STABILITY! YOU'RE SAYING THIS BEYBLADE HAS *BOTH* QUALITIES?
WITH BALANCE BETTER THAN ANY WE'VE SEEN!
HE MAY HAVE THE *PERFECT* BALANCE SYSTEM!

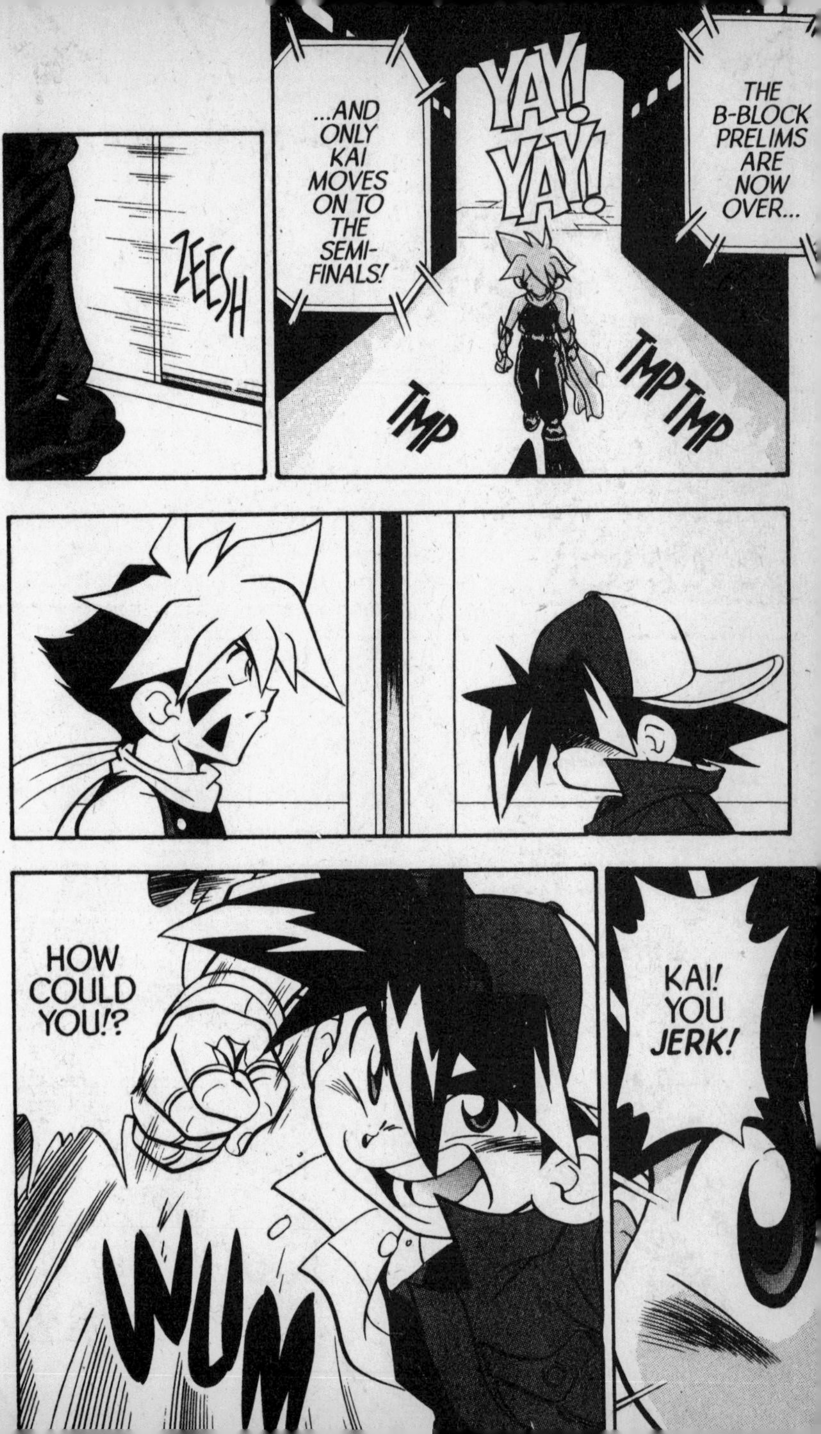
THE B-BLOCK PRELIMS ARE NOW OVER...
YAY! YAY!
...AND ONLY KAI MOVES ON TO THE SEMI-FINALS!
TMP TMP
TMP
ZEESH
KAI! YOU JERK!
HOW COULD YOU!?
WUM

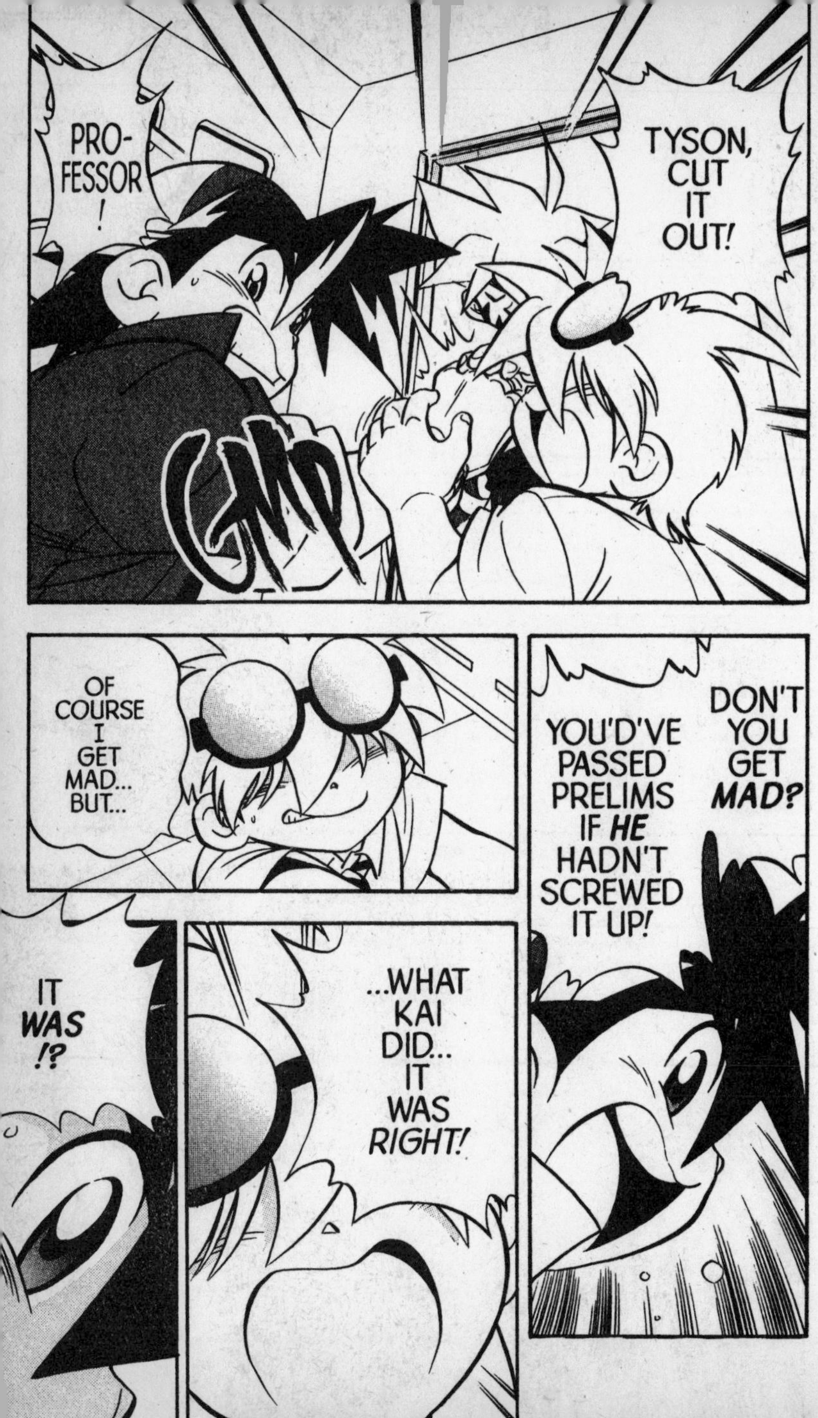
TYSON, CUT IT OUT!
PRO-FESSOR!
GMP
DON'T YOU GET MAD?
YOU'D'VE PASSED PRELIMS IF HE HADN'T SCREWED IT UP!
OF COURSE I GET MAD... BUT...
...WHAT KAI DID... IT WAS RIGHT!
IT WAS!?

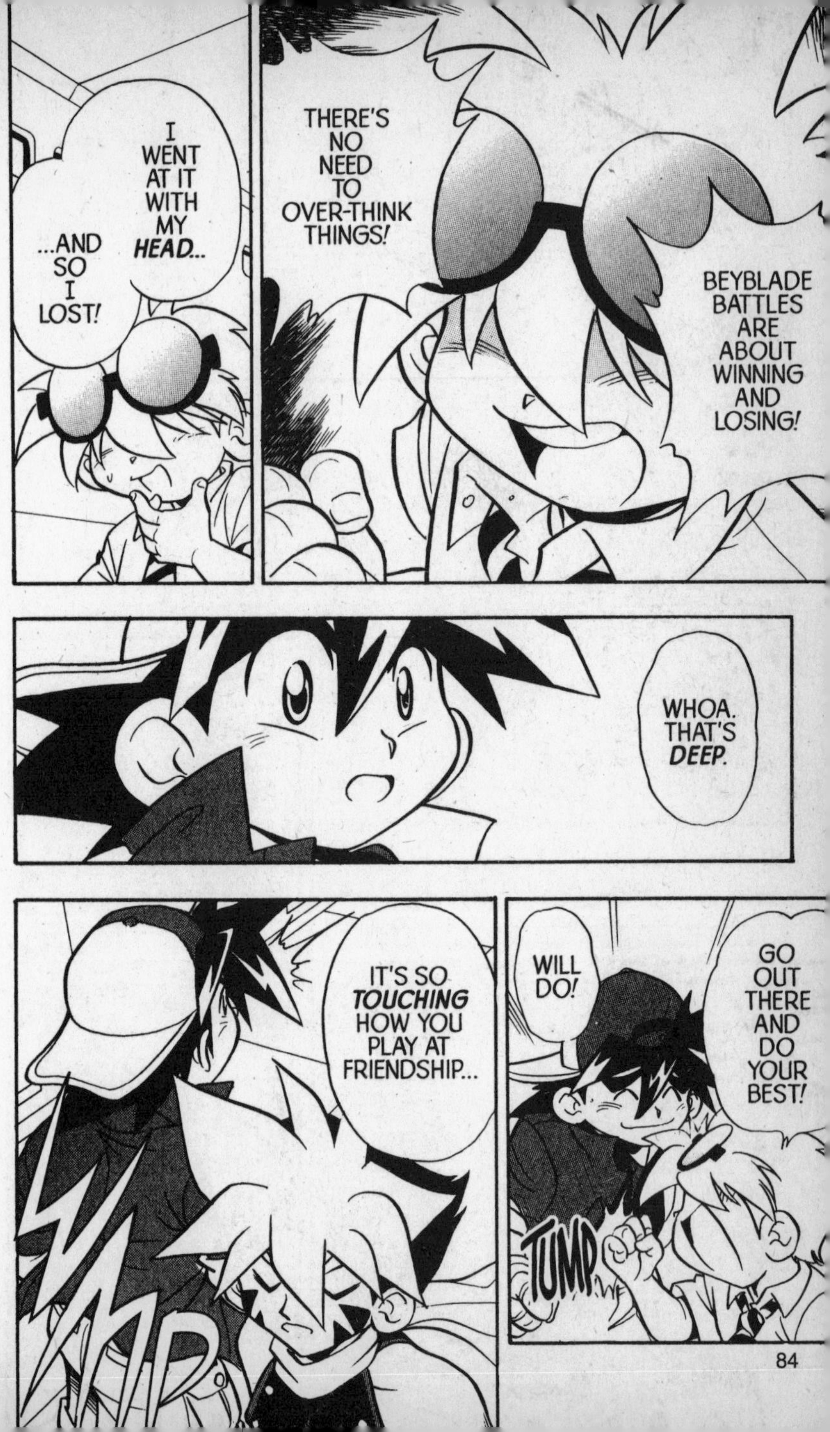
THERE'S NO NEED TO OVER-THINK THINGS!
BEYBLADE BATTLES ARE ABOUT WINNING AND LOSING!
I WENT AT IT WITH MY *HEAD*...
...AND SO I LOST!
WHOA. THAT'S *DEEP*.
GO OUT THERE AND DO YOUR BEST!
WILL DO!
TUMP
IT'S SO *TOUCHING* HOW YOU PLAY AT FRIENDSHIP...
WHAP

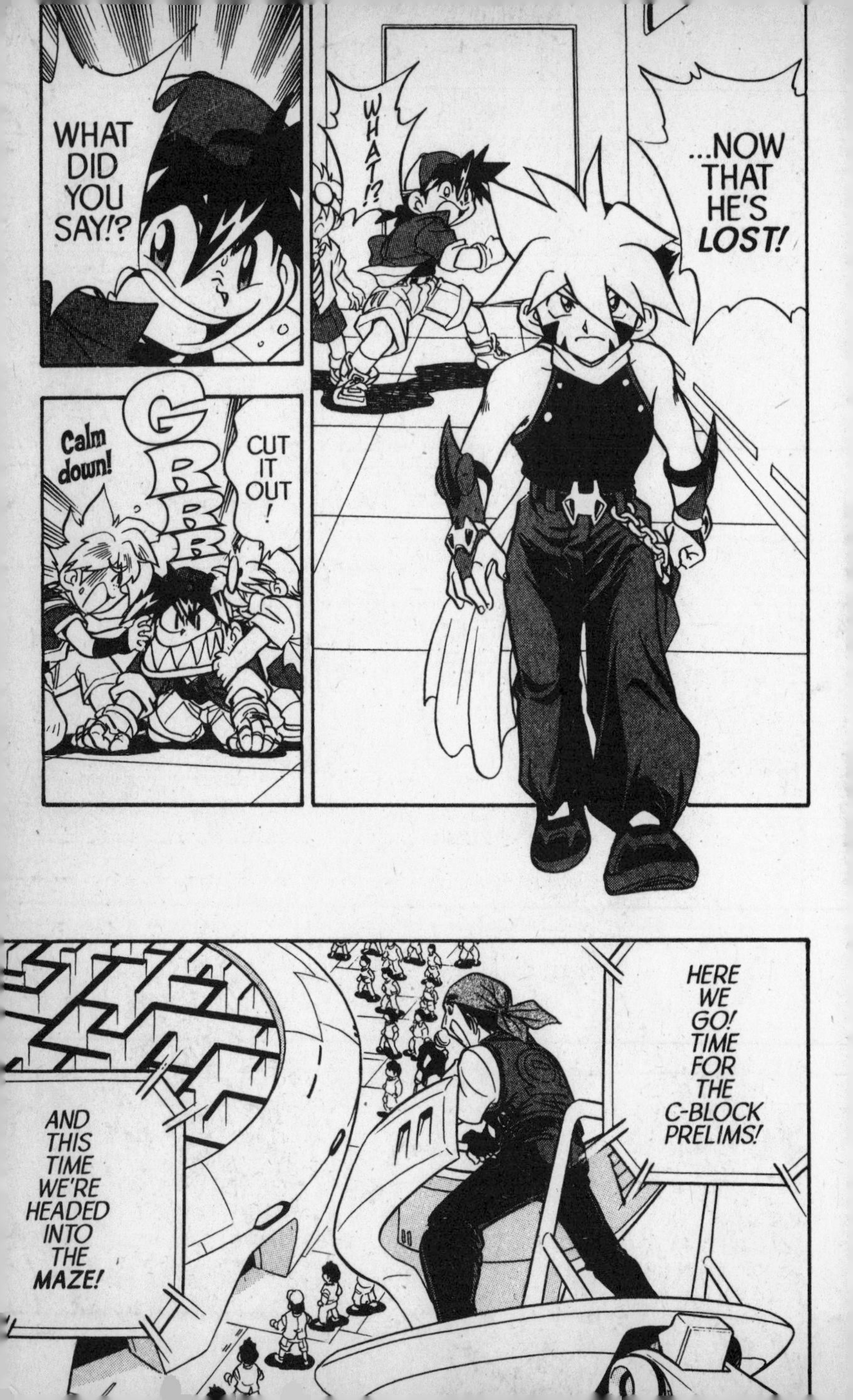
...NOW THAT HE'S LOST!
WHAT!?
WHAT DID YOU SAY!?
CUT IT OUT!
GRRRR
Calm down!
HERE WE GO! TIME FOR THE C-BLOCK PRELIMS!
AND THIS TIME WE'RE HEADED INTO THE MAZE!

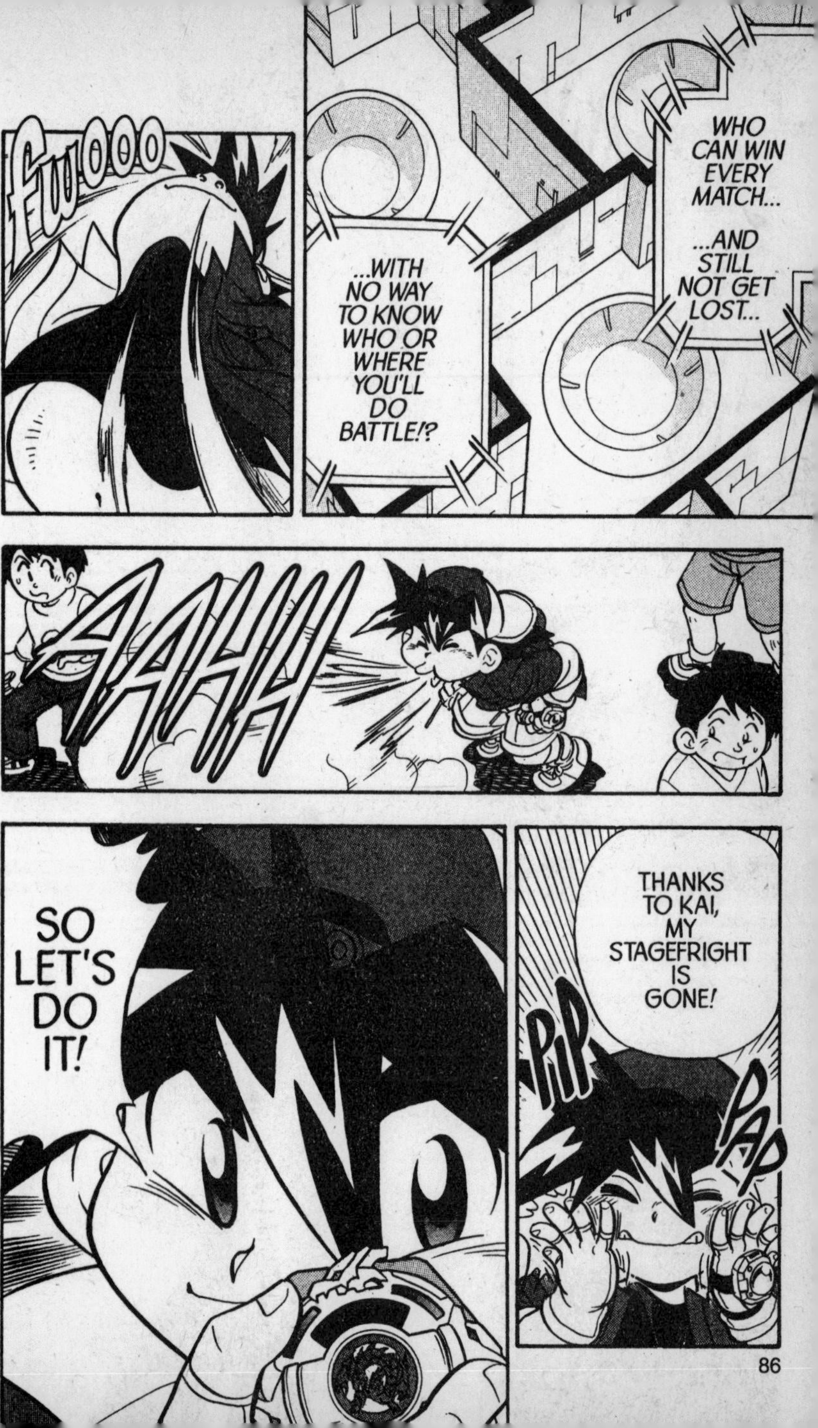
WHO CAN WIN EVERY MATCH...
...AND STILL NOT GET LOST...
...WITH NO WAY TO KNOW WHO OR WHERE YOU'LL DO BATTLE!?
FWOOO
AAHH
THANKS TO KAI, MY STAGEFRIGHT IS GONE!
PIP
PAP
SO LET'S DO IT!

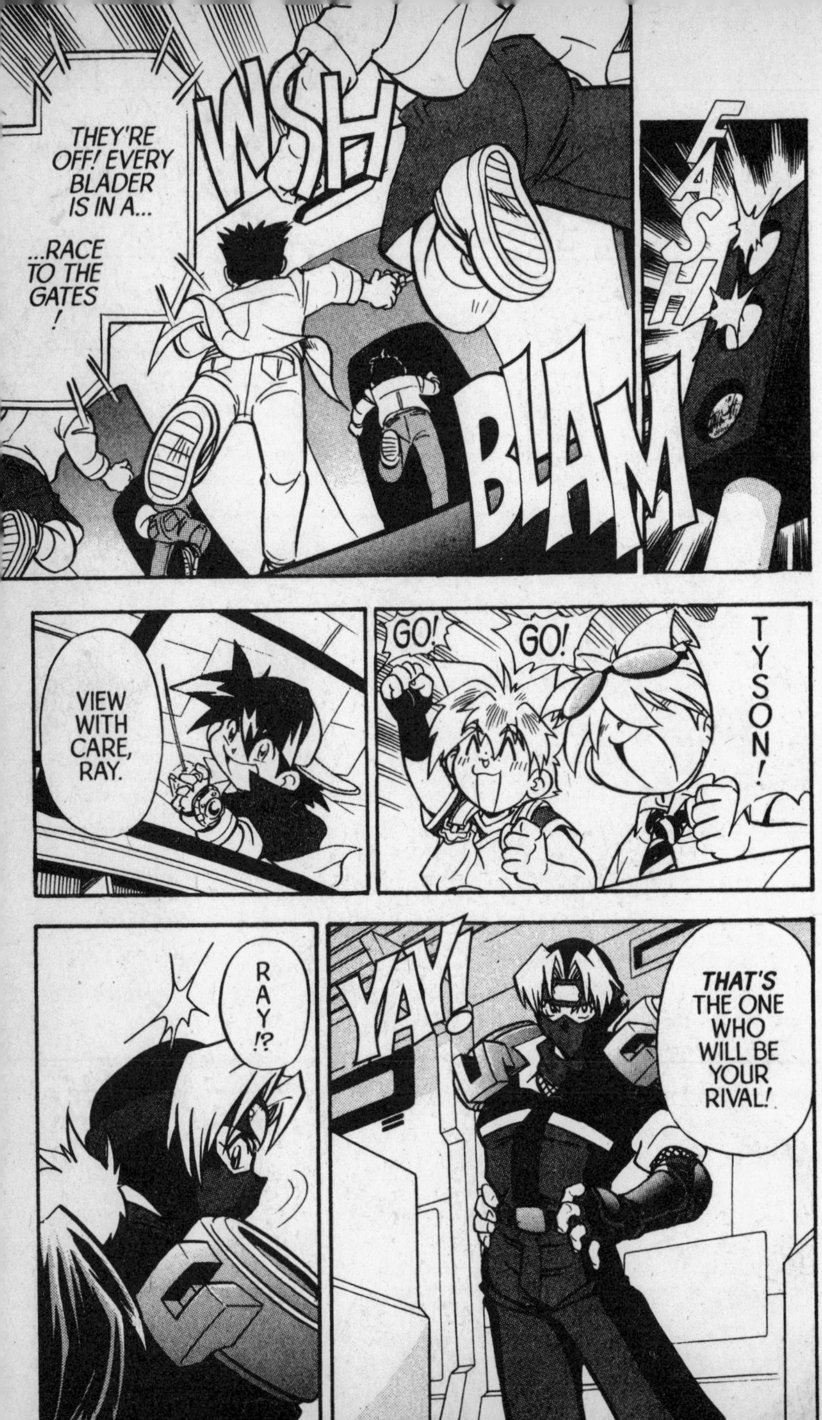
FASH
THEY'RE OFF! EVERY BLADER IS IN A...
...RACE TO THE GATES!
WSH
BLAM
GO!
GO!
TYSON!
VIEW WITH CARE, RAY.
YAY!
THAT'S THE ONE WHO WILL BE YOUR RIVAL!
RAY!?

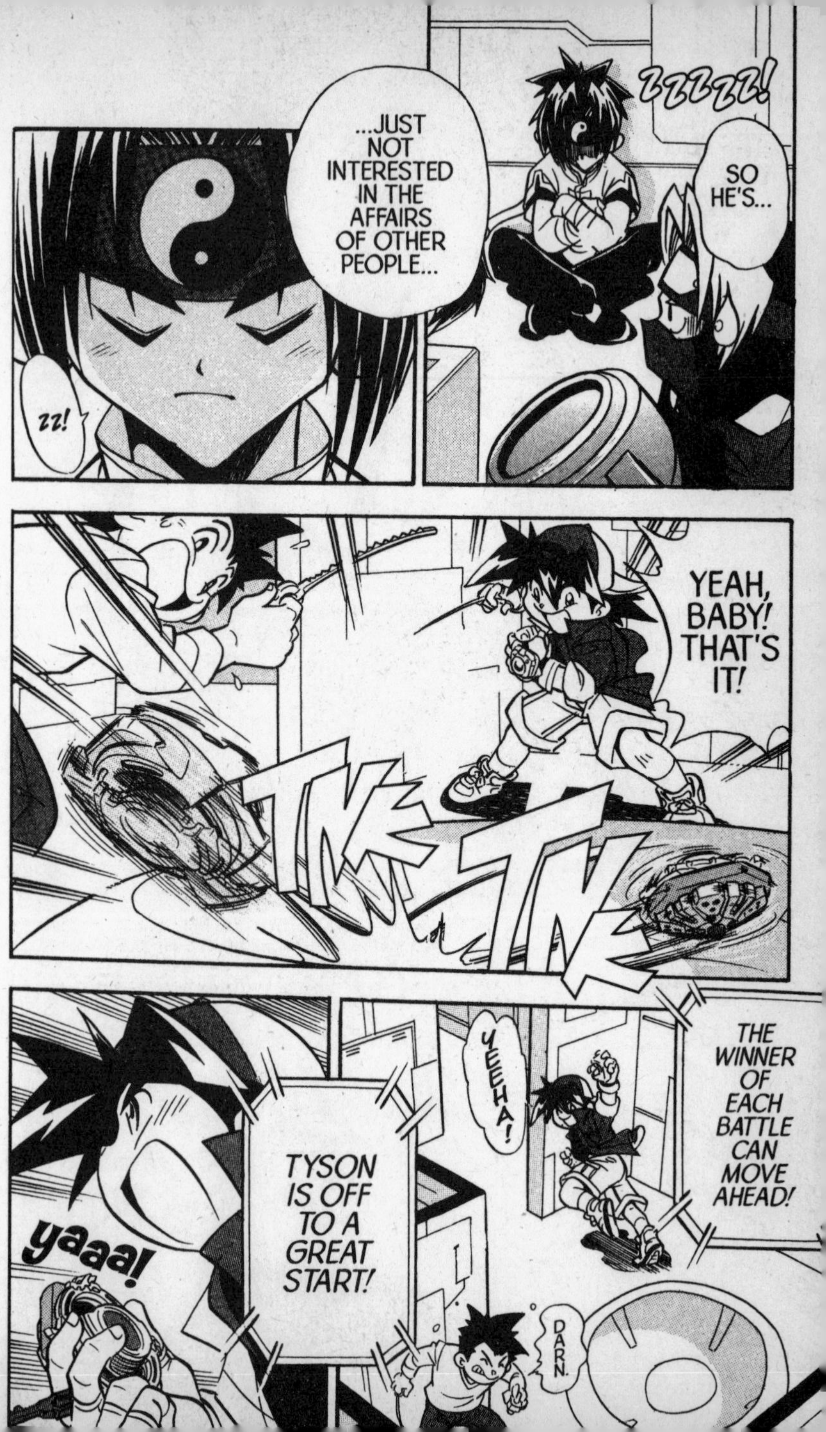
ZZZZZZ!
SO HE'S...
...JUST NOT INTERESTED IN THE AFFAIRS OF OTHER PEOPLE...
ZZ!
YEAH, BABY! THAT'S IT!
THE WINNER OF EACH BATTLE CAN MOVE AHEAD!
YEEHA!
DARN.
TYSON IS OFF TO A GREAT START!
yaaa!

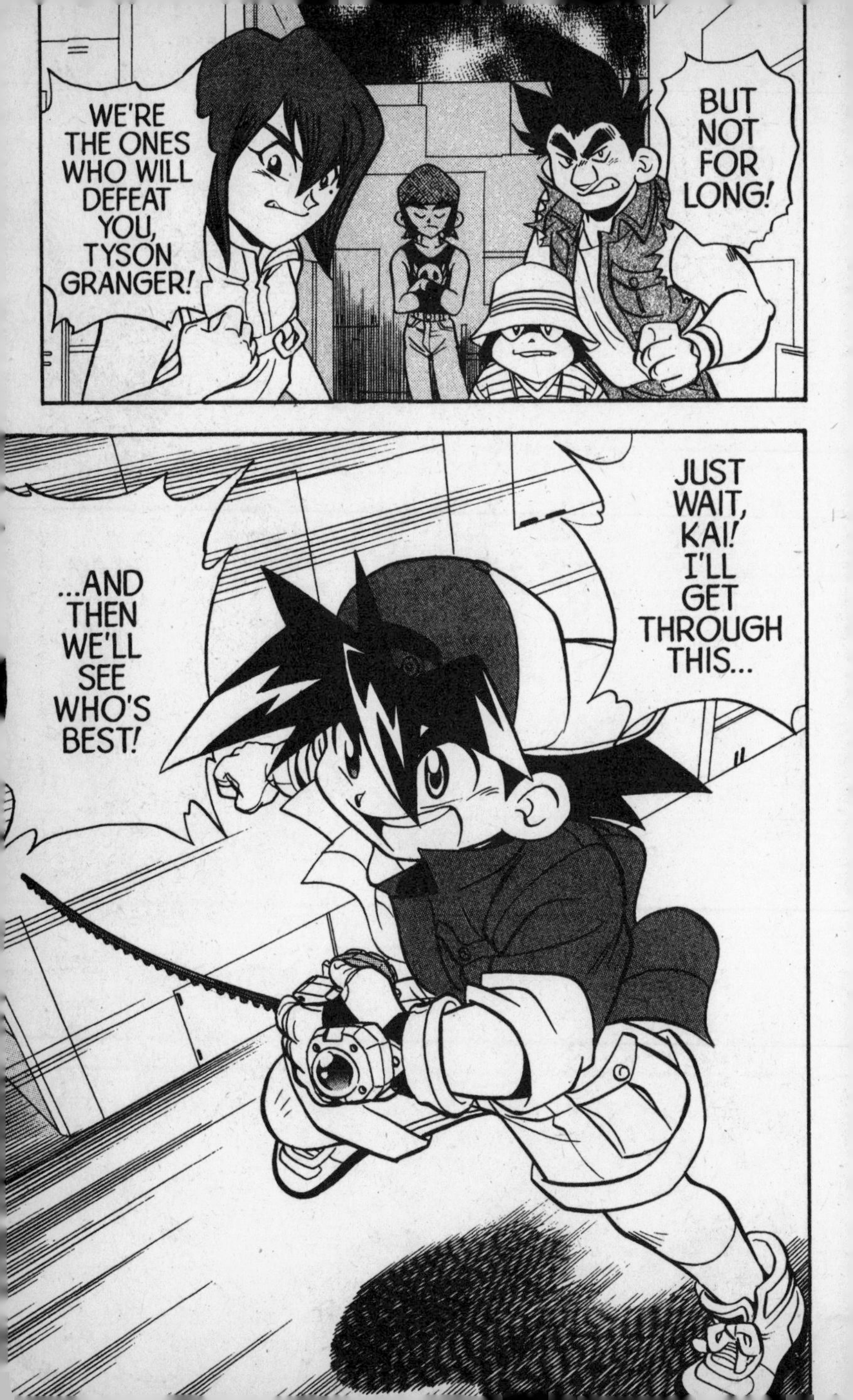
BUT NOT FOR LONG!
WE'RE THE ONES WHO WILL DEFEAT YOU, TYSON GRANGER!
JUST WAIT, KAI! I'LL GET THROUGH THIS...
...AND THEN WE'LL SEE WHO'S BEST!

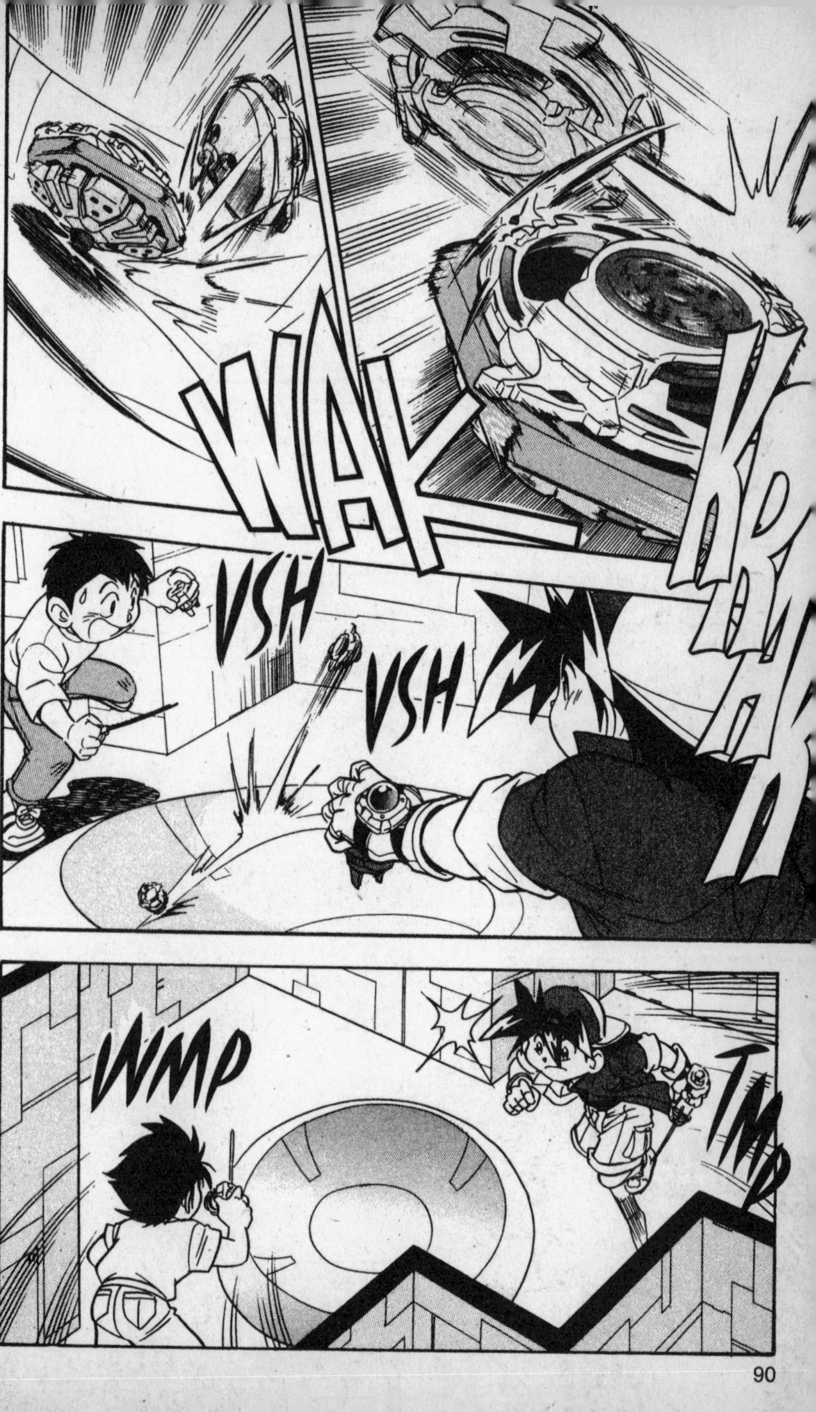
WAK
VSH
VSH
TMP
WMP

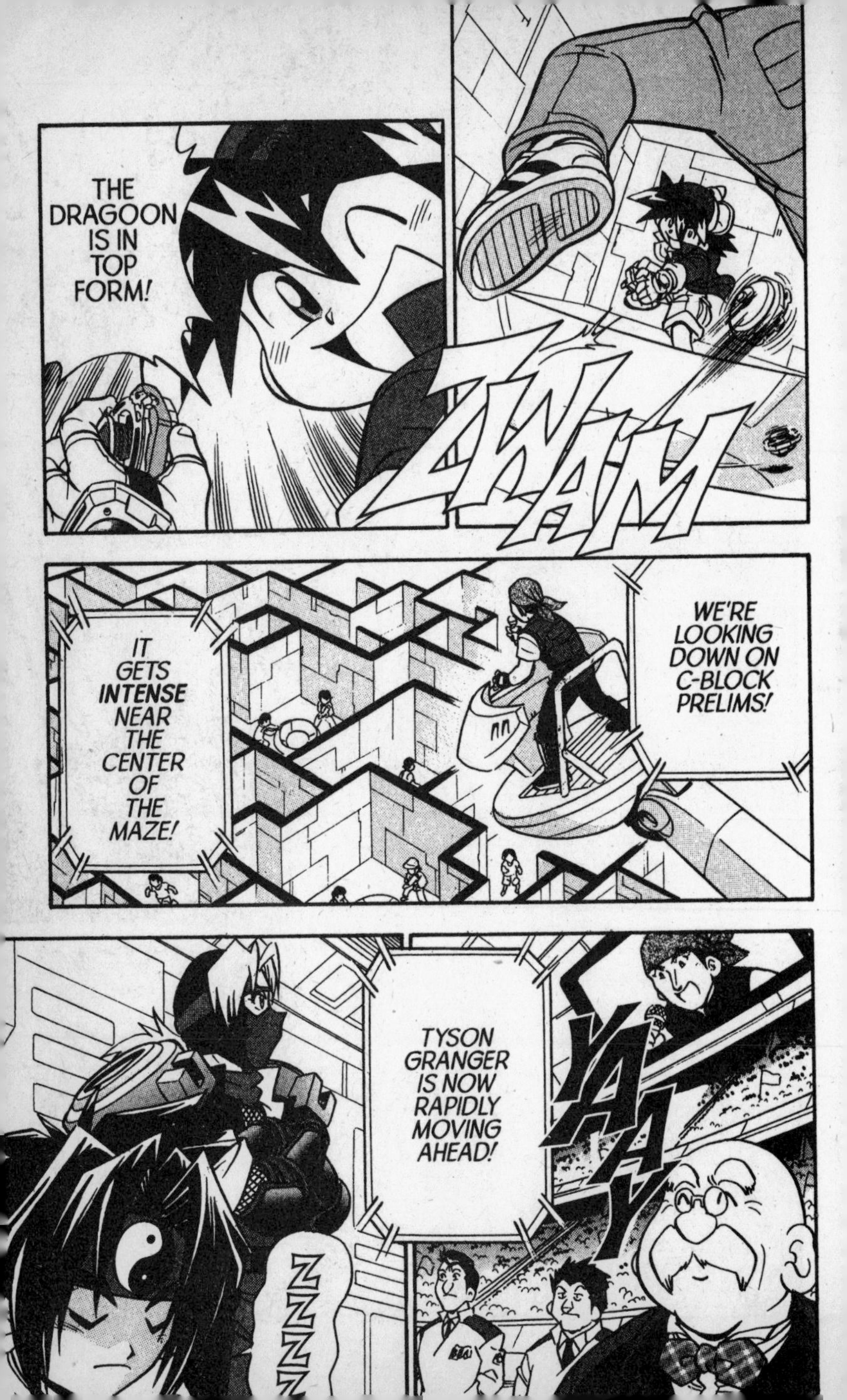
ZWAM
THE DRAGOON IS IN TOP FORM!
WE'RE LOOKING DOWN ON C-BLOCK PRELIMS!
IT GETS INTENSE NEAR THE CENTER OF THE MAZE!
YAAA
TYSON GRANGER IS NOW RAPIDLY MOVING AHEAD!

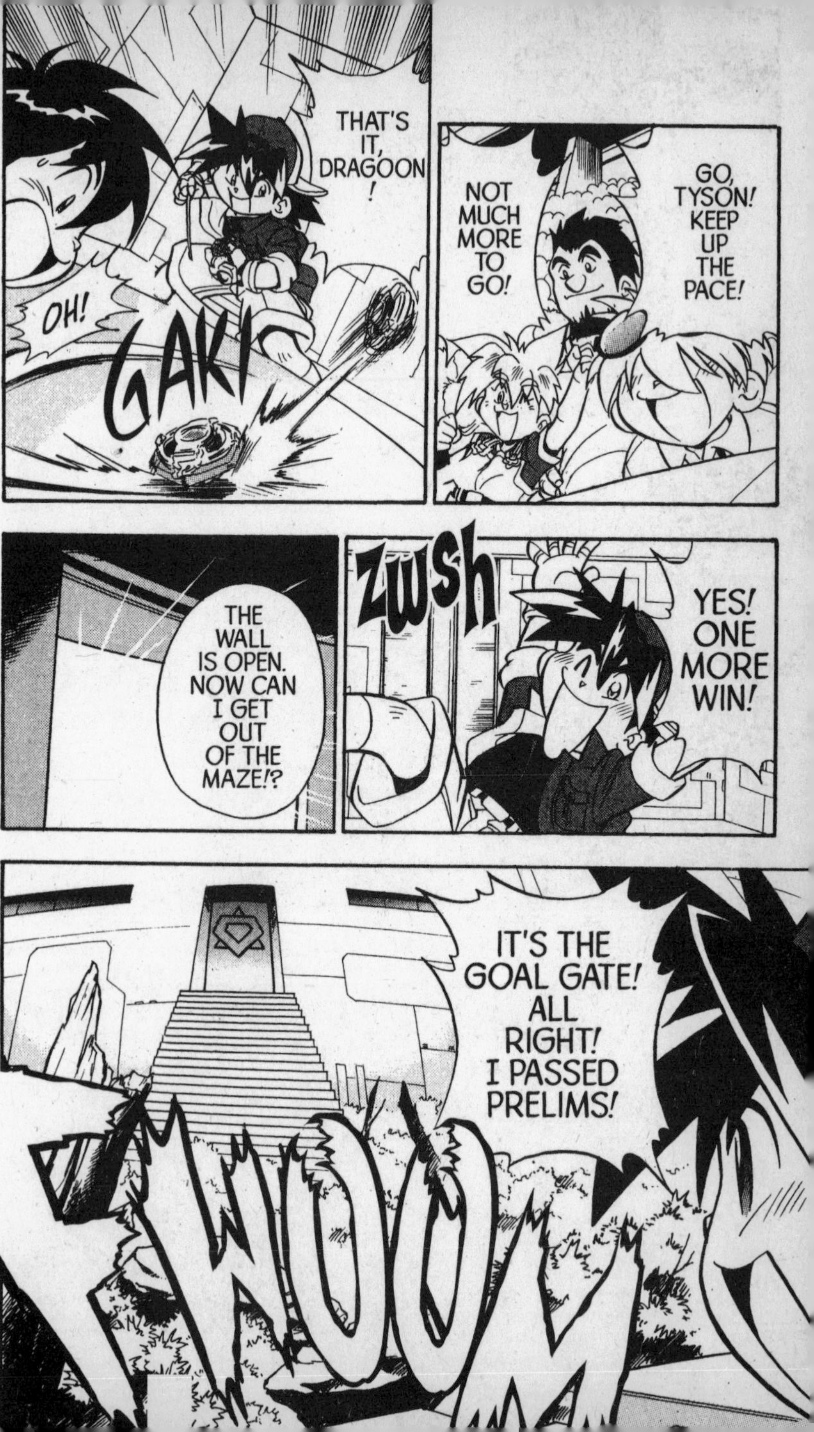
GO, TYSON! KEEP UP THE PACE!
NOT MUCH MORE TO GO!
THAT'S IT, DRAGOON!
OH!
GAKI
ZWSH
YES! ONE MORE WIN!
THE WALL IS OPEN. NOW CAN I GET OUT OF THE MAZE!?
IT'S THE GOAL GATE! ALL RIGHT! I PASSED PRELIMS!
WHOOM

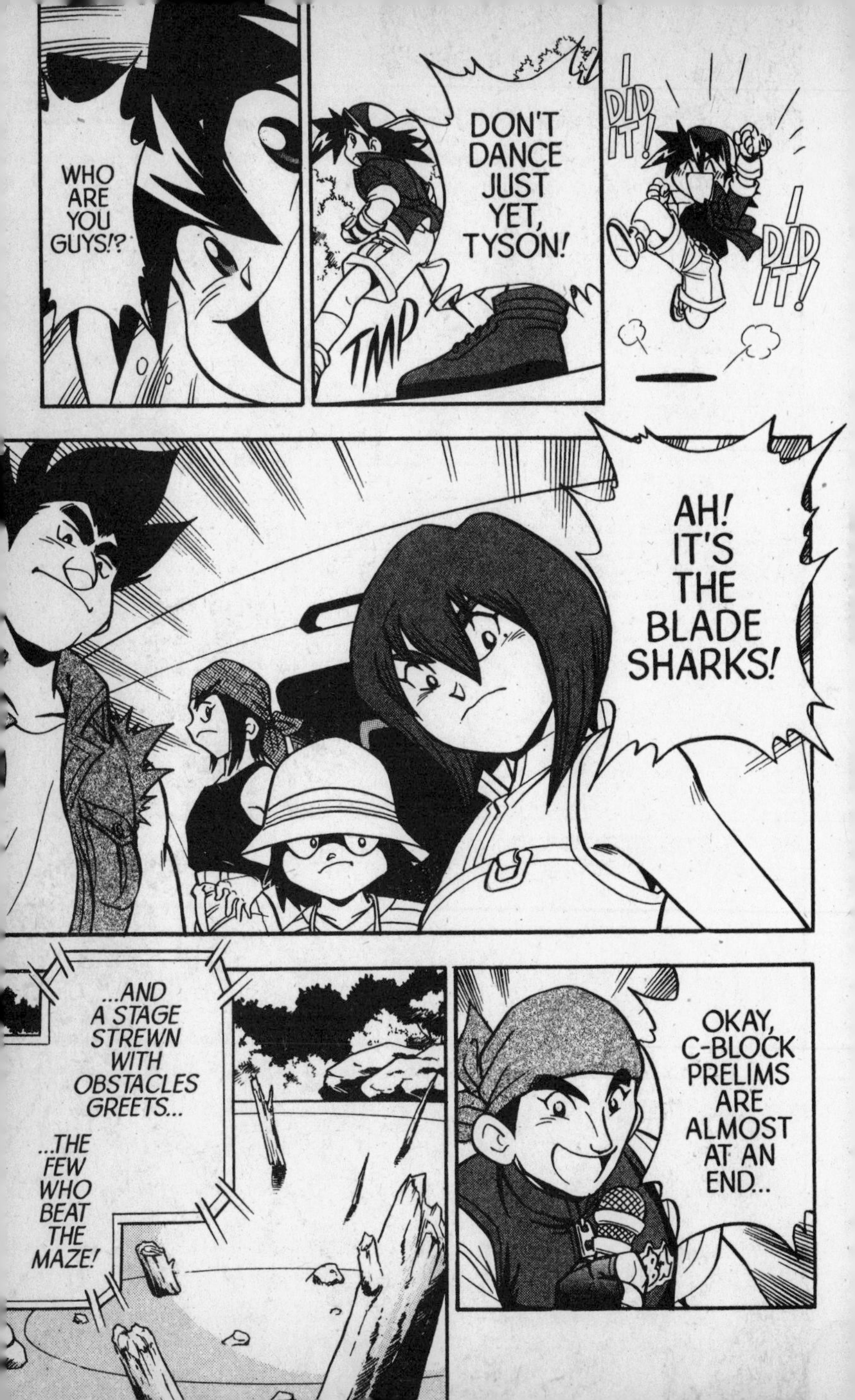
I DID IT!
I DID IT!
DON'T DANCE JUST YET, TYSON!
TMP
WHO ARE YOU GUYS!?
AH! IT'S THE BLADE SHARKS!
OKAY, C-BLOCK PRELIMS ARE ALMOST AT AN END...
...AND A STAGE STREWN WITH OBSTACLES GREETS...
...THE FEW WHO BEAT THE MAZE!

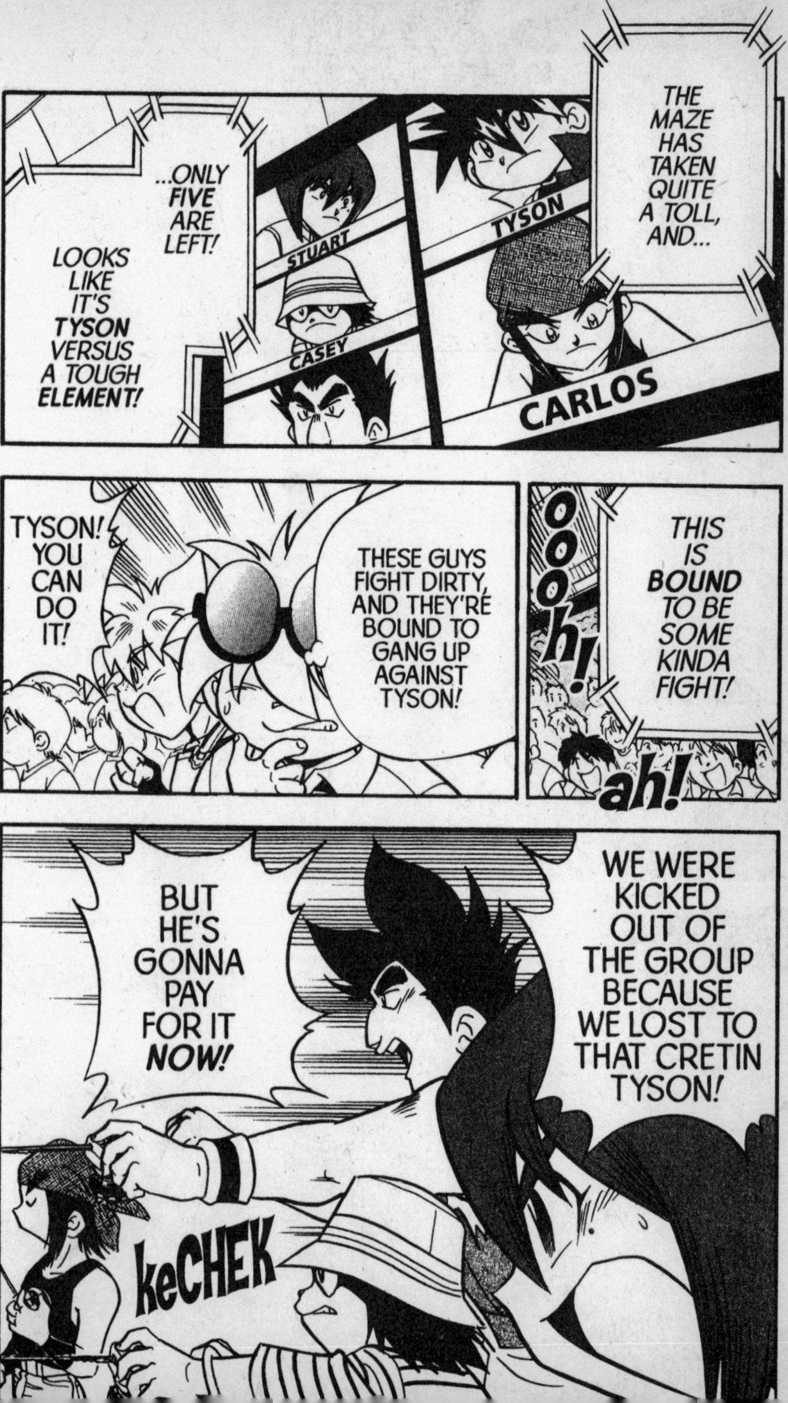
THE MAZE HAS TAKEN QUITE A TOLL, AND...
TYSON
CARLOS
STUART
CASEY
...ONLY **FIVE** ARE LEFT!
LOOKS LIKE IT'S **TYSON** VERSUS A TOUGH **ELEMENT!**
THIS IS **BOUND** TO BE SOME KINDA FIGHT!
Oooh!
ah!
THESE GUYS FIGHT DIRTY, AND THEY'RE BOUND TO GANG UP AGAINST TYSON!
TYSON! YOU CAN DO IT!
WE WERE KICKED OUT OF THE GROUP BECAUSE WE LOST TO THAT CRETIN TYSON!
BUT HE'S GONNA PAY FOR IT ***NOW!***
keCHEK

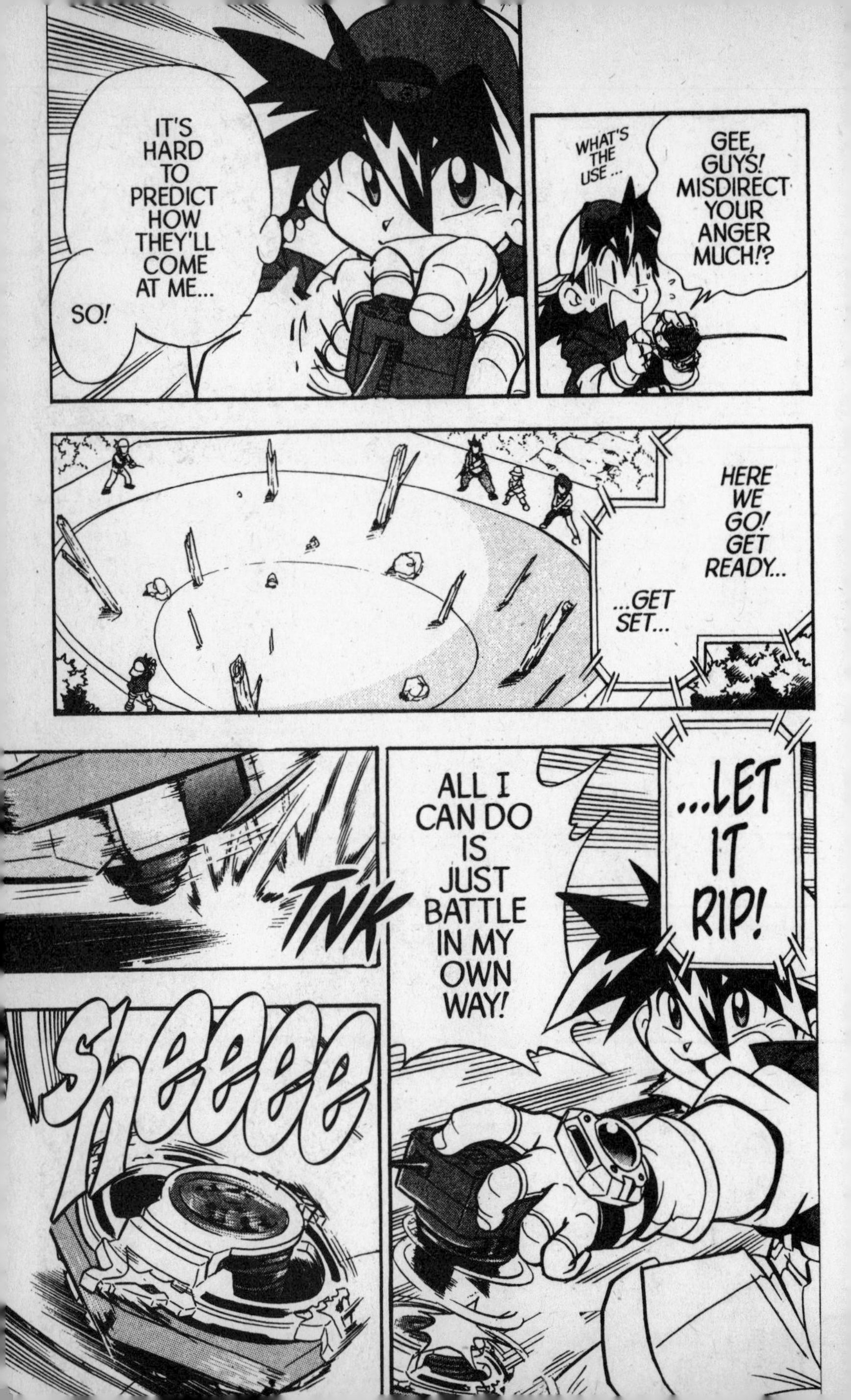
GEE, GUYS! MISDIRECT YOUR ANGER MUCH!?
WHAT'S THE USE ...
IT'S HARD TO PREDICT HOW THEY'LL COME AT ME... SO!
HERE WE GO! GET READY...
...GET SET...
...LET IT RIP!
ALL I CAN DO IS JUST BATTLE IN MY OWN WAY!
TNK
Sheeee

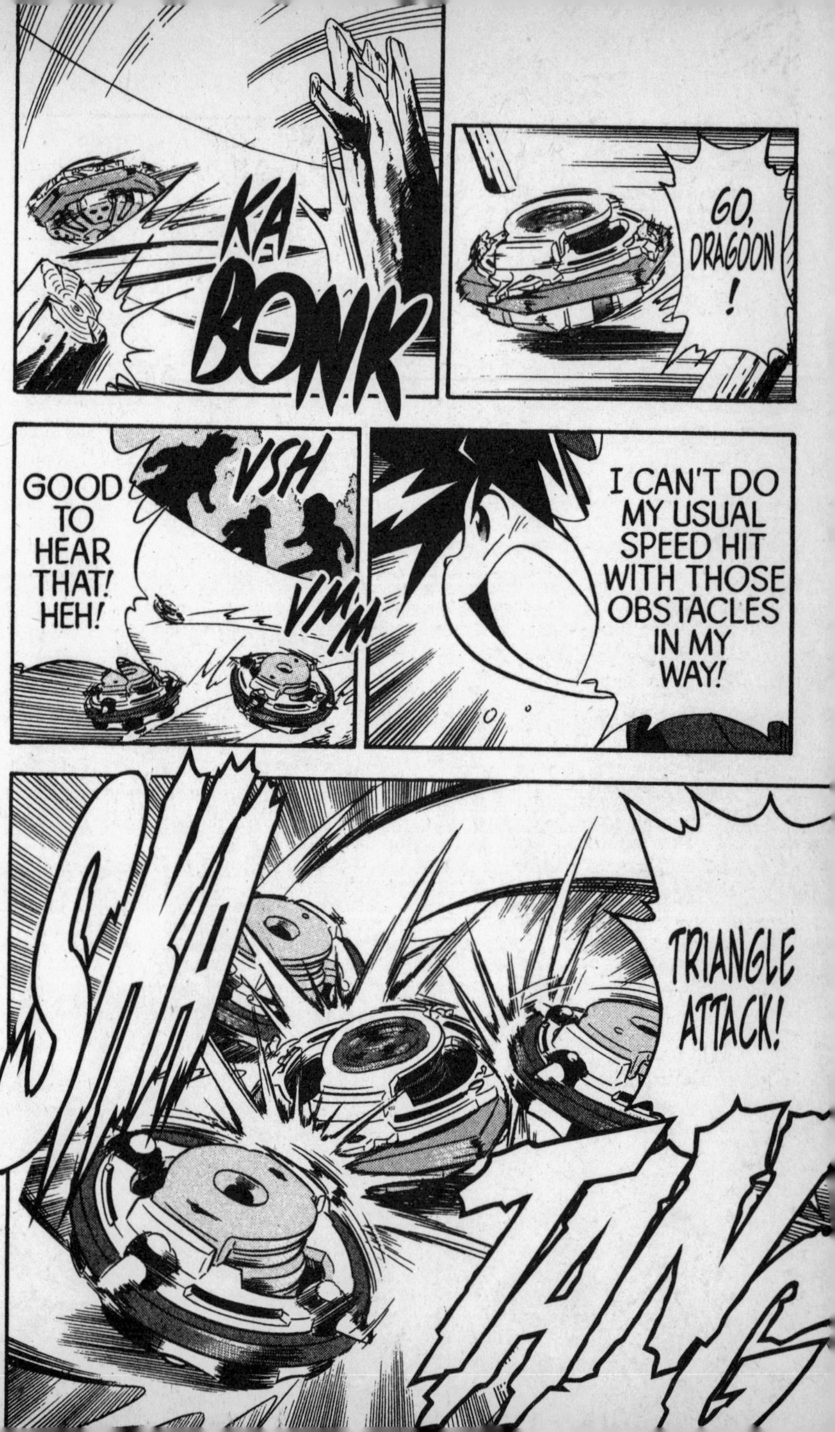
GO, DRAGOON!
KA BONK
I CAN'T DO MY USUAL SPEED HIT WITH THOSE OBSTACLES IN MY WAY!
GOOD TO HEAR THAT! HEH!
VSH
VMM
TRIANGLE ATTACK!

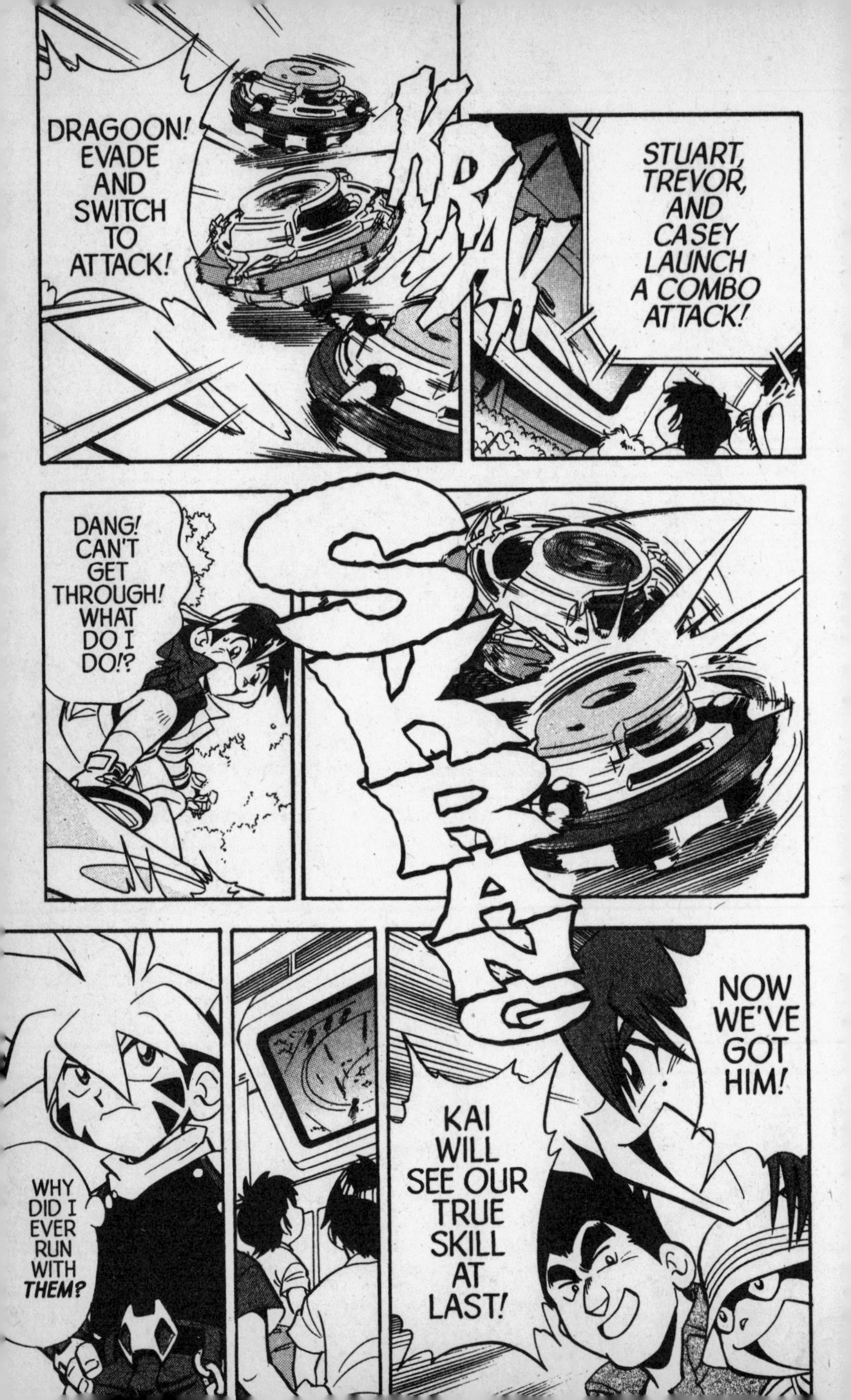
STUART, TREVOR, AND CASEY LAUNCH A COMBO ATTACK!
KRAK
DRAGOON! EVADE AND SWITCH TO ATTACK!
SKRANG
DANG! CAN'T GET THROUGH! WHAT DO I DO!?
NOW WE'VE GOT HIM!
KAI WILL SEE OUR TRUE SKILL AT LAST!
WHY DID I EVER RUN WITH *THEM*?

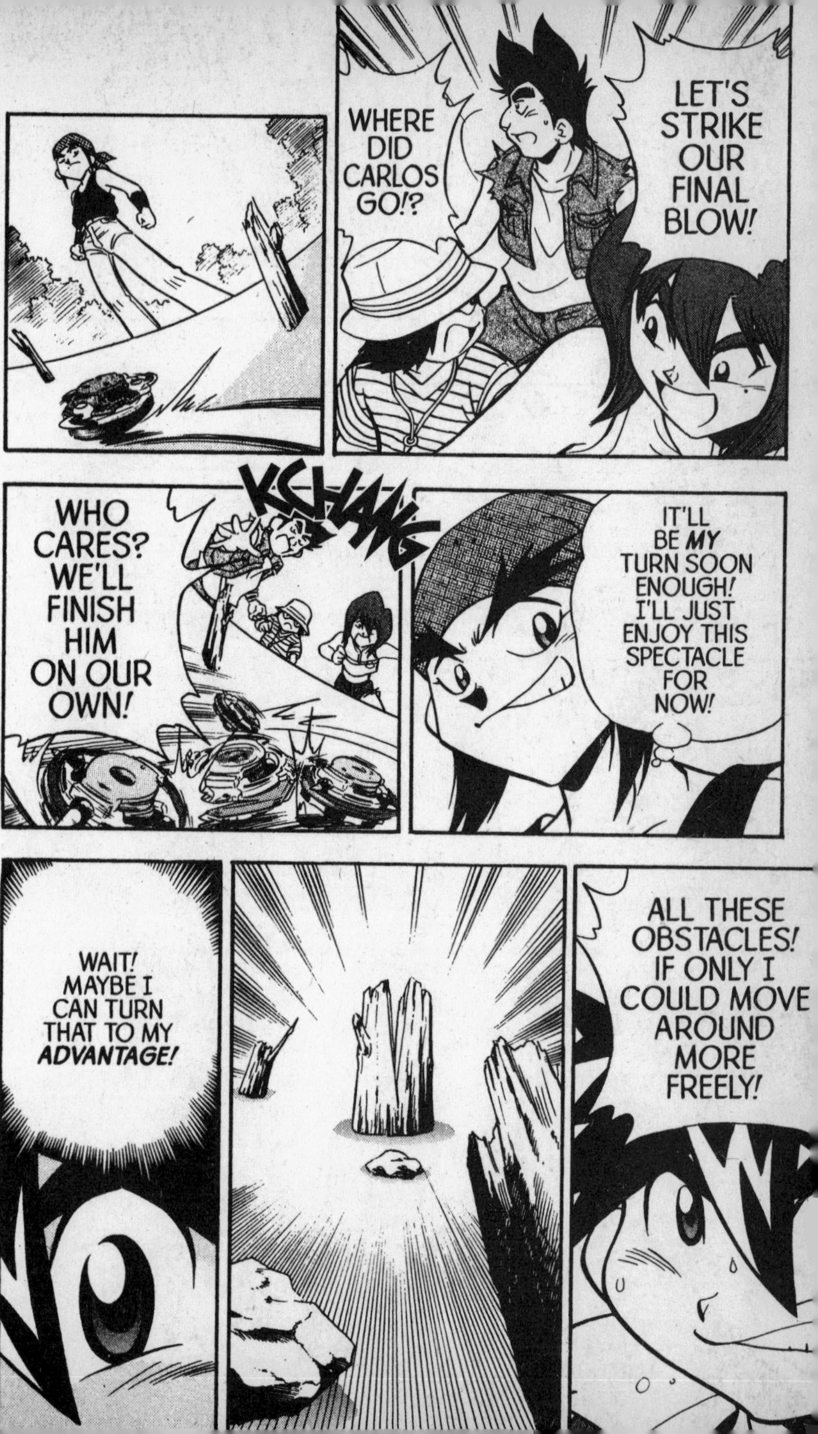
LET'S STRIKE OUR FINAL BLOW!
WHERE DID CARLOS GO!?
IT'LL BE MY TURN SOON ENOUGH! I'LL JUST ENJOY THIS SPECTACLE FOR NOW!
KCHANG
WHO CARES? WE'LL FINISH HIM ON OUR OWN!
ALL THESE OBSTACLES! IF ONLY I COULD MOVE AROUND MORE FREELY!
WAIT! MAYBE I CAN TURN THAT TO MY ADVANTAGE!

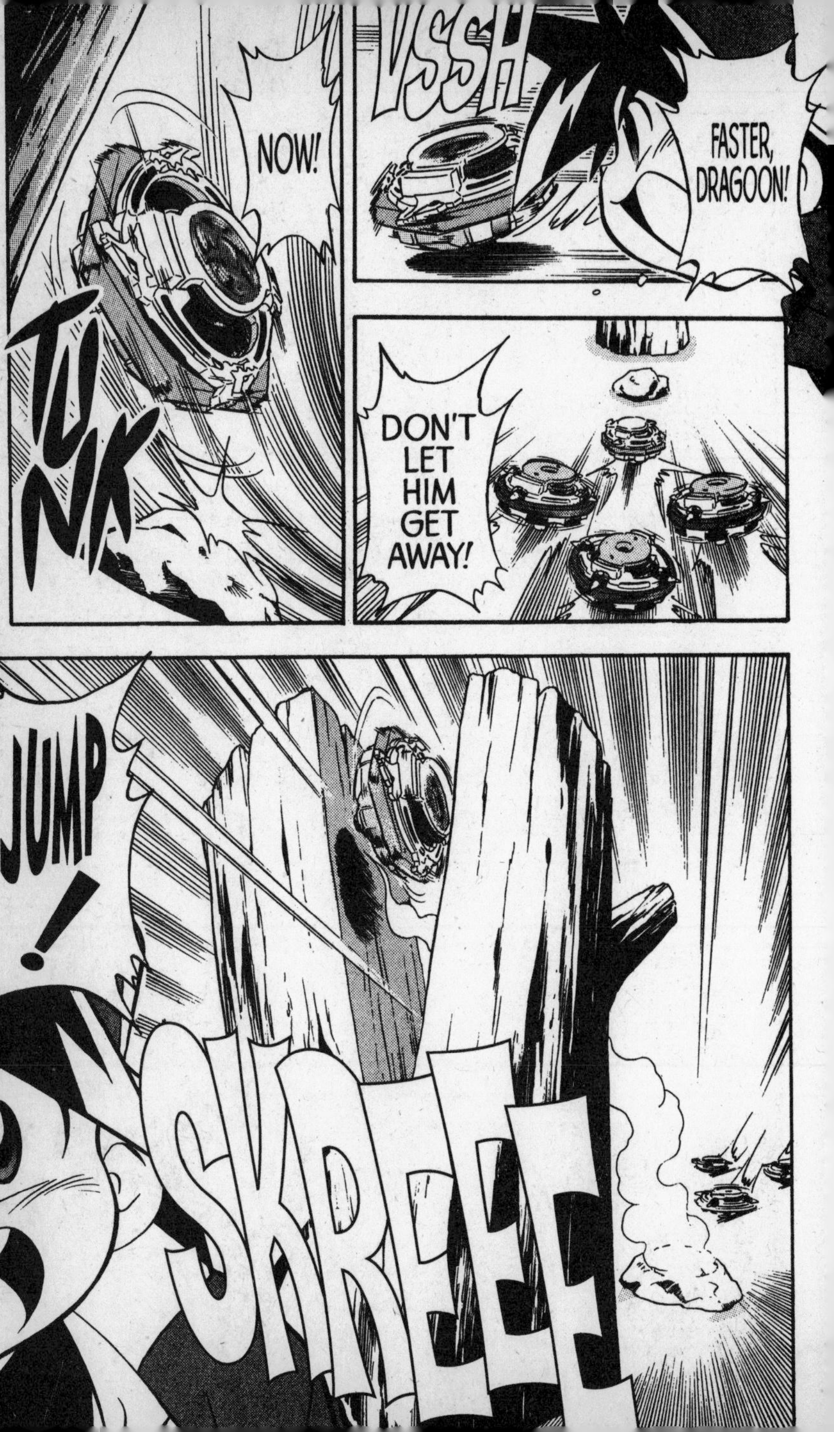
VSSH
FASTER, DRAGOON!
DON'T LET HIM GET AWAY!
NOW!
TUNK
JUMP!
SKREEE

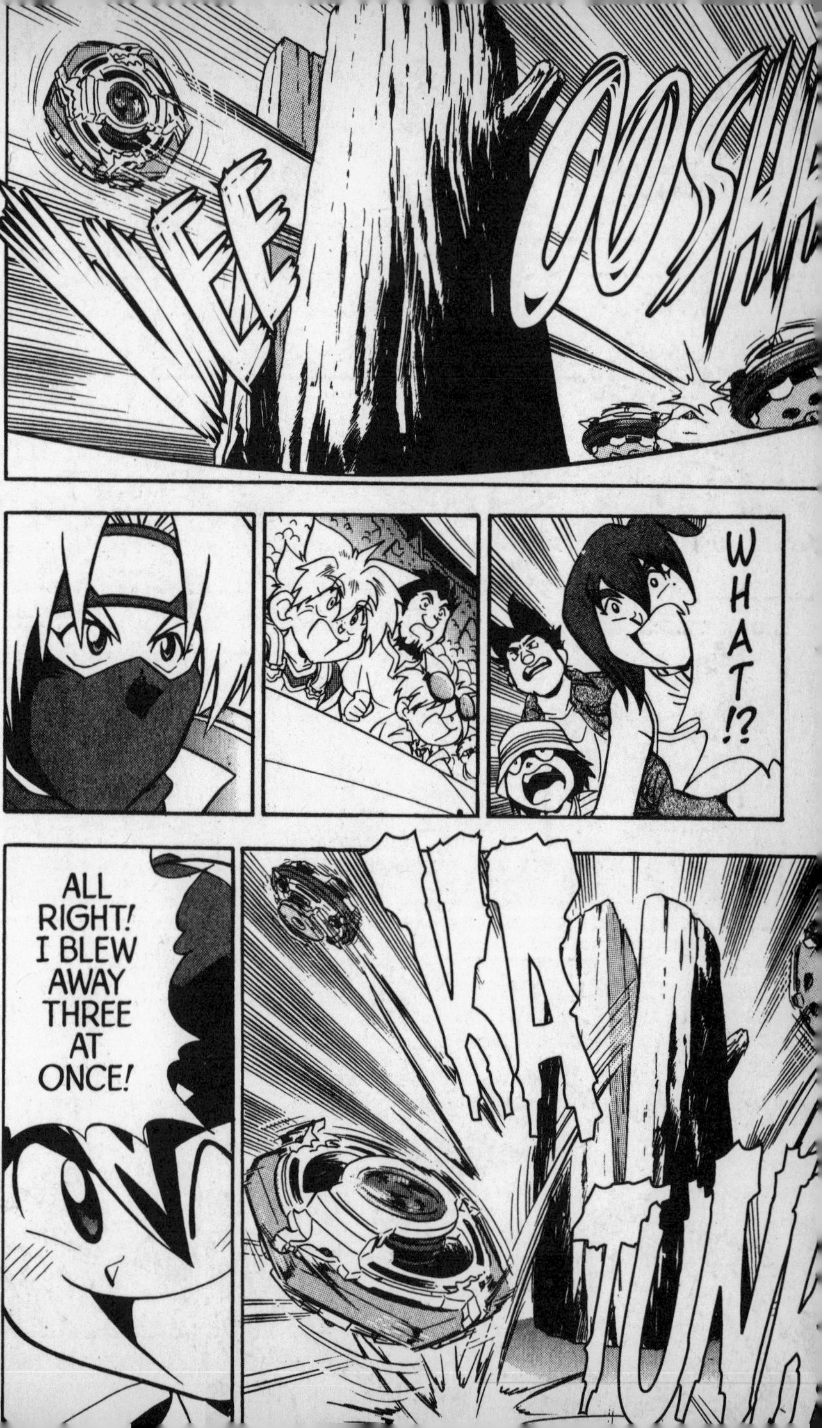
WHAT!?
ALL RIGHT! I BLEW AWAY THREE AT ONCE!

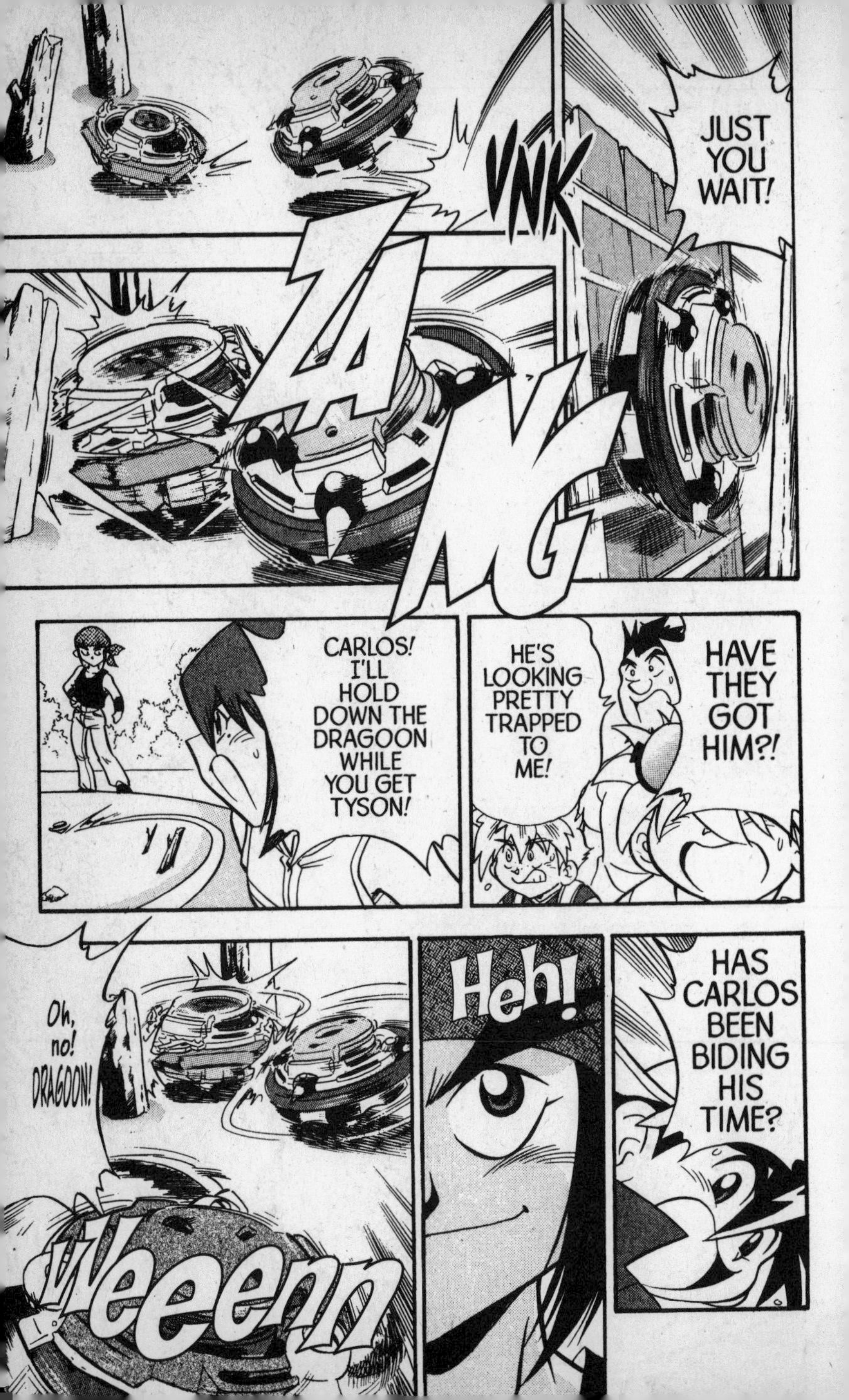
JUST YOU WAIT!
VNK
ZANG
HAVE THEY GOT HIM?!
HE'S LOOKING PRETTY TRAPPED TO ME!
CARLOS! I'LL HOLD DOWN THE DRAGOON WHILE YOU GET TYSON!
HAS CARLOS BEEN BIDING HIS TIME?
Heh!
Oh, no! DRAGOON!
Weeenn

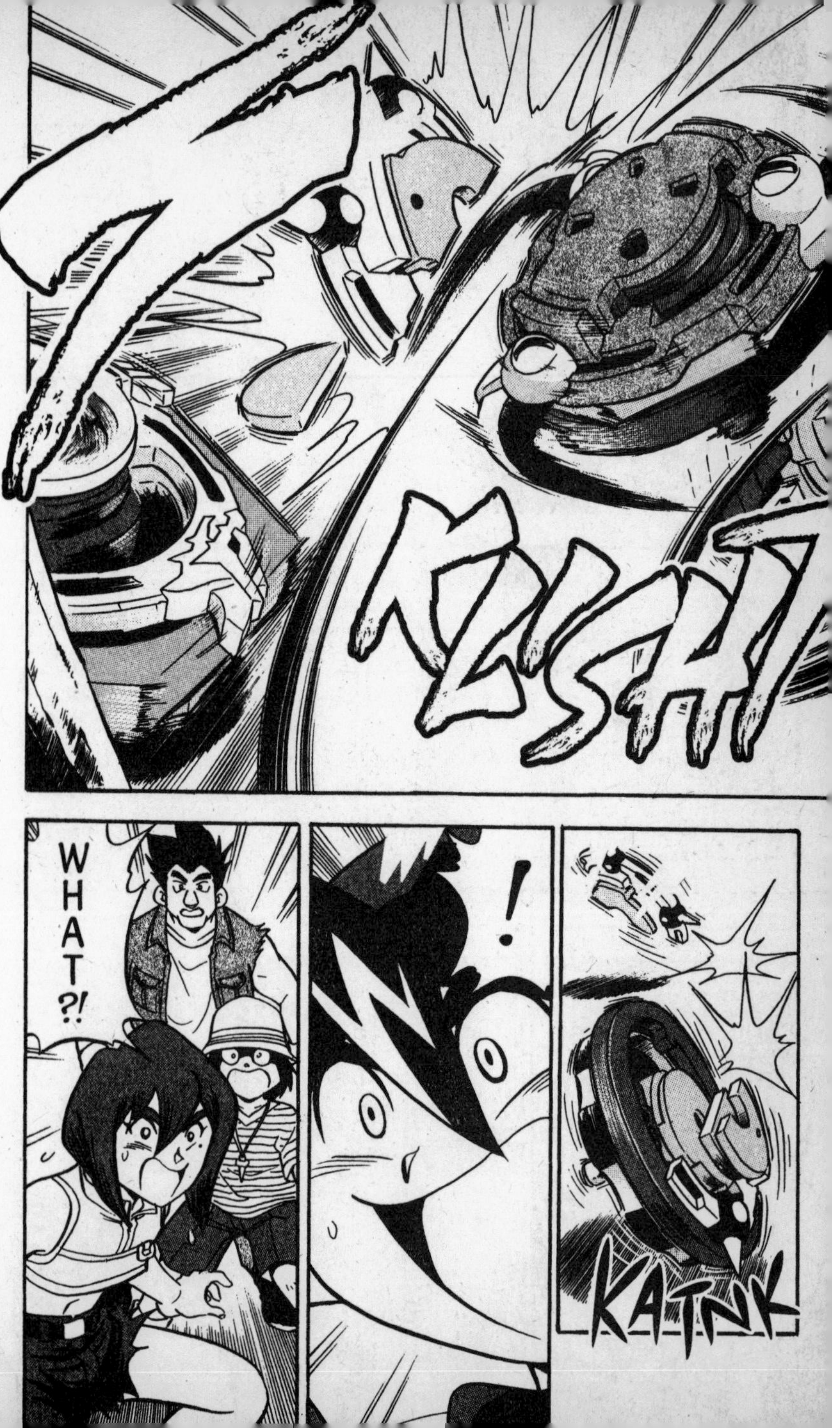
KLISH
KATNK
!
WHAT?!

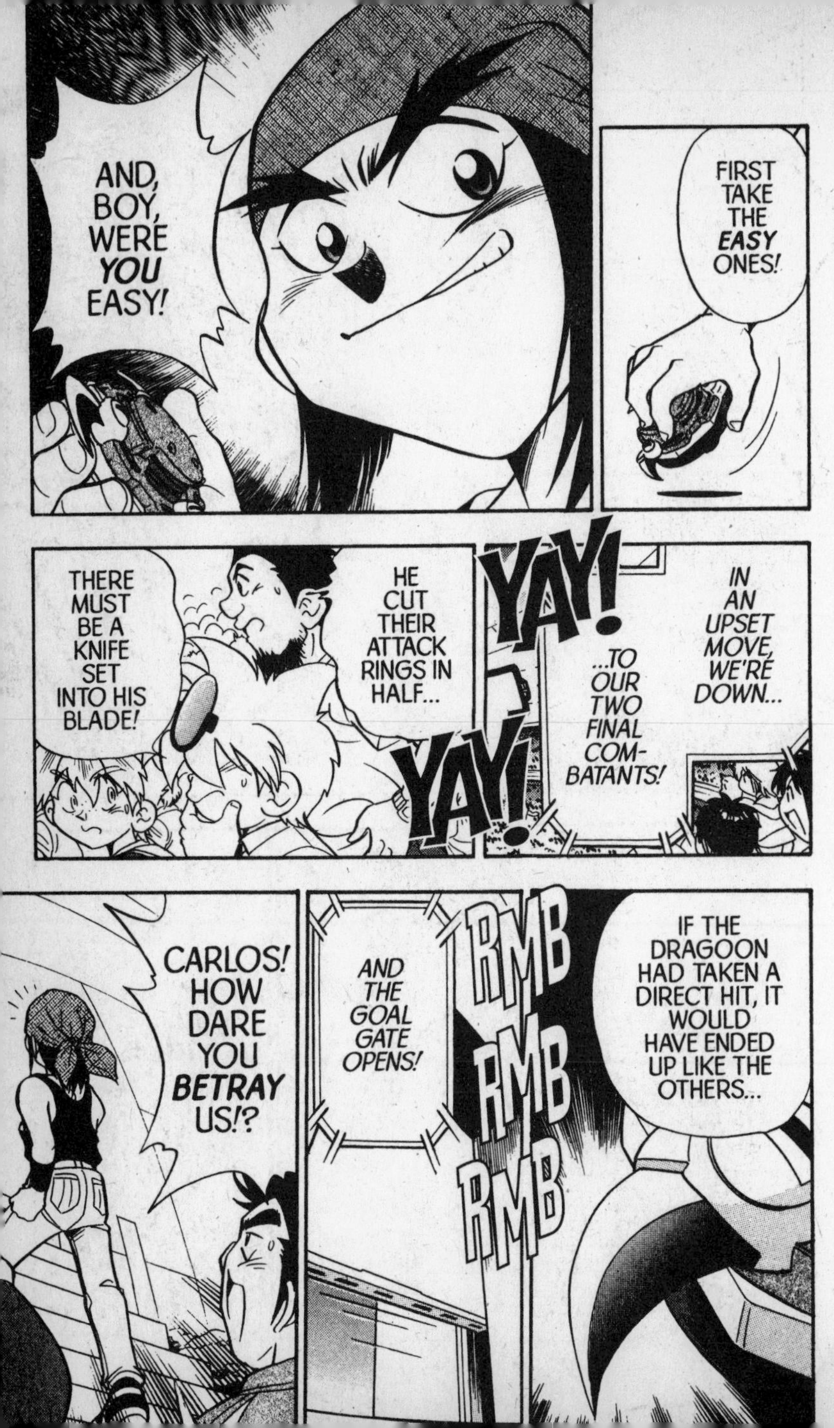
FIRST TAKE THE *EASY* ONES!
AND, BOY, WERE *YOU* EASY!
IN AN UPSET MOVE, WE'RE DOWN...
...TO OUR TWO FINAL COM-BATANTS!
YAY!
YAY!
HE CUT THEIR ATTACK RINGS IN HALF...
THERE MUST BE A KNIFE SET INTO HIS BLADE!
IF THE DRAGOON HAD TAKEN A DIRECT HIT, IT WOULD HAVE ENDED UP LIKE THE OTHERS...
RMB
RMB
RMB
AND THE GOAL GATE OPENS!
CARLOS! HOW DARE YOU ***BETRAY*** US!?

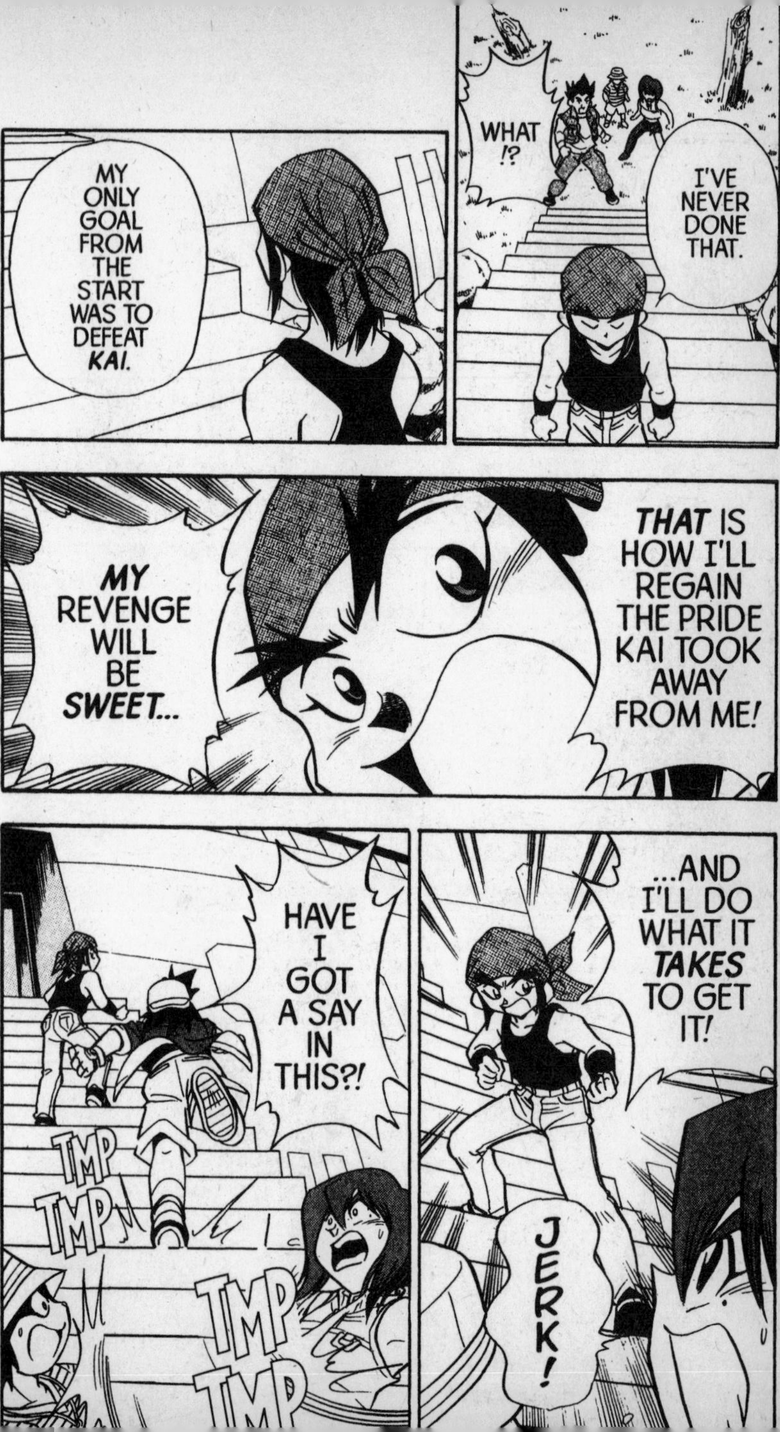
I'VE NEVER DONE THAT.
WHAT !?
MY ONLY GOAL FROM THE START WAS TO DEFEAT *KAI.*
THAT IS HOW I'LL REGAIN THE PRIDE KAI TOOK AWAY FROM ME!
MY REVENGE WILL BE ***SWEET...***
...AND I'LL DO WHAT IT ***TAKES*** TO GET IT!
JERK!
HAVE I GOT A SAY IN THIS?!
TMP TMP
TMP TMP

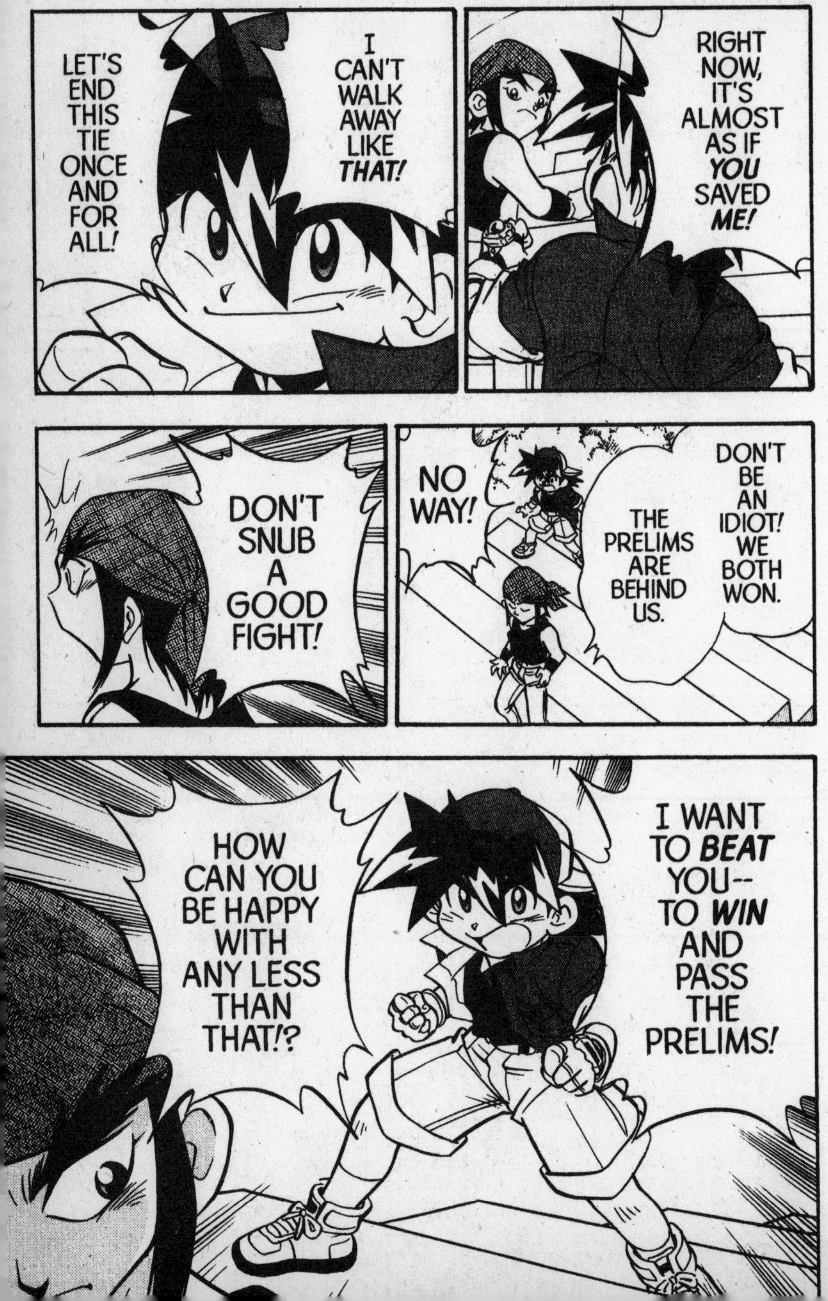
RIGHT NOW, IT'S ALMOST AS IF YOU SAVED ME!
I CAN'T WALK AWAY LIKE THAT!
LET'S END THIS TIE ONCE AND FOR ALL!
DON'T BE AN IDIOT! WE BOTH WON.
THE PRELIMS ARE BEHIND US.
NO WAY!
DON'T SNUB A GOOD FIGHT!
I WANT TO BEAT YOU-- TO WIN AND PASS THE PRELIMS!
HOW CAN YOU BE HAPPY WITH ANY LESS THAN THAT!?

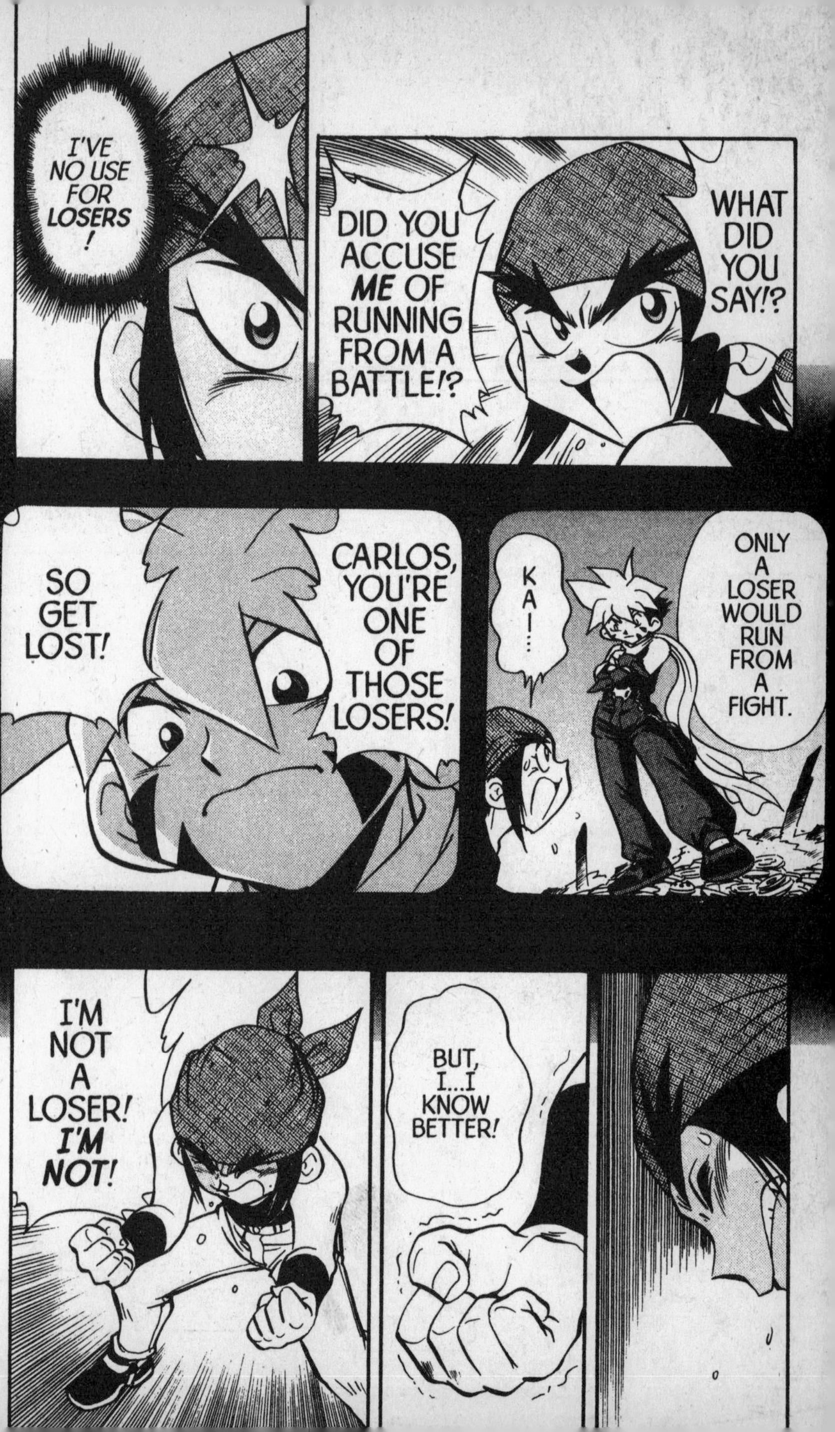
WHAT DID YOU SAY!?
DID YOU ACCUSE *ME* OF RUNNING FROM A BATTLE!?
I'VE NO USE FOR *LOSERS*!
ONLY A LOSER WOULD RUN FROM A FIGHT.
KAI!...
CARLOS, YOU'RE ONE OF THOSE LOSERS!
SO GET LOST!
BUT, I...I KNOW BETTER!
I'M NOT A LOSER! *I'M NOT*!

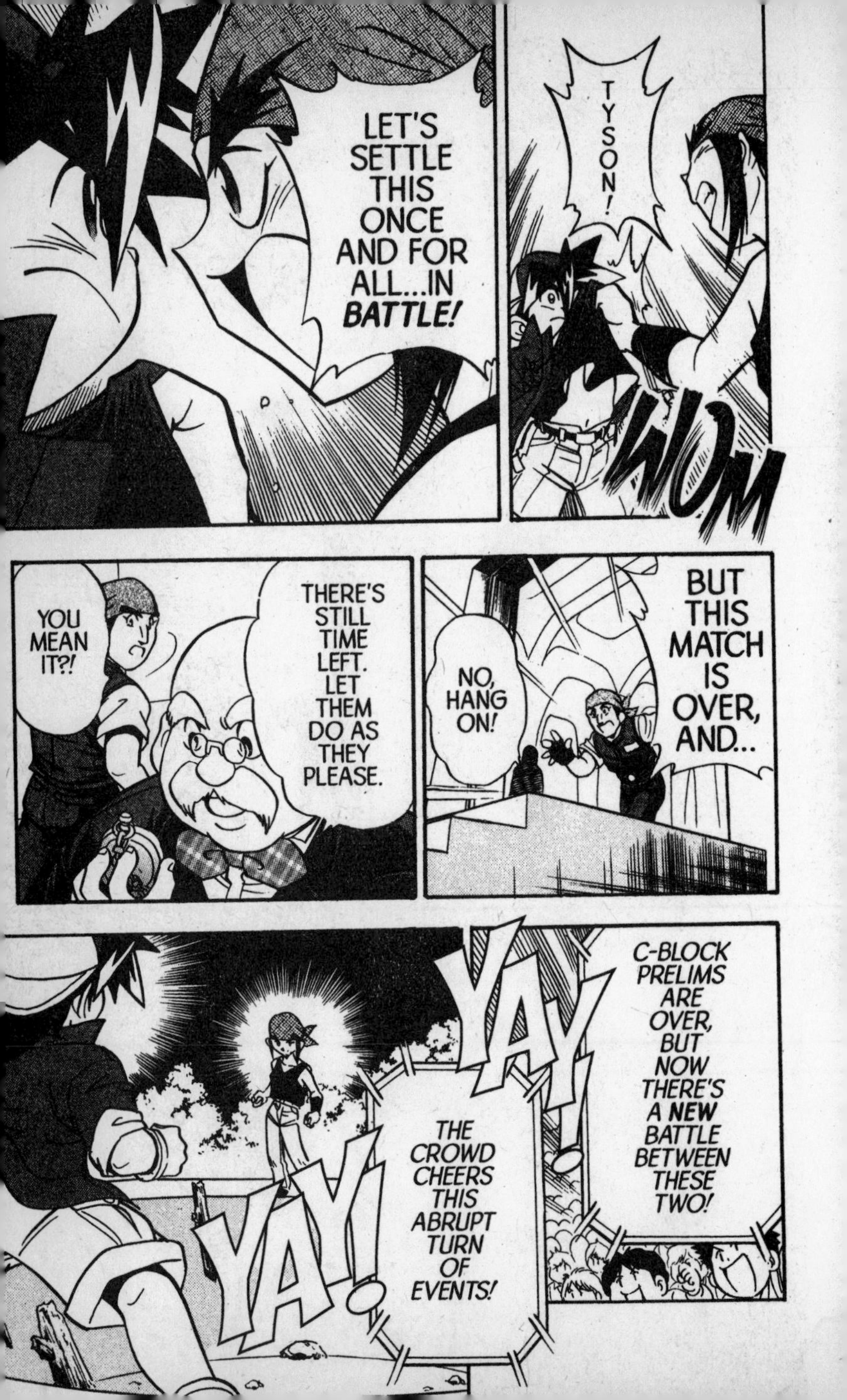
TYSON!
WUM
LET'S SETTLE THIS ONCE AND FOR ALL...IN *BATTLE!*
BUT THIS MATCH IS OVER, AND...
NO, HANG ON!
THERE'S STILL TIME LEFT. LET THEM DO AS THEY PLEASE.
YOU MEAN IT?!
C-BLOCK PRELIMS ARE OVER, BUT NOW THERE'S A ***NEW*** *BATTLE BETWEEN THESE TWO!*
YAY
THE CROWD CHEERS THIS ABRUPT TURN OF EVENTS!
YAY!

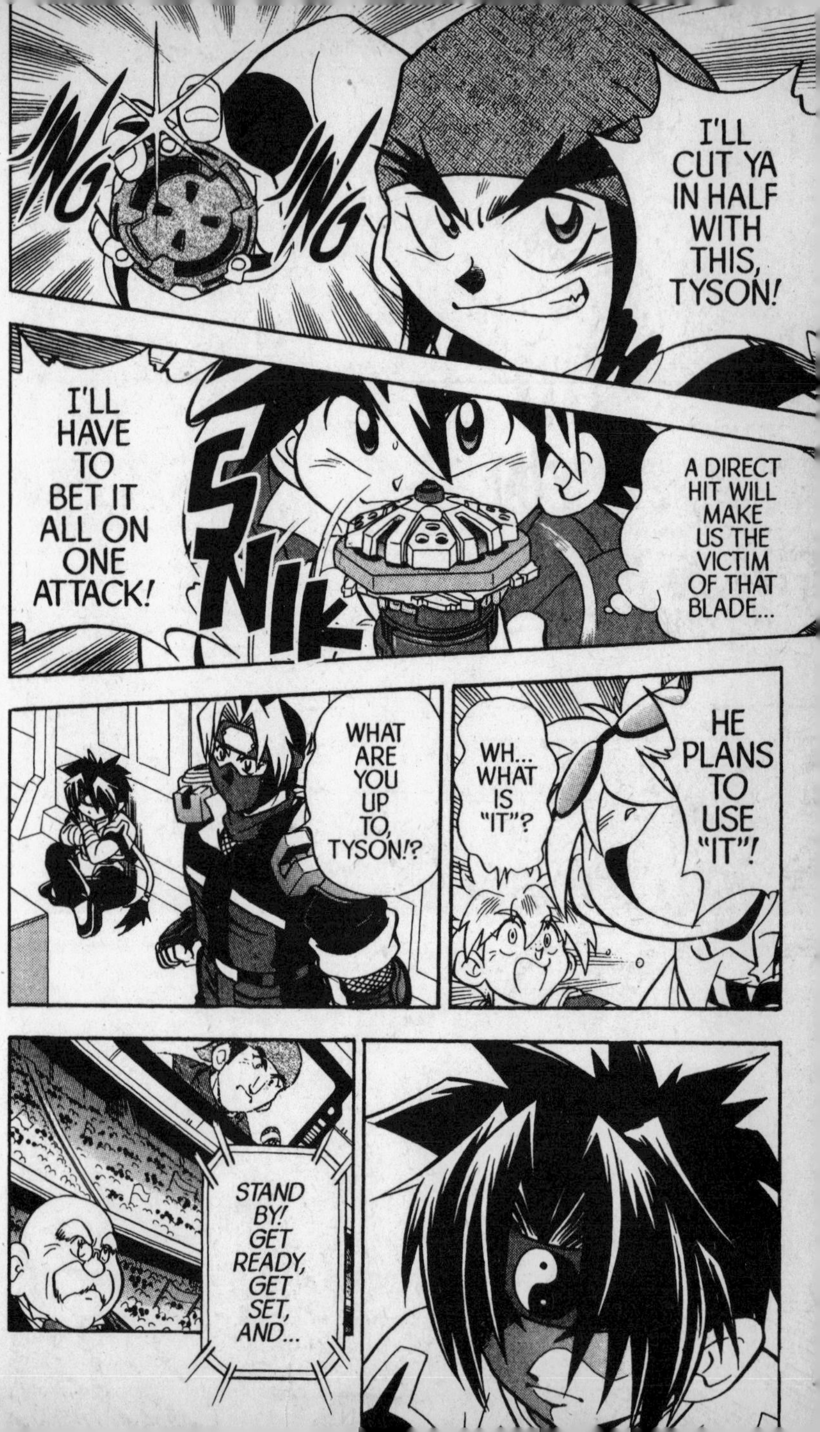
I'LL CUT YA IN HALF WITH THIS, TYSON!
A DIRECT HIT WILL MAKE US THE VICTIM OF THAT BLADE...
SNIK
I'LL HAVE TO BET IT ALL ON ONE ATTACK!
HE PLANS TO USE "IT"!
WH... WHAT IS "IT"?
WHAT ARE YOU UP TO, TYSON!?
STAND BY! GET READY, GET SET, AND...

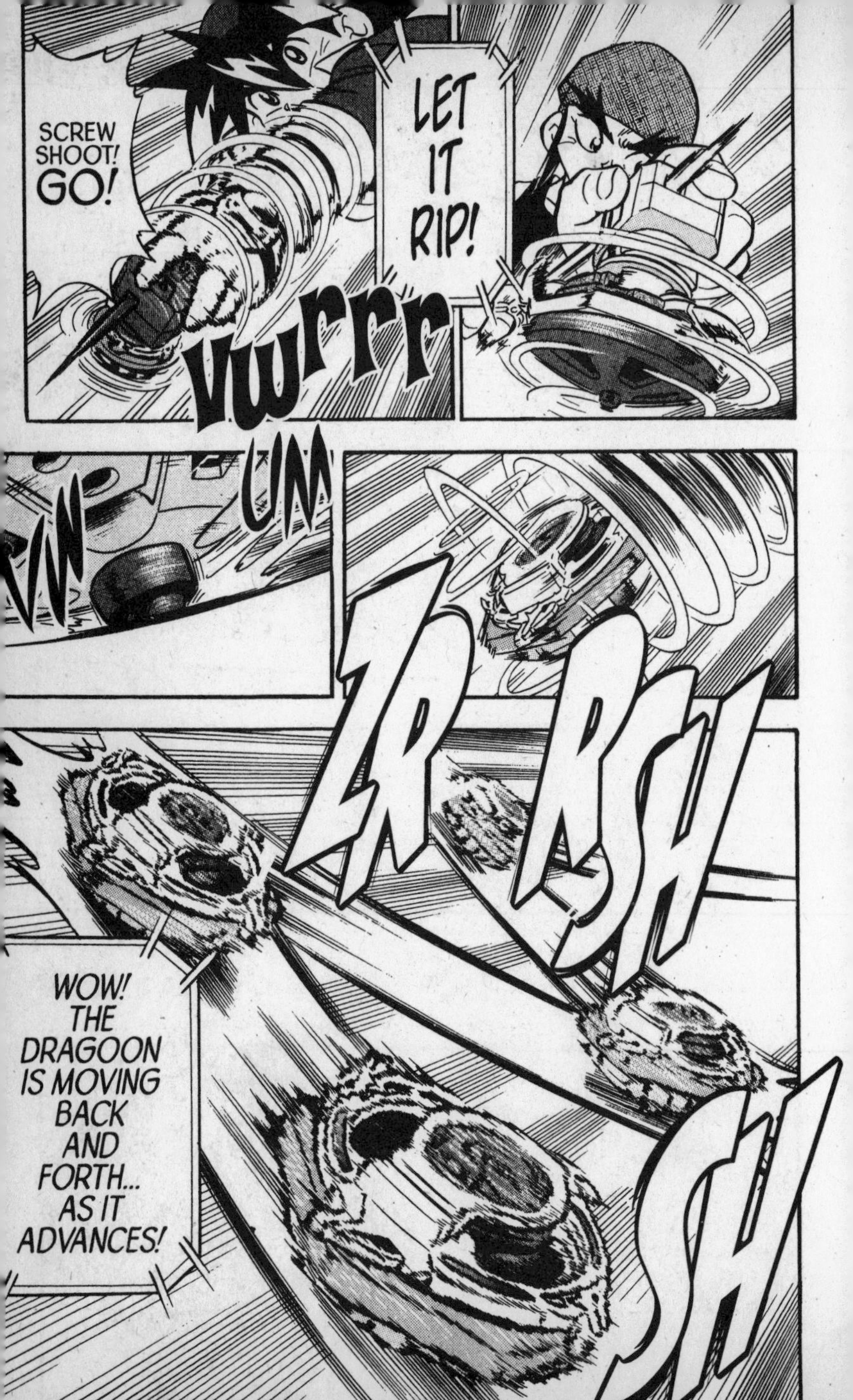
LET IT RIP!
SCREW SHOOT! GO!
VWRRR
UM
ZR
RSH
WOW! THE DRAGOON IS MOVING BACK AND FORTH... AS IT ADVANCES!
SH

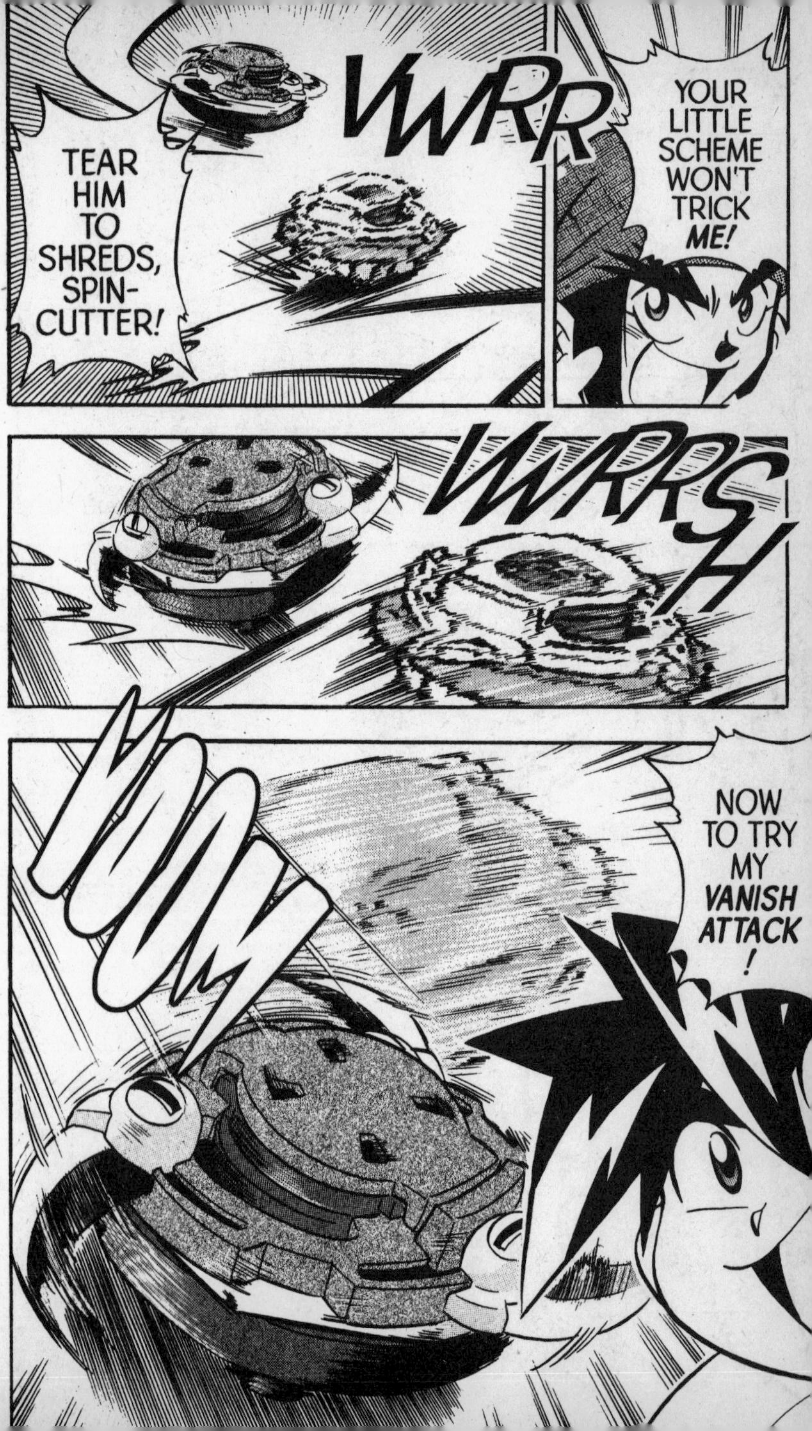
YOUR LITTLE SCHEME WON'T TRICK *ME!*
VWRR
TEAR HIM TO SHREDS, SPIN-CUTTER!
VWRRSH
NOW TO TRY MY *VANISH ATTACK!*
VOOM

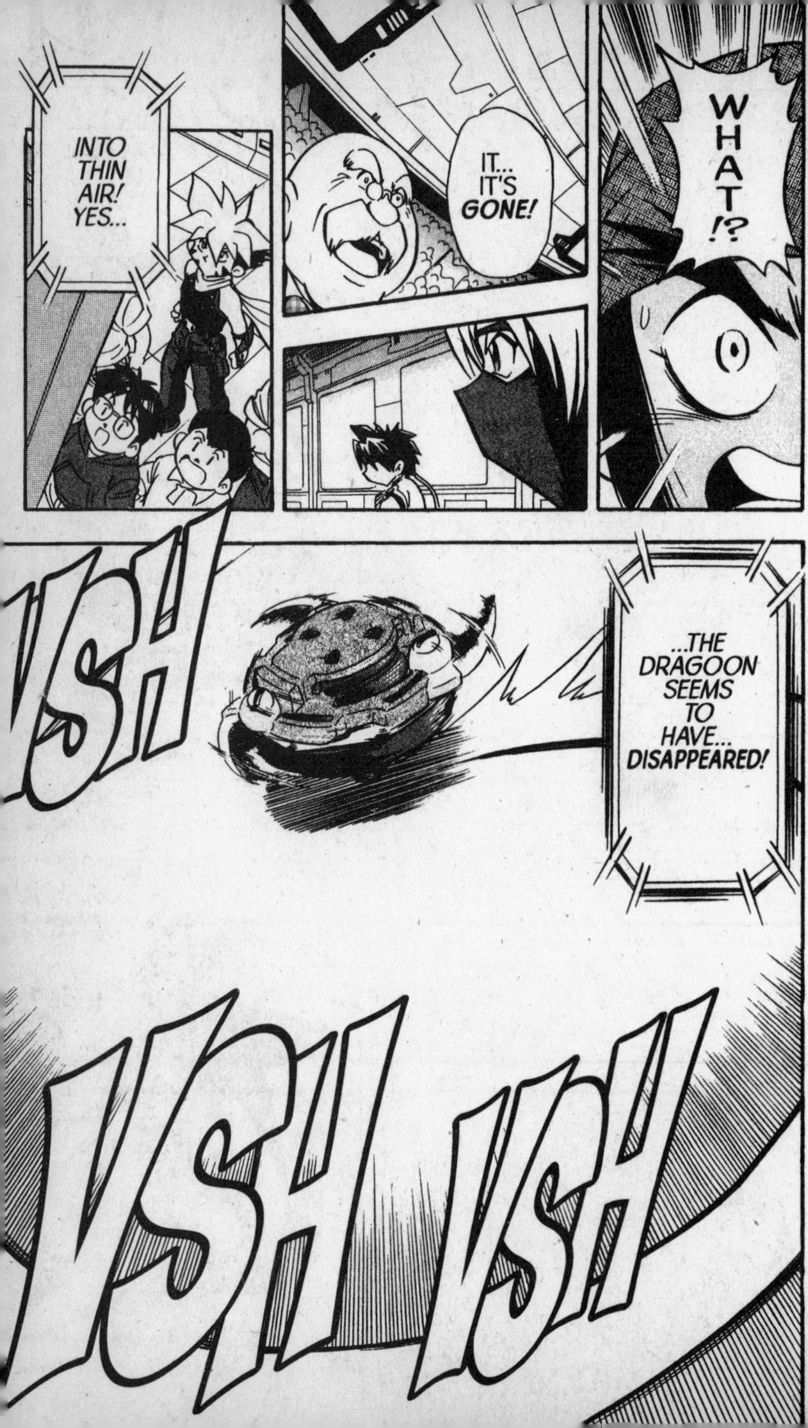
WHAT!?
IT... IT'S GONE!
INTO THIN AIR! YES...
...THE DRAGOON SEEMS TO HAVE... DISAPPEARED!
SH
VSH VSH

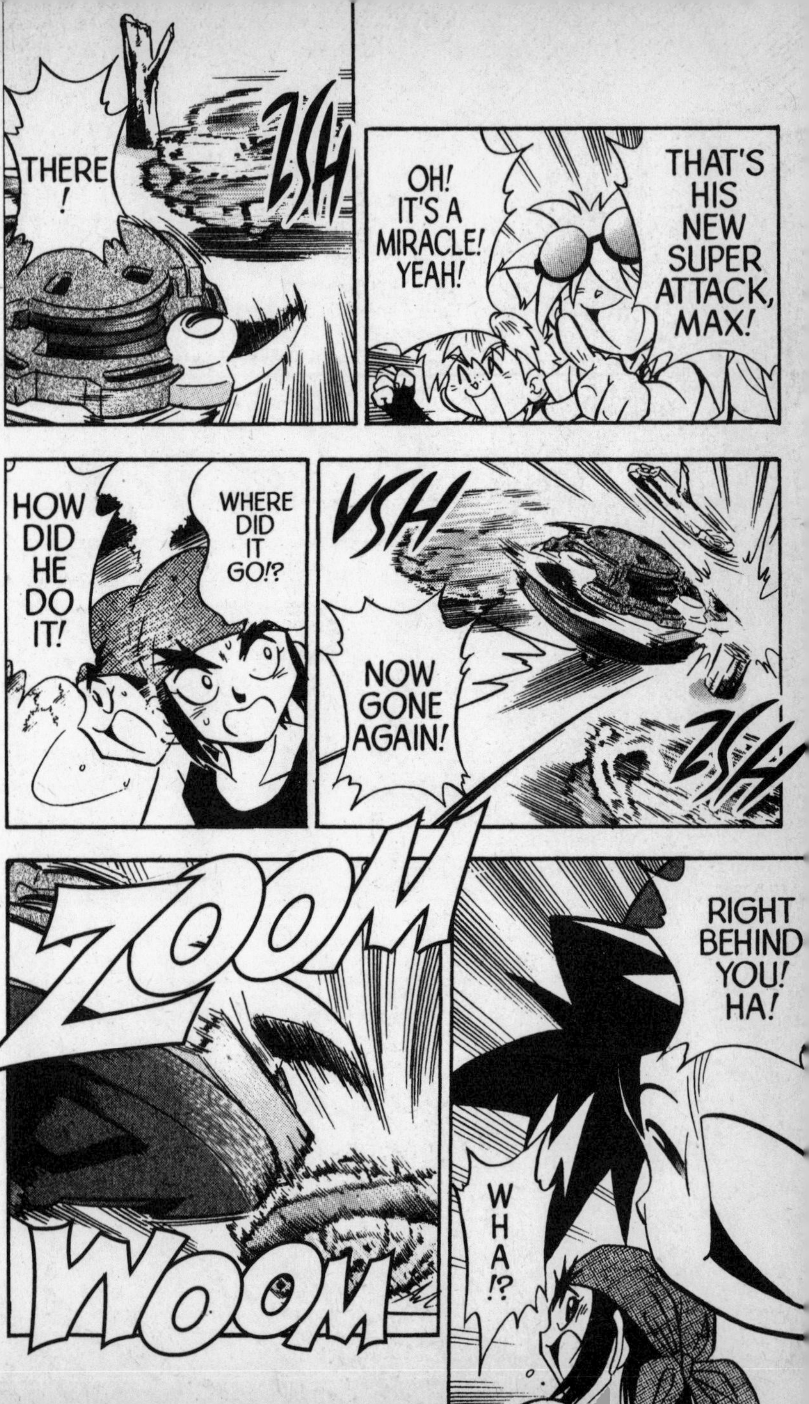

THAT'S HIS NEW SUPER ATTACK, MAX!
OH! IT'S A MIRACLE! YEAH!
ZSH
THERE!
VSH
NOW GONE AGAIN!
ZSH
WHERE DID IT GO!?
HOW DID HE DO IT!
RIGHT BEHIND YOU! HA!
WHA!?
ZOOM
WOOM

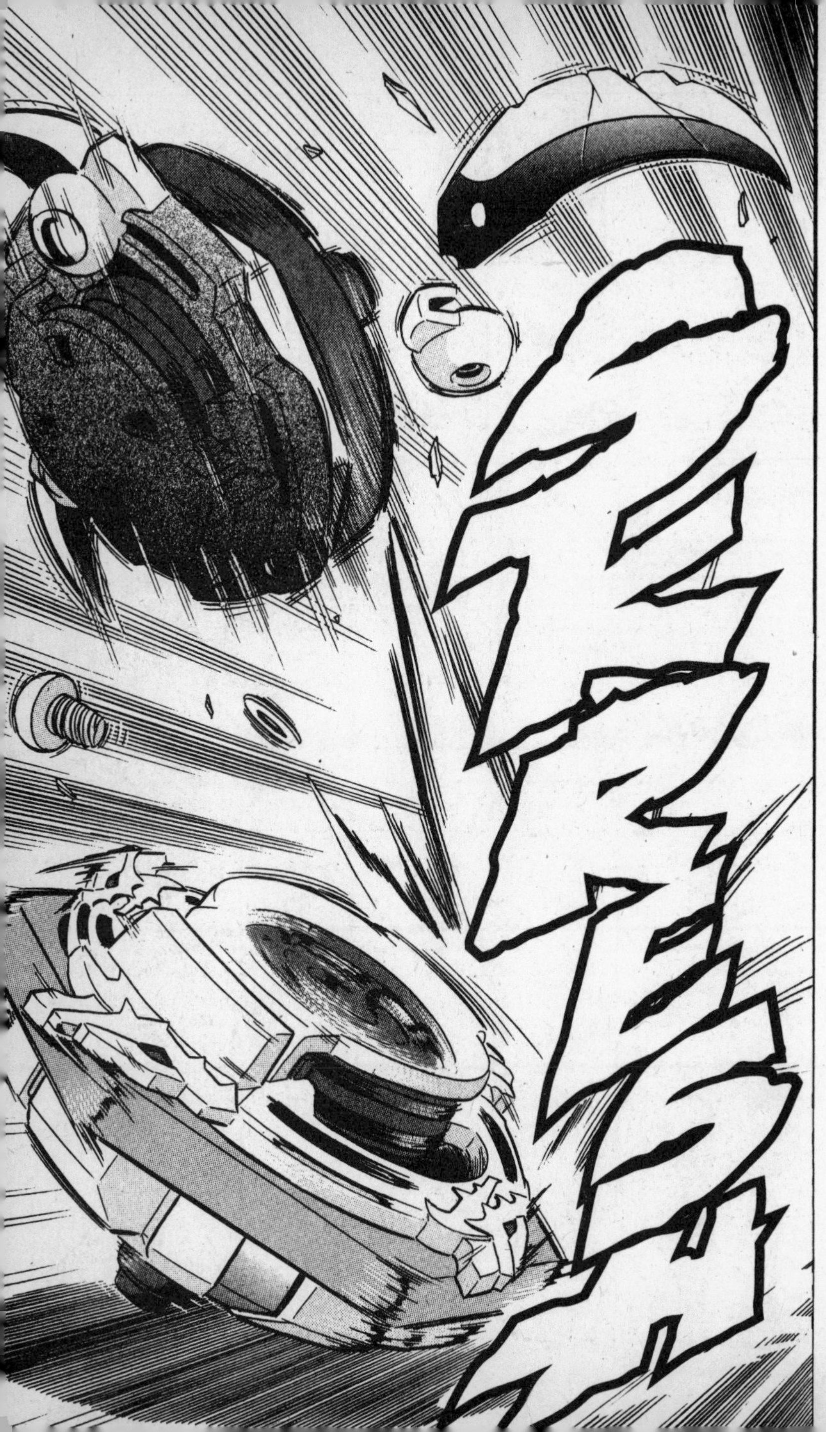

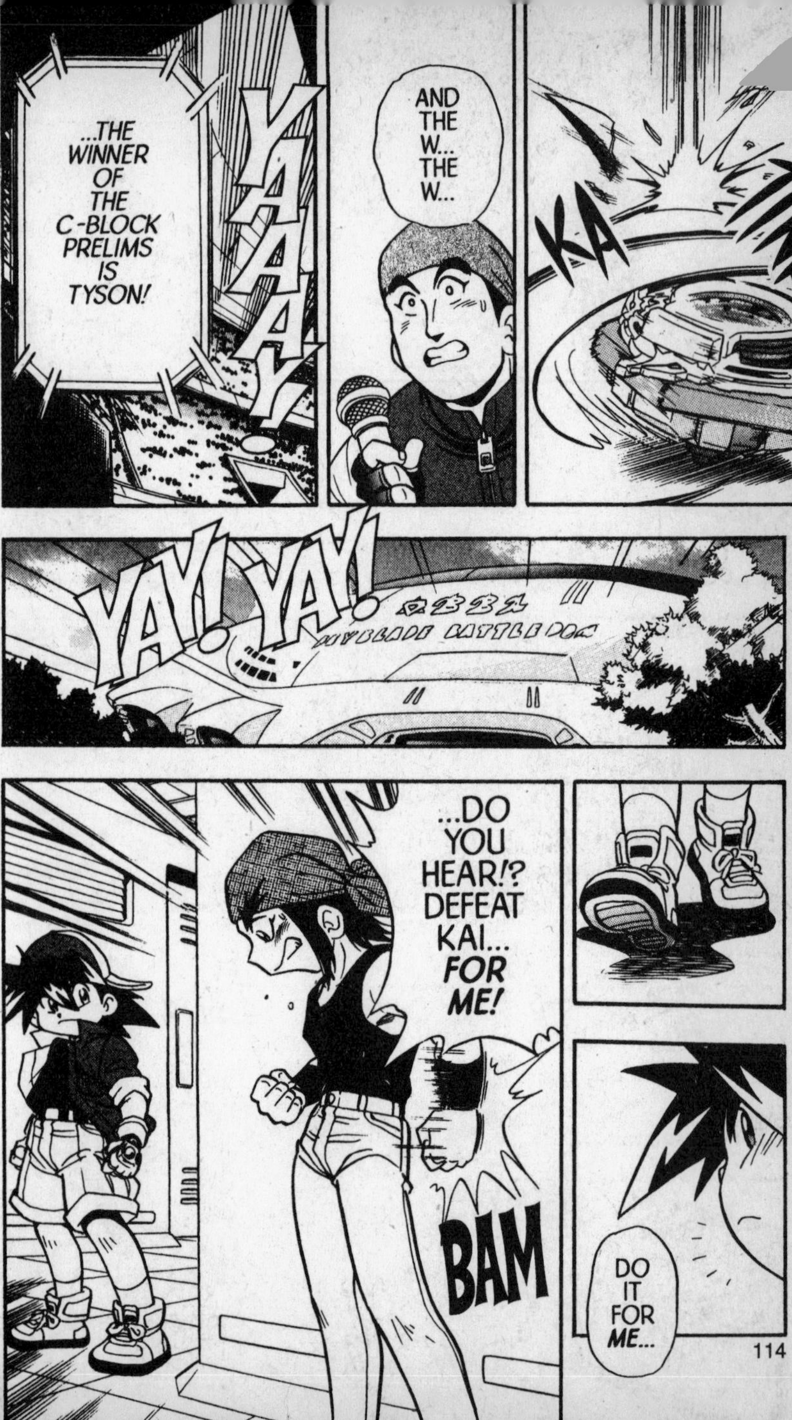
KA-TIN
AND THE W... THE W...
...THE WINNER OF THE C-BLOCK PRELIMS IS TYSON!
YAAAAY!
YAY! YAY!
DO IT FOR ME...
...DO YOU HEAR!? DEFEAT KAI... FOR ME!
BAM

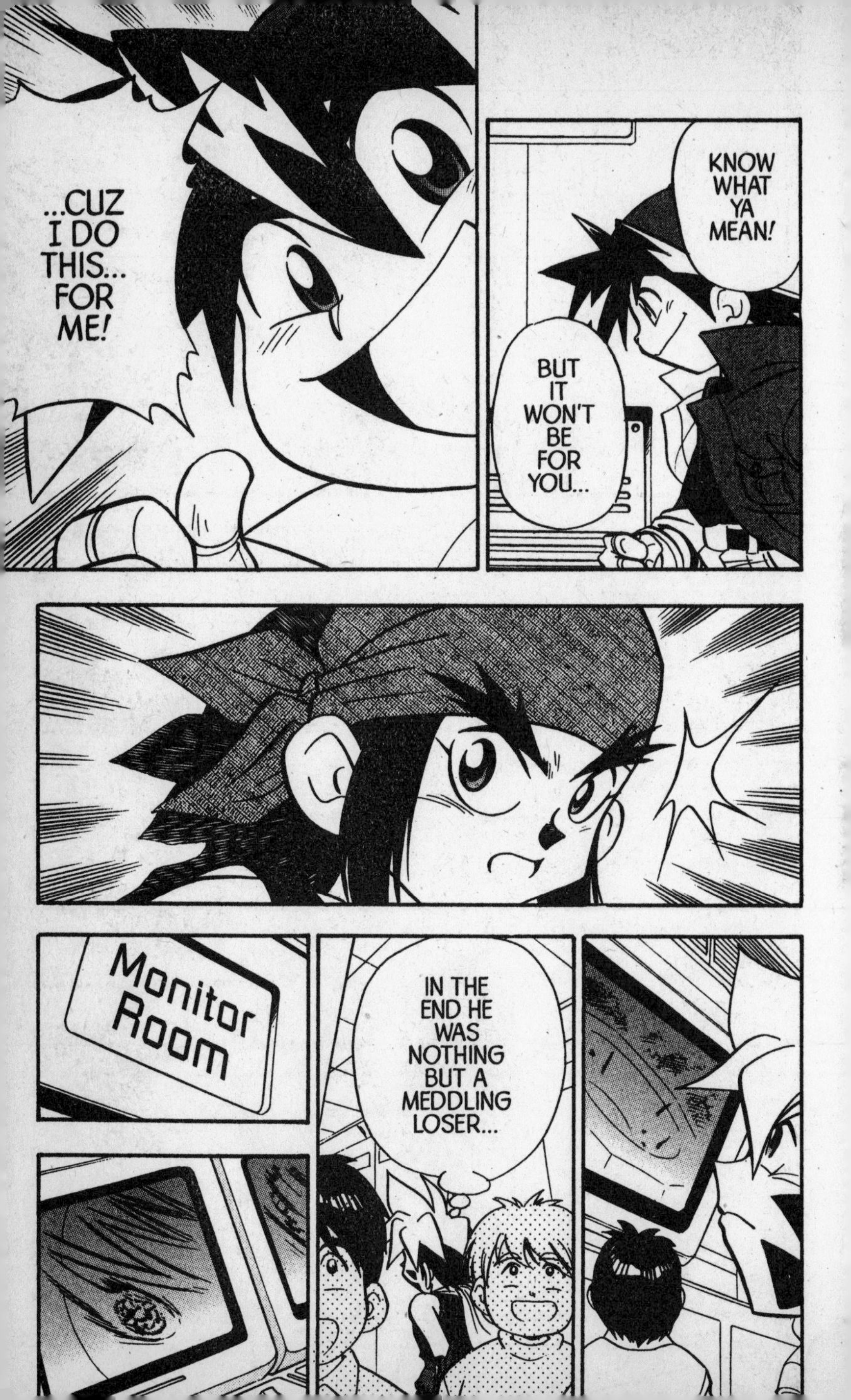

KNOW WHAT YA MEAN!
BUT IT WON'T BE FOR YOU...
...CUZ I DO THIS... FOR ME!
IN THE END HE WAS NOTHING BUT A MEDDLING LOSER...
Monitor Room

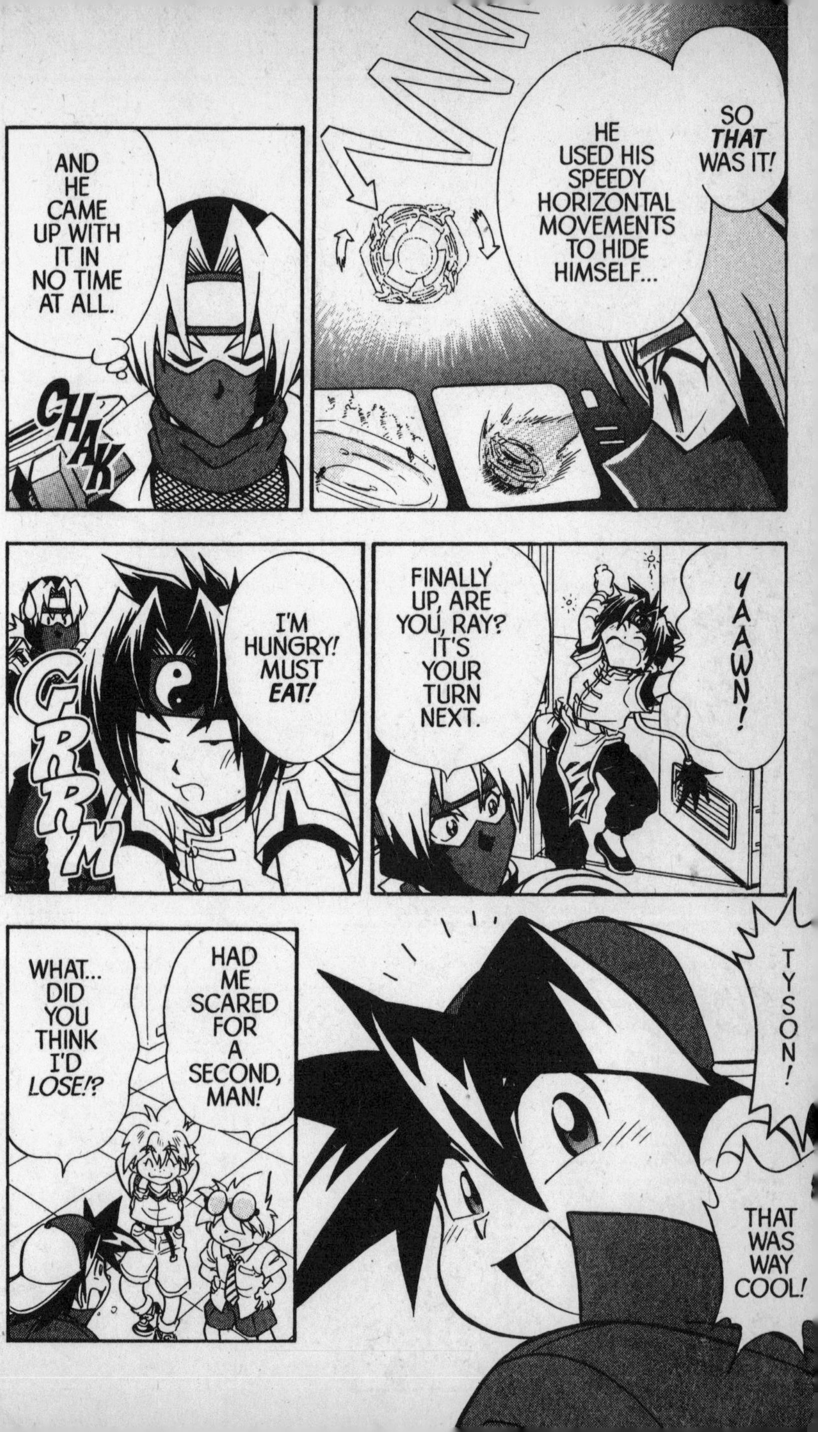
SO *THAT* WAS IT!
HE USED HIS SPEEDY HORIZONTAL MOVEMENTS TO HIDE HIMSELF...
AND HE CAME UP WITH IT IN NO TIME AT ALL.
CHAK
YAAWN!
FINALLY UP, ARE YOU, RAY? IT'S YOUR TURN NEXT.
I'M HUNGRY! MUST *EAT!*
GRRM
TYSON!
THAT WAS WAY COOL!
HAD ME SCARED FOR A SECOND, MAN!
WHAT... DID YOU THINK I'D *LOSE!?*

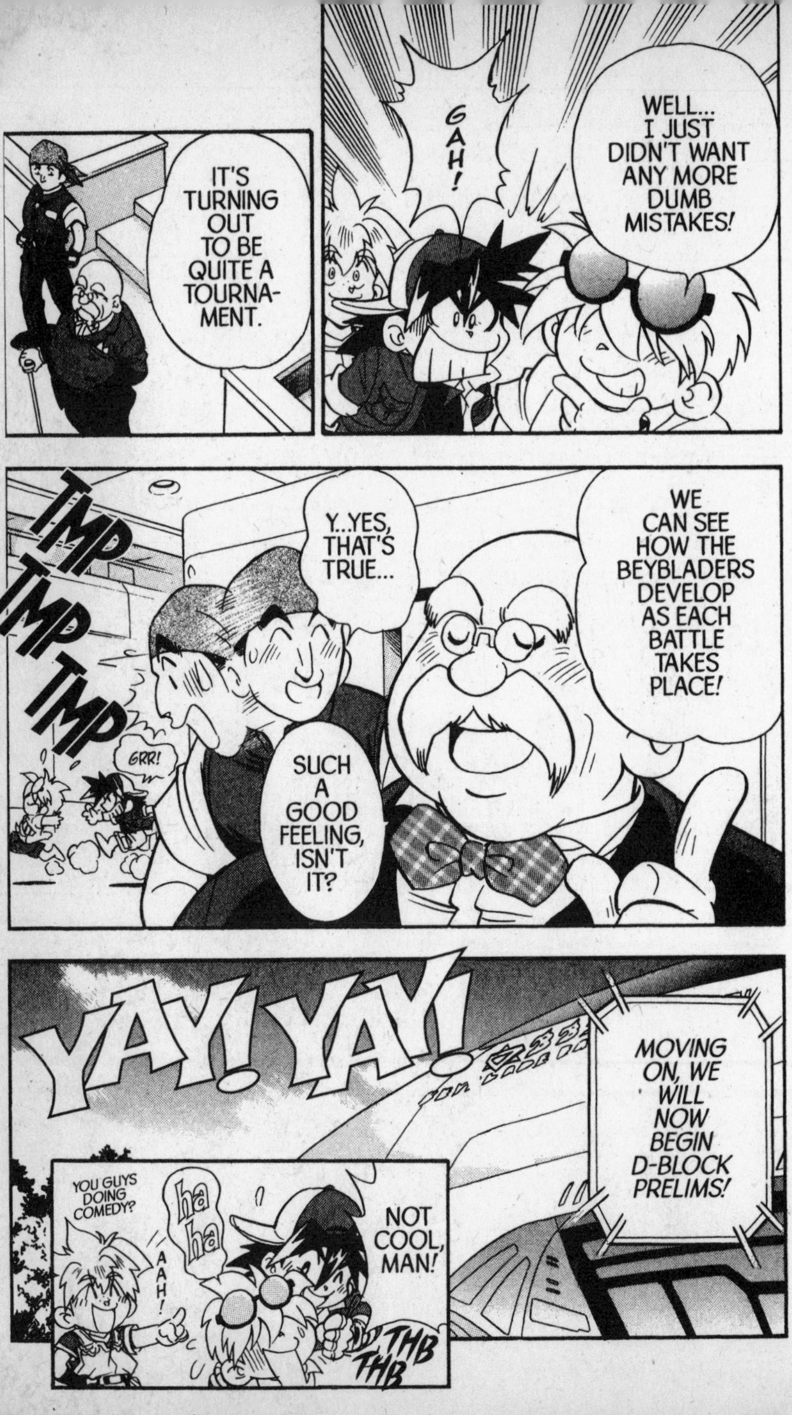
WELL... I JUST DIDN'T WANT ANY MORE DUMB MISTAKES!
GAH!
IT'S TURNING OUT TO BE QUITE A TOURNAMENT.
WE CAN SEE HOW THE BEYBLADERS DEVELOP AS EACH BATTLE TAKES PLACE!
Y...YES, THAT'S TRUE...
SUCH A GOOD FEELING, ISN'T IT?
TMP TMP TMP TMP
GRR!
MOVING ON, WE WILL NOW BEGIN D-BLOCK PRELIMS!
YAY! YAY!
NOT COOL, MAN!
ha ha
AAH!
YOU GUYS DOING COMEDY?
THB THB

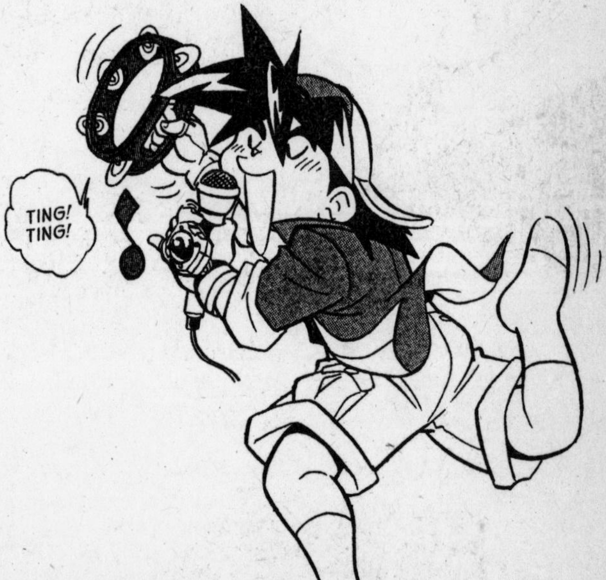
TING! TING!

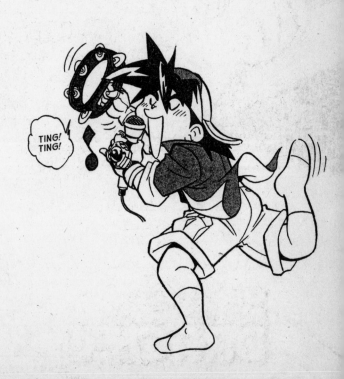

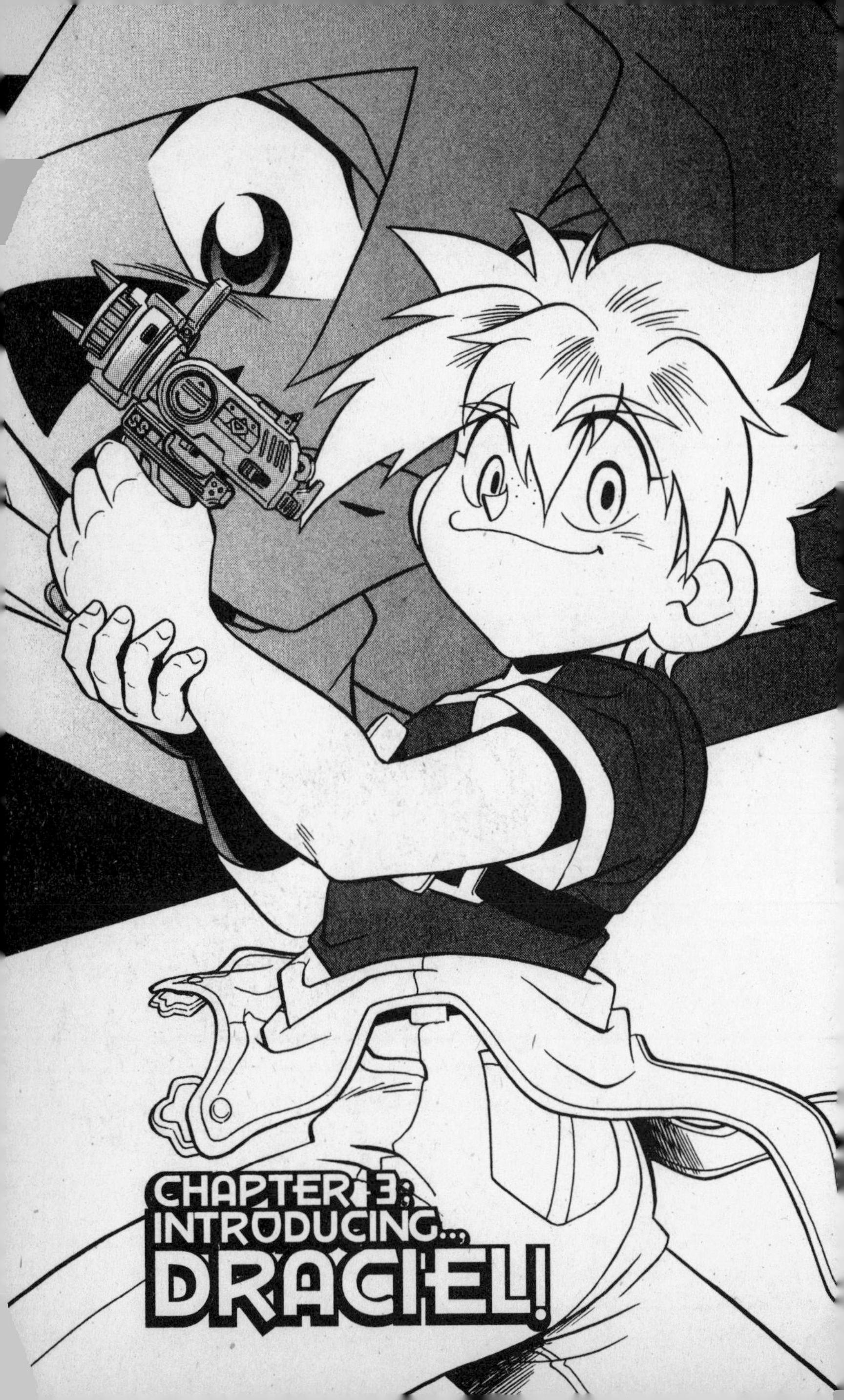
CHAPTER 3:
INTRODUCING...,
DRACIEL!

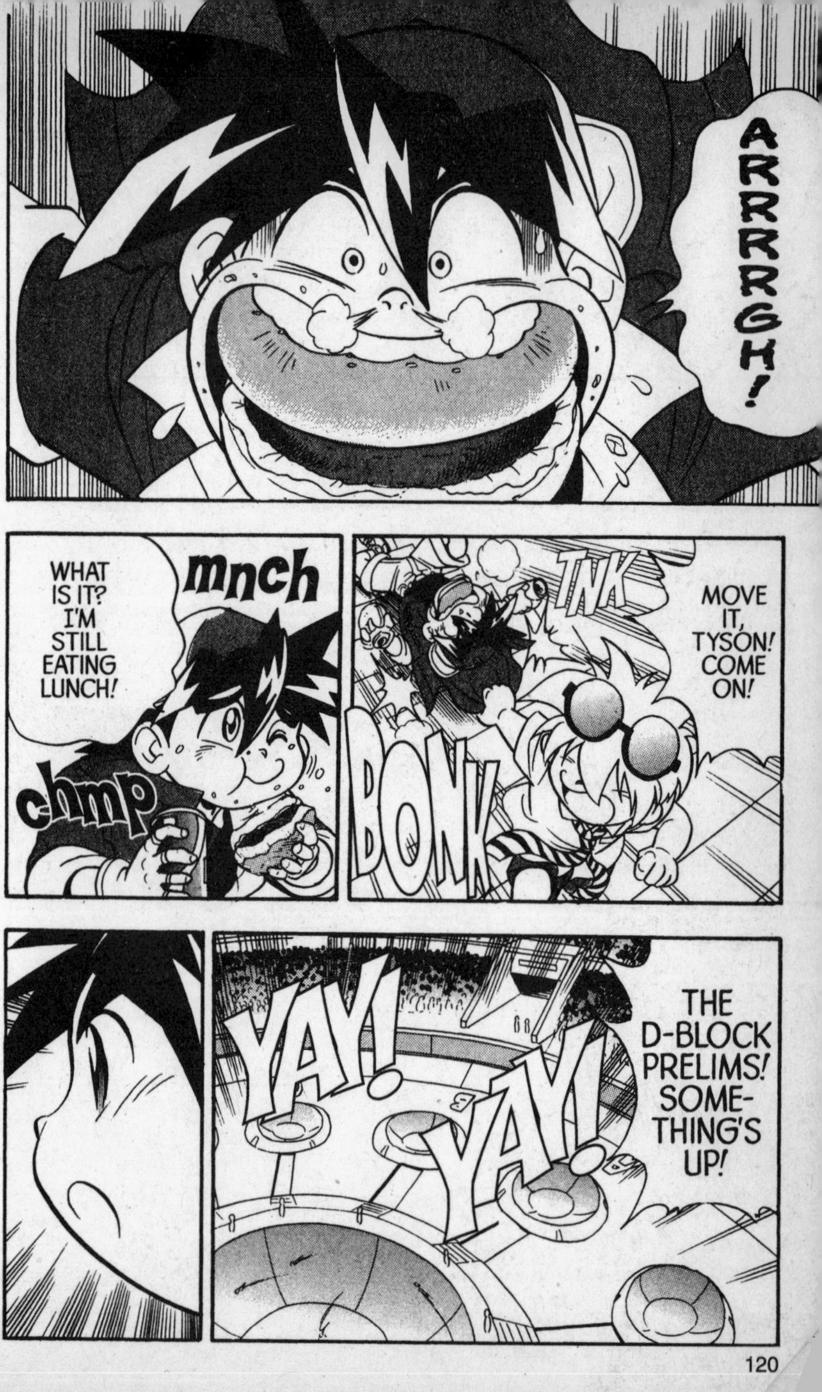
ARRRRGH!
MOVE IT, TYSON! COME ON!
TNK
BONK
mnch
WHAT IS IT? I'M STILL EATING LUNCH!
chmp
THE D-BLOCK PRELIMS! SOME-THING'S UP!
YAY!
YAY!

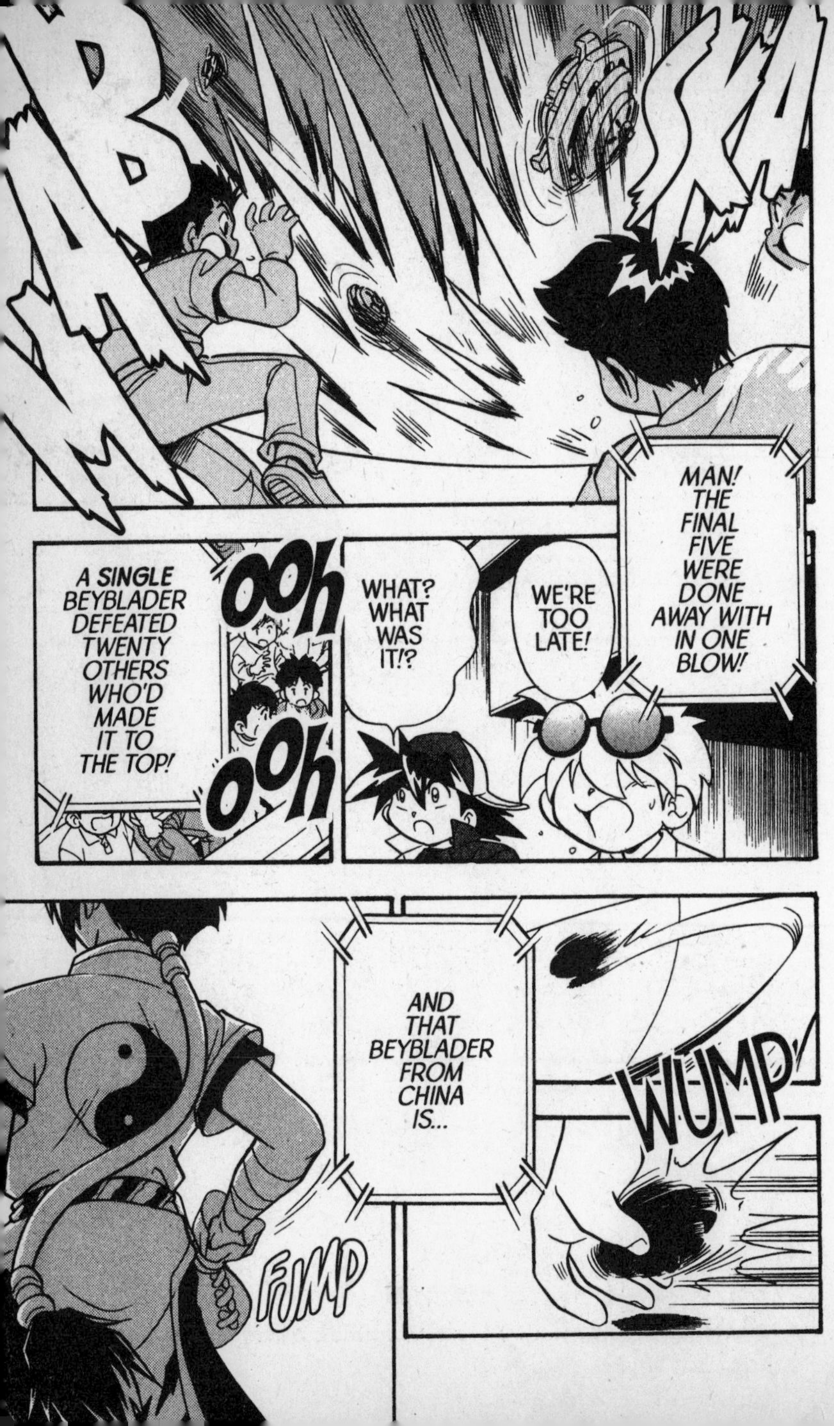
MAN! THE FINAL FIVE WERE DONE AWAY WITH IN ONE BLOW!
WE'RE TOO LATE!
WHAT? WHAT WAS IT!?
OOH
OOH
A SINGLE BEYBLADER DEFEATED TWENTY OTHERS WHO'D MADE IT TO THE TOP!
WUMP
AND THAT BEYBLADER FROM CHINA IS...
FUMP

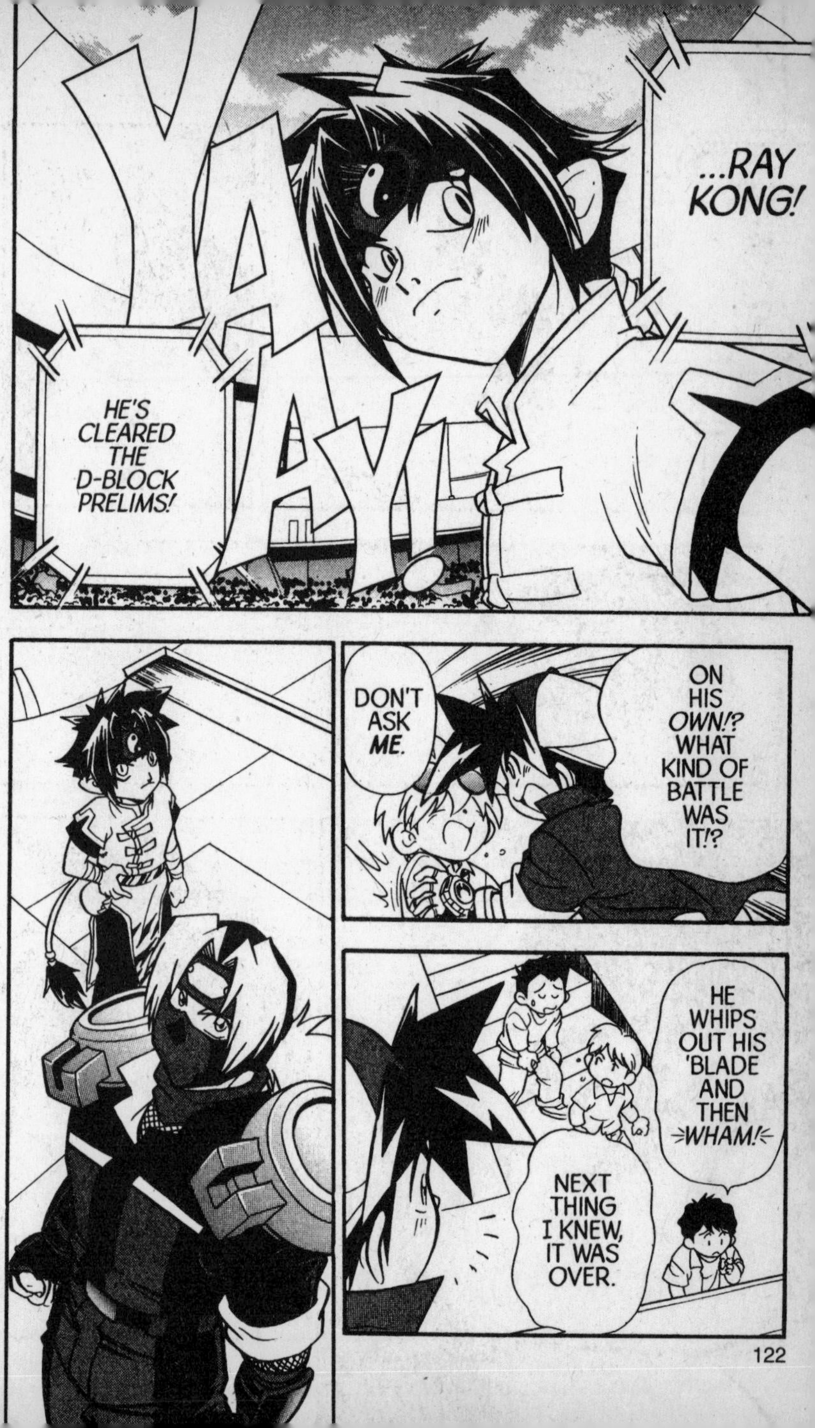
...RAY KONG!
YAY!
HE'S CLEARED THE D-BLOCK PRELIMS!
ON HIS *OWN!?* WHAT KIND OF BATTLE WAS IT!?
DON'T ASK *ME.*
HE WHIPS OUT HIS 'BLADE AND THEN *WHAM!*
NEXT THING I KNEW, IT WAS OVER.

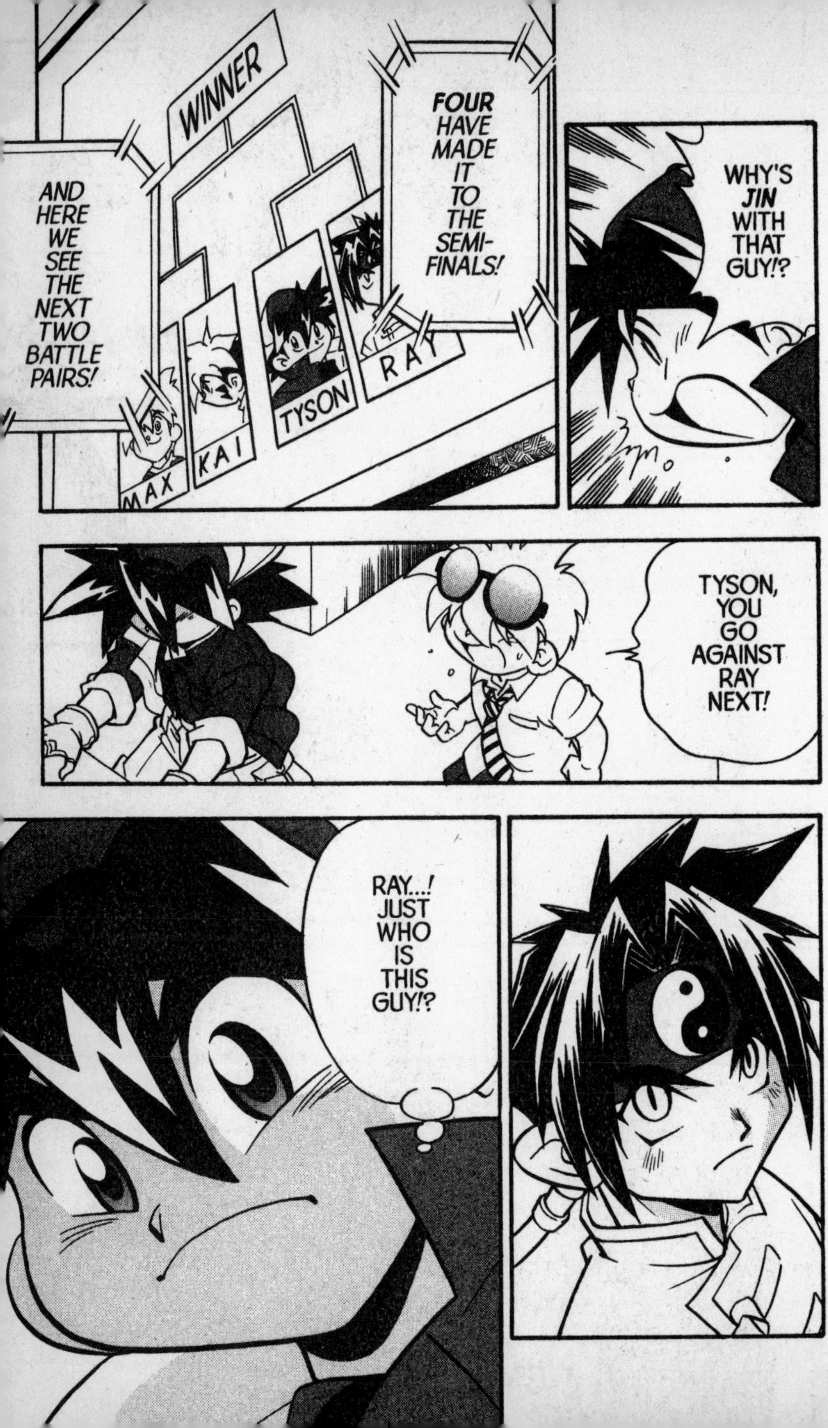
WHY'S JIN WITH THAT GUY!?
FOUR HAVE MADE IT TO THE SEMI-FINALS!
WINNER
RAY
TYSON
KAI
MAX
AND HERE WE SEE THE NEXT TWO BATTLE PAIRS!
TYSON, YOU GO AGAINST RAY NEXT!
RAY...! JUST WHO IS THIS GUY!?

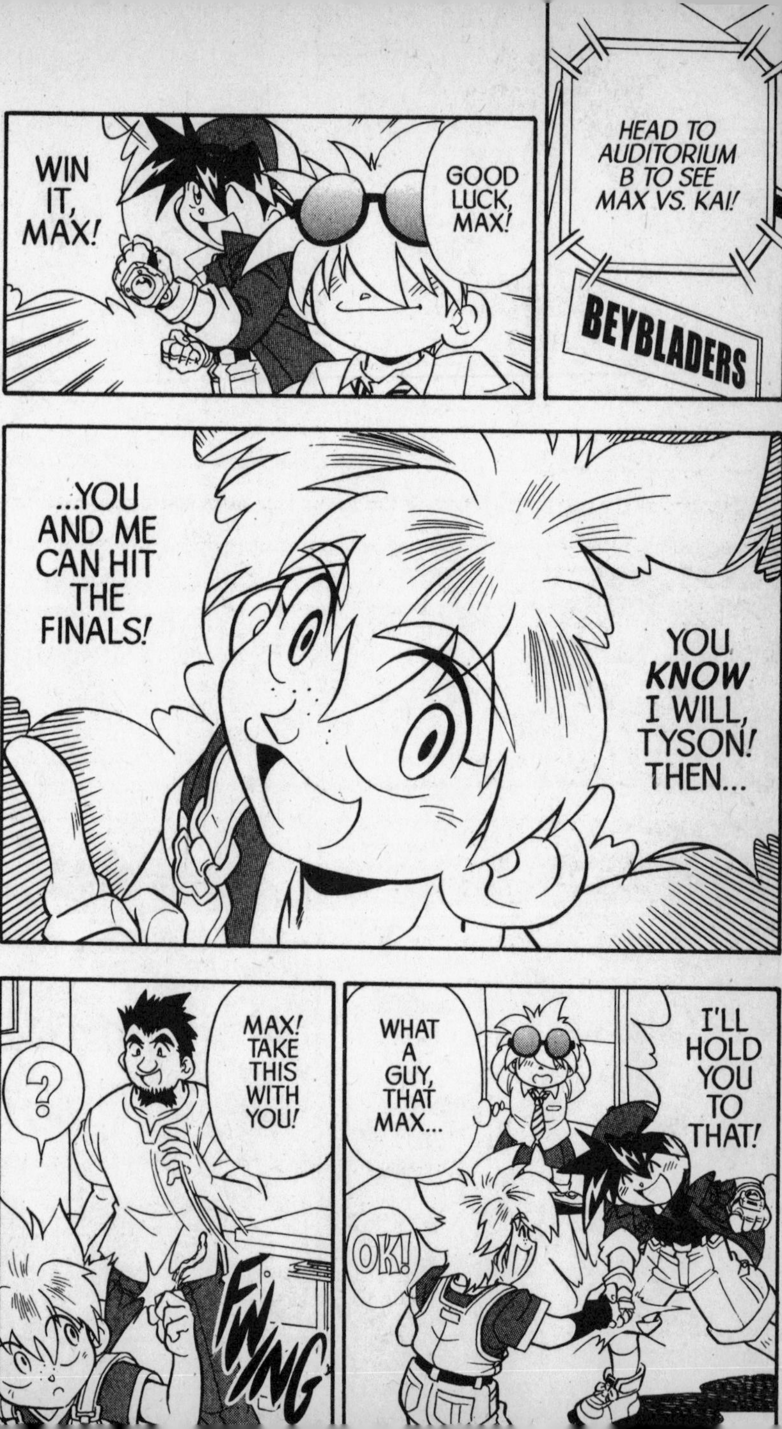
HEAD TO AUDITORIUM B TO SEE MAX VS. KAI!
BEYBLADERS
GOOD LUCK, MAX!
WIN IT, MAX!
YOU *KNOW* I WILL, TYSON! THEN...
...YOU AND ME CAN HIT THE FINALS!
I'LL HOLD YOU TO THAT!
WHAT A GUY, THAT MAX...
OK!
MAX! TAKE THIS WITH YOU!
?
FWING

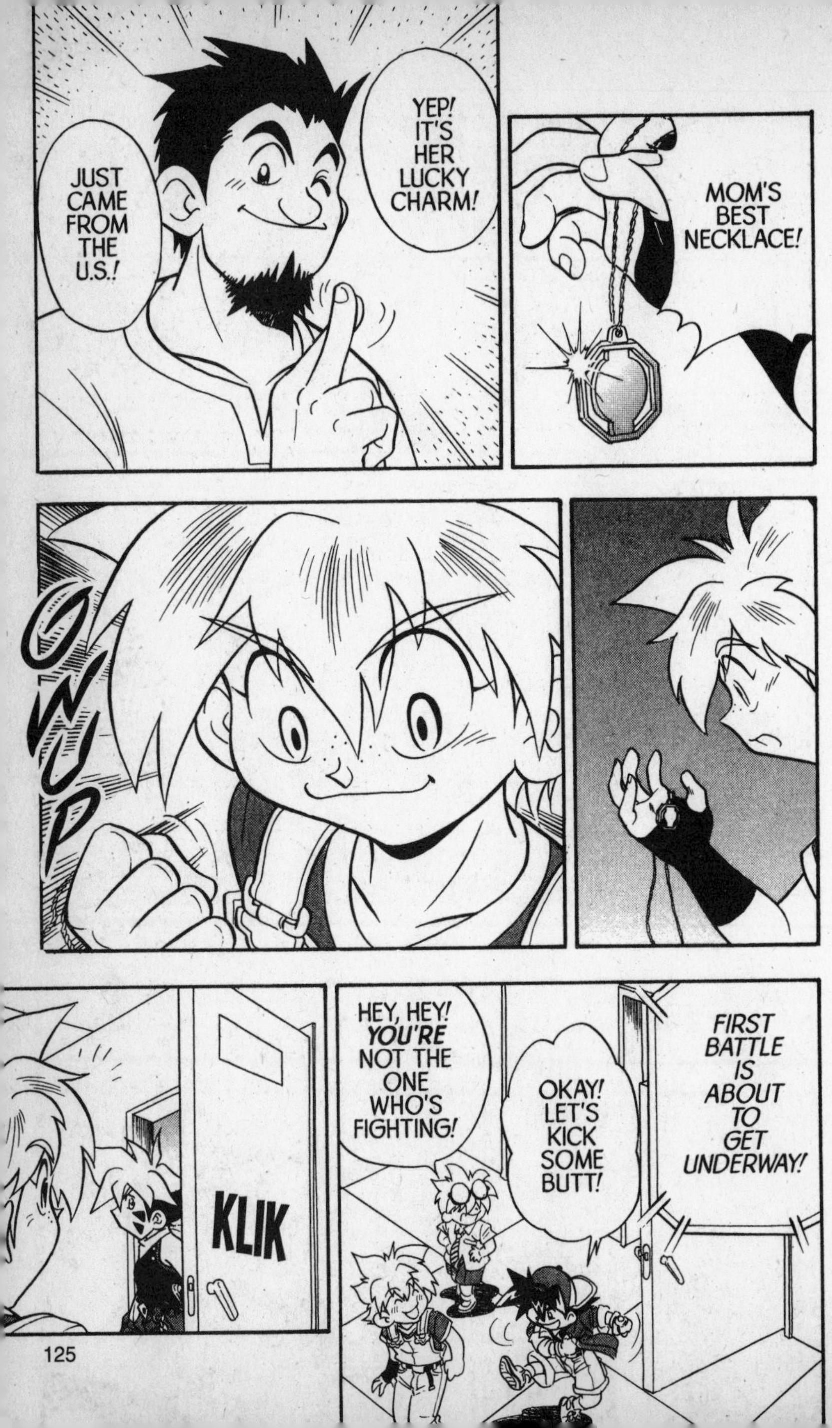
MOM'S BEST NECKLACE!
YEP! IT'S HER LUCKY CHARM!
JUST CAME FROM THE U.S.!
GWUP
FIRST BATTLE IS ABOUT TO GET UNDERWAY!
OKAY! LET'S KICK SOME BUTT!
HEY, HEY! *YOU'RE* NOT THE ONE WHO'S FIGHTING!
KLIK

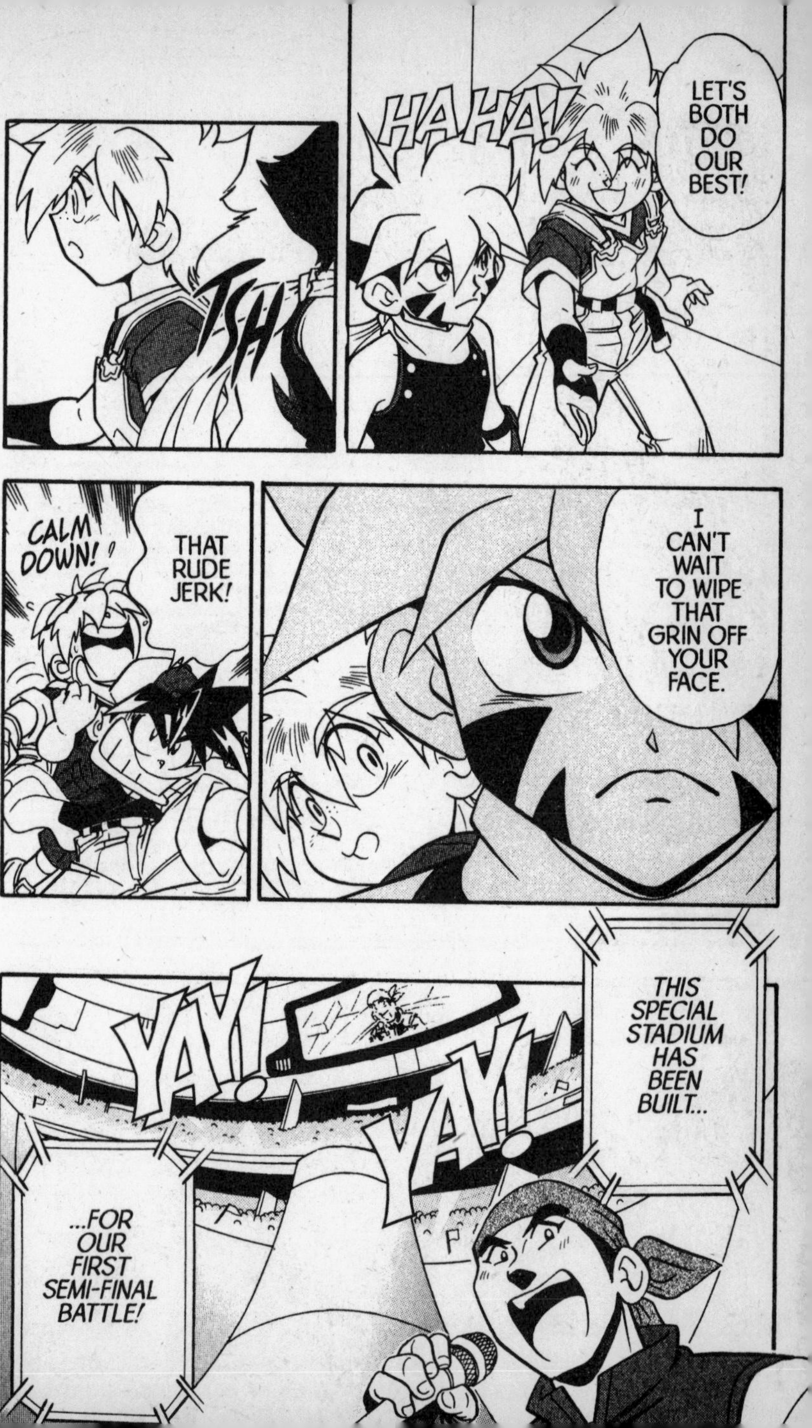
LET'S BOTH DO OUR BEST!
HAHA!
TSH
I CAN'T WAIT TO WIPE THAT GRIN OFF YOUR FACE.
THAT RUDE JERK!
CALM DOWN!
THIS SPECIAL STADIUM HAS BEEN BUILT...
YAY!
YAY!
...FOR OUR FIRST SEMI-FINAL BATTLE!

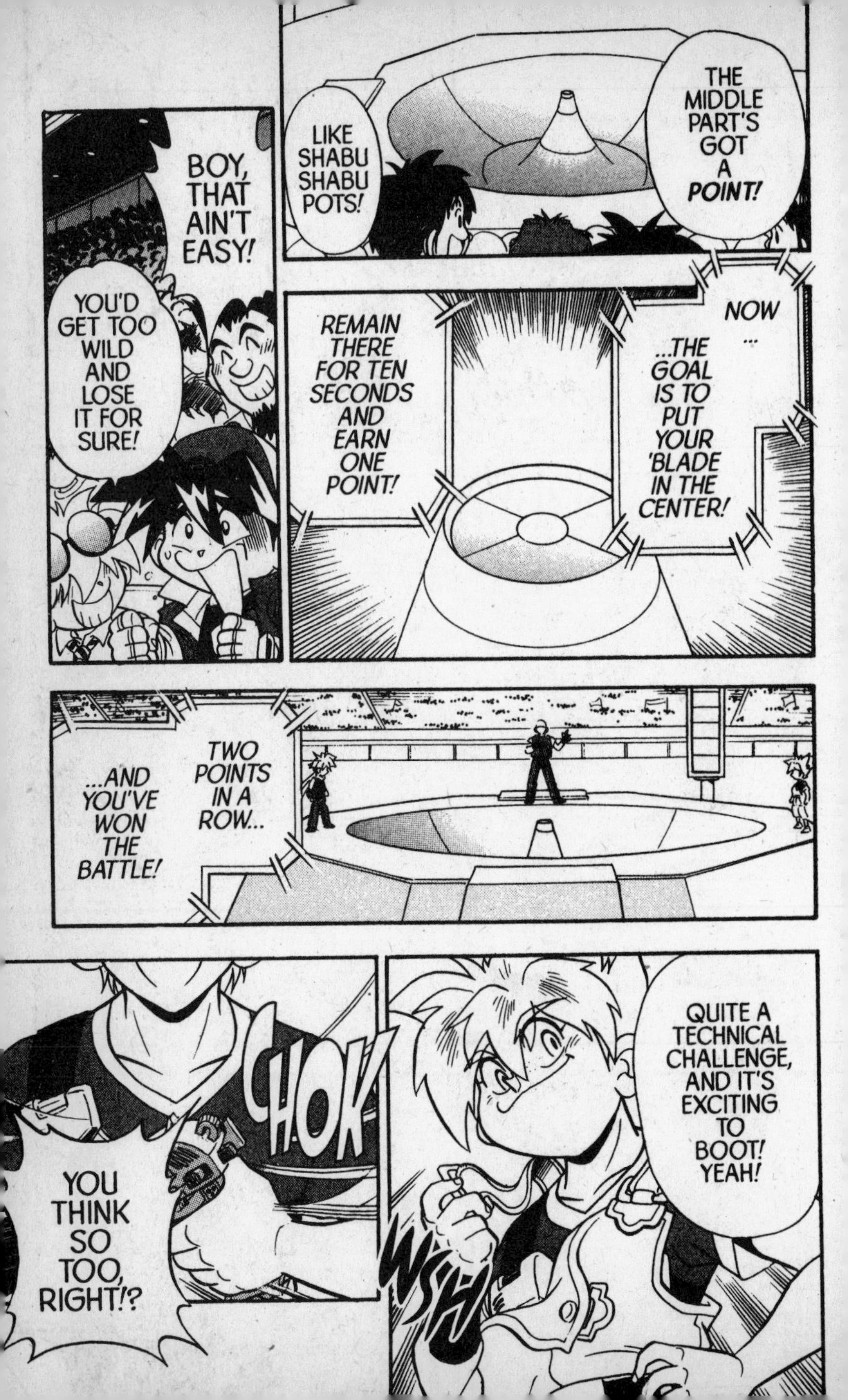
THE MIDDLE PART'S GOT A POINT!
LIKE SHABU SHABU POTS!
NOW ...
...THE GOAL IS TO PUT YOUR 'BLADE IN THE CENTER!
REMAIN THERE FOR TEN SECONDS AND EARN ONE POINT!
BOY, THAT AIN'T EASY!
YOU'D GET TOO WILD AND LOSE IT FOR SURE!
TWO POINTS IN A ROW...
...AND YOU'VE WON THE BATTLE!
QUITE A TECHNICAL CHALLENGE, AND IT'S EXCITING TO BOOT! YEAH!
WSH
CHOK
YOU THINK SO TOO, RIGHT!?

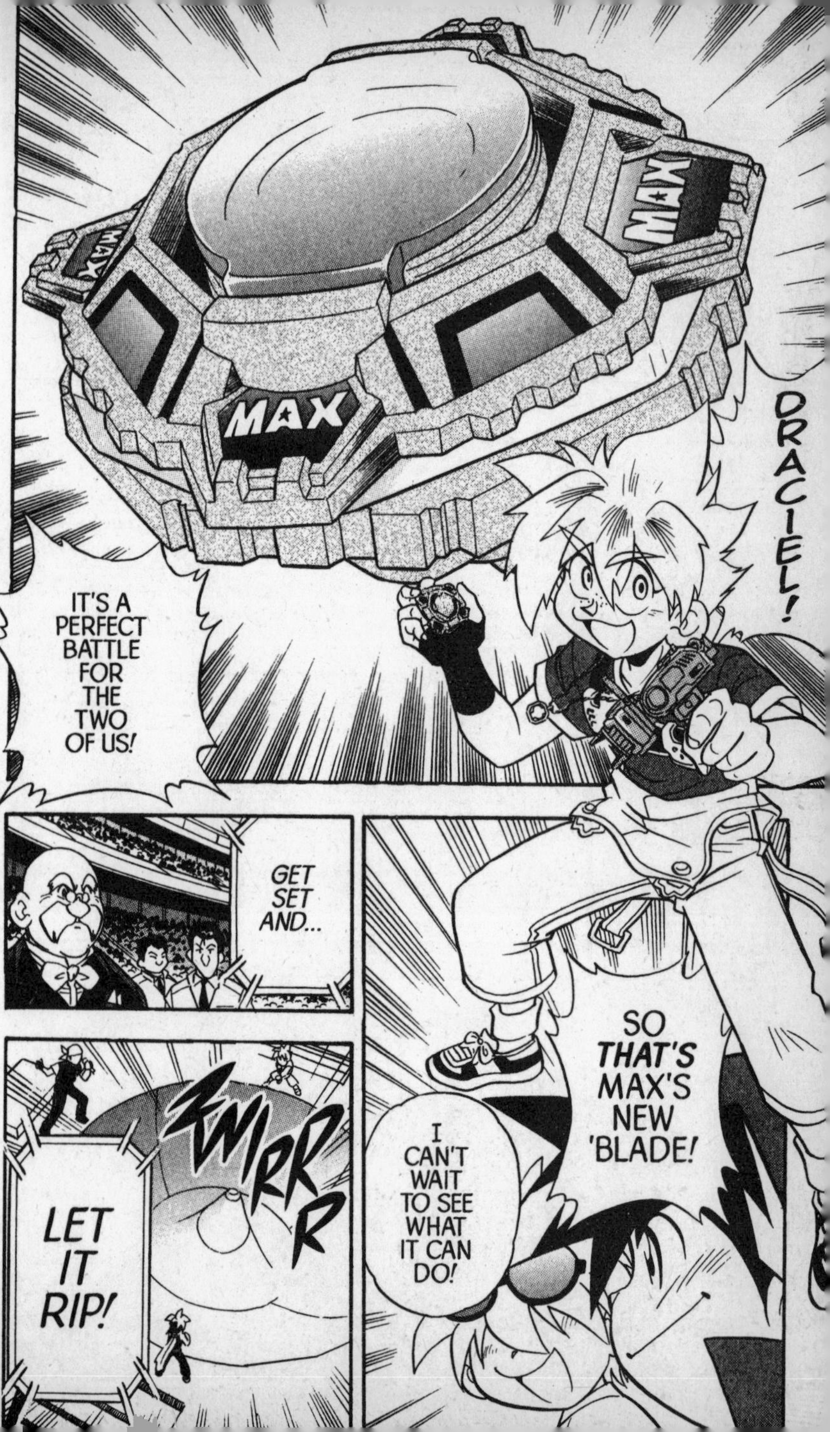
DRACIEL!
IT'S A PERFECT BATTLE FOR THE TWO OF US!
SO THAT'S MAX'S NEW 'BLADE!
I CAN'T WAIT TO SEE WHAT IT CAN DO!
GET SET AND...
ZWIRRR
LET IT RIP!

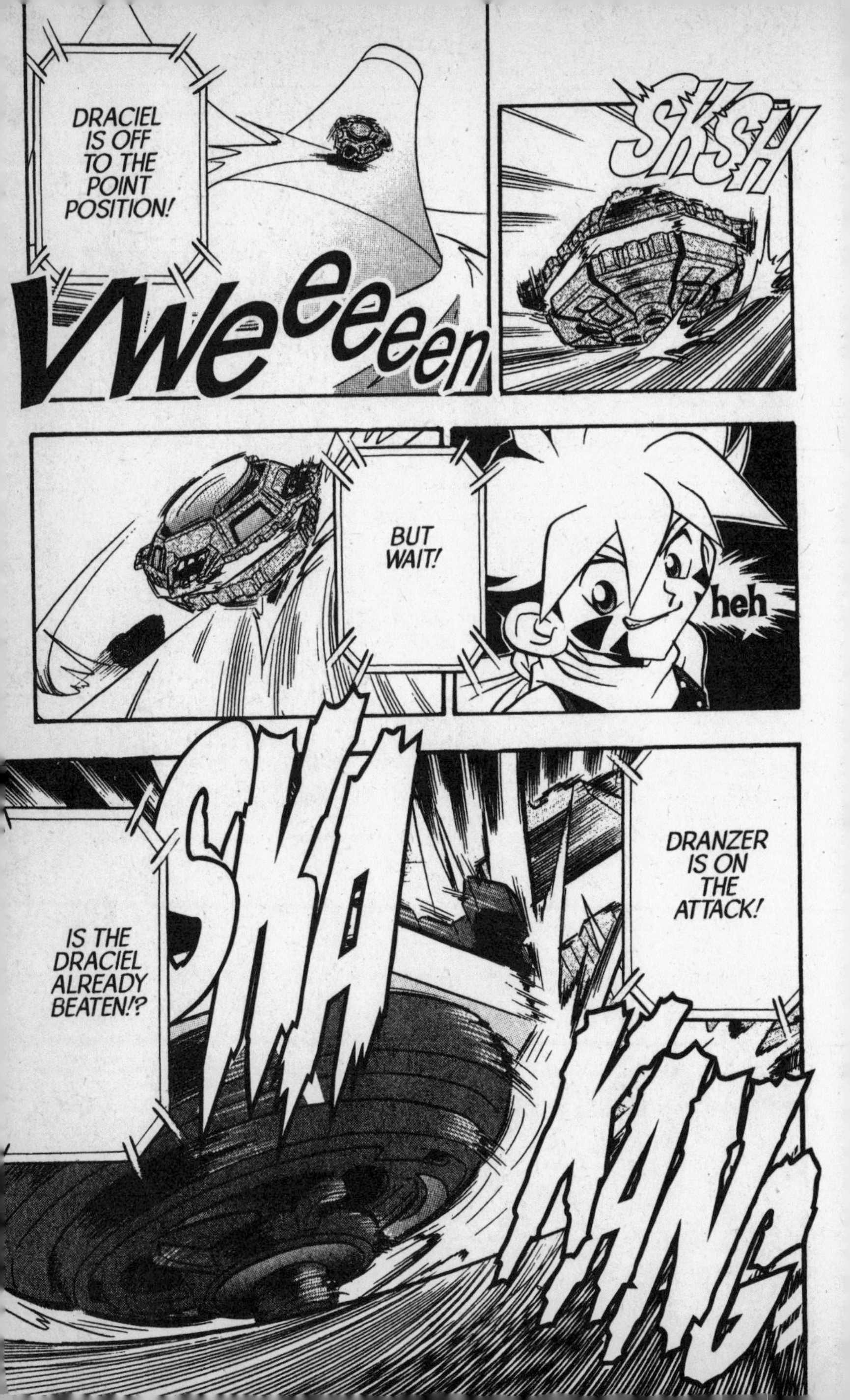
SKSH
DRACIEL IS OFF TO THE POINT POSITION!
VWeeeeen
BUT WAIT!
heh
DRANZER IS ON THE ATTACK!
SHAKANG
IS THE DRACIEL ALREADY BEATEN!?

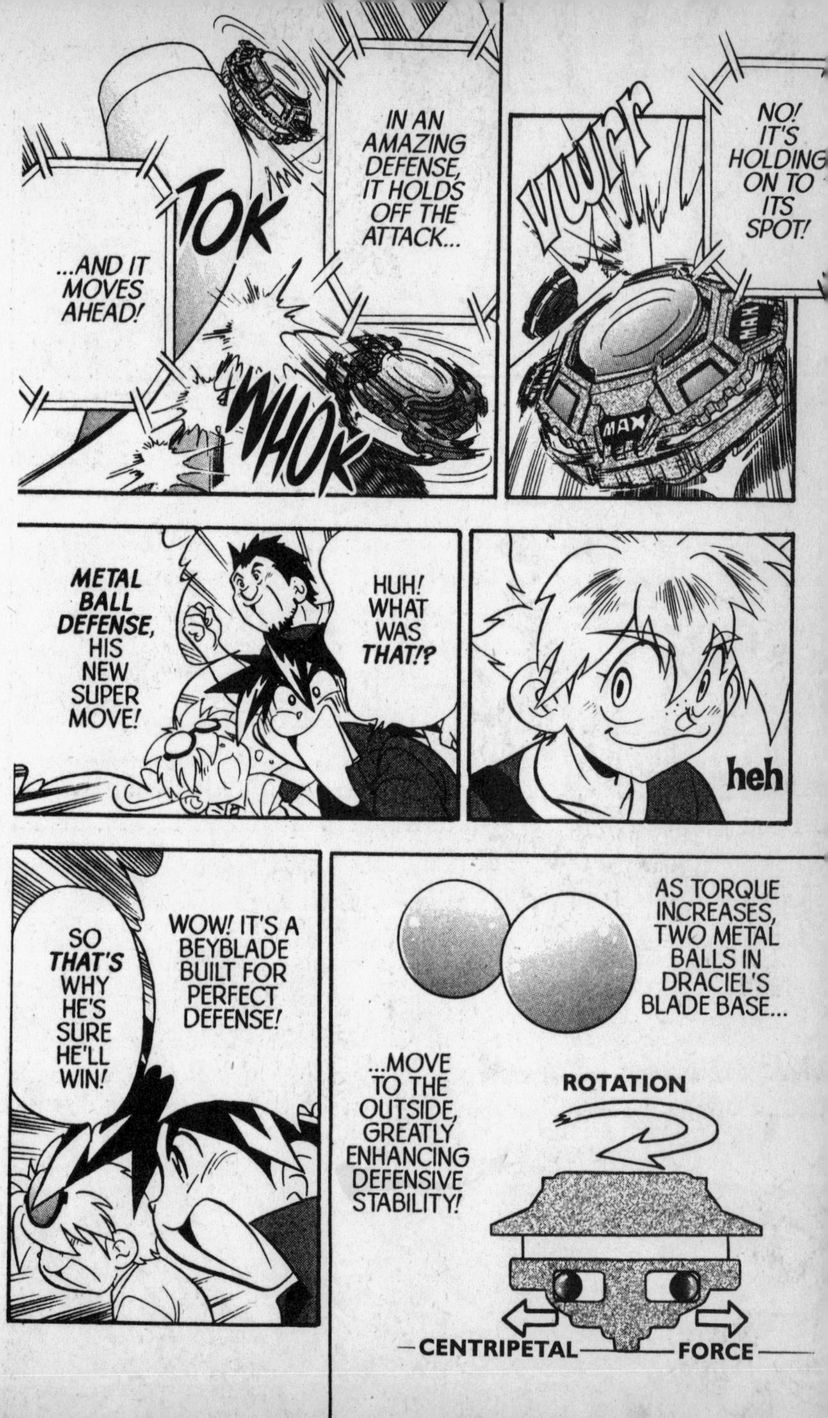
VWURR
NO! IT'S HOLDING ON TO ITS SPOT!
IN AN AMAZING DEFENSE, IT HOLDS OFF THE ATTACK...
TOK
...AND IT MOVES AHEAD!
WHOK
heh
HUH! WHAT WAS *THAT!?*
METAL BALL DEFENSE, HIS NEW SUPER MOVE!
AS TORQUE INCREASES, TWO METAL BALLS IN DRACIEL'S BLADE BASE...
ROTATION
...MOVE TO THE OUTSIDE, GREATLY ENHANCING DEFENSIVE STABILITY!
CENTRIPETAL FORCE
WOW! IT'S A BEYBLADE BUILT FOR PERFECT DEFENSE!
SO ***THAT'S*** WHY HE'S SURE HE'LL WIN!

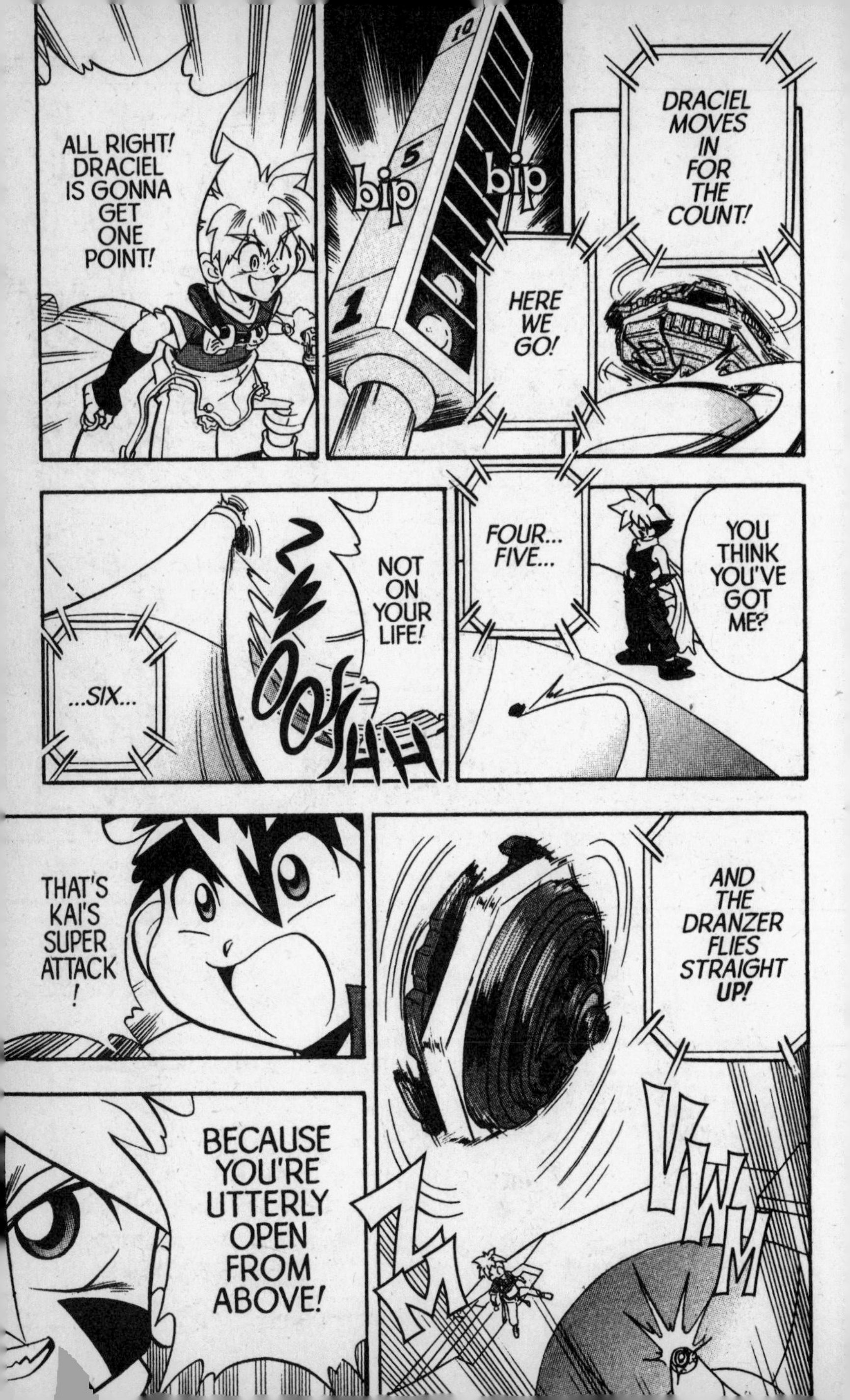
DRACIEL MOVES IN FOR THE COUNT!
HERE WE GO!
bip
bip
ALL RIGHT! DRACIEL IS GONNA GET ONE POINT!
YOU THINK YOU'VE GOT ME?
FOUR... FIVE...
NOT ON YOUR LIFE!
...SIX...
AND THE DRANZER FLIES STRAIGHT UP!
THAT'S KAI'S SUPER ATTACK!
BECAUSE YOU'RE UTTERLY OPEN FROM ABOVE!

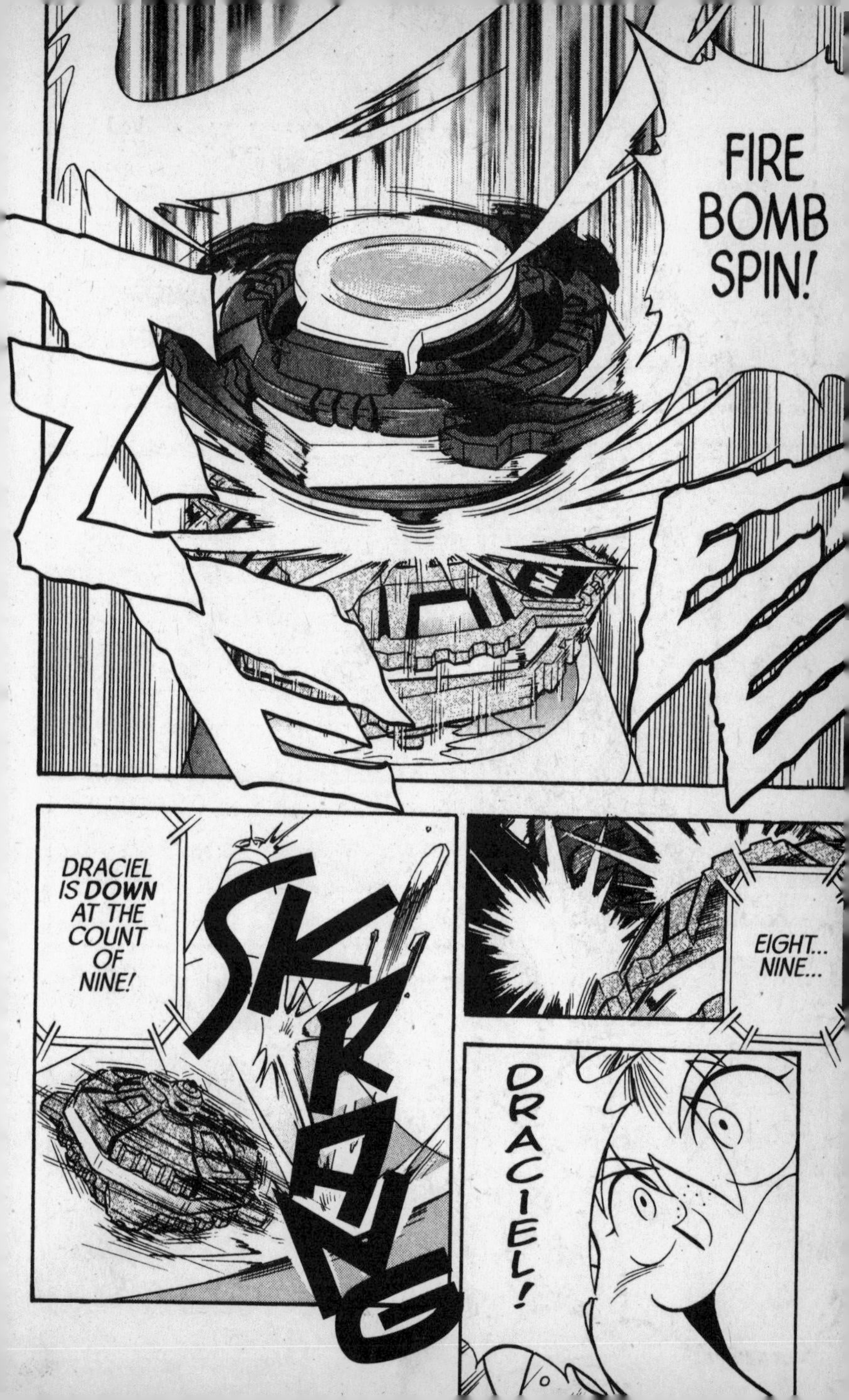
FIRE BOMB SPIN!
EIGHT... NINE...
DRACIEL IS DOWN AT THE COUNT OF NINE!
DRACIEL!

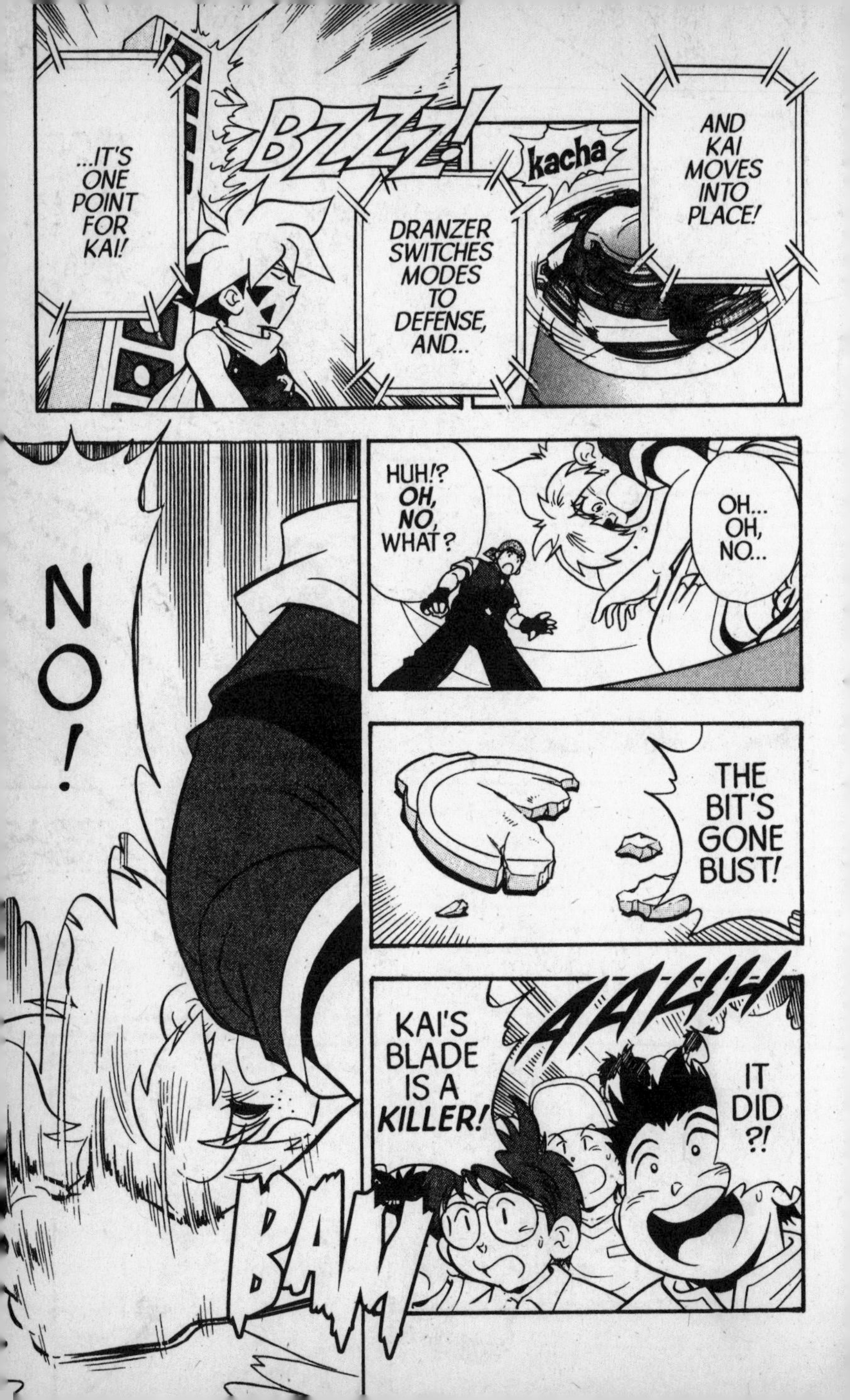
AND KAI MOVES INTO PLACE!
kacha
DRANZER SWITCHES MODES TO DEFENSE, AND...
BZZZ!
...IT'S ONE POINT FOR KAI!
OH... OH, NO...
HUH!? OH, NO, WHAT?
THE BIT'S GONE BUST!
AAHH
IT DID?!
KAI'S BLADE IS A KILLER!
NO!
BAM

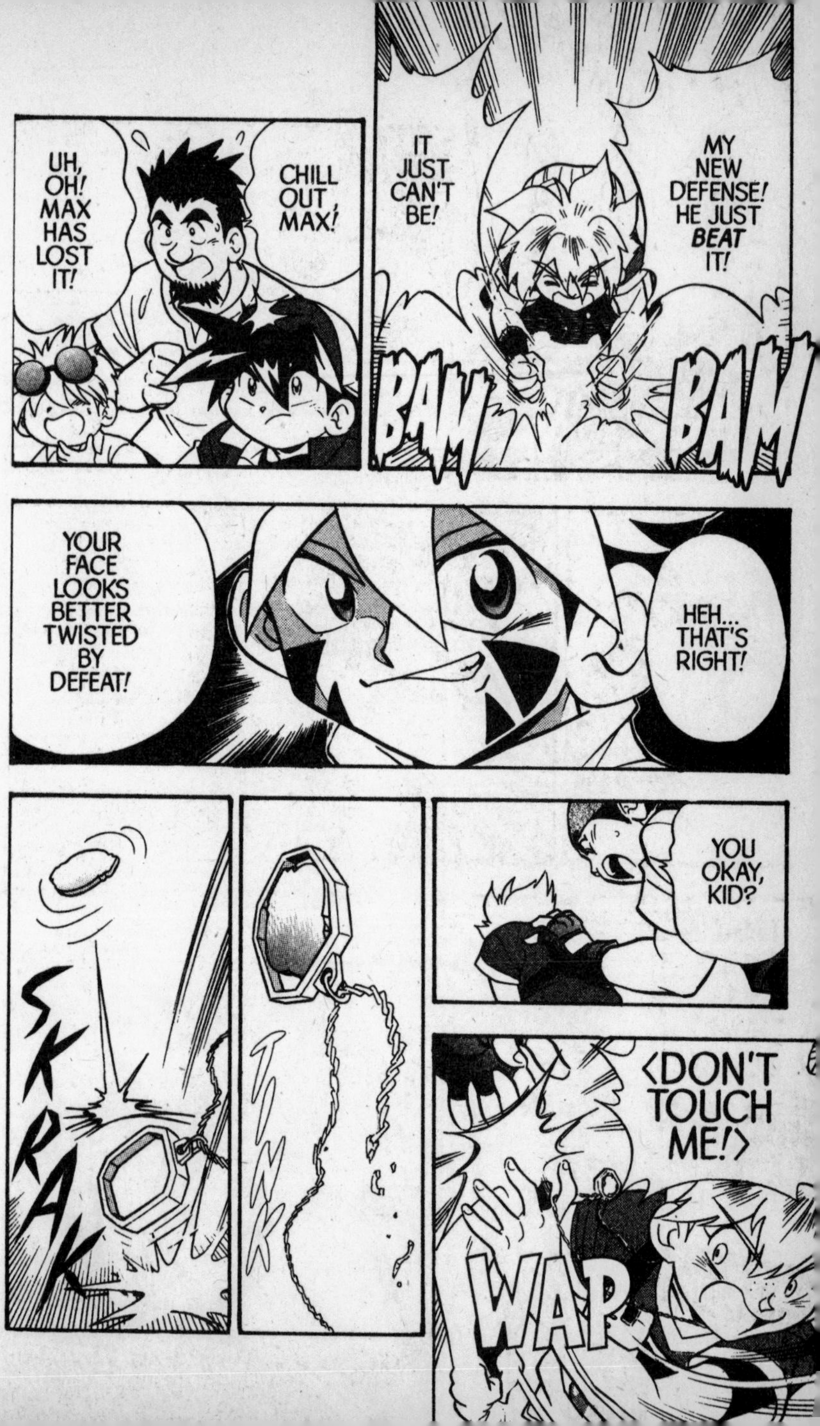
MY NEW DEFENSE! HE JUST *BEAT* IT!
IT JUST CAN'T BE!
BAM
BAM
CHILL OUT, MAX!
UH, OH! MAX HAS LOST IT!
HEH... THAT'S RIGHT!
YOUR FACE LOOKS BETTER TWISTED BY DEFEAT!
YOU OKAY, KID?
<DON'T TOUCH ME!>
WAP
TINK
SKRAK

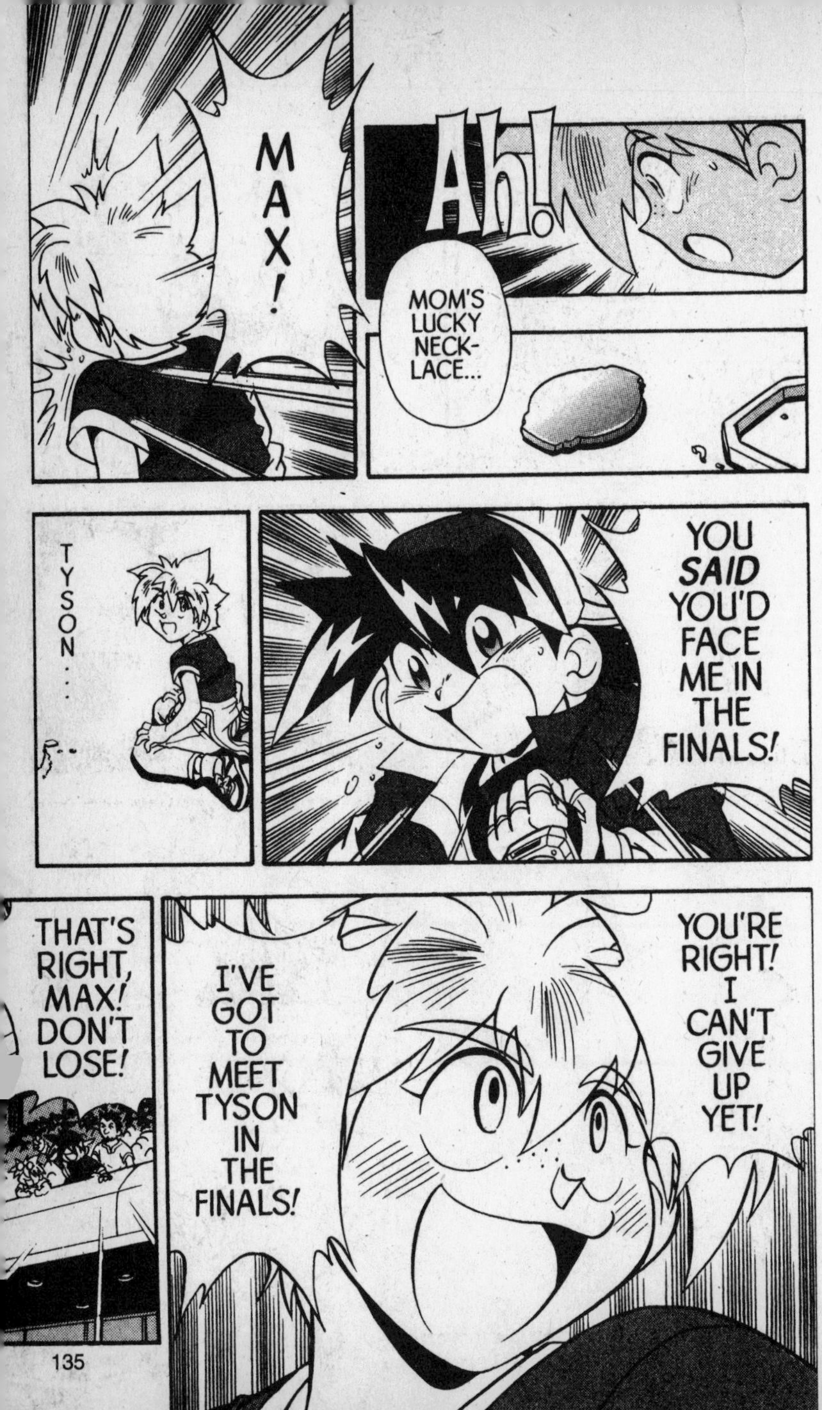
Ah!
MOM'S LUCKY NECK-LACE...
MAX!
YOU SAID YOU'D FACE ME IN THE FINALS!
TYSON...
YOU'RE RIGHT! I CAN'T GIVE UP YET!
I'VE GOT TO MEET TYSON IN THE FINALS!
THAT'S RIGHT, MAX! DON'T LOSE!

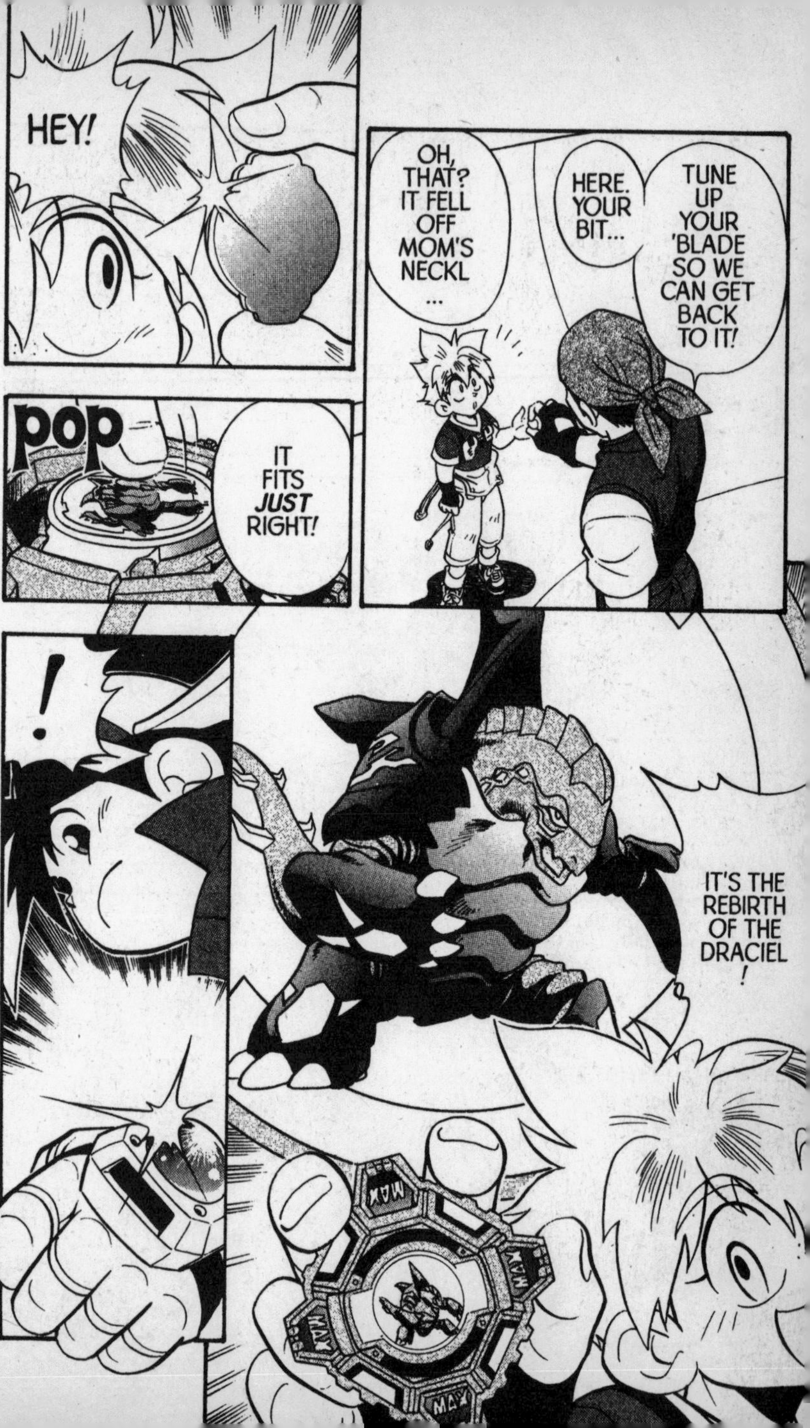
HEY!
TUNE UP YOUR 'BLADE SO WE CAN GET BACK TO IT!
HERE. YOUR BIT...
OH, THAT? IT FELL OFF MOM'S NECKL...
pop
IT FITS ***JUST*** RIGHT!
IT'S THE REBIRTH OF THE DRACIEL!
!
MAX

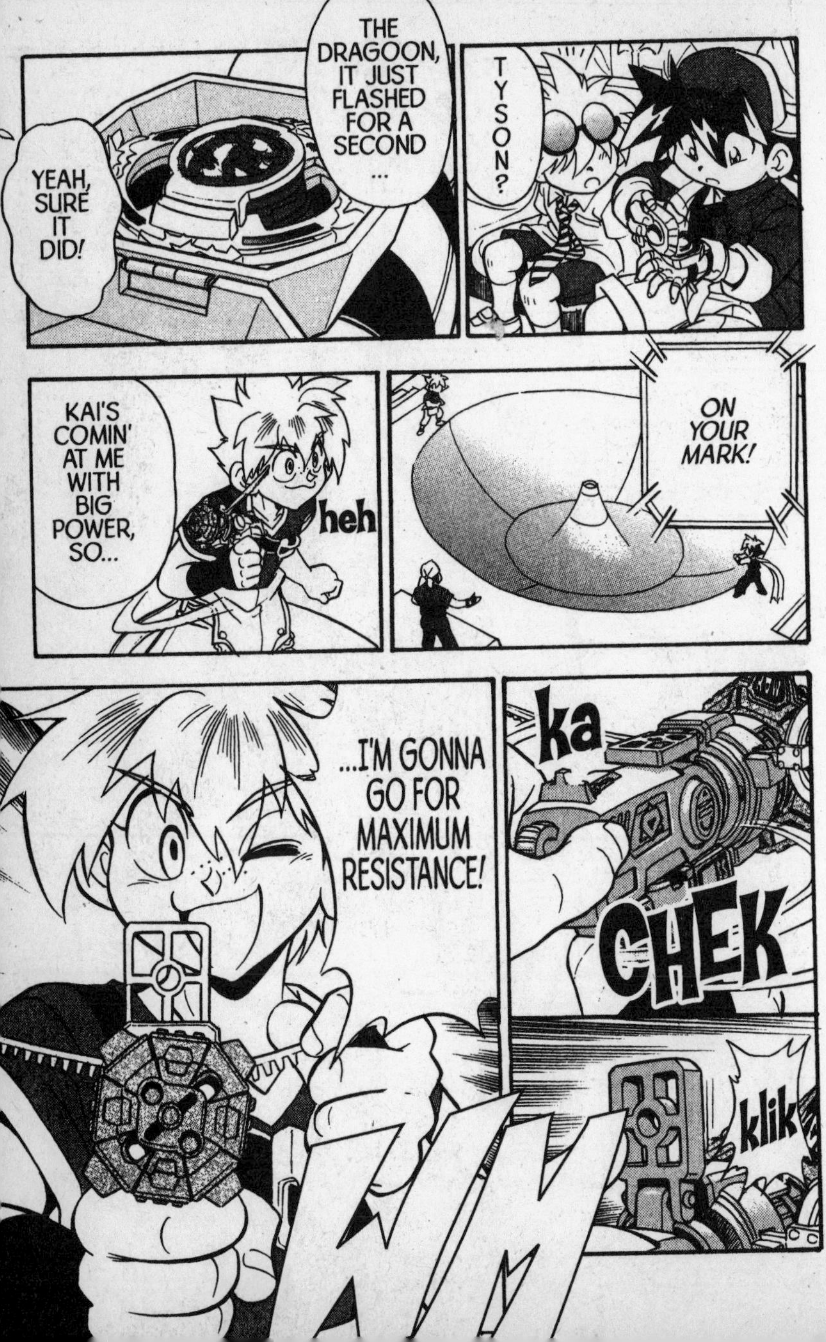
TYSON?
THE DRAGOON, IT JUST FLASHED FOR A SECOND ...
YEAH, SURE IT DID!
ON YOUR MARK!
KAI'S COMIN' AT ME WITH BIG POWER, SO...
heh
ka
CHEK
klik
...I'M GONNA GO FOR MAXIMUM RESISTANCE!

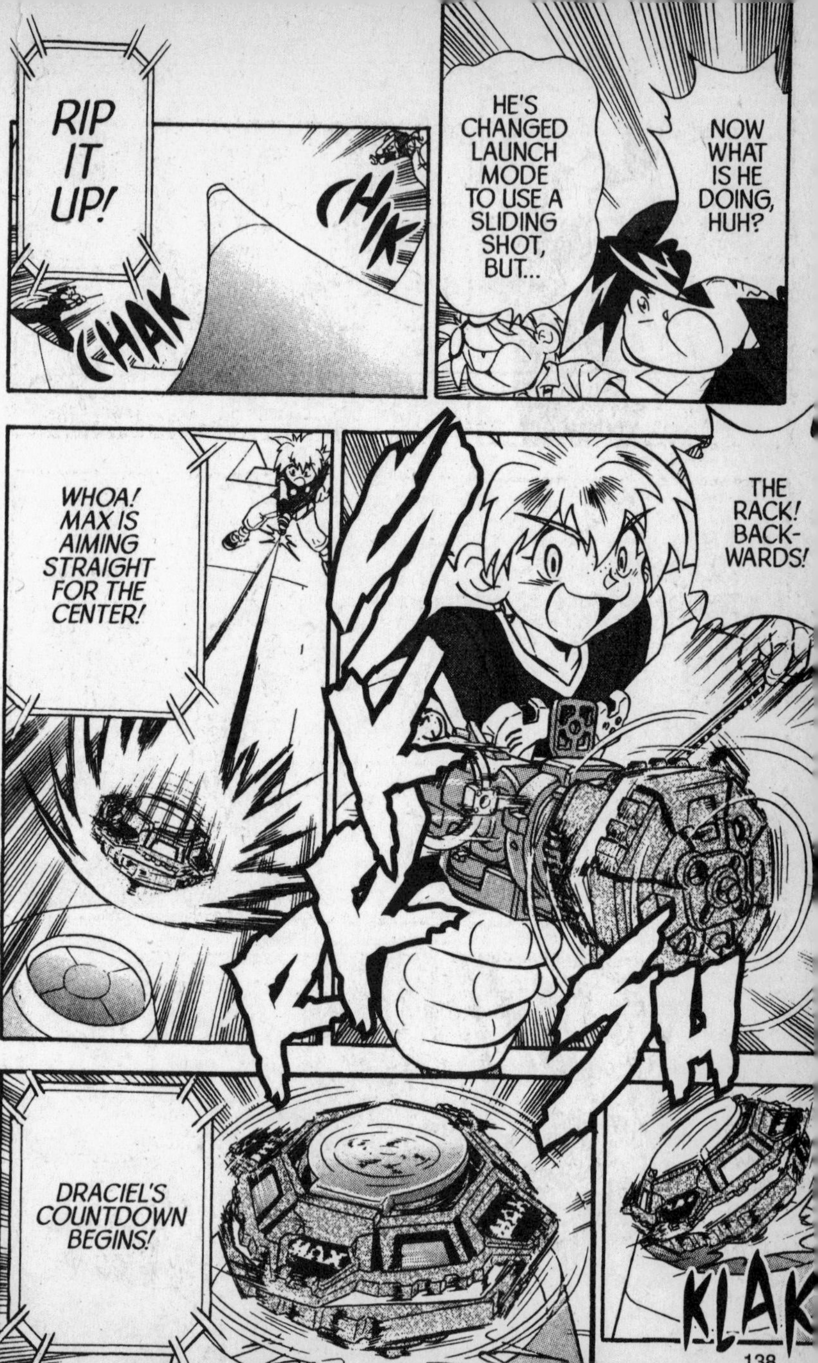
NOW WHAT IS HE DOING, HUH?
HE'S CHANGED LAUNCH MODE TO USE A SLIDING SHOT, BUT...
RIP IT UP!
CHIK
CHAK
THE RACK! BACKWARDS!
WHOA! MAX IS AIMING STRAIGHT FOR THE CENTER!
KLAK
DRACIEL'S COUNTDOWN BEGINS!

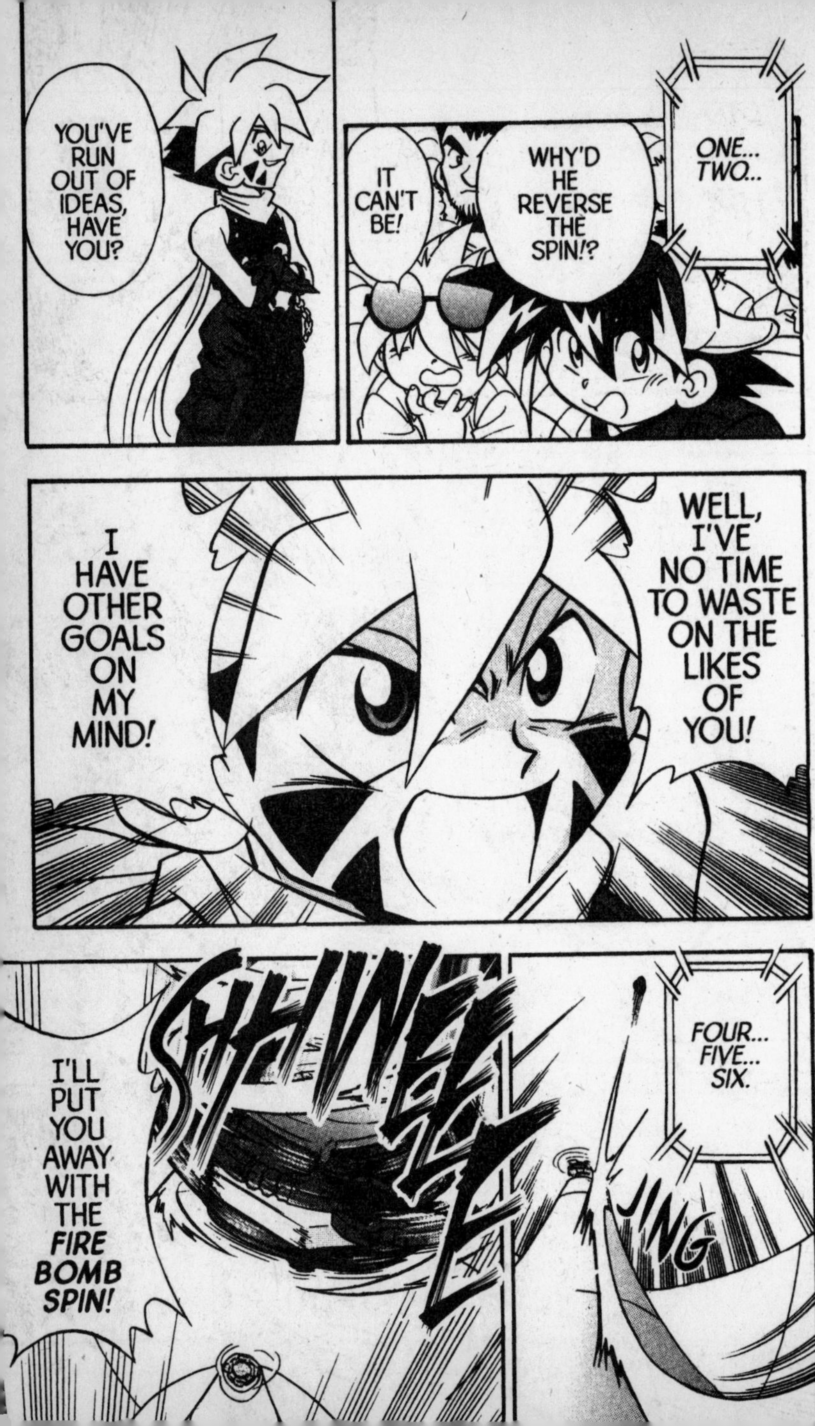
ONE... TWO...
WHY'D HE REVERSE THE SPIN!?
IT CAN'T BE!
YOU'VE RUN OUT OF IDEAS, HAVE YOU?
WELL, I'VE NO TIME TO WASTE ON THE LIKES OF YOU!
I HAVE OTHER GOALS ON MY MIND!
FOUR... FIVE... SIX.
JING
I'LL PUT YOU AWAY WITH THE *FIRE BOMB SPIN!*

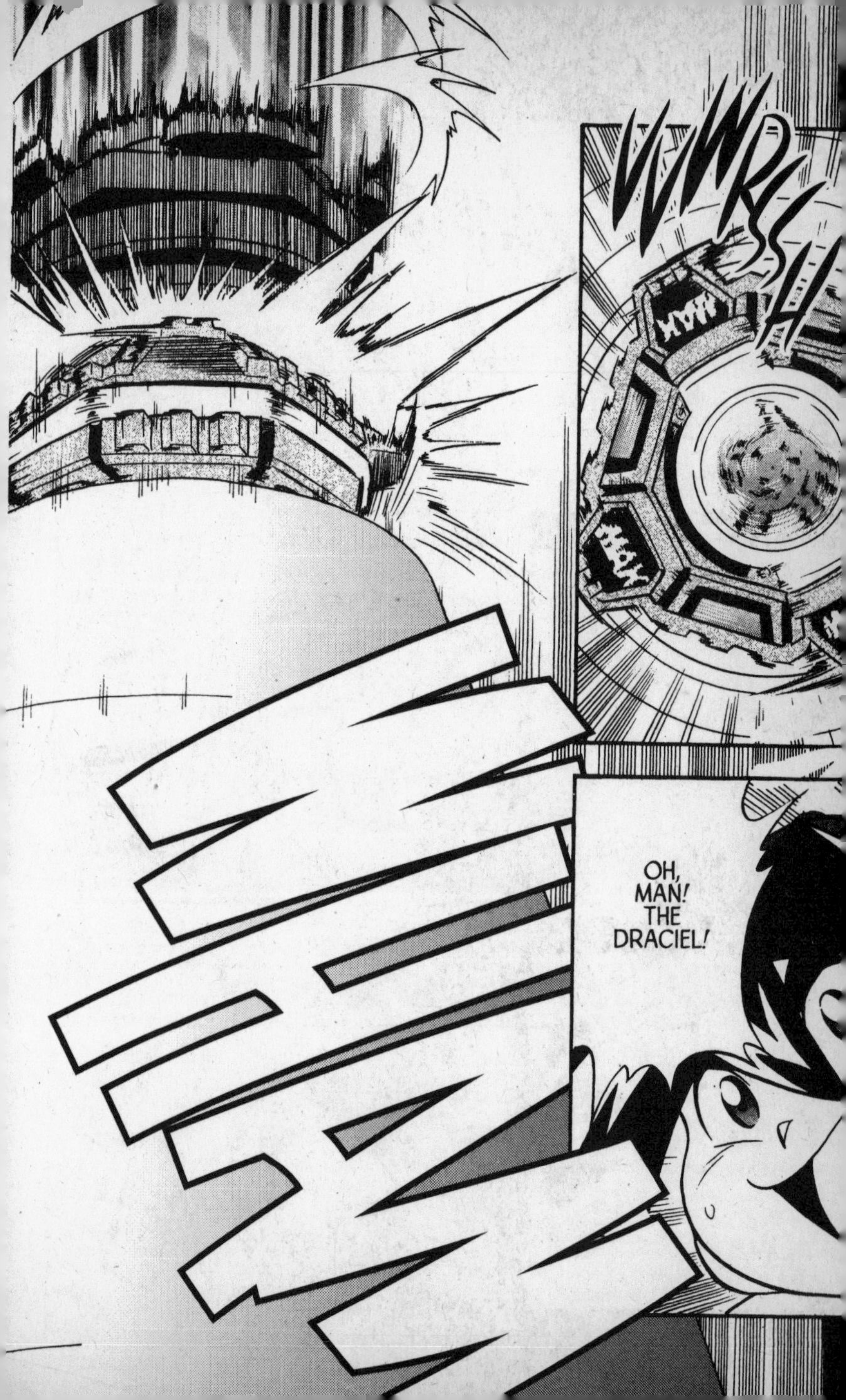
OH, MAN! THE DRACIEL!

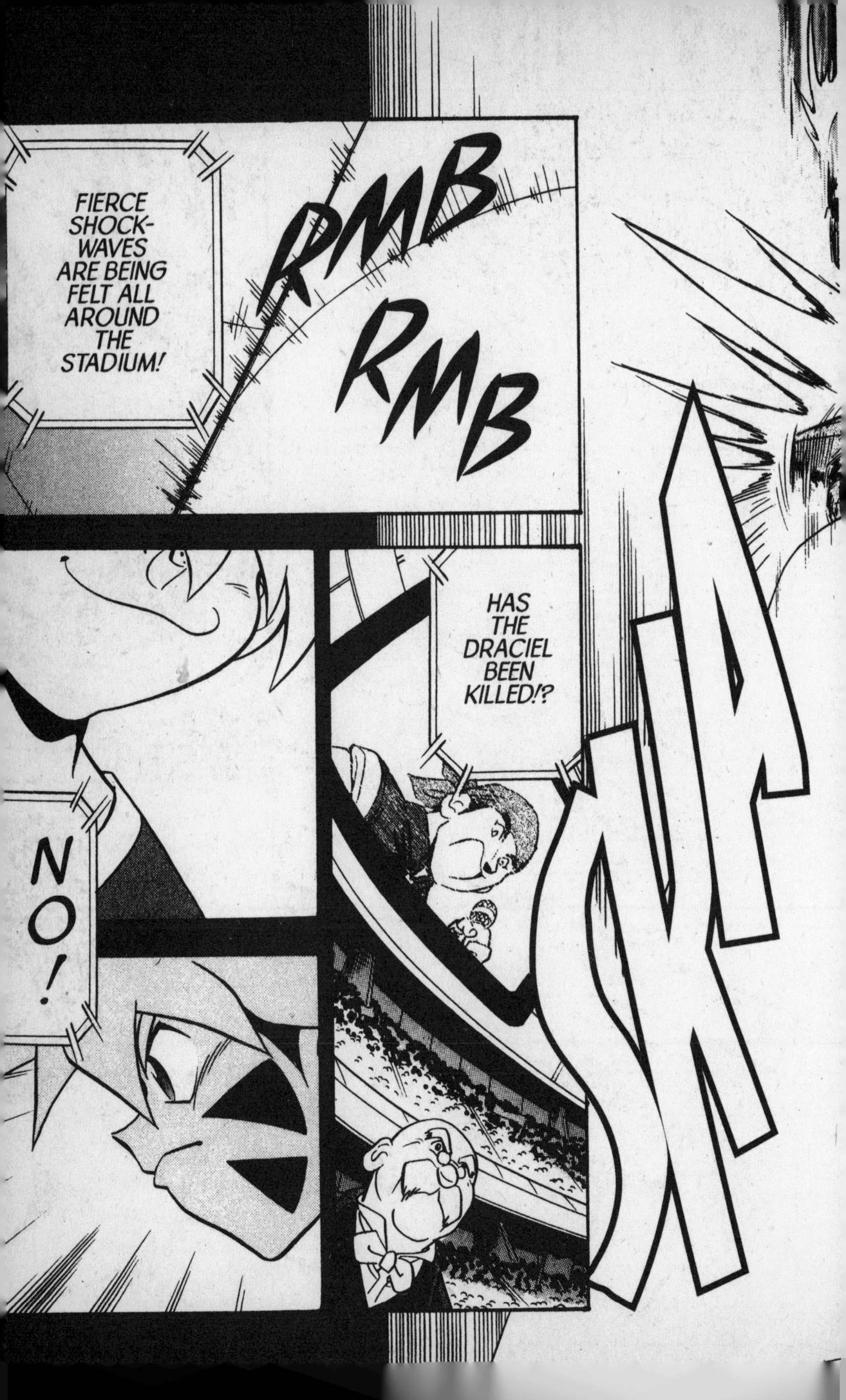

RMB
RMB
FIERCE SHOCK-WAVES ARE BEING FELT ALL AROUND THE STADIUM!
HAS THE DRACIEL BEEN KILLED!?
NO!

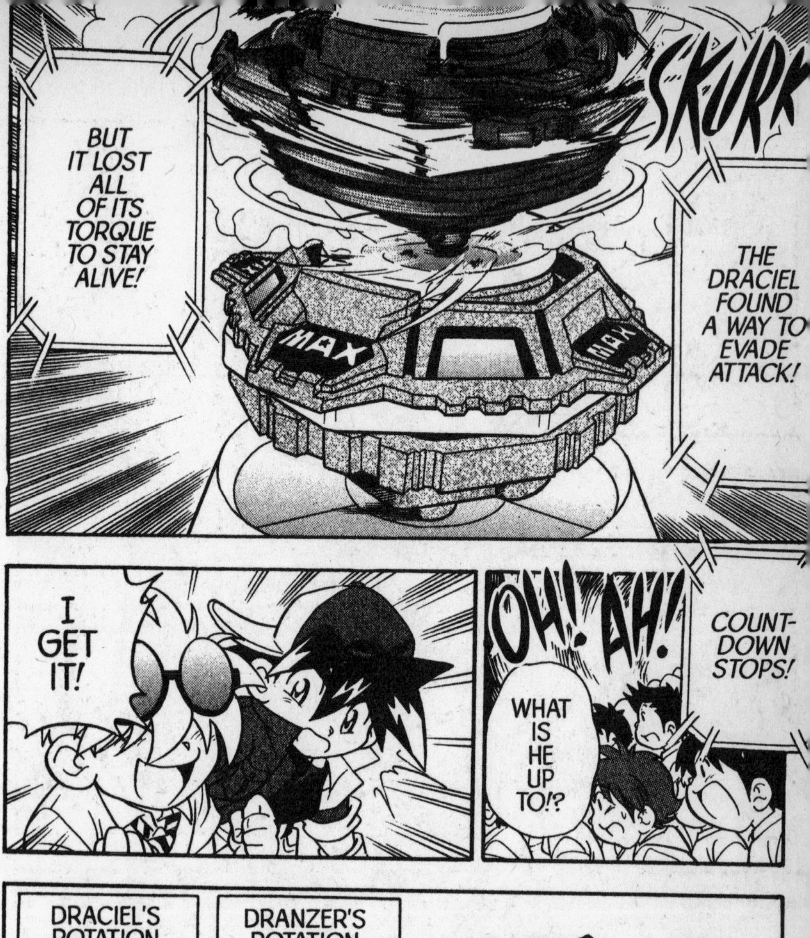
SKURK
THE DRACIEL FOUND A WAY TO EVADE ATTACK!
BUT IT LOST ALL OF ITS TORQUE TO STAY ALIVE!
COUNT-DOWN STOPS!
OH! AH!
WHAT IS HE UP TO!?
I GET IT!
THE DRACIEL STOOD UP TO DRANZER'S FIERCE ATTACK WITH AN OPPOSING SPIN!
DRANZER
DRACIEL
DRANZER'S ROTATION
DRACIEL'S ROTATION
gwm
IN OTHER WORDS, DRACIEL GAVE UP ITS OWN TORQUE IN ORDER TO ABSORB THE FORCE OF DRANZER'S SPIN!

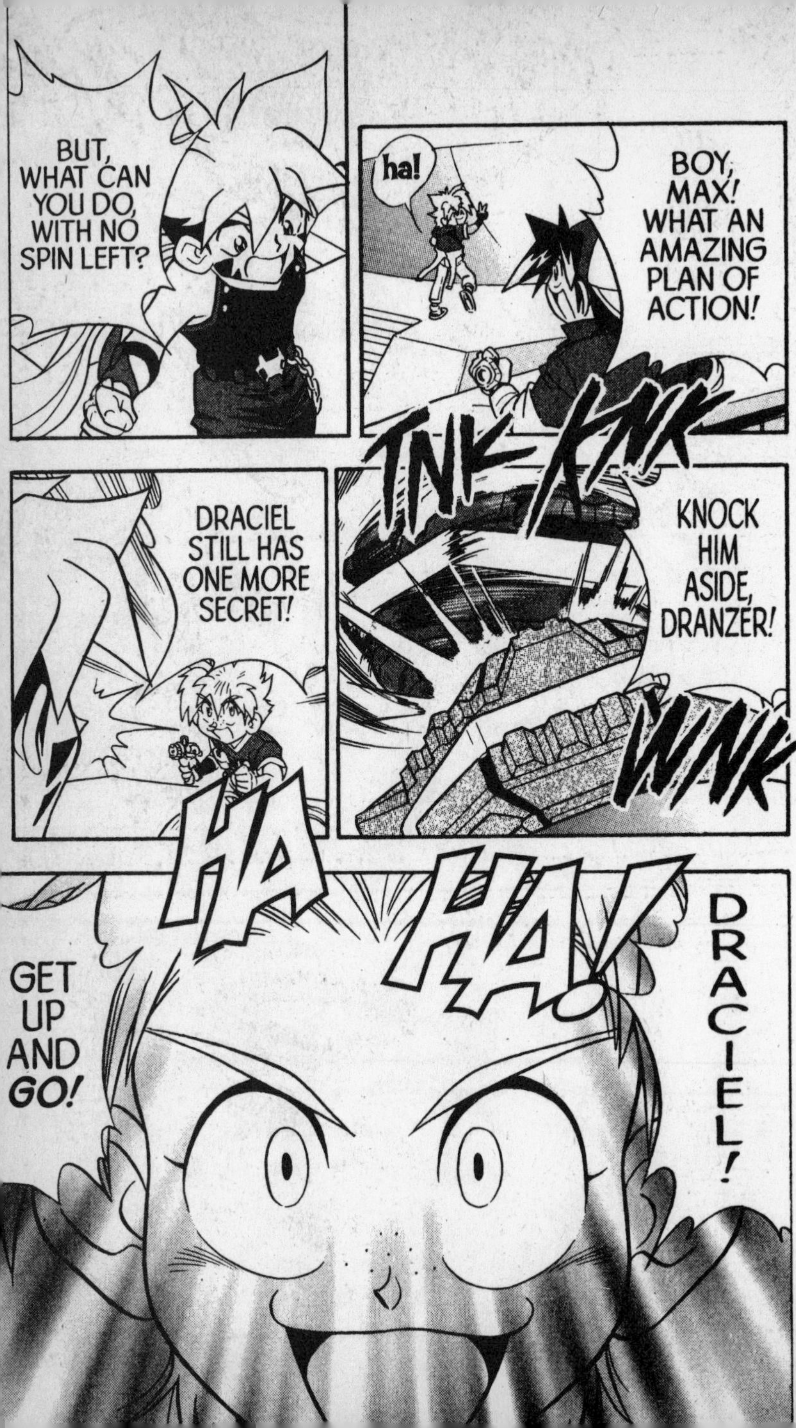
BOY, MAX! WHAT AN AMAZING PLAN OF ACTION!
ha!
BUT, WHAT CAN YOU DO, WITH NO SPIN LEFT?
TNK KNK
KNOCK HIM ASIDE, DRANZER!
WNK
DRACIEL STILL HAS ONE MORE SECRET!
HA HA!
DRACIEL!
GET UP AND GO!

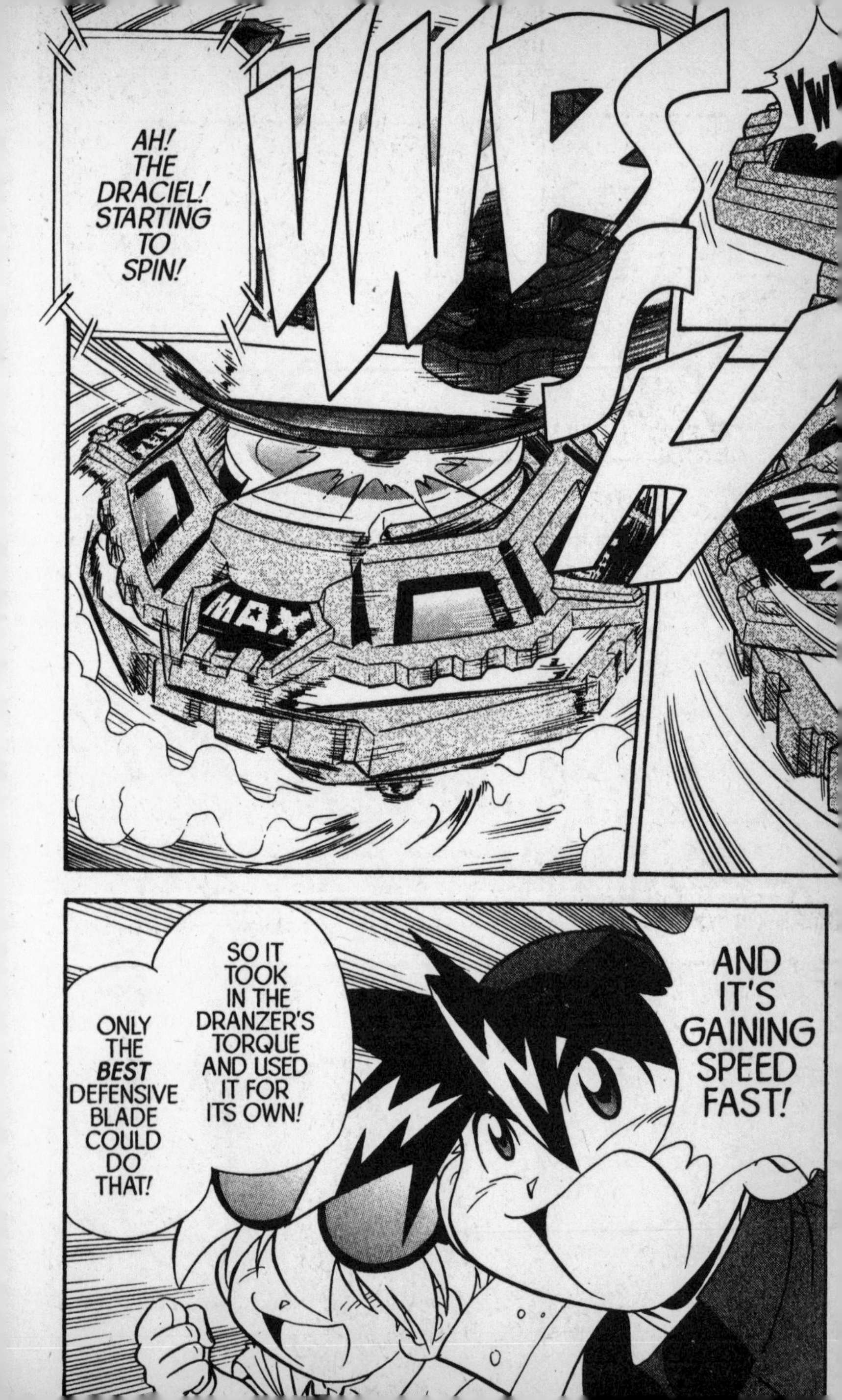
AH! THE DRACIEL! STARTING TO SPIN!
AND IT'S GAINING SPEED FAST!
SO IT TOOK IN THE DRANZER'S TORQUE AND USED IT FOR ITS OWN!
ONLY THE *BEST* DEFENSIVE BLADE COULD DO THAT!

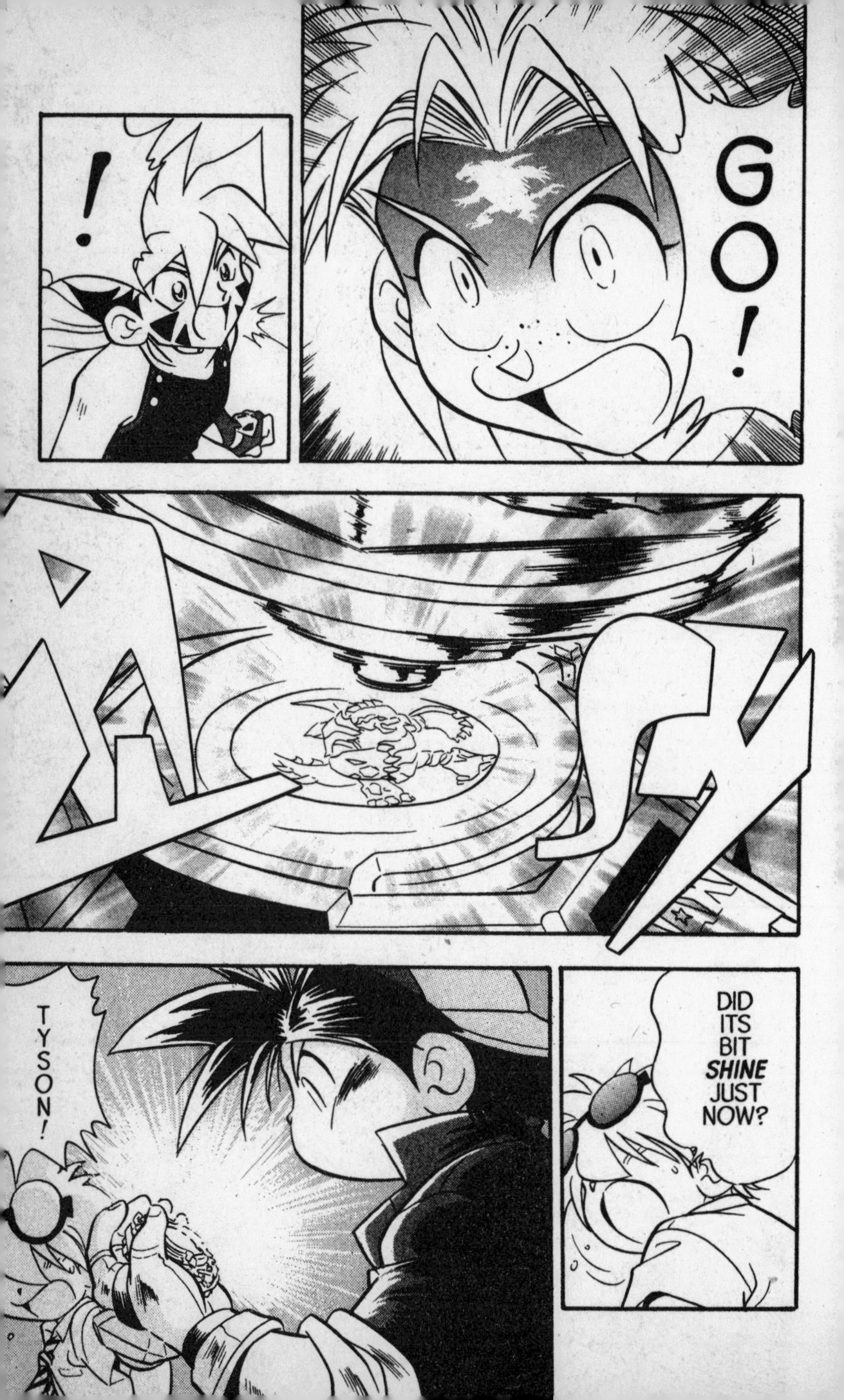
GO!
!
DID ITS BIT SHINE JUST NOW?
TYSON!

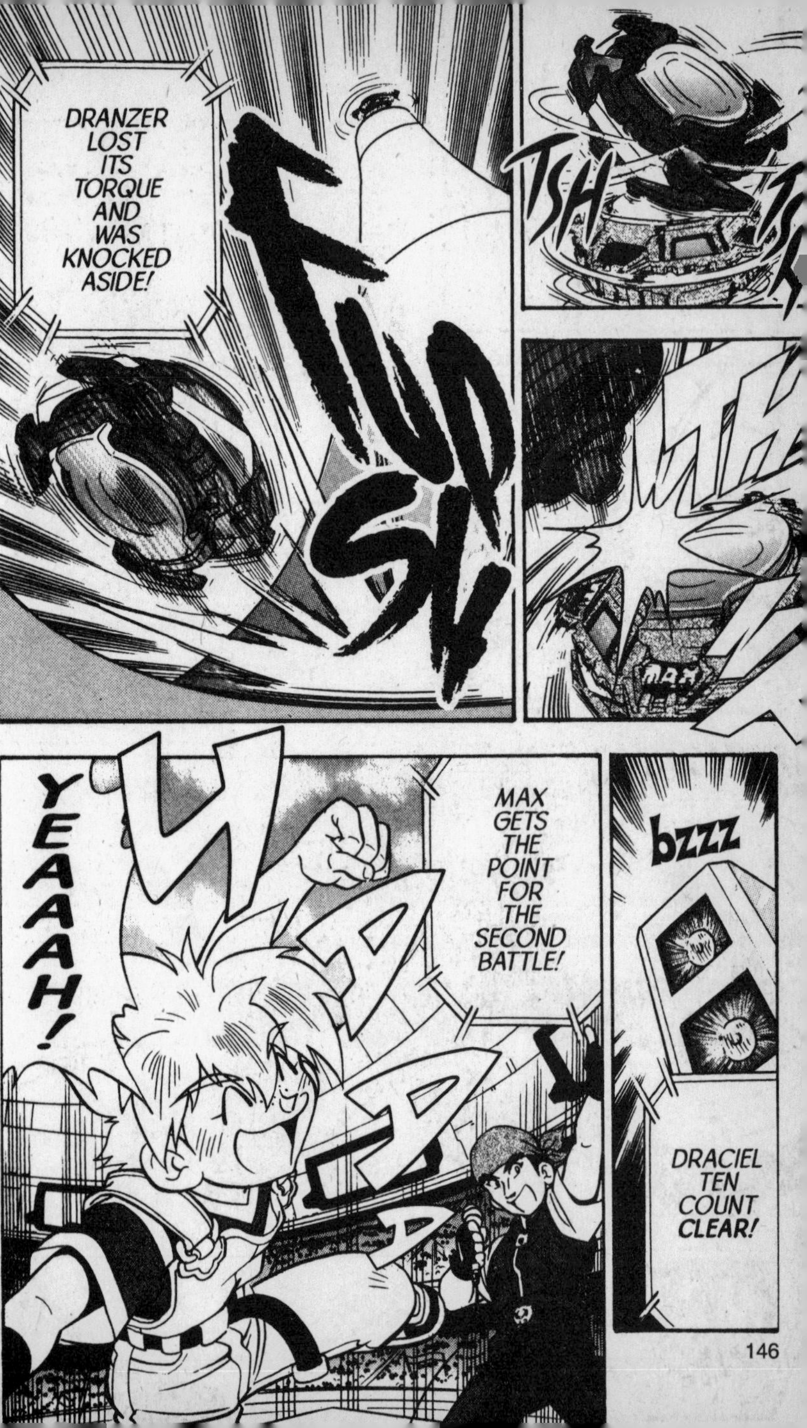

TSH TSK
DRANZER LOST ITS TORQUE AND WAS KNOCKED ASIDE!
bzzz
DRACIEL TEN COUNT CLEAR!
MAX GETS THE POINT FOR THE SECOND BATTLE!
YEAAAAH!

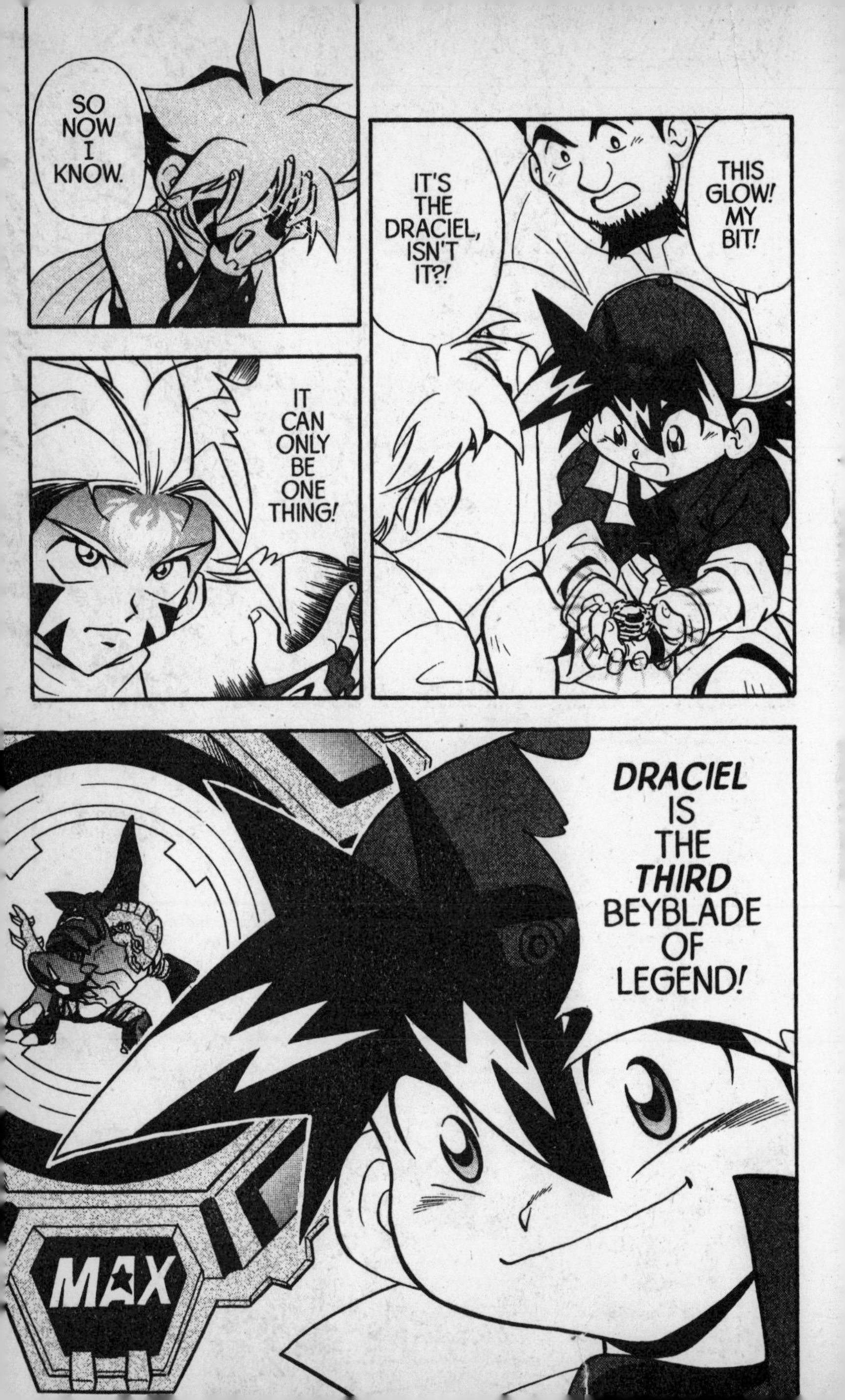
THIS GLOW! MY BIT!
IT'S THE DRACIEL, ISN'T IT?!
SO NOW I KNOW.
IT CAN ONLY BE ONE THING!
DRACIEL IS THE THIRD BEYBLADE OF LEGEND!
MAX

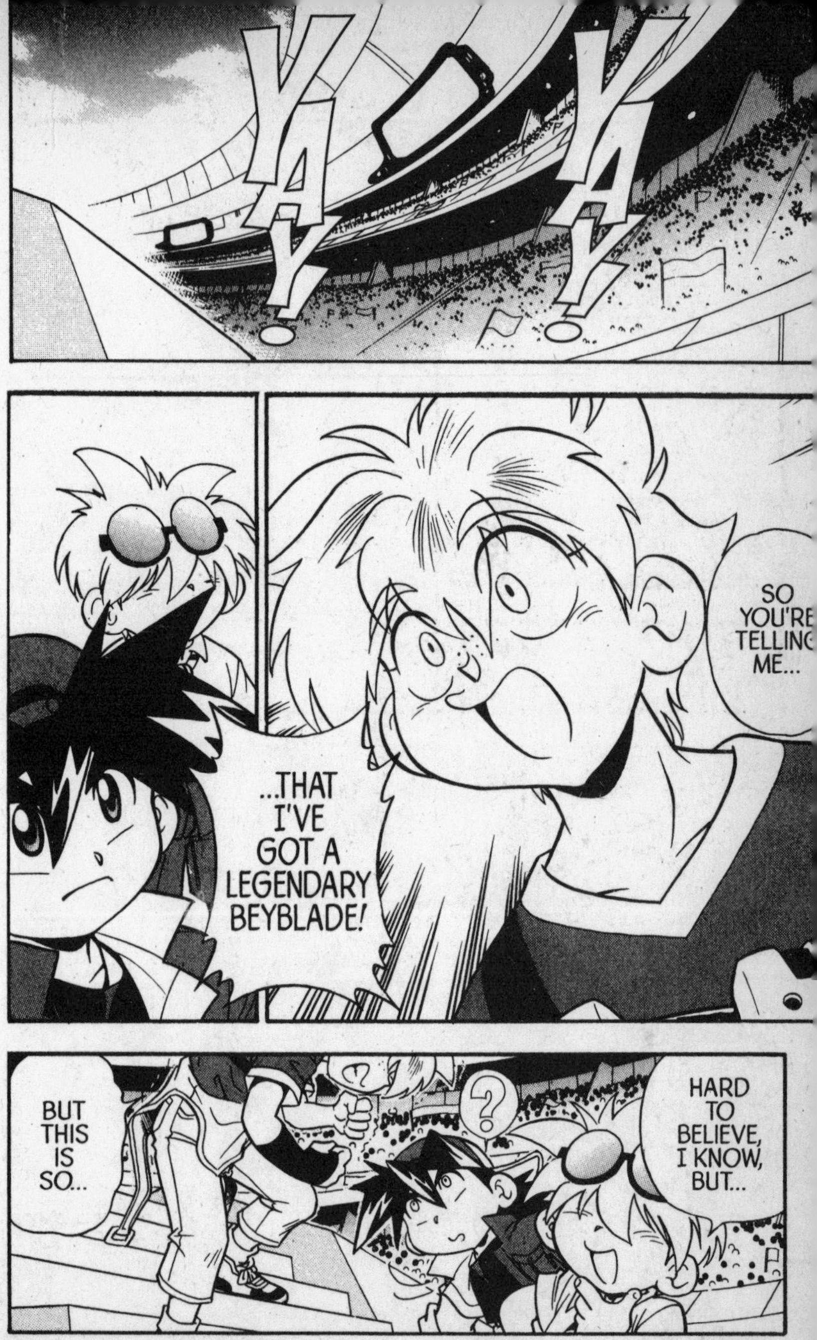
YAY!
YAY!
SO YOU'RE TELLING ME...
...THAT I'VE GOT A LEGENDARY BEYBLADE!
HARD TO BELIEVE, I KNOW, BUT...
?
BUT THIS IS SO...

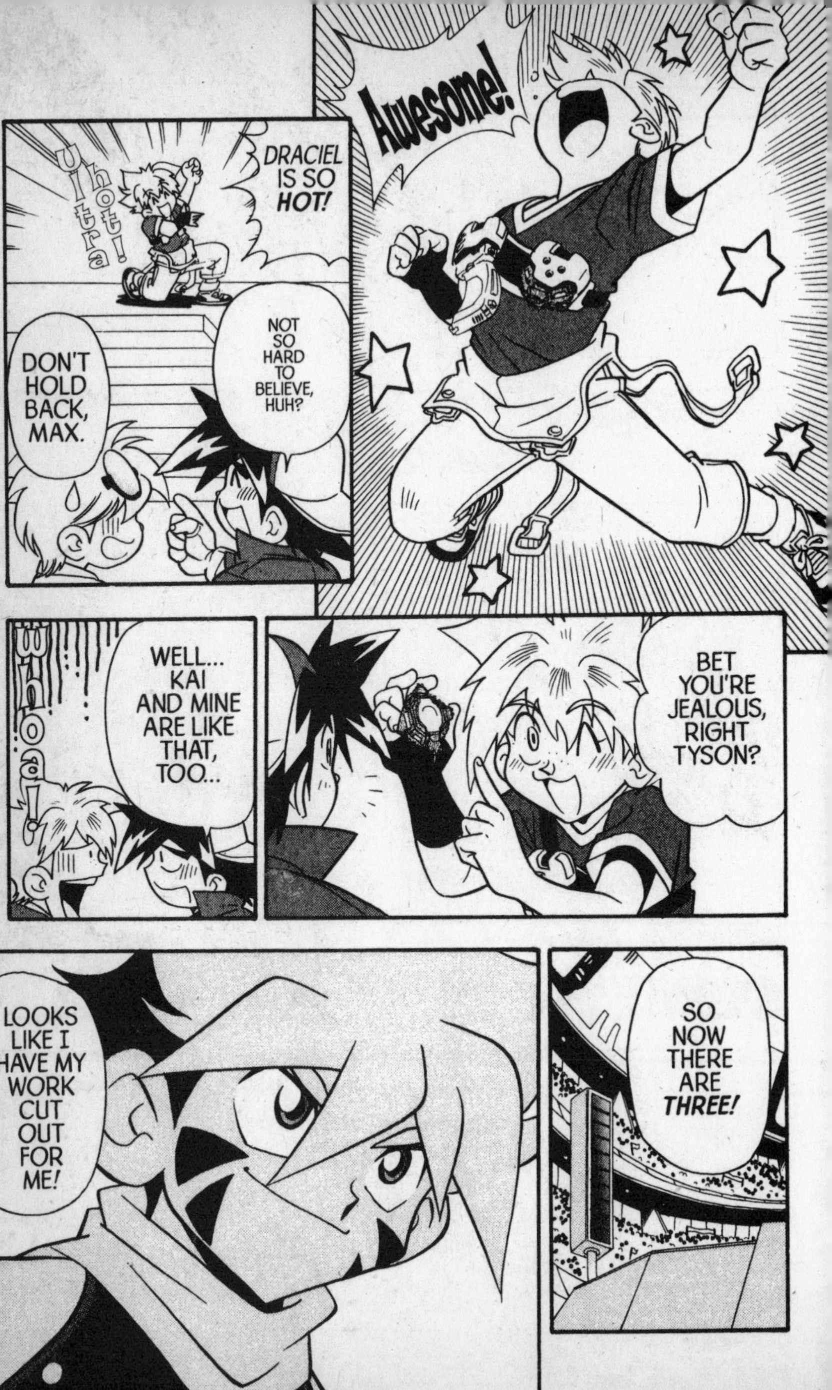
Awesome!
DRACIEL IS SO *HOT!*
Ultra hot!
NOT SO HARD TO BELIEVE, HUH?
DON'T HOLD BACK, MAX.
BET YOU'RE JEALOUS, RIGHT TYSON?
WELL... KAI AND MINE ARE LIKE THAT, TOO...
Whoa!
SO NOW THERE ARE *THREE!*
LOOKS LIKE I HAVE MY WORK CUT OUT FOR ME!

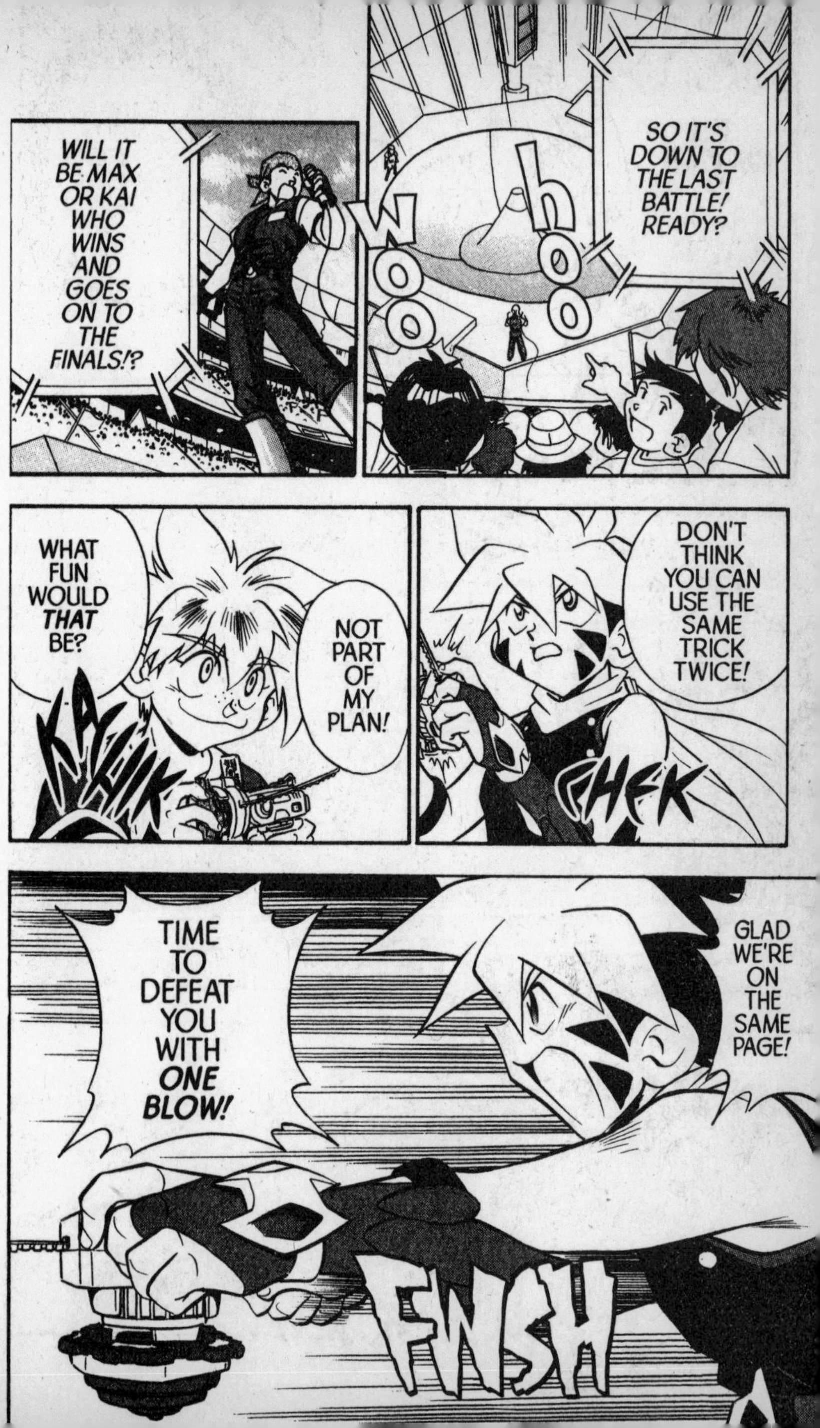
SO IT'S DOWN TO THE LAST BATTLE! READY?
Woohoo
WILL IT BE MAX OR KAI WHO WINS AND GOES ON TO THE FINALS!?
DON'T THINK YOU CAN USE THE SAME TRICK TWICE!
CHEK
NOT PART OF MY PLAN!
WHAT FUN WOULD *THAT* BE?
KA-CHIK
GLAD WE'RE ON THE SAME PAGE!
TIME TO DEFEAT YOU WITH *ONE BLOW!*
FWSH

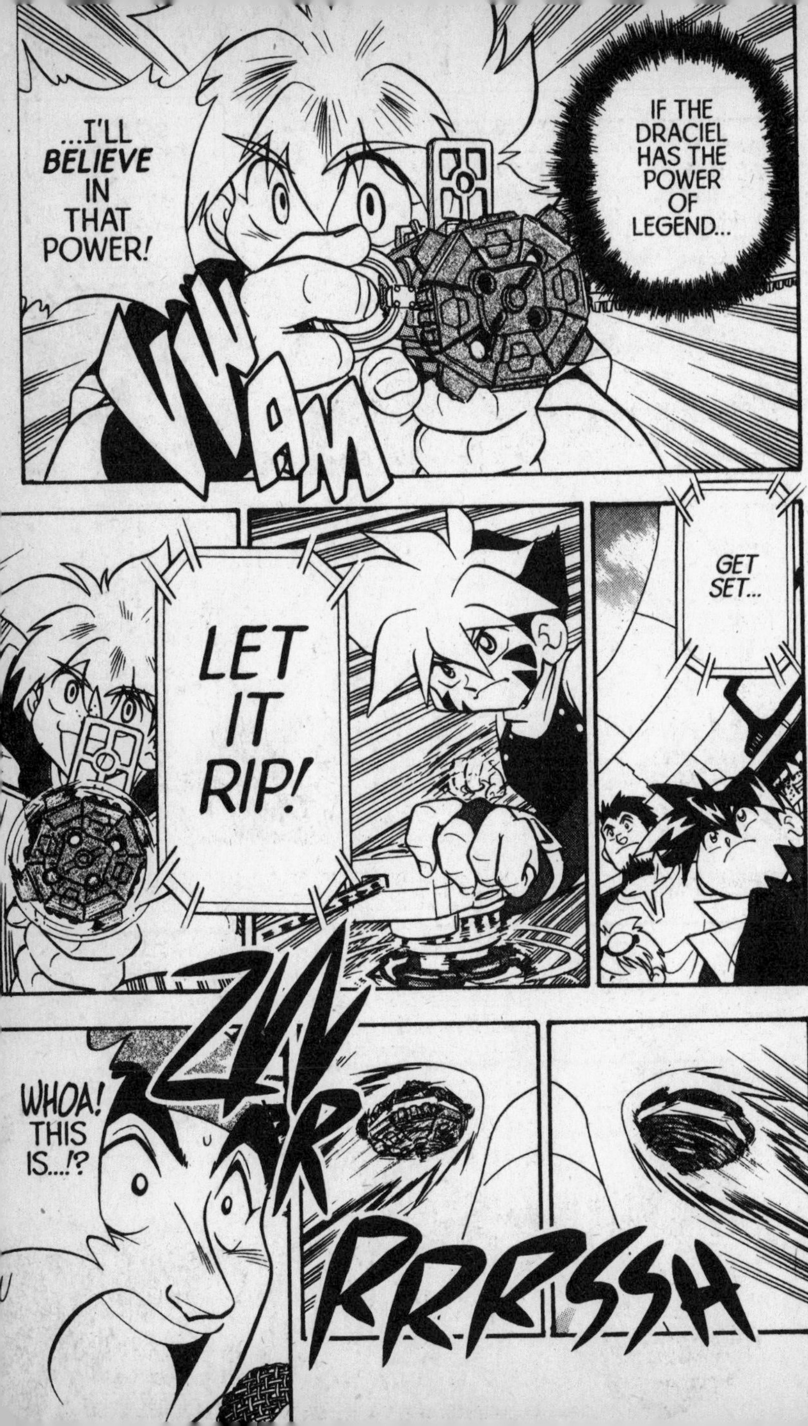
IF THE DRACIEL HAS THE POWER OF LEGEND...
...I'LL *BELIEVE* IN THAT POWER!
VWAM
GET SET...
LET IT RIP!
ZWR
WHOA! THIS IS...!?
RRRSSH

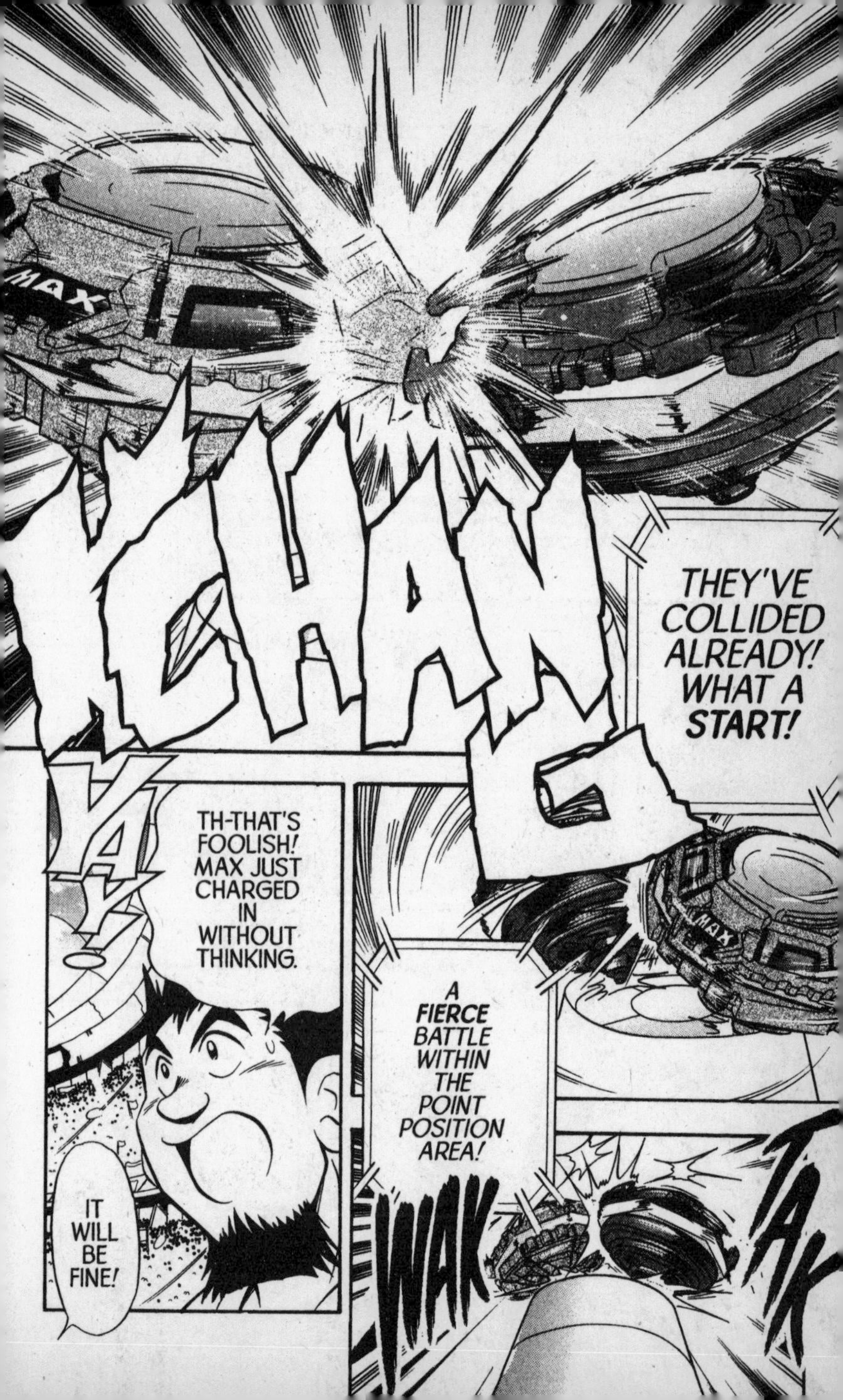
CHANG
THEY'VE COLLIDED ALREADY! WHAT A START!
A FIERCE BATTLE WITHIN THE POINT POSITION AREA!
WAK
TAK
TH-THAT'S FOOLISH! MAX JUST CHARGED IN WITHOUT THINKING.
IT WILL BE FINE!

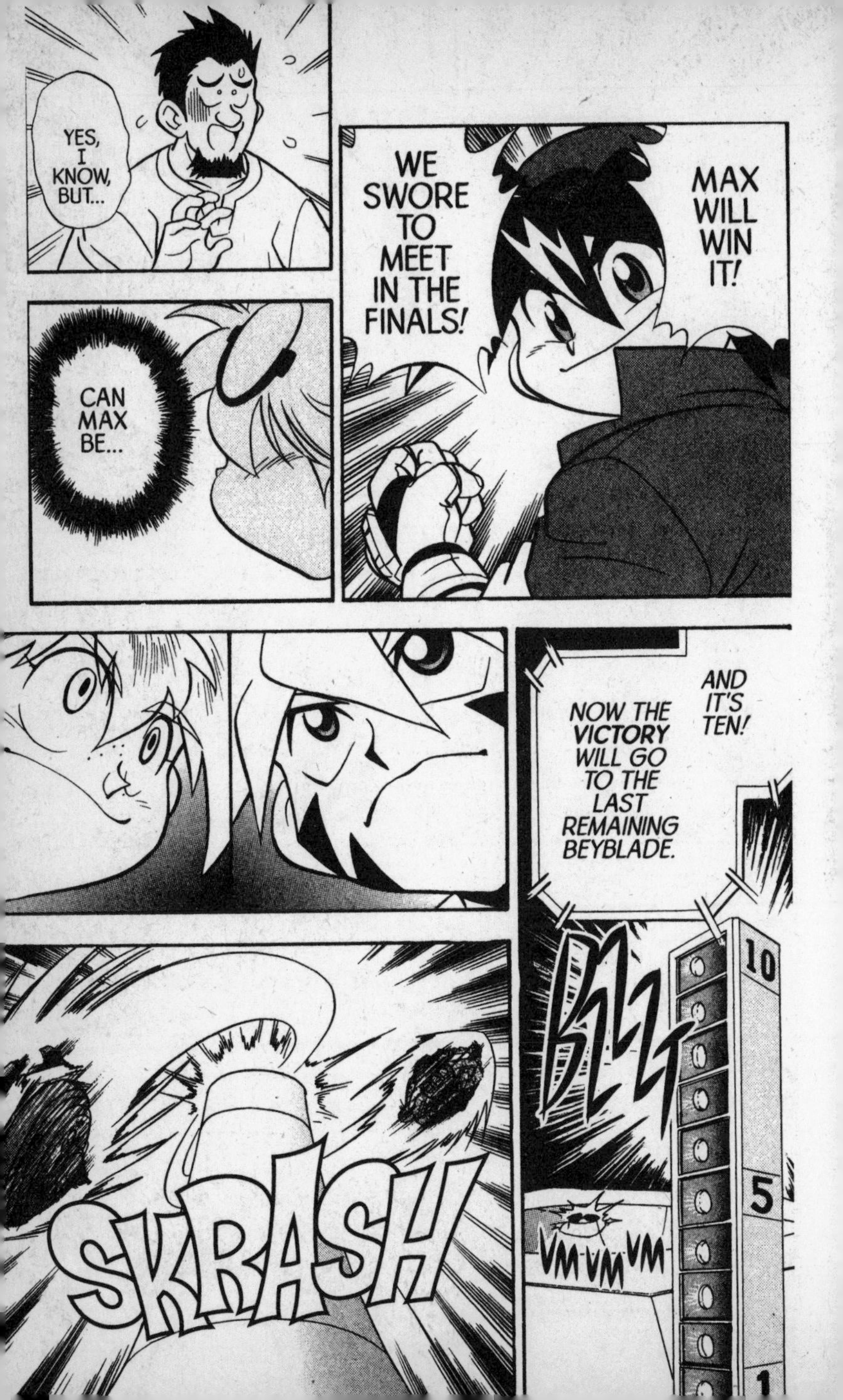
MAX WILL WIN IT!
WE SWORE TO MEET IN THE FINALS!
YES, I KNOW, BUT...
CAN MAX BE...
AND IT'S TEN!
NOW THE VICTORY WILL GO TO THE LAST REMAINING BEYBLADE.
10
5
1
VM VM VM
SKRASH

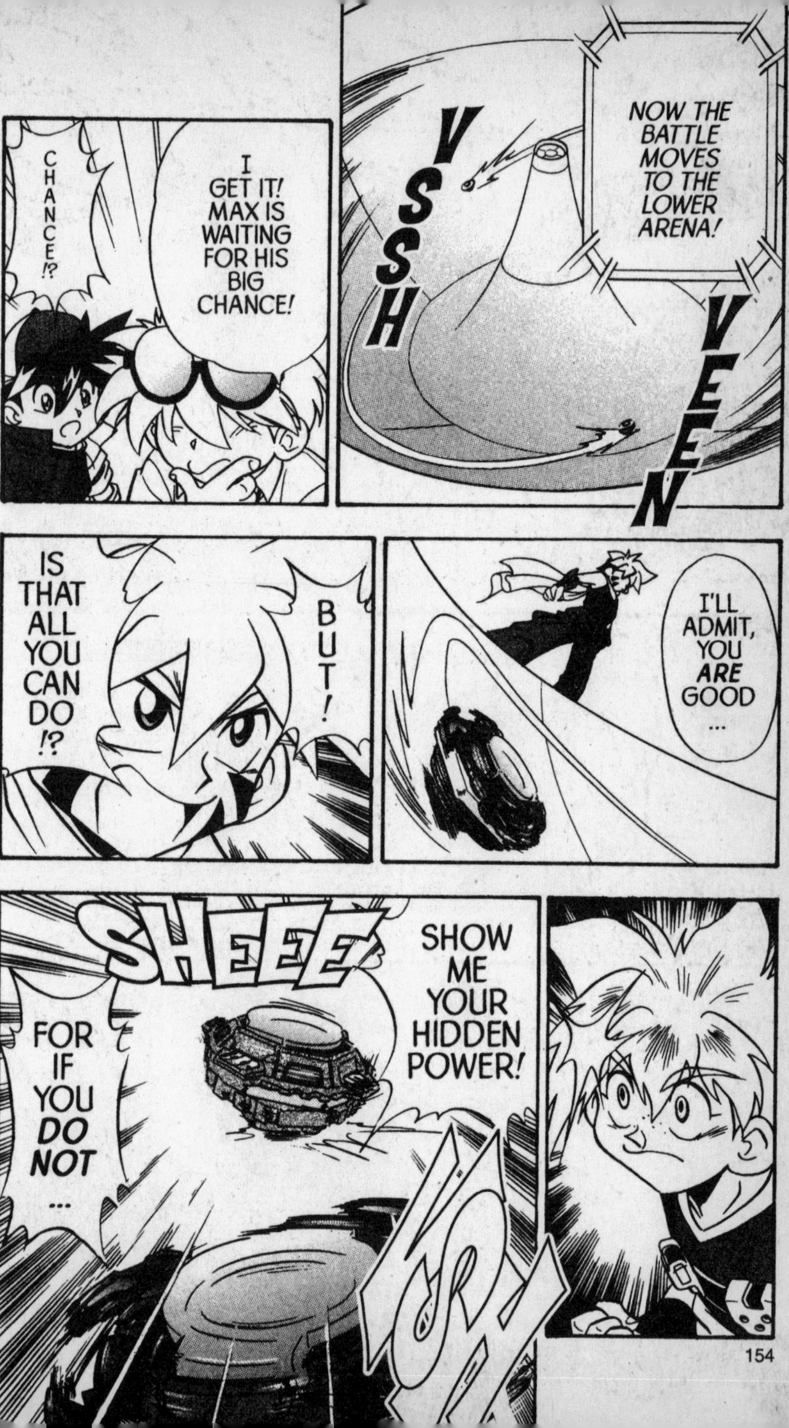
NOW THE BATTLE MOVES TO THE LOWER ARENA!
VSSH
VEEEN
I GET IT! MAX IS WAITING FOR HIS BIG CHANCE!
CHANCE!?
I'LL ADMIT, YOU *ARE* GOOD ...
BUT!
IS THAT ALL YOU CAN DO!?
SHOW ME YOUR HIDDEN POWER!
SHEEE
FOR IF YOU *DO NOT* ...

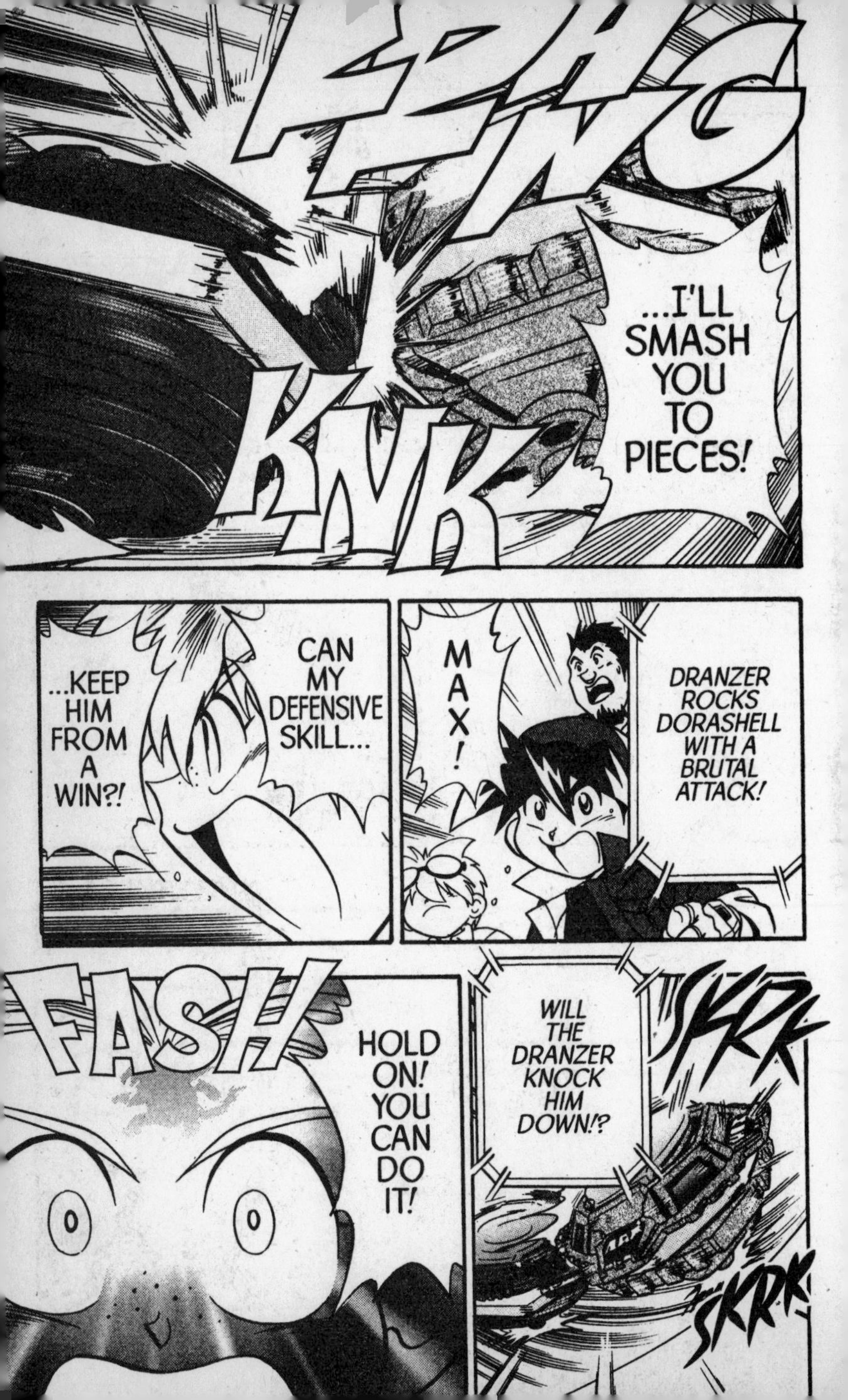
KNK
...I'LL SMASH YOU TO PIECES!
DRANZER ROCKS DORASHELL WITH A BRUTAL ATTACK!
MAX!
CAN MY DEFENSIVE SKILL...
...KEEP HIM FROM A WIN?!
SKRK
WILL THE DRANZER KNOCK HIM DOWN!?
SKRK
FASH
HOLD ON! YOU CAN DO IT!

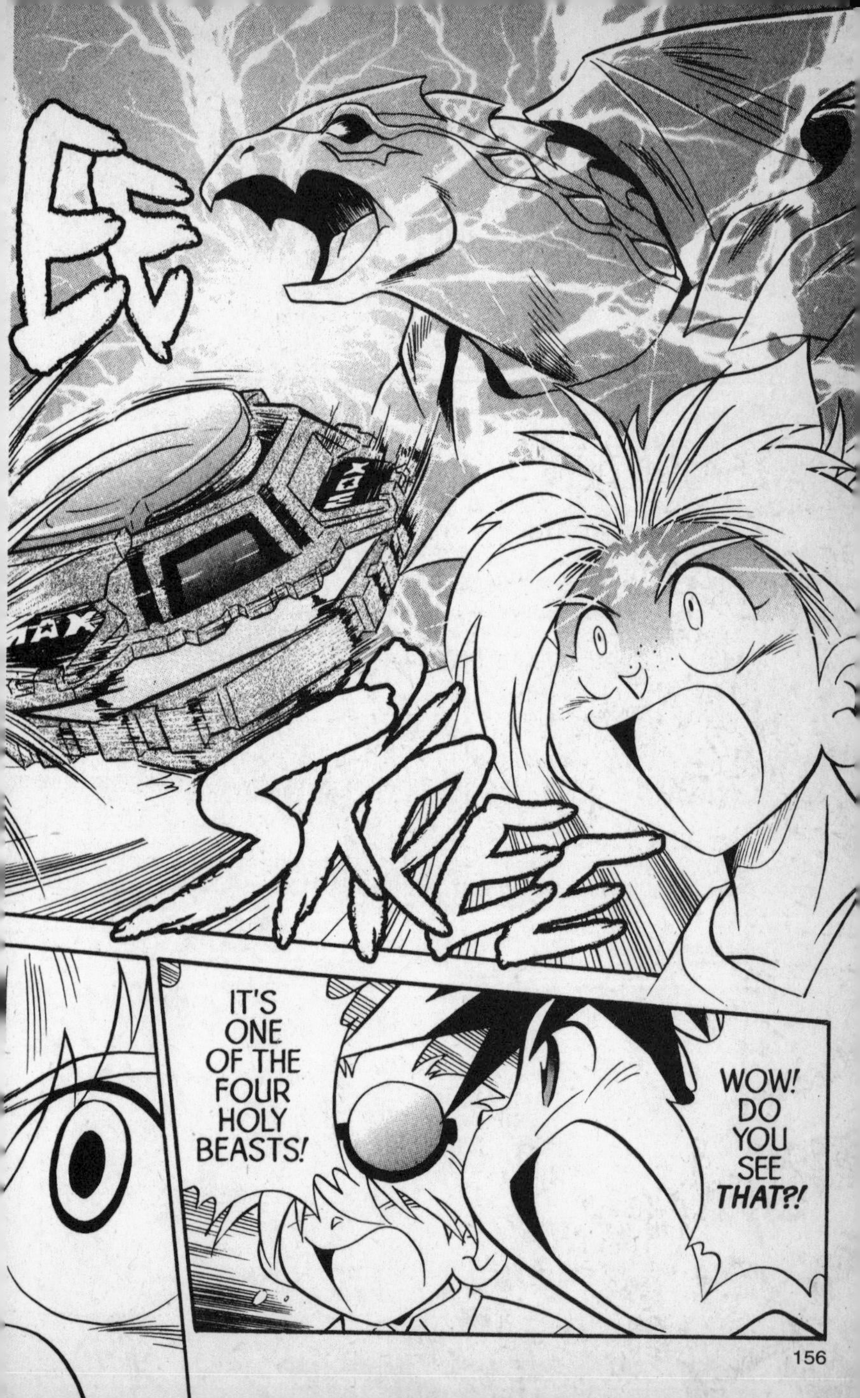
WOW! DO YOU SEE THAT?!
IT'S ONE OF THE FOUR HOLY BEASTS!

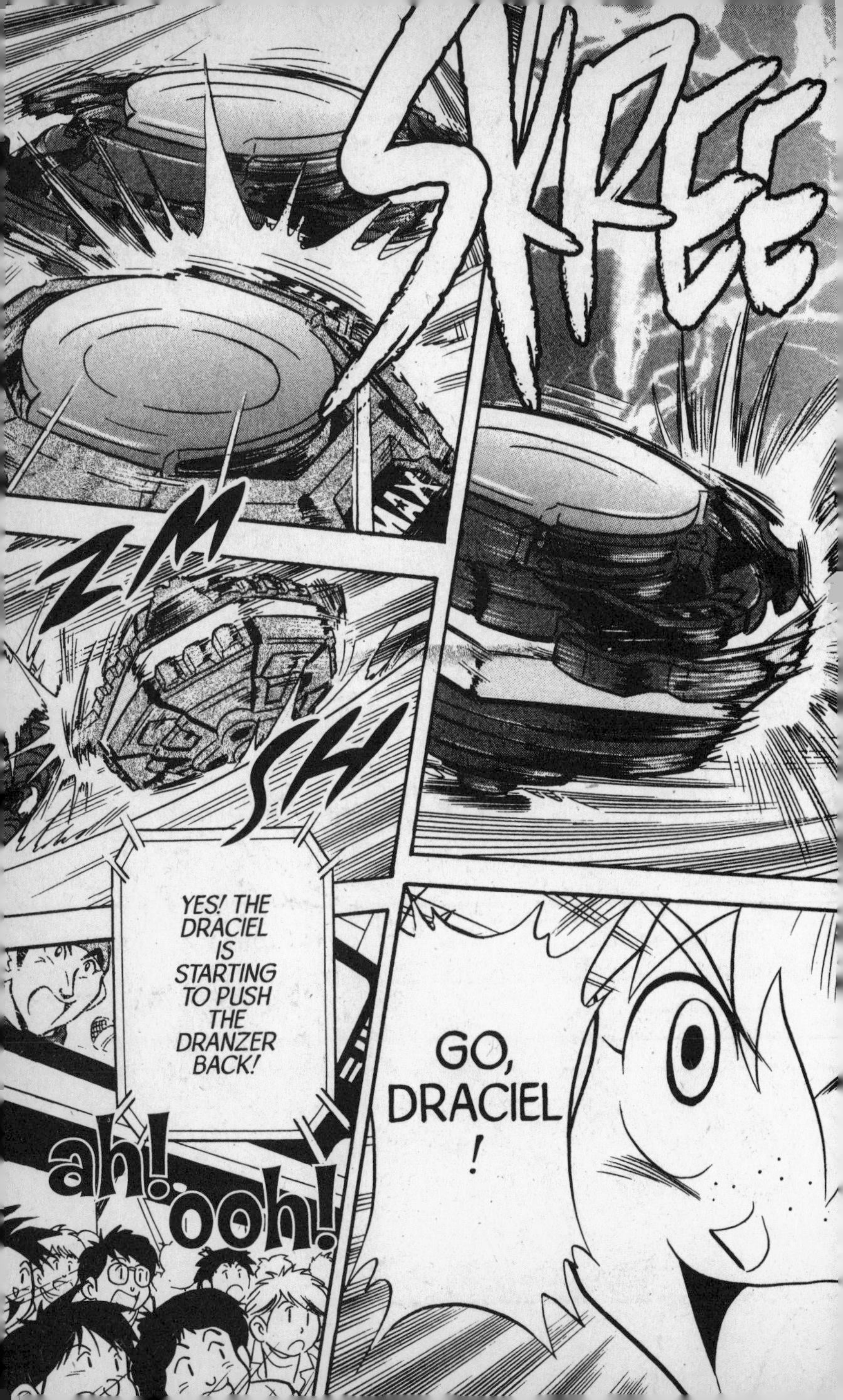
SKREE
ZMM
SHH
GO, DRACIEL!
YES! THE DRACIEL IS STARTING TO PUSH THE DRANZER BACK!
ah! ooh!

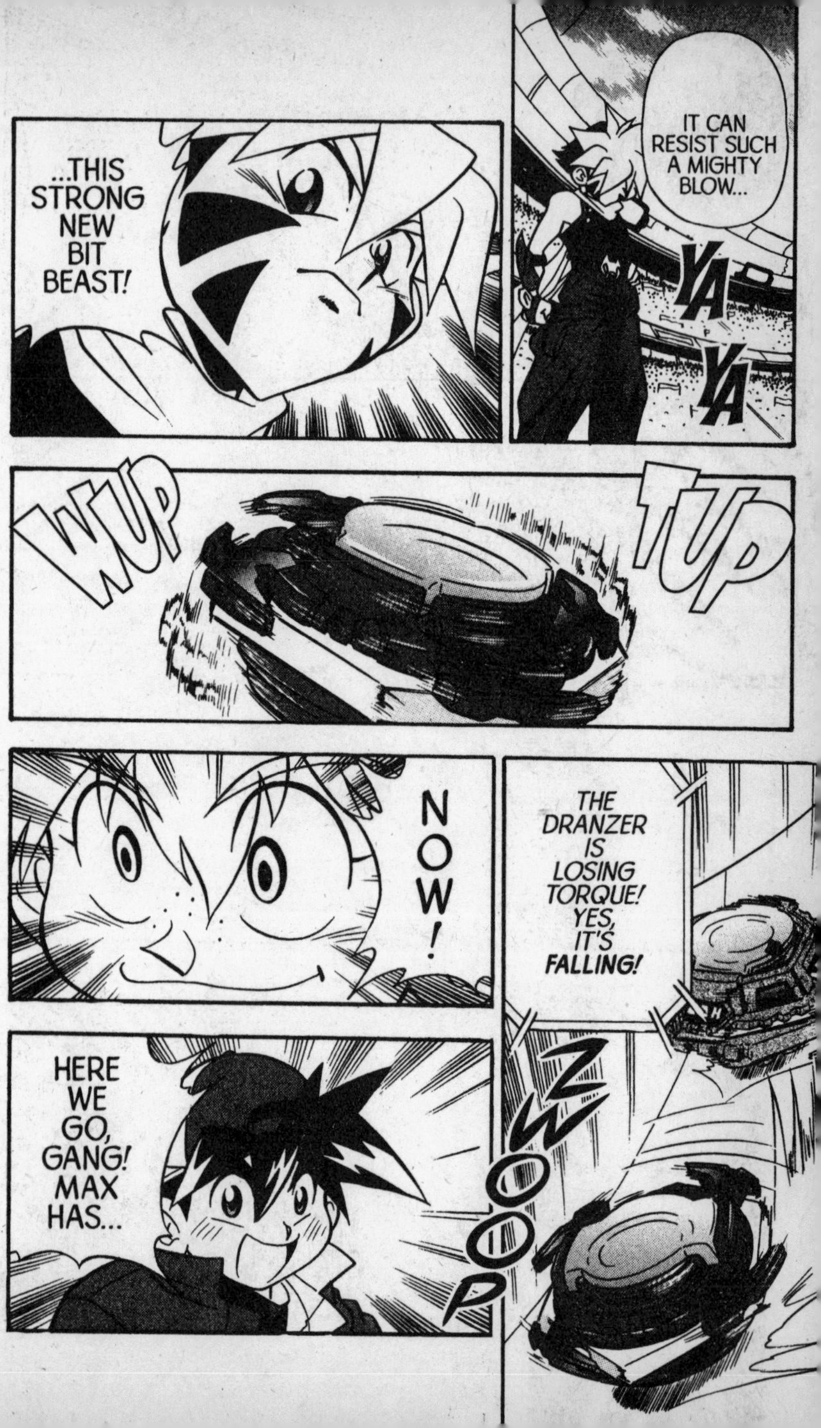
IT CAN RESIST SUCH A MIGHTY BLOW...
YA YA
...THIS STRONG NEW BIT BEAST!
TUP
WUP
THE DRANZER IS LOSING TORQUE! YES, IT'S FALLING!
ZWOOOP
NOW!
HERE WE GO, GANG! MAX HAS...

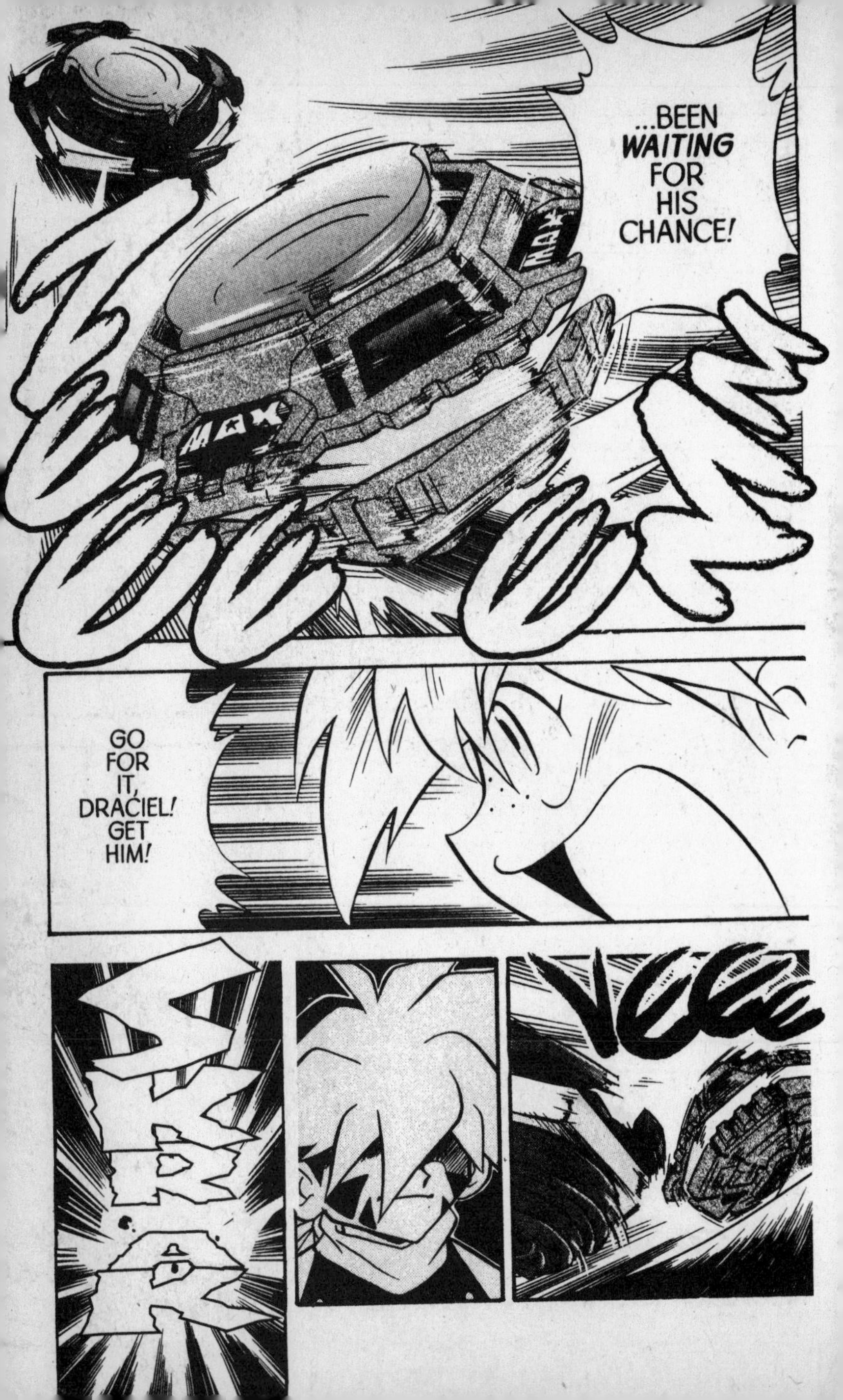
...BEEN WAITING FOR HIS CHANCE!
GO FOR IT, DRACIEL! GET HIM!

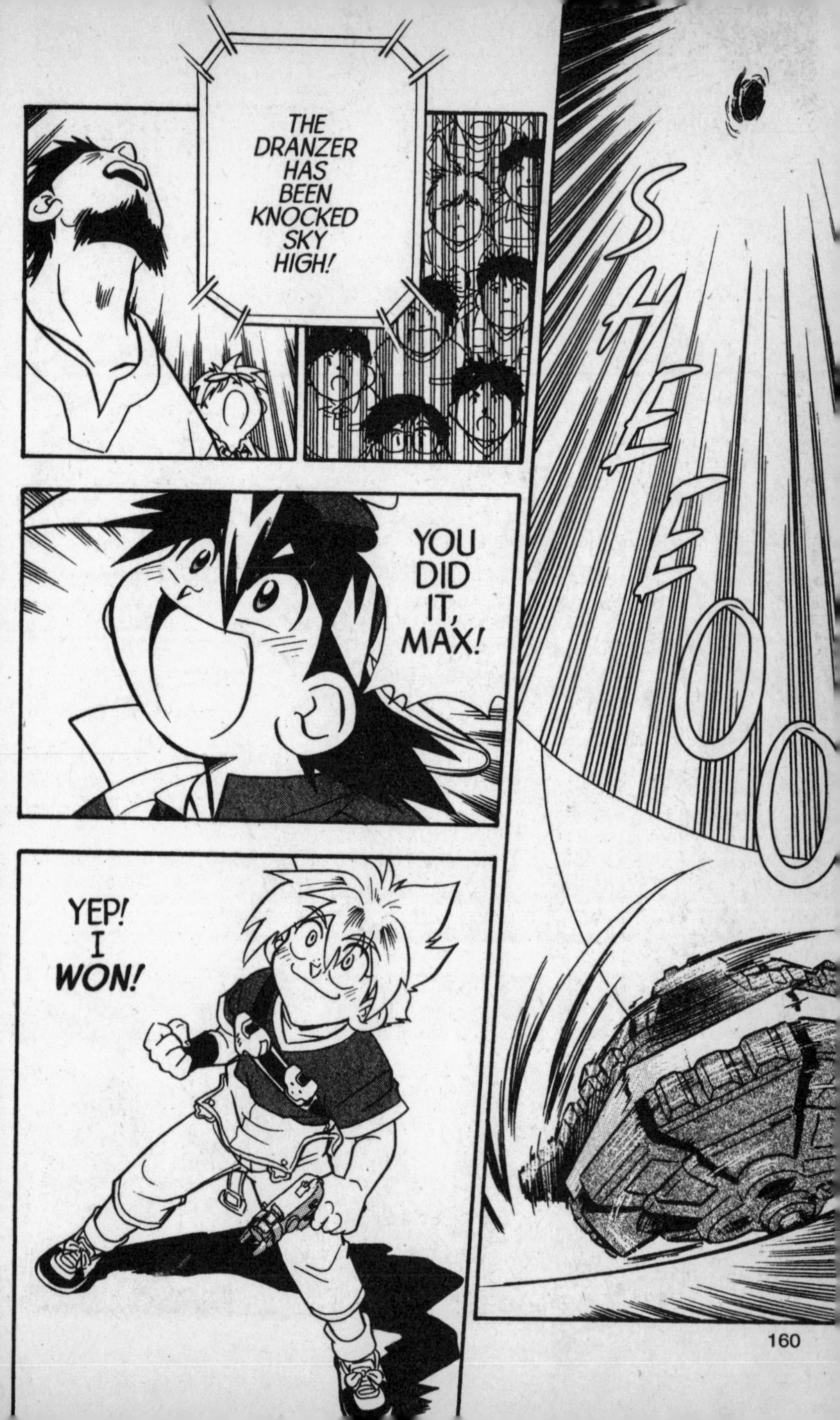
SHEEOOO
THE DRANZER HAS BEEN KNOCKED SKY HIGH!
YOU DID IT, MAX!
YEP! I WON!

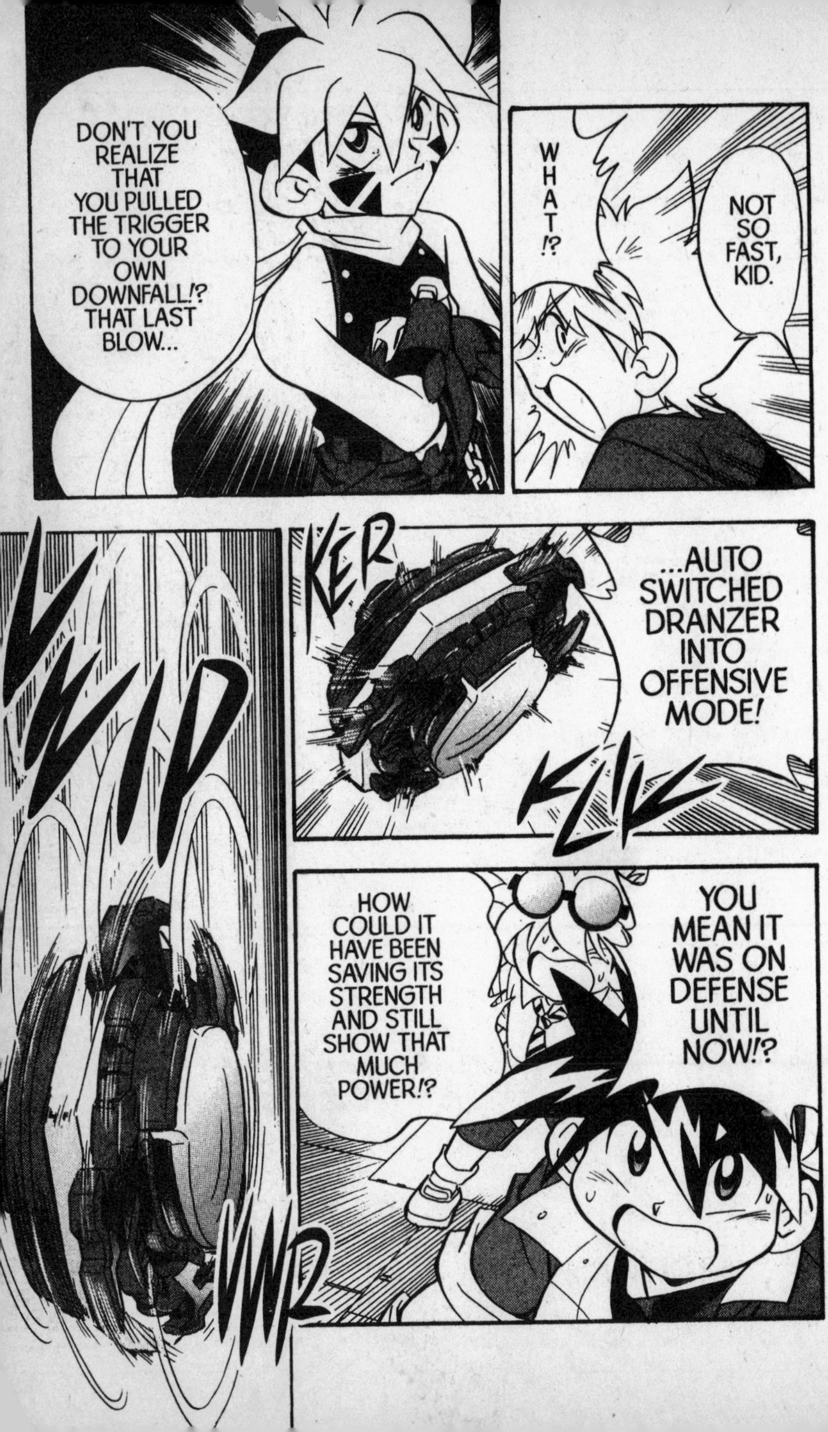
NOT SO FAST, KID.
WHAT!?
DON'T YOU REALIZE THAT YOU PULLED THE TRIGGER TO YOUR OWN DOWNFALL!? THAT LAST BLOW...
...AUTO SWITCHED DRANZER INTO OFFENSIVE MODE!
KER
KLIK
YOU MEAN IT WAS ON DEFENSE UNTIL NOW!?
HOW COULD IT HAVE BEEN SAVING ITS STRENGTH AND STILL SHOW THAT MUCH POWER!?
WHIP
VWR

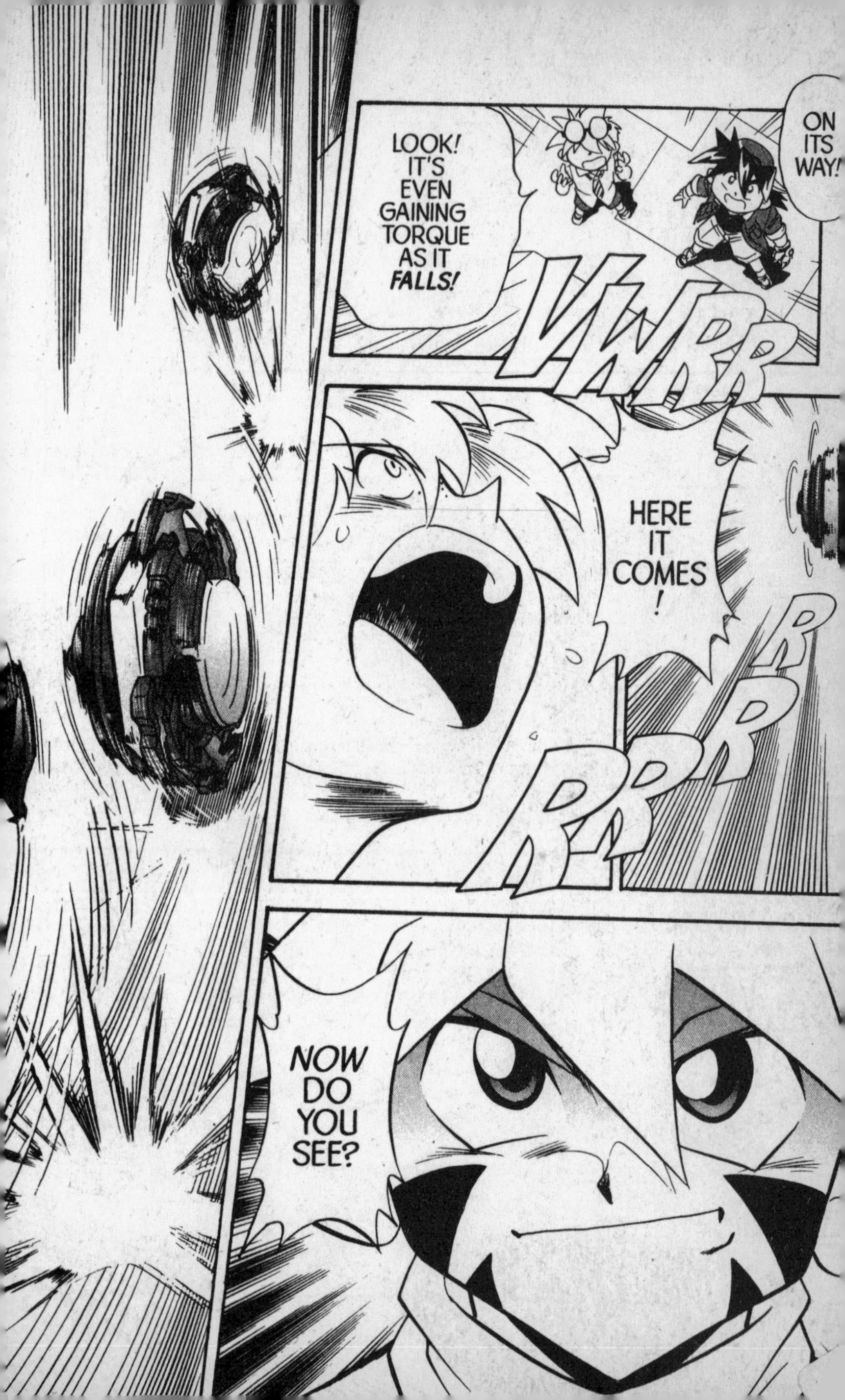
ON ITS WAY!
LOOK! IT'S EVEN GAINING TORQUE AS IT *FALLS!*
VWRR
HERE IT COMES!
RRRRR
NOW DO YOU SEE?

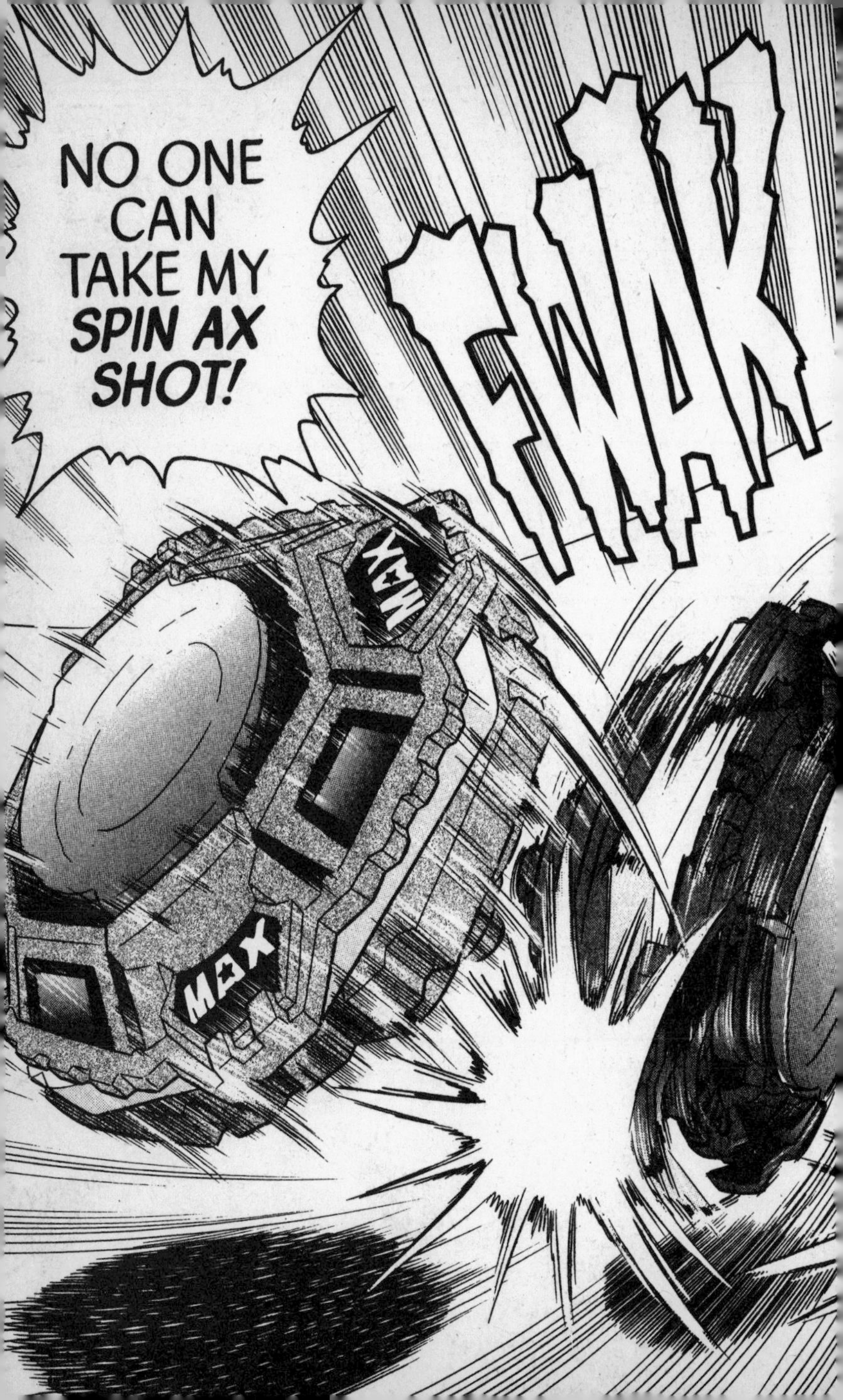
NO ONE CAN TAKE MY SPIN AX SHOT!
GWAK
MAX
MAX

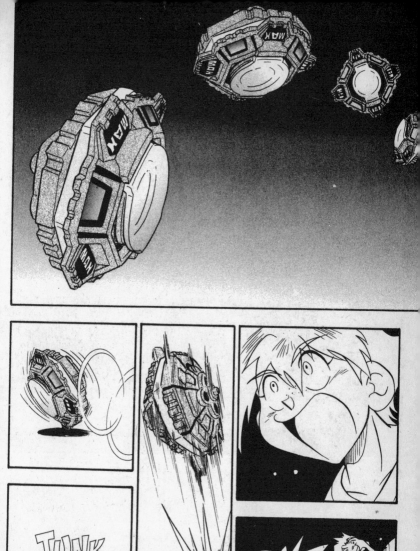

TUNK

WAM

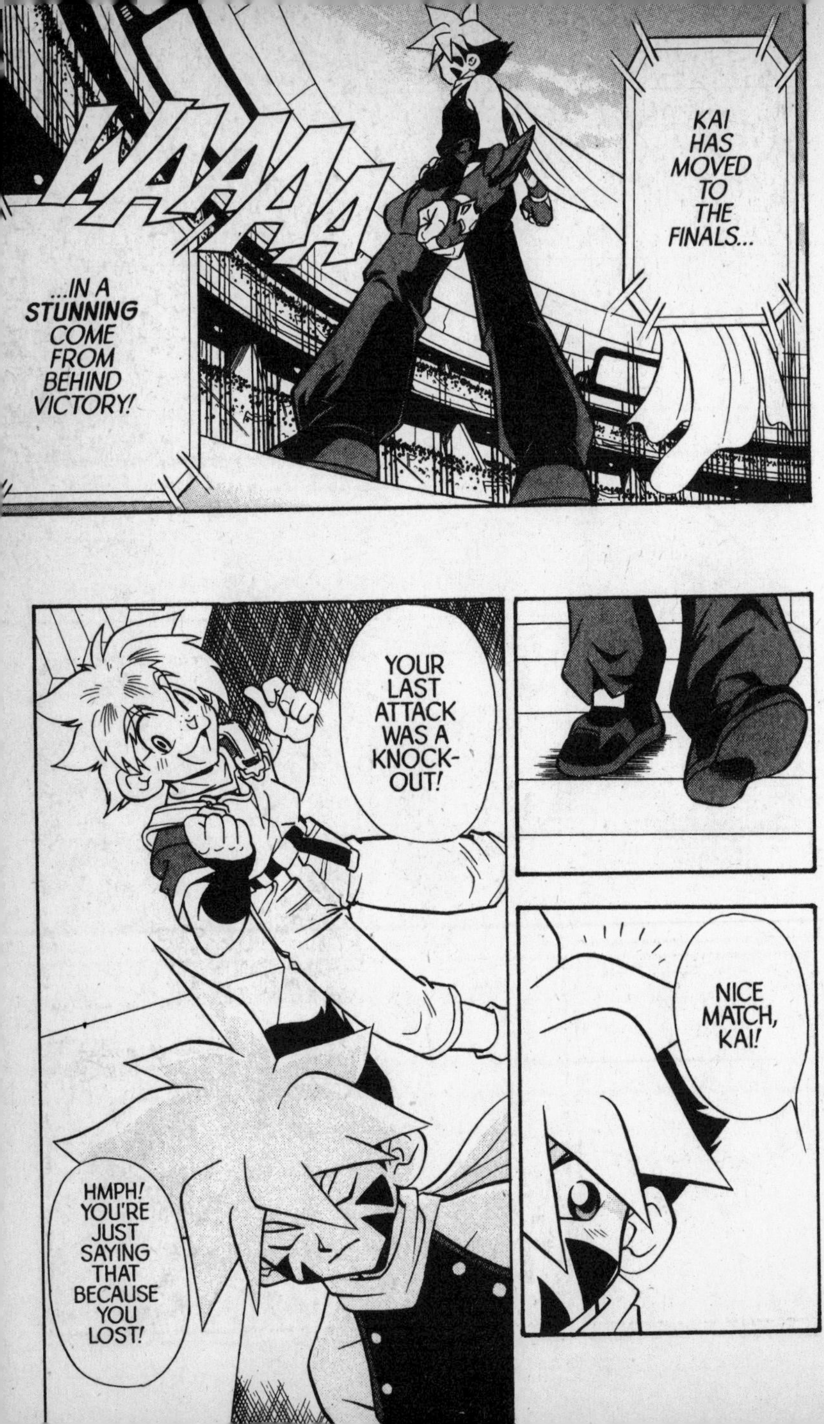
KAI HAS MOVED TO THE FINALS...
WAAAA
...IN A STUNNING COME FROM BEHIND VICTORY!
NICE MATCH, KAI!
YOUR LAST ATTACK WAS A KNOCK-OUT!
HMPH! YOU'RE JUST SAYING THAT BECAUSE YOU LOST!

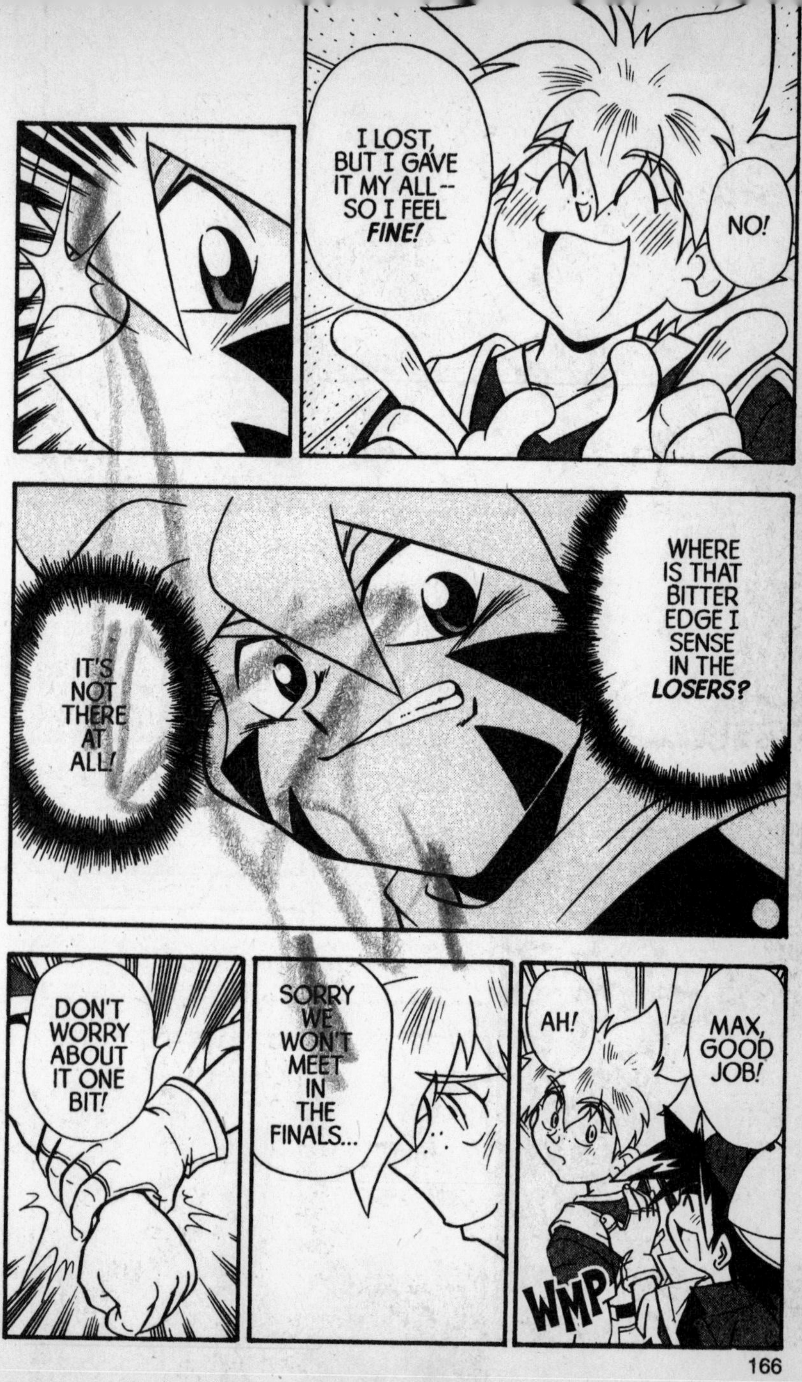
I LOST, BUT I GAVE IT MY ALL -- SO I FEEL FINE!
NO!
WHERE IS THAT BITTER EDGE I SENSE IN THE LOSERS?
IT'S NOT THERE AT ALL!
MAX, GOOD JOB!
AH!
WMP
SORRY WE WON'T MEET IN THE FINALS...
DON'T WORRY ABOUT IT ONE BIT!

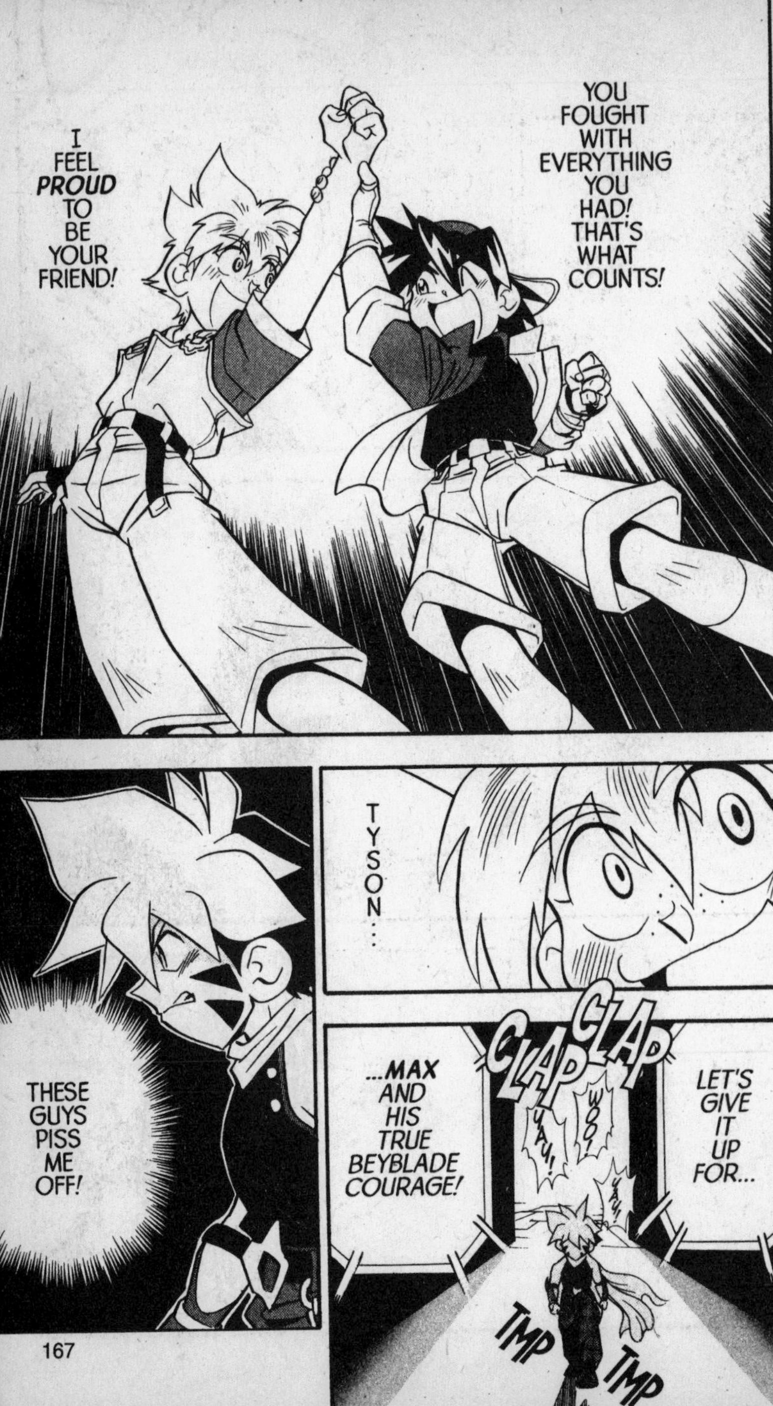
YOU FOUGHT WITH EVERYTHING YOU HAD! THAT'S WHAT COUNTS!
I FEEL **PROUD** TO BE YOUR FRIEND!
TYSON...
LET'S GIVE IT UP FOR...
...**MAX** AND HIS TRUE BEYBLADE COURAGE!
CLAP CLAP
WOO!
YAAY!
YAAY!
TMP TMP
THESE GUYS PISS ME OFF!

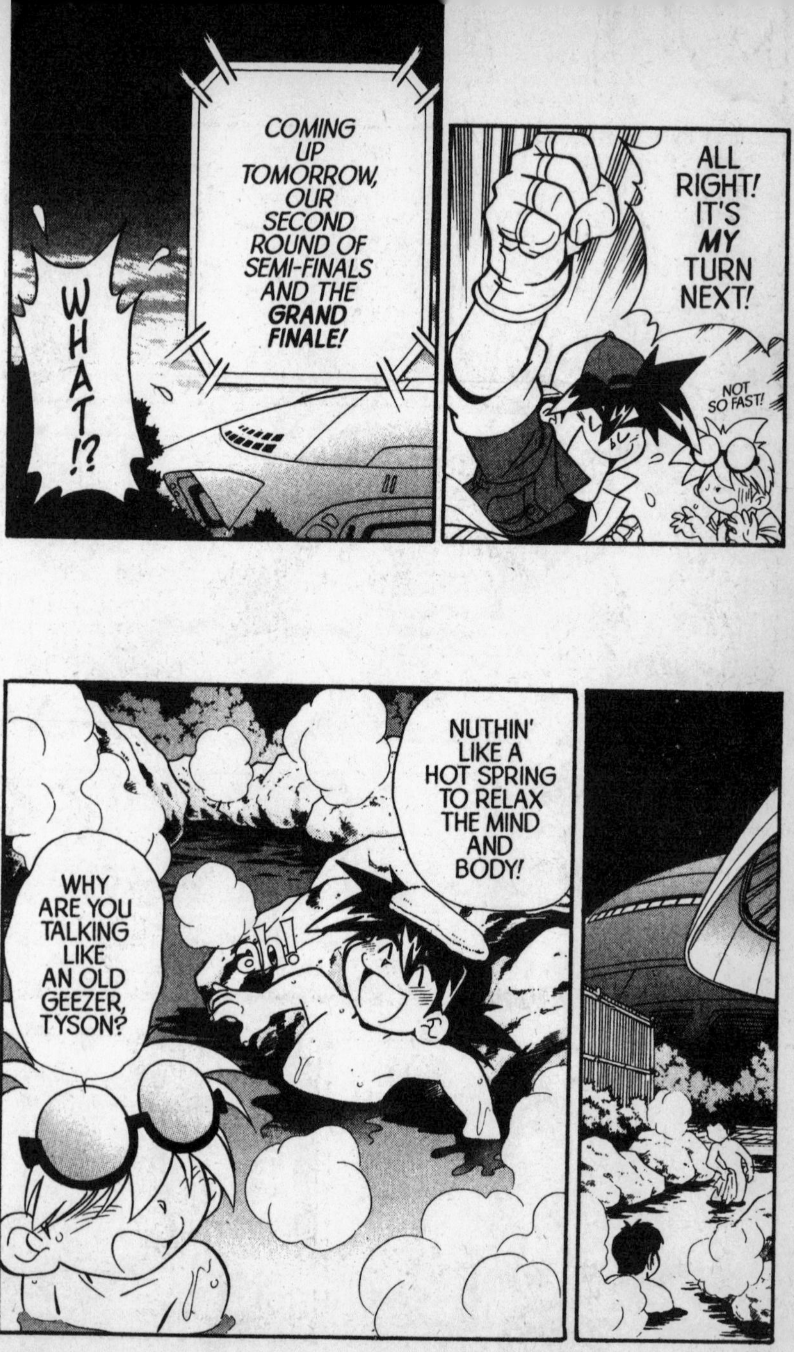
ALL RIGHT! IT'S MY TURN NEXT!
NOT SO FAST!
COMING UP TOMORROW, OUR SECOND ROUND OF SEMI-FINALS AND THE GRAND FINALE!
WHAT!?
NUTHIN' LIKE A HOT SPRING TO RELAX THE MIND AND BODY!
ah!
WHY ARE YOU TALKING LIKE AN OLD GEEZER, TYSON?

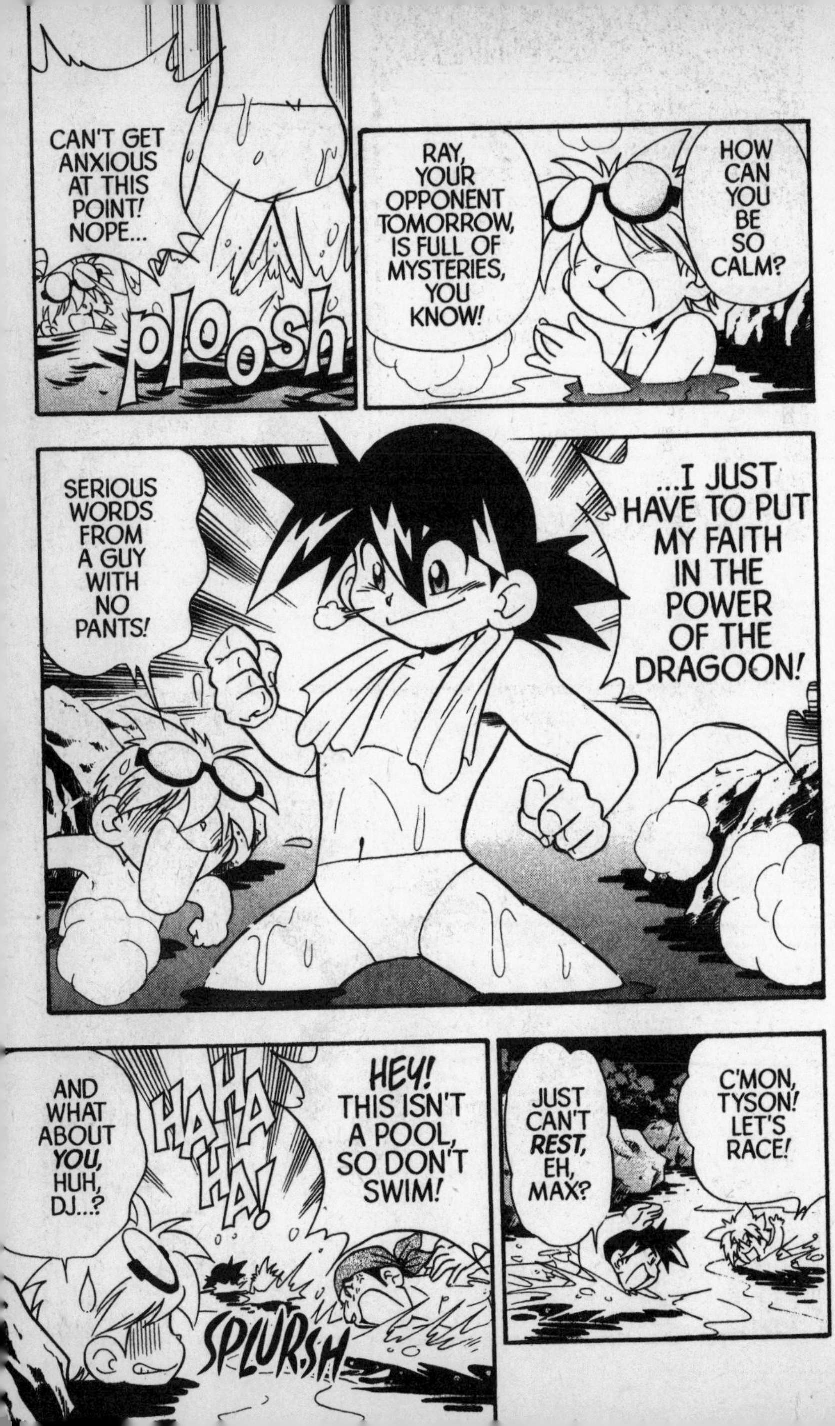
HOW CAN YOU BE SO CALM?
RAY, YOUR OPPONENT TOMORROW, IS FULL OF MYSTERIES, YOU KNOW!
CAN'T GET ANXIOUS AT THIS POINT! NOPE...
ploosh
...I JUST HAVE TO PUT MY FAITH IN THE POWER OF THE DRAGOON!
SERIOUS WORDS FROM A GUY WITH NO PANTS!
C'MON, TYSON! LET'S RACE!
JUST CAN'T *REST,* EH, MAX?
HEY! THIS ISN'T A POOL, SO DON'T SWIM!
HA HA HA HA!
AND WHAT ABOUT *YOU,* HUH, DJ...?
SPLURSH

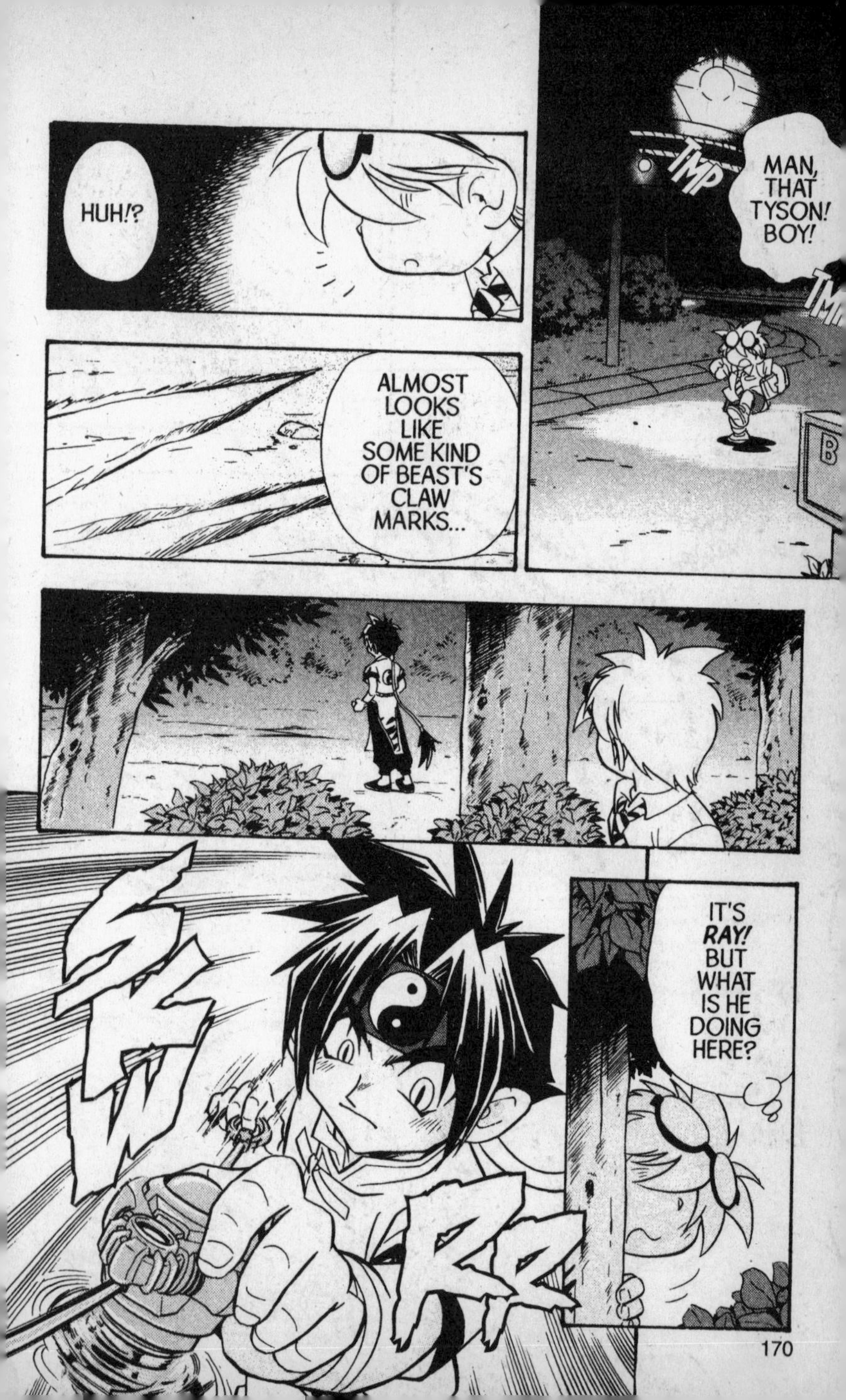

TMP
MAN, THAT TYSON! BOY!
HUH!?
ALMOST LOOKS LIKE SOME KIND OF BEAST'S CLAW MARKS...
IT'S *RAY!* BUT WHAT IS HE DOING HERE?

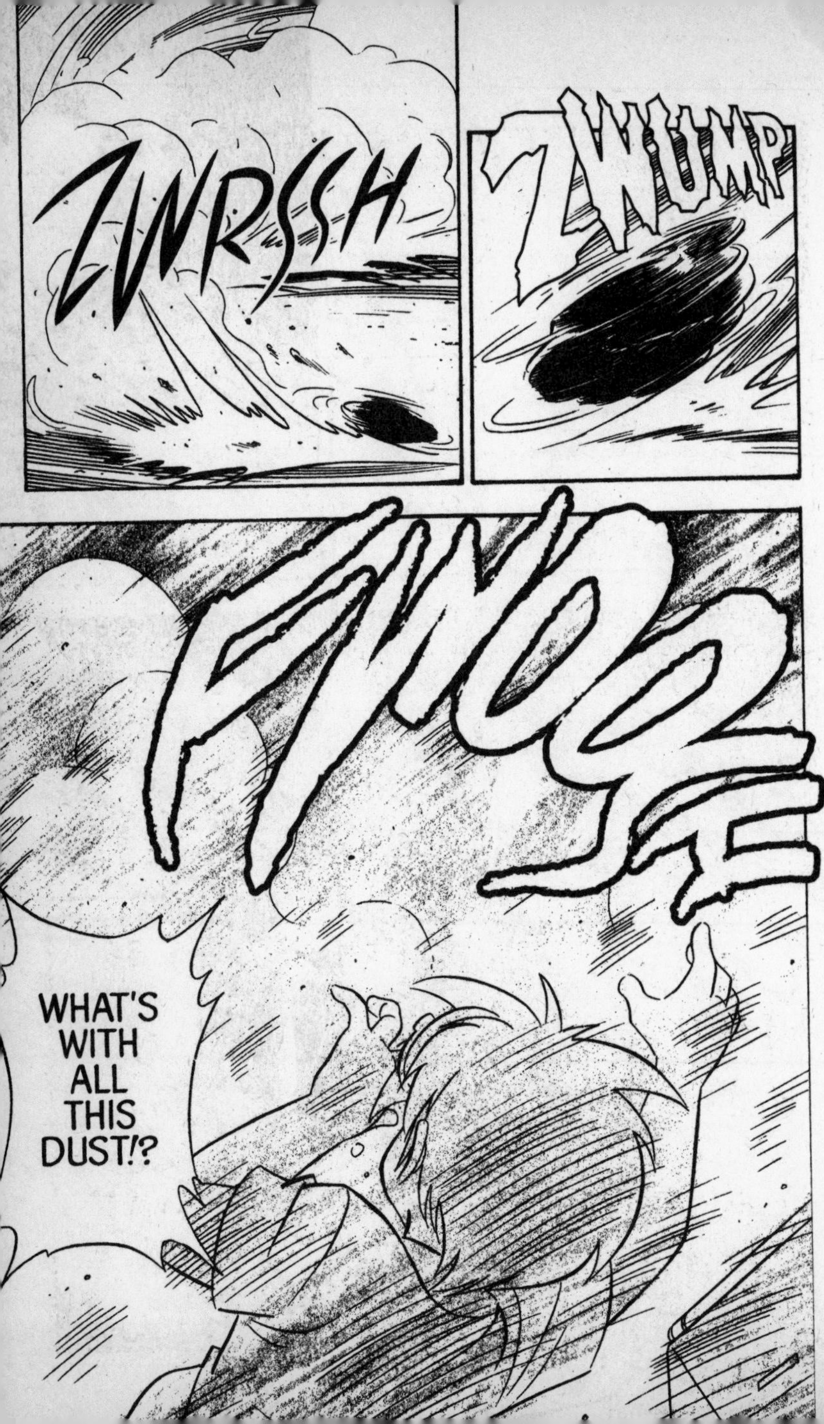
ZWUMP
ZWRSSH
FWOOSH
WHAT'S WITH ALL THIS DUST!?

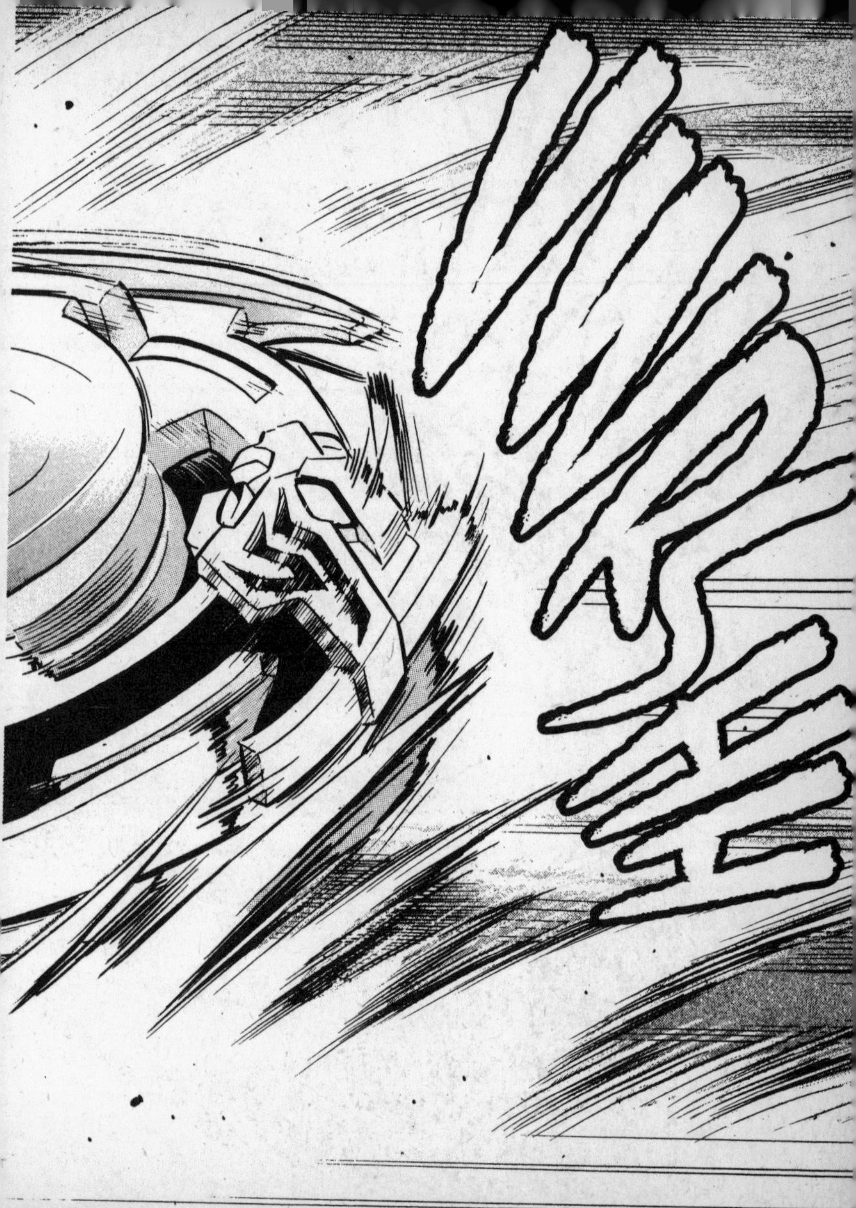

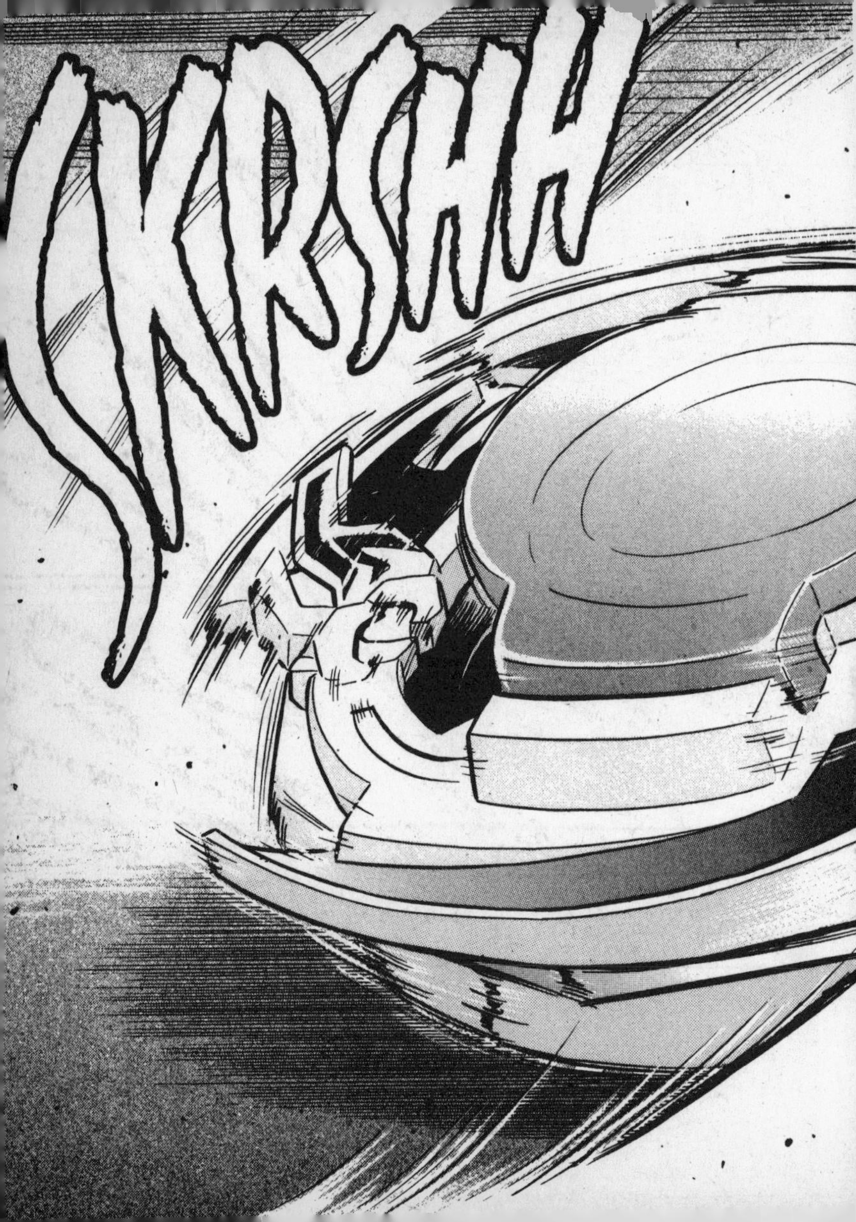
SKRSCHH

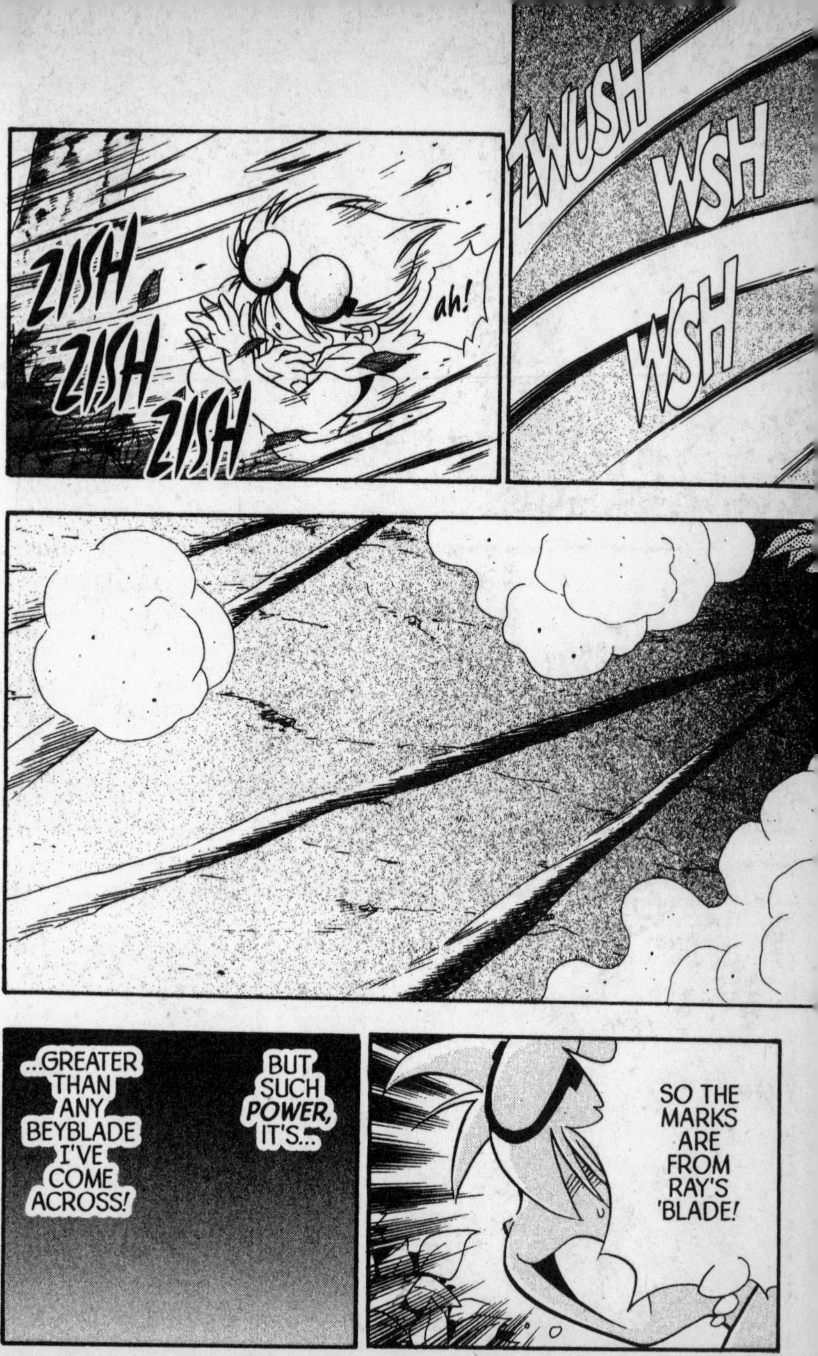
ZWUSH
WSH
WSH
ZISH ZISH ZISH
ah!
SO THE MARKS ARE FROM RAY'S 'BLADE!
BUT SUCH *POWER*, IT'S...
...GREATER THAN ANY BEYBLADE I'VE COME ACROSS!

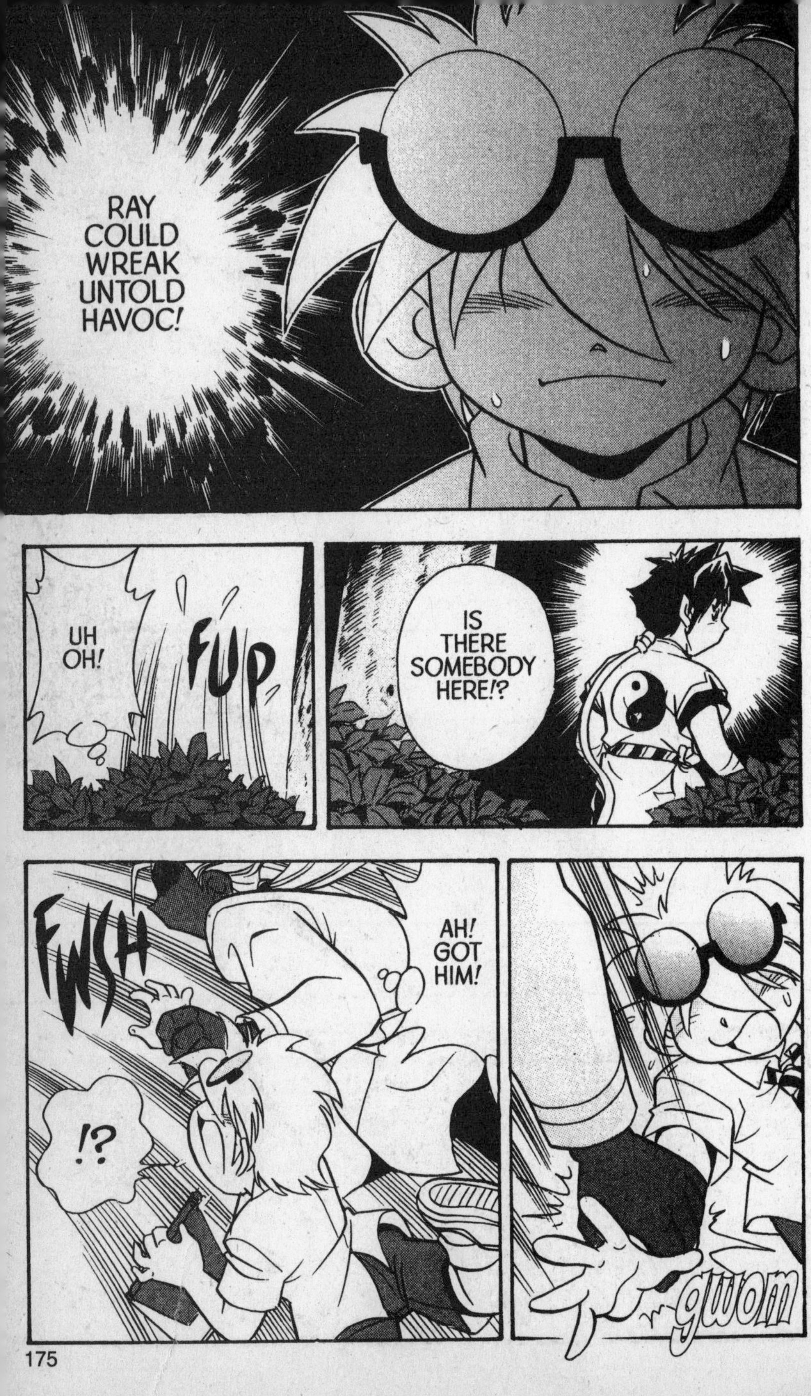
RAY COULD WREAK UNTOLD HAVOC!
IS THERE SOMEBODY HERE!?
FUP
UH OH!
gwom
AH! GOT HIM!
FWSH
!?

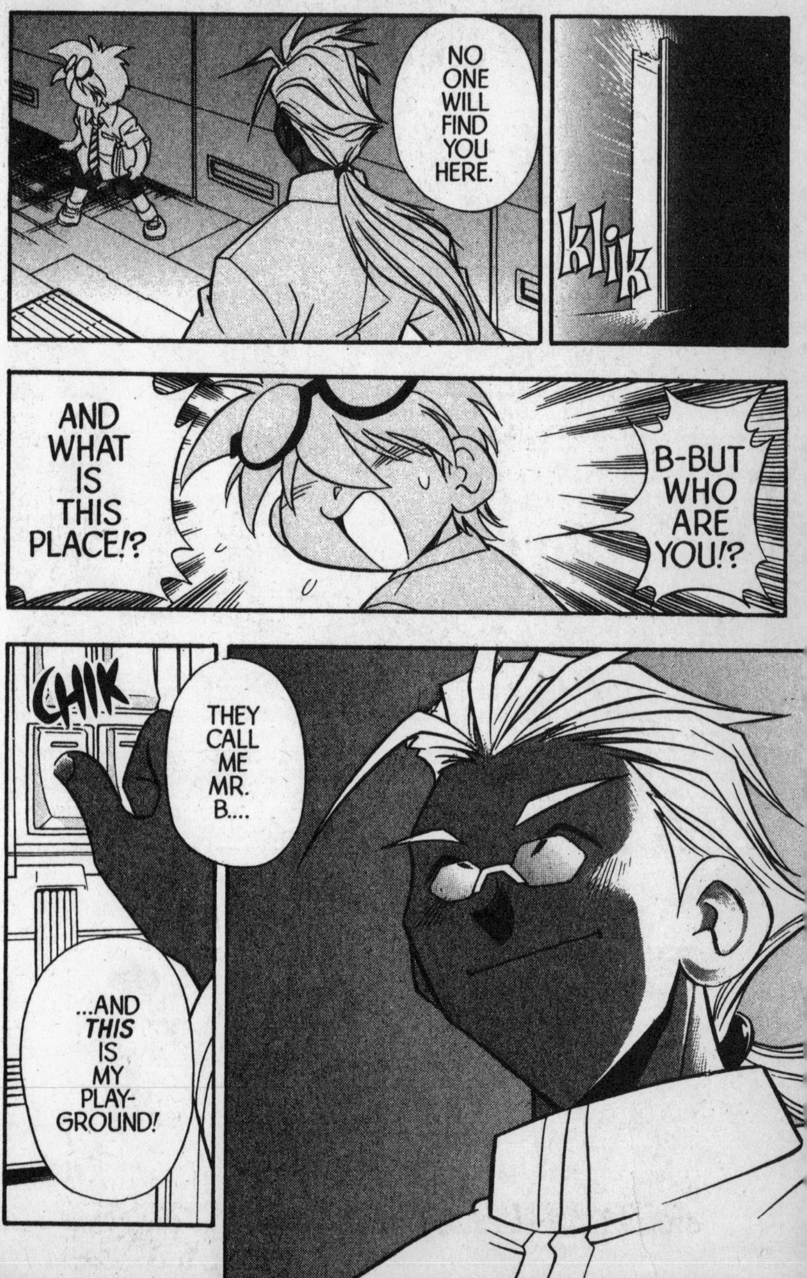
klik
NO ONE WILL FIND YOU HERE.
B-BUT WHO ARE YOU!?
AND WHAT IS THIS PLACE!?
THEY CALL ME MR. B....
CHIK
...AND *THIS* IS MY PLAY-GROUND!

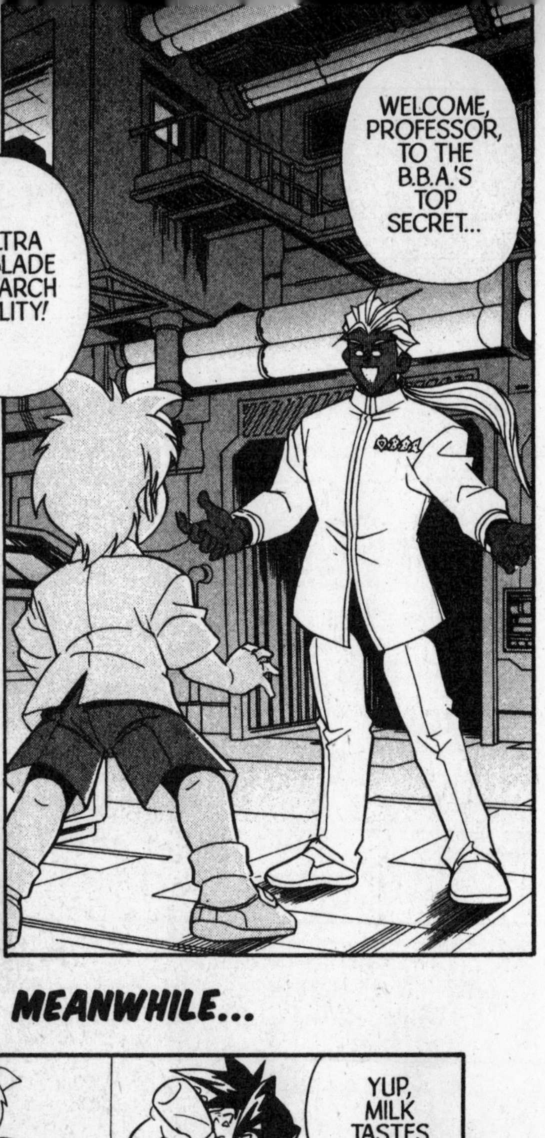
WELCOME, PROFESSOR, TO THE B.B.A.'S TOP SECRET...

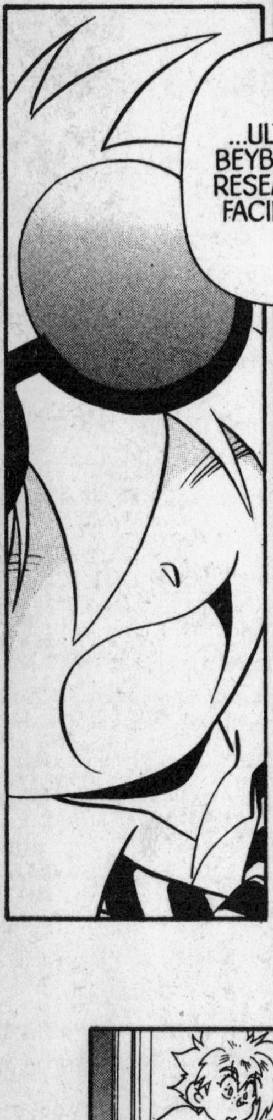
...ULTRA BEYBLADE RESEARCH FACILITY!

MEANWHILE...

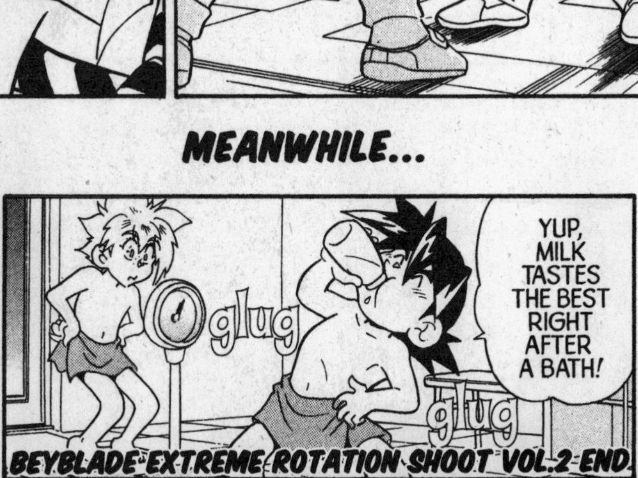
YUP, MILK TASTES THE BEST RIGHT AFTER A BATH!
glug
glug
BEYBLADE EXTREME ROTATION SHOOT VOL.2 END

CONTINUED IN VOL. 3

EDITOR'S RECOMMENDATIONS

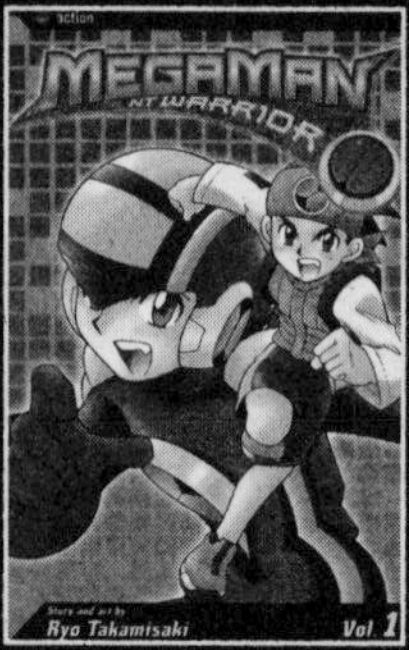

MEGAMAN
NT WARRIOR
Ryo Takamisaki
Vol. 1

MEGAMAN
By Ryo Takamisaki. Our hero, Lan Hikari, synchronizes with *MEGAMAN* and becomes a super-charged dynamo. In and outside of the computer world they do their best to thwart the evil organization, World Three, from taking over the world.

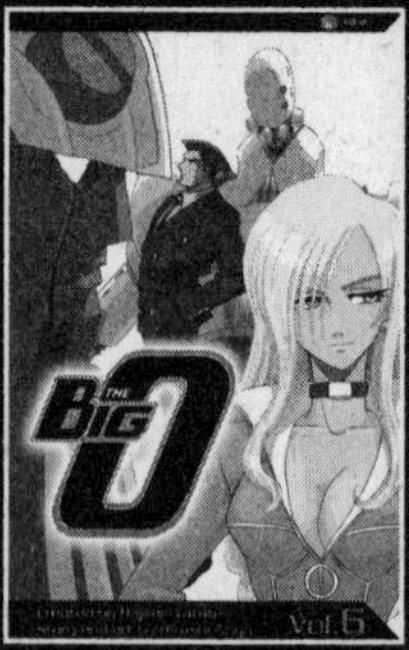

THE BIG O
Vol.6

THE BIG O
Created by Hajime Yatate with story and art by Hitoshi Ariga. More than a straight adaptation of the hit Cartoon Network series, the manga includes the prequel to events in *THE BIG O* anime, plus many completely new stories.

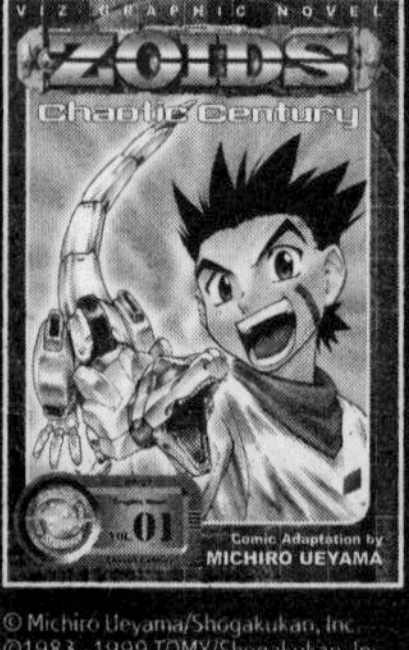

ZOIDS
Chaotic Century
Vol.01
Comic Adaptation by
MICHIRO UEYAMA

ZOIDS: CHAOTIC CENTURY
By Michiro Ueyama. Together, boy and machine fight for peace on Planet Zi. The anime was great. You'll love this series from VIZ, as well.

BEYBLADE™

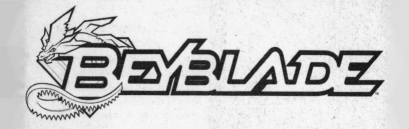

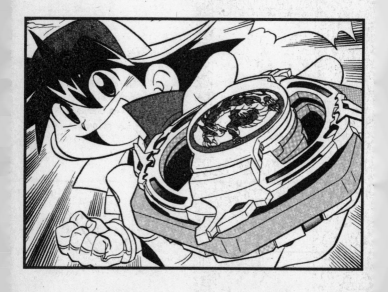

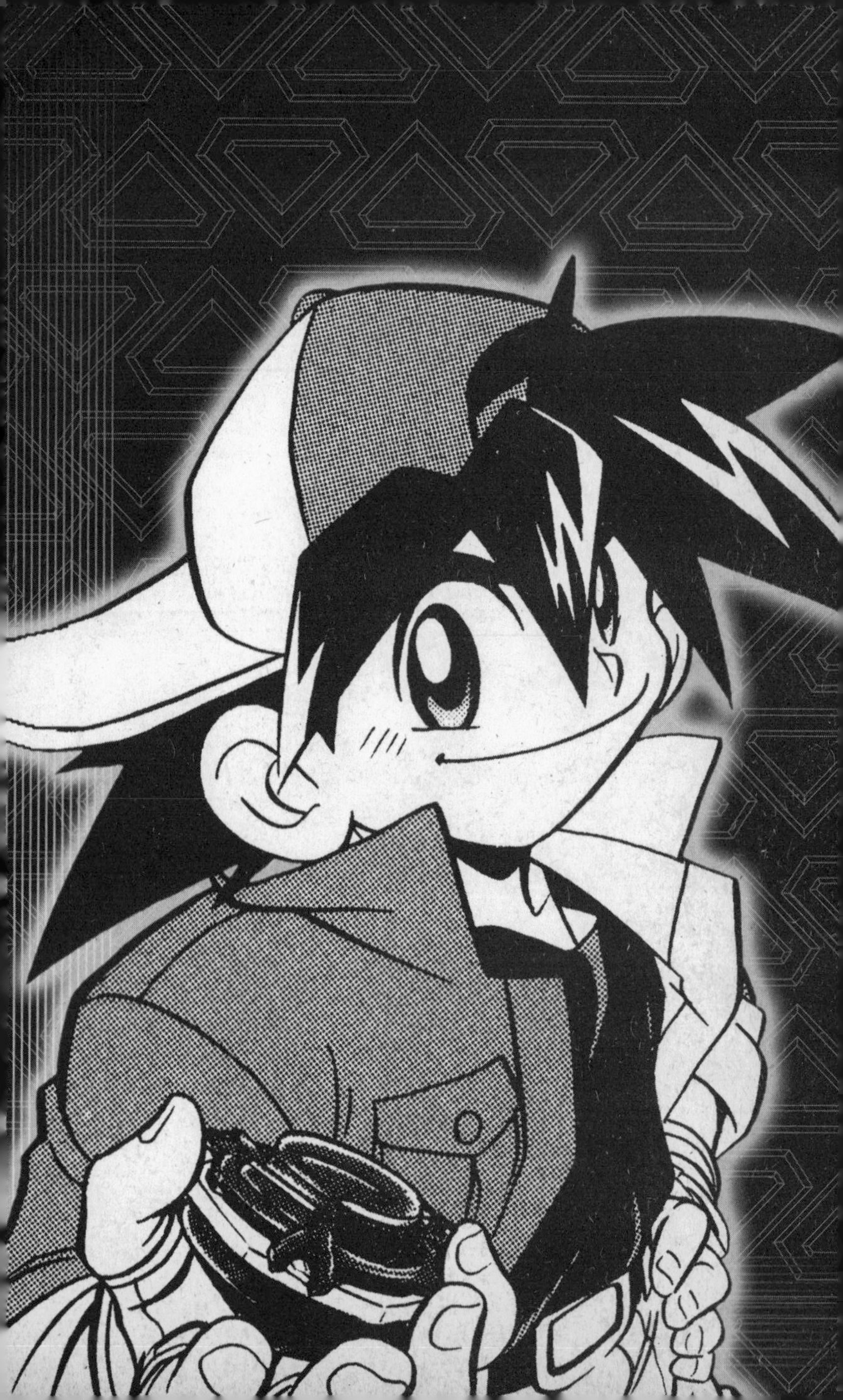

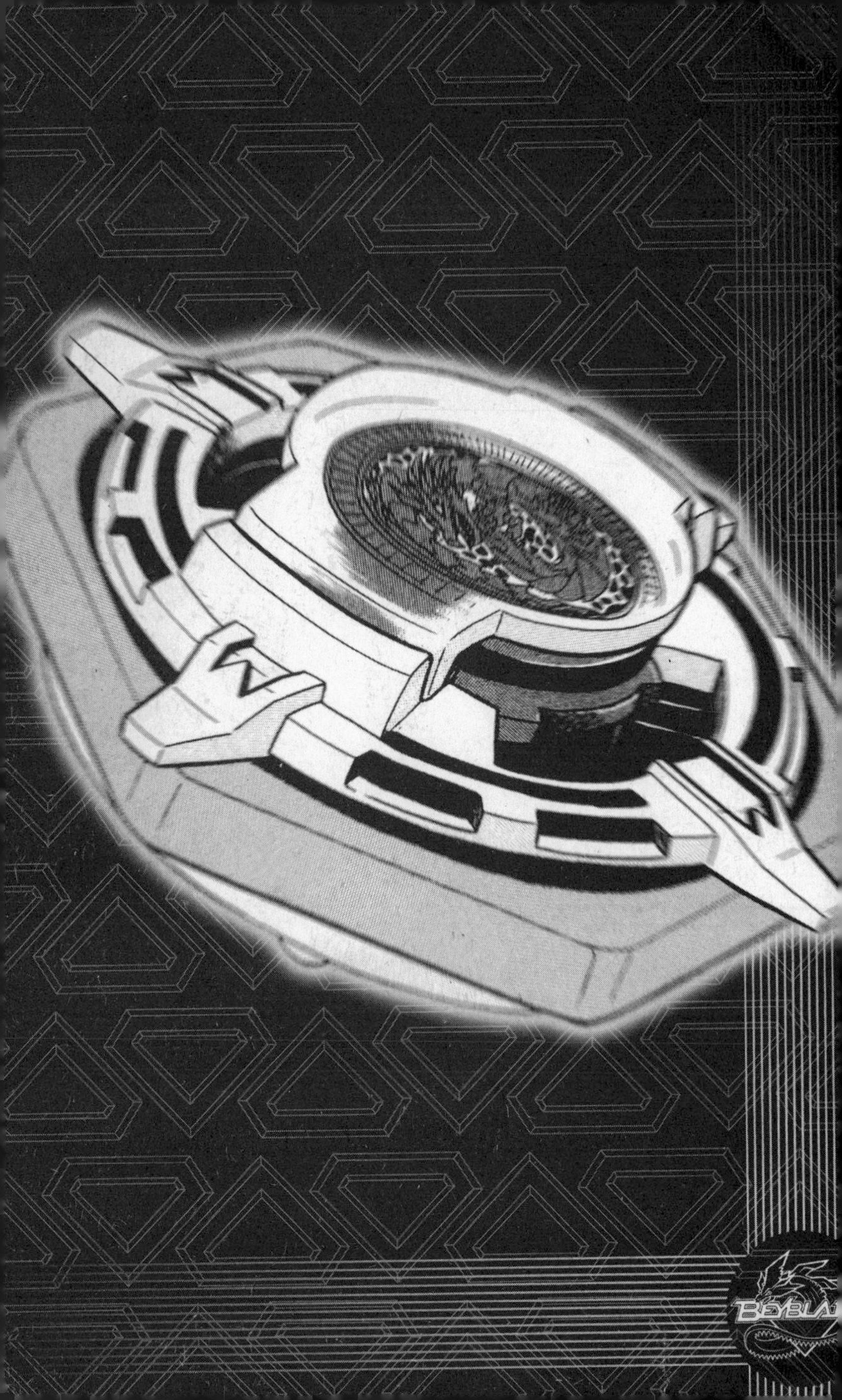

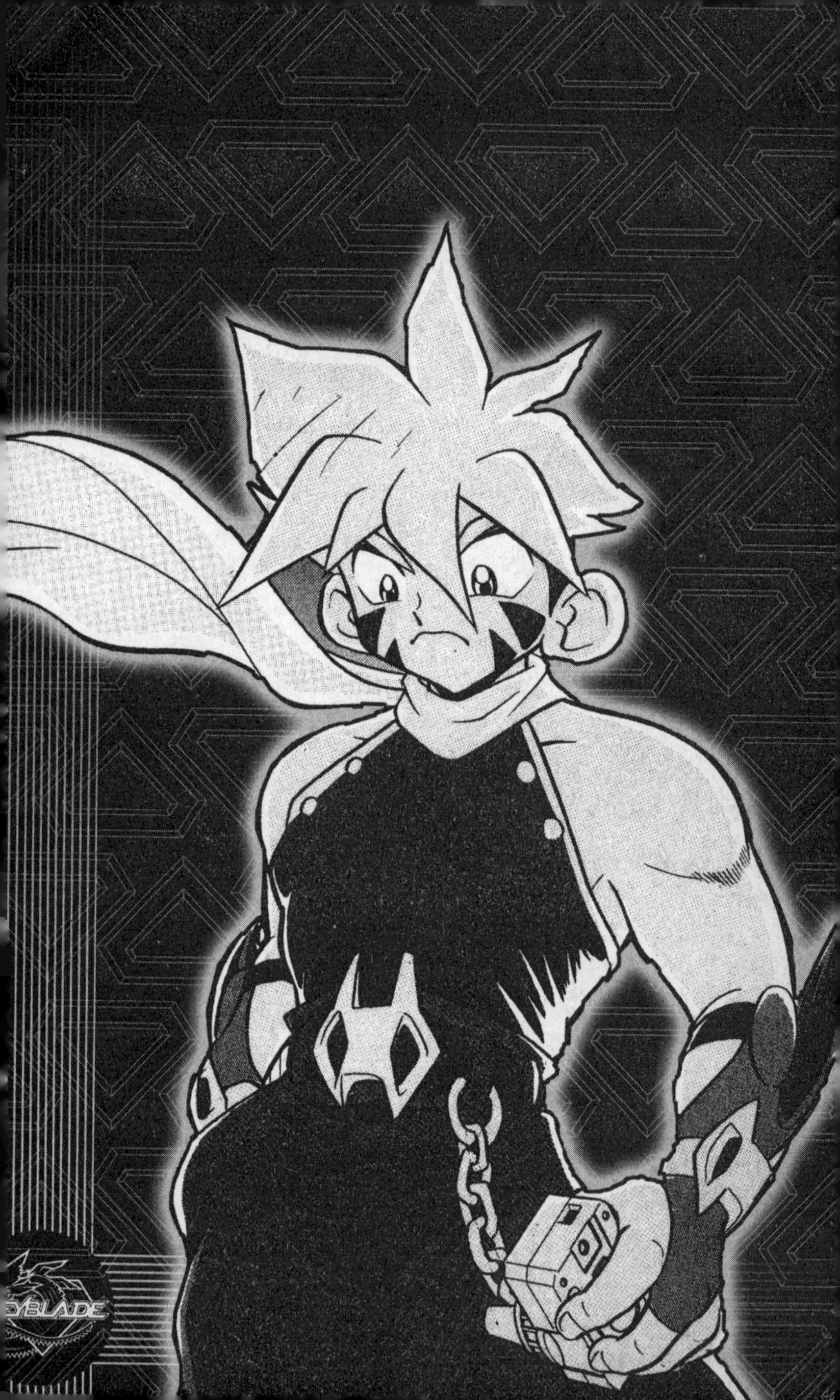

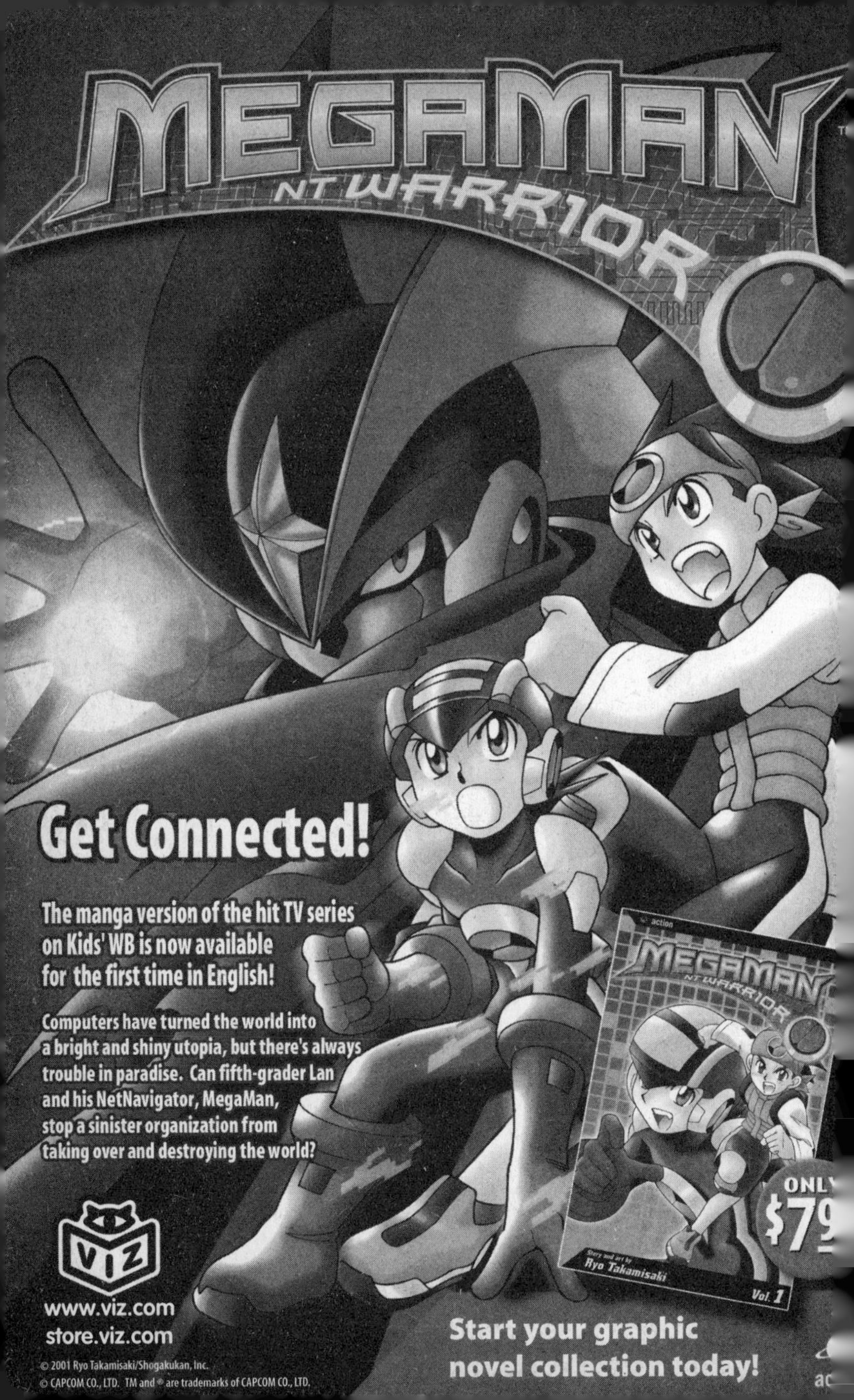

MEGAMAN
NT WARRIOR
Get Connected!
The manga version of the hit TV series on Kids' WB is now available for the first time in English!
Computers have turned the world into a bright and shiny utopia, but there's always trouble in paradise. Can fifth-grader Lan and his NetNavigator, MegaMan, stop a sinister organization from taking over and destroying the world?
action
MEGAMAN
NT WARRIOR
Ryo Takamisaki
Vol. 1
ONLY
VIZ
www.viz.com
store.viz.com
Start your graphic novel collection today!
© 2001 Ryo Takamisaki/Shogakukan, Inc.
© CAPCOM CO., LTD. TM and ® are trademarks of CAPCOM CO., LTD.

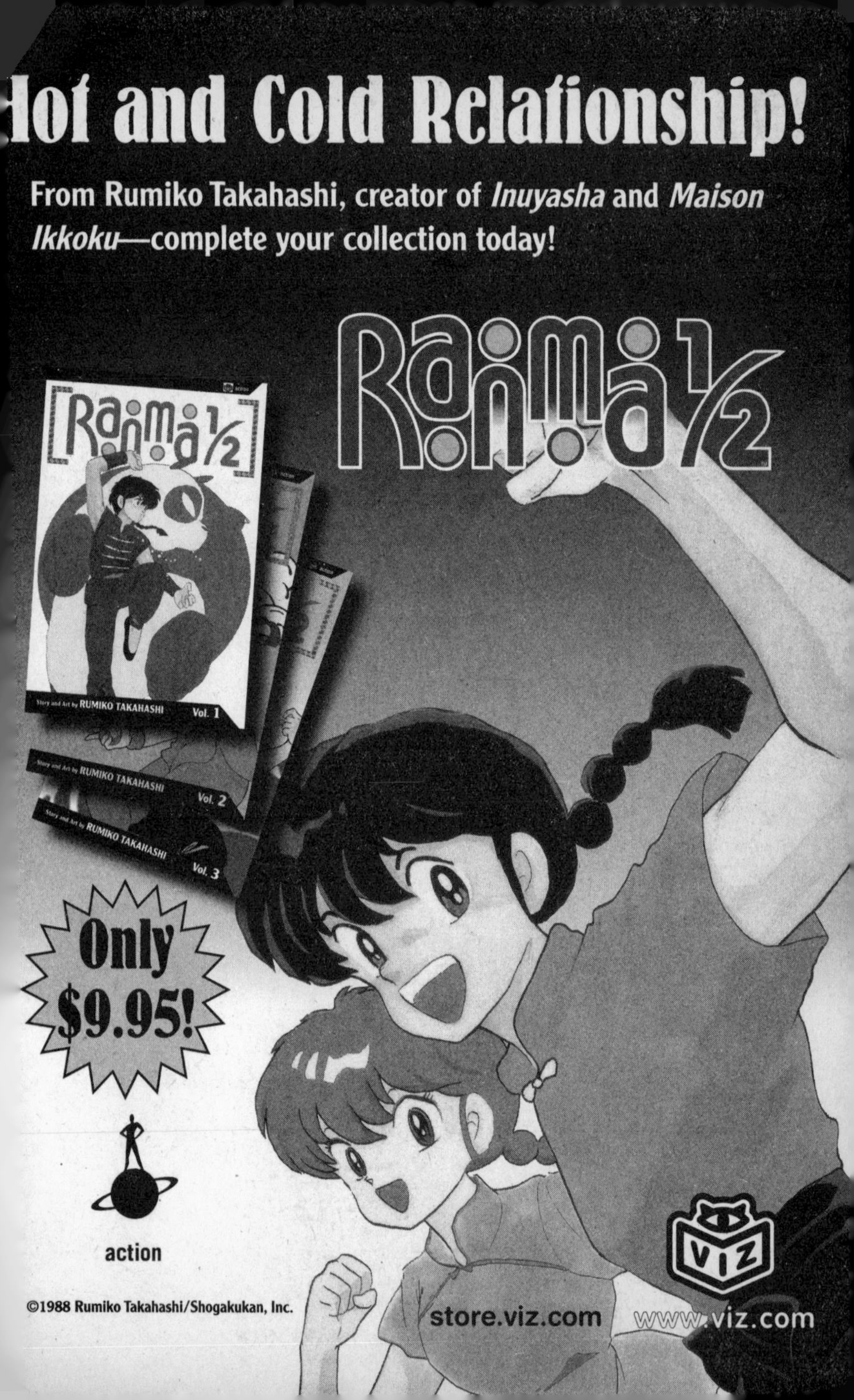
Hot and Cold Relationship!
From Rumiko Takahashi, creator of *Inuyasha* and *Maison Ikkoku*—complete your collection today!
Ranma 1/2
Ranma 1/2
Story and Art by RUMIKO TAKAHASHI Vol. 1
Story and Art by RUMIKO TAKAHASHI Vol. 2
Story and Art by RUMIKO TAKAHASHI Vol. 3
Only $9.95!
action
VIZ
©1988 Rumiko Takahashi/Shogakukan, Inc.
store.viz.com
www.viz.com

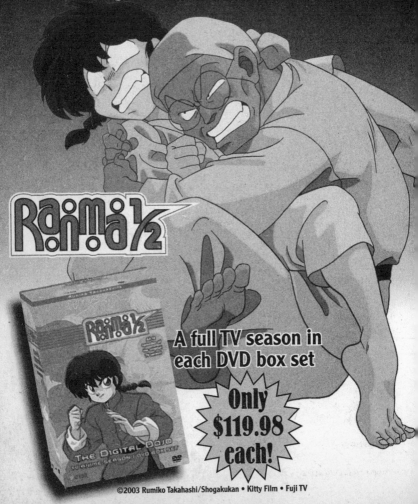

Set Your Anime Collection on Fire!
FLAME OF RECCA™
Meet Recca Hanabishi--an average teen with the not-so-average goal of becoming a ninja. After encountering a mysterious woman who threatens death unless he unleashes his hidden power to conjure up flame, will Recca have the strength to defeat this shadowy figure? Or will he go up in smoke?
Now available on DVD!
FLAME OF RECCA
Only $24.98!
A NINJA'S TEST
FRESH FROM JAPAN
日本最新
©NOBUYUKI ANZAI / SHOGAKUKAN • FUJI TV • PIERROT
www.viz.com

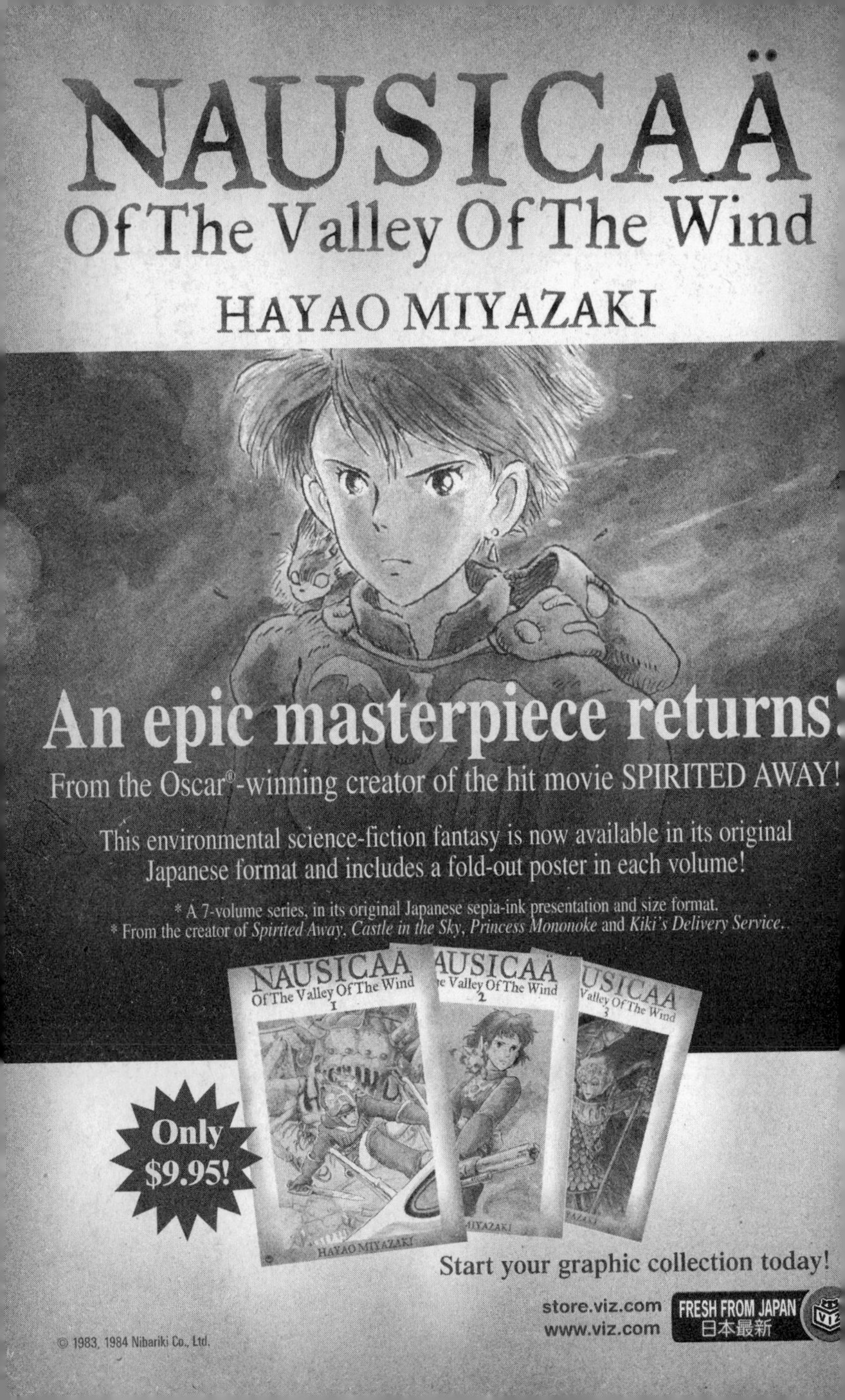
NAUSICAÄ
Of The Valley Of The Wind
HAYAO MIYAZAKI
An epic masterpiece returns!
From the Oscar®-winning creator of the hit movie SPIRITED AWAY!
This environmental science-fiction fantasy is now available in its original Japanese format and includes a fold-out poster in each volume!
* A 7-volume series, in its original Japanese sepia-ink presentation and size format.
* From the creator of Spirited Away, Castle in the Sky, Princess Mononoke and Kiki's Delivery Service.
NAUSICAÄ Of The Valley Of The Wind 1
Only $9.95!
Start your graphic collection today!
store.viz.com
www.viz.com
FRESH FROM JAPAN
日本最新
© 1983, 1984 Nibariki Co., Ltd.

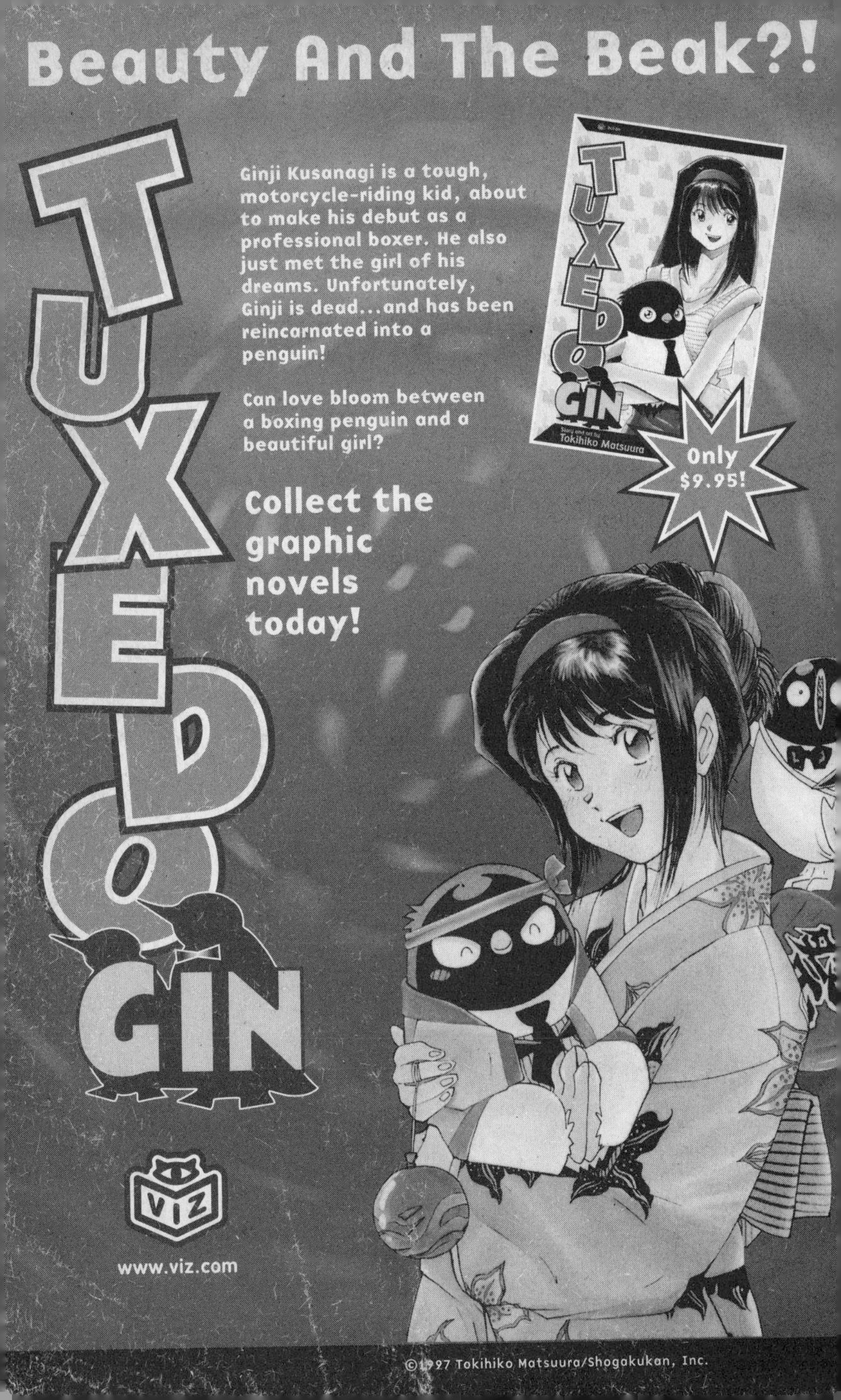
Beauty And The Beak?!
TUXEDO GIN
Ginji Kusanagi is a tough, motorcycle-riding kid, about to make his debut as a professional boxer. He also just met the girl of his dreams. Unfortunately, Ginji is dead...and has been reincarnated into a penguin!
Can love bloom between a boxing penguin and a beautiful girl?
Collect the graphic novels today!
Only $9.95!
Tokihiko Matsuura
VIZ
www.viz.com
©1997 Tokihiko Matsuura/Shogakukan, Inc.

COMPLETE OUR SURVEY AND LET US KNOW WHAT YOU THINK!

☐ Please do NOT send me information about VIZ products, news and events, special offers, or other information.

☐ Please do NOT send me information from VIZ's trusted business partners.

Name: _____

Address: _____

City: _____ **State:** _____ **Zip:** _____

E-mail: _____

☐ Male ☐ Female **Date of Birth** (mm/dd/yyyy): ___ / ___ / ___ (Under 13? Parental consent required)

What race/ethnicity do you consider yourself? (please check one)

☐ Asian/Pacific Islander ☐ Black/African American ☐ Hispanic/Latino

☐ Native American/Alaskan Native ☐ White/Caucasian ☐ Other: _____

What VIZ product did you purchase? (check all that apply and indicate title purchased)

☐ DVD/VHS _____

☐ Graphic Novel _____

☐ Magazines _____

☐ Merchandise _____

Reason for purchase: (check all that apply)

☐ Special offer ☐ Favorite title ☐ Gift

☐ Recommendation ☐ Other _____

Where did you make your purchase? (please check one)

☐ Comic store ☐ Bookstore ☐ Mass/Grocery Store

☐ Newsstand ☐ Video/Video Game Store ☐ Other: _____

☐ Online (site: _____)

What other VIZ properties have you purchased/own? _____

_____

How many anime and/or manga titles have you purchased in the last year? How many were VIZ titles? **(please check one from each column)**

ANIME	MANGA	VIZ
☐ None	☐ None	☐ None
☐ 1-4	☐ 1-4	☐ 1-4
☐ 5-10	☐ 5-10	☐ 5-10
☐ 11+	☐ 11+	☐ 11+

I find the pricing of VIZ products to be: **(please check one)**

☐ Cheap ☐ Reasonable ☐ Expensive

What genre of manga and anime would you like to see from VIZ? **(please check two)**

☐ Adventure ☐ Comic Strip ☐ Science Fiction ☐ Fighting

☐ Horror ☐ Romance ☐ Fantasy ☐ Sports

What do you think of VIZ's new look?

☐ Love It ☐ It's OK ☐ Hate It ☐ Didn't Notice ☐ No Opinion

Which do you prefer? **(please check one)**

☐ Reading right-to-left

☐ Reading left-to-right

Which do you prefer? **(please check one)**

☐ Sound effects in English

☐ Sound effects in Japanese with English captions

☐ Sound effects in Japanese only with a glossary at the back

THANK YOU! Please send the completed form to:

VIZ Survey
42 Catharine St.
Poughkeepsie, NY 12601

All information provided will be used for internal purposes only. We promise not to sell or otherwise divulge your information.